ISSUES
AND
PRACTICES
IN
SPECIAL
EDUCATION

ISSUES AND PRACTICES IN SPECIAL EDUCATION

DONALD S. MAROZAS
AND
DEBORAH C. MAY

With editorial assistance from:
Victor Greco
Kimberly Leonard

Longman
New York & London

Issues and Practices in Special Education

Longman, 10 Bank Street, White Plains, N.Y. 10606

Associated companies:
Longman Group Ltd., London
Longman Cheshire Pty., Melbourne
Longman Paul Pty., Auckland
Copp Clark Pitman, Toronto
Pitman Publishing Inc., New York

Executive editor: Raymond T. O'Connell
Production editor: Helen B. Ambrosio
Text design: Lynn Luchetti
Cover design: Jill Francis Wood
Production supervisor: Pamela Teisler

Library of Congress Cataloging-in-Publication Data

Marozas, Donald S.
    Issues and practices in special education.

    Bibliography: p.
    Includes index.
    1. Special education.   I. May, Deborah C.   II. Greco,
Victor.   III. Leonard, Kimberly.   IV. Title.
LC3965.M279 1988   371.9   87-22584
ISBN 0-582-28639-5

4 5 6 7 8 9 10-AL-95949392

Credits

"Educating All Students in Regular Education," by William Stainback and Susan Stainback. *TASH Newsletter,* 13. Copyright 1987 by the Association for Persons with Severe Handicaps. Reprinted by permission.

"Our Towns: When Classes for Gifted Swell with Ungifted," by Michael Winerip, Copyright © 1986 by the New York Times Company. Reprinted by permission.

From "Characteristics of Superior and Average Special Education Teachers," by David L. Westling, Mark A. Koorland and Terry L. Rose. *Exceptional Children,* 47, 1981, pp. 357–363. Copyright 1981 by The Council for Exceptional Children. Reprinted by permission.

"Paraprofessionals in Special Education," by Richard White, SOCIAL POLICY, published by Social Policy Corporation, New York, New York 10036. Copyright 1984 by Social Policy Corporation.

From CONTEMPORARY ISSUES IN SPECIAL EDUCATION (2nd. ed.) by R. E. Schmid and L. M. Nagata. McGraw-Hill, Inc. Copyright 1983 by McGraw-Hill, Inc. Reprinted by permission.

THE WILSON STRESS PROFILE FOR TEACHERS, by Christopher F. Wilson. Copyright 1979. Reprinted by permission.

From J. R. Yates, "Teacher Training Associated with Serving Bilingual Exceptional Students," *Teacher Education and Special Education,* (1982), 5:3, pp. 64–66. Reprinted with permission of the Teacher Education Division of The Council for Exceptional Children and Special Press.

From M. H. Diebold & L. L. Trentham, "Special Educator Predictions of Regular Class Teacher Attitudes Concerning Mainstreaming," *Teacher Education and Special Education* (1987), *10*:1, 19–25. Copyright 1987 by Special Press. Reprinted with permission of the Teacher Education Division of The Council for Exceptional Children and Special Press.

"The Research Base for Early Intervention," by N. J. Anastasiow. *Early Childhood,* 10, 1986, pp. 99–105. Reprinted with permission of *Early Childhood* and author.

From "Avoiding Misconceptions of Mainstreaming, the LRE, and Normalization" by Gunnar Dybwad, *Exceptional Children,* 47, 1980, pp. 85–88. Copyright 1980 by The Council for Exceptional Children. Reprinted by permission.

"Setting Free the Captives: The Power of Community Integration in Liberating Institutionalized Adults from the Bonds of Their Past," by M. J. Baker and R. S. Salon. *Journal of the*

Contents

Preface

In the rapidly changing field of special education, many issues and practices are still evolving, and there are few absolute answers. To ignore these issues is a mistake.

We have written this book because of our strong commitment to discussing the practical, ethical, and legal questions affecting special education today. This book, *Issues and Practices in Special Education,* is designed to help the reader to understand the issues and trends that affect the field of special education. It is not our intent to present a comprehensive review of all relevant issues, nor to approach the text from a perspective with which all educators will agree. Rather, we intend to provide enough information about each issue to provoke critical thought and discussion. The word *issues* itself implies disagreement.

In each chapter, the authors review some of the existing literature and raise many questions that remain unresolved; conclusions must be drawn by the reader. It is our intent that this book be used as a text in seminars and issues courses that focus on these rapidly changing topics, as well as a supplement to introductory courses and texts that tend to stress the more factual aspects of special education.

The text includes reprints of articles on selected chapter topics. In addition, both real and hypothetical situations, case histories, and discussion questions are included to encourage thought and discussion.

This text is presented with the hope that special educators, both present and future, will become more knowledgeable about the issues that influence their profession, and in turn, will work toward a resolution of those issues.

Obviously, many people supported and assisted us during the preparation of this book. We thank all of them, with particular gratitude to our families, friends, and colleagues: to Victor Greco and Kim Leonard for their editorial assistance; and to Liz Ancker, Kelly Shay, Sue Daley, and Dot Purdy for their typing assistance. At Longman, we are grateful to Karen Bermingham and Ray O'Connell for their help during all phases of this project.

Finally, this book is truly a coauthored book, where both authors contributed equally to the contents. There should be no first or second author, but, since we have been told that the publishing field still cannot print two names in one space, we are listed alphabetically.

Donald S. Marozas

Deborah C. May

CHAPTER 1

Programming Issues

INTRODUCTION

Special education serves a wide range of student populations, including, but not limited to, severely handicapped, gifted, and mainstreamed mildly handicapped students. As a result of this diversity, each area of exceptionality entails its own problems and issues. Some of the issues and practices for these exceptionality areas may overlap to a degree, but in many cases they are unique to the exceptionality under discussion.

Chapter one is divided into three sections. Section one, *Merging Regular and Special Education,* focuses on the possibility of combining special and regular education service delivery systems. This discussion includes a rationale for opposing the merger concept. An article by the Stainbacks, entitled *Educating All Students in Regular Education,* is included as part of this section. The authors advocate bringing special education students into the regular classroom as a part of a team effort between regular and special education. According to the Stainbacks, the instructional needs of such students do not warrant the operation of a dual system of education.

Section two, *Educating Individuals with Severe Handicaps,* addresses the programmatic needs of severely handicapped students. The evolution and provision of services for this population are discussed, together with such specific programmatic issues as assessment practices, instructional approaches, and teacher preparation.

The chapter concludes with a discussion of educational programs for gifted students in the section *Educational Programs for Gifted Students: Necessity or Luxury?* The issues presented include the problems with identification, reasons for opposition to programs for the gifted, and program alternatives. Section three includes a reprint of an article from the *New York Times* entitled *Our Towns: When Classes for Gifted Swell with Ungifted.* The author notes that increasing numbers of students are included in honors programs, even though many cannot perform at grade level in some subject areas.

Programmatic issues and trends vary according to population. Despite this diversity, special educators must join forces to resolve these issues and assure the best possible education for all exceptional students.

MERGING REGULAR AND SPECIAL EDUCATION

Why Merge?

The structure of the special education delivery system was initially questioned when Dunn (1968) wrote his landmark article discussing the efficacy of special education for mildly handicapped learners. Since then, the special education service delivery system has frequently been challenged, often by special educators themselves (Hobbs 1975; Lilly 1979; Reynolds, Wang, and Walberg 1987; Stainback and Stainback 1984). Recently, Assistant Education Secretary Madeleine Will (State officials 1987) called for the integration of regular and special education. Stainback and Stainback (1984) went a step further, suggesting a merger which would abolish special education as a separate entity. Other authors (Reynolds, Wang, and Walberg 1987) have proposed restructuring programs for mildly handicapped students and forming a coalition between special education and remedial or compensatory education (Moran 1984).

One reason for advocating a merger of these two educational systems is concern that the categories presently used to classify mildly handicapped students in special education are neither valid nor reliable (Reynolds, Wang, and Walberg 1987). A review of special education placement practices undertaken by the National Academy of Science (Heller, Holtzman, and Messick 1982) led to the conclusion that little empirical justification existed for the categorical labeling of students with mild academic difficulties. In addition, classification of mildly handicapped learners is often not only unreliable (Stainback and Stainback 1984), but of minimal instructional value (Gardner 1982, Potter et al. 1983), since similar instructional practices have been effective with mildly retarded, learning disabled and remedial students (Heller, Holtzman, and Messick 1982).

According to the Stainbacks, the instructional needs of students do not warrant the operation of a dual system of education. They stated, "There are not two distinct types of students—special and regular" (Stainback and Stainback 1984, 102). Students are individuals with unique characteristics. Mildly and moderately handicapped learners reflect not so much discrete disabilities as a continuum of cognitive and adaptive skills that vary with the learning situation (Gerber, cited in Reynolds, Wang, and Walberg 1987).

Categorical labeling of academically handicapped students has also been shown inefficient in terms of both time and money. Nearly fifty percent of the special education budget is used for assessment and staffing for learning disabled students (Shepard and Smith 1981). The cost of identifying a student as learning disabled may run over six hundred dollars per placement, while the cost of placing a student in a compensatory education program on the basis of low achievement scores has been estimated at about five dollars (Shepard 1983). According to Reschly (as reported in Reynolds, Wang, and Walberg 1987, 342), "The amount of time and energy now devoted to preplacement and reevaluations . . . represents excessively costly and ineffective use of resources." When one considers that research has suggested categorical labels are largely irrelevant for classroom instruction (Gardner 1982), the costs of labeling appear even more extreme.

The existing dichotomy between regular and special education has also been criticized on the grounds that it fosters competition among professionals and unnecessary duplication of services (Stainback and Stainback 1984). Separating the two systems has often produced differing viewpoints about education, and a resultant lack of mutual understanding among educators (Lortie 1978). The breakdown in professional relationships may be seen even on the research level: information of use to *all* educators often goes unrecognized by some because it is associated with the "other" system (Stainback and Stainback 1984).

The treatment of similar problems by separate groups is common within special education. Reynolds and Wang (1983) describe this as disjointed incrementalism, a situation in which several programs, each designed to be independent of the others, are launched one by one. Each distinct program has its own set of rules and guidelines for eligibility, accountability, and funding. As a result of this tight program definition, many students fall through the cracks (Reynolds, Wang, and Walberg 1987). It seems that, because of bureaucratic divisions, it is difficult for educators to work toward mutual needs and goals (McLaughlin 1982).

Aside from the difficulties and problems inherent in maintaining the present dual system, another rationale for merging regular and special education stems from the limited empirical support for special programs. Dunn (1968) offered evidence which challenged the appropriateness of self-contained special education programs for some mildly handicapped students. More recent reviews of achievement outcomes also suggest that segregation has a negative effect on low achievers (Moran 1984).

Madden and Slavin (1983), for example, conducted a large-scale review of studies comparing special and regular education for academically handicapped students. They concluded that, with minimal accommodations in the mainstream classroom, regular class placement resulted in better achievement outcomes. One explanation is that students in special classes are often less involved in academic tasks than their regular class peers (Madden and Slavin 1983). Special class placements have been described as negatively influencing academic focus and time on task (Leinhardt and Pallay 1982), with reduced teacher expectations that often shift curricular emphasis from academic performance to social development (Madden and Slavin 1983).

What Is Involved in Merging?

Just what do these proposals advocating the merger of regular and special education entail? The Stainbacks' proposal (Stainback and Stainback 1984) is perhaps the most intricate; it includes delivering services to all handicapped students, even those who are severely and/or multiply handicapped in regular education. One of the primary steps in their plan involves refocusing the training and assigning of school personnel. According to the new system, educators would be trained and assigned according to instructional categories rather than student categories. Teachers might, for example, specialize in reading, science, self-care skills, or alternative communication systems. Resource specialists and consultants, however, would continue to play important roles within this system.

In addition, under the Stainback and Stainback proposal, much of the current emphasis on classification, homogenous grouping and tracking would be reduced. The rationale for heterogeneous grouping stems from research which suggests that most students can succeed in heterogeneous groupings given individualized, cooperative learning programs (Stainback and Stainback 1984).

Will's report (State officials 1987) suggests two ways to integrate regular and special education. First, she recommends implementing more special education for handicapped students in regular education classrooms; and second, she encourages the provision of individualized support to students who, while not identified as handicapped, nevertheless have learning problems. Seven million dollars in federal discretionary grants will be awarded to projects that try to implement these ideas.

Heterogeneous grouping of students is also supported by Reynolds, Wang, and Walberg (1987). They recommend such instructional approaches as curriculum-based identification systems (Tucker 1985) and the Adaptive Learning Environments Model (Wang and Birch 1984) as ways of helping to ensure success with broader groupings of children. The use of teacher assistance teams and other collaborative models (Chalfant, Pysh, and Moultrie 1979) is also suggested. Moran (1984) proposes that any plan to integrate low achievers into the mainstream must include inservice training for teachers. These inservice programs should include training in practices for enhancing instruction and increasing students' academic learning time (Leinhardt and Pallay 1982).

Proposals for merging regular and special education assume that all students are individuals with different learning styles and needs. Individualized educational programming and services are thus seen as important for all students (Stainback and Stainback 1984). Reynolds, Wang, and Walberg (1987) suggest extending the rights to due process and Individualized Educational Plans (IEPs) to all students. The deficit model of education should be abandoned and replaced by a model more compatible with instructional equity (Moran 1984). The most appropriate and effective instructional methods are likely to be those that recognize the unique academic and social needs of all students, and that are therefore responsive to those needs within the context of the regular classroom (Madden and Slavin 1983).

In order to provide appropriate and effective services for all students, Reynolds, Wang, and Walberg (1987) propose a three-step approach; they refer to their proposal as "Rights Without Labels." First, to ensure that only children with clearly identifiable handicaps receive further evaluations, prereferral screenings are conducted. Second, curriculum-based assessment procedures are used to ensure that appropriate educational programs are provided to all students. Third, some special education resources are reallocated to provide appropriate educational services for special needs students in mainstream settings (Reynolds, Wang, and Walberg 1987).

Perhaps the most complex question to resolve in all of these plans is funding. At the present time, funding in special education is based primarily on categories of exceptionality (Stainback and Stainback 1984), but a variety of creative alternatives have been proposed. Hobbs (1980) recommends a shift from funding by category to funding by services, and suggests that funding be dispersed for services delivered, whether those services consist of individual instruction, social skills training, speech therapy, or other services.

Reynolds, Wang, and Walberg (1987) advocate a "waiver for performance" strategy, whereby specific rules and regulations would be waived for local educational agencies (LEAs). LEAs would then be free to experiment with integrated education for formerly segregated students without losing their government funding. The LEAs, in return, would provide data on the performance of students in experimental programs.

Another funding alternative is offered by Shepard (1987), who suggests that state and federal governments pay the total cost for educating the most severely handicapped students (approximately four percent of the budget), while each district puts forth an equal dollar amount for services to low achieving students. Such a policy would not only guarantee continued services for severely handicapped students, but for low achievers as well. Greater programming flexibility could be achieved; categorical labels for mild learning problems could be avoided; and the number of at-risk children served could be expanded at no increased cost to the district. Stainback and Stainback (1984) emphasize the need to proceed slowly toward funding reorganization, and suggest that research money be set aside to study a variety of funding options.

While some federal grant money will be awarded to support projects that address this merger, strict regulations keep funding sources for special education separate from regular education money. However, a joint policy statement from the Office of Special Education and Rehabilitative Services and the Office of Elementary and Secondary Programs will suggest ways that special program teachers can avoid violating these regulations while serving more students (State officials 1987).

Opposition to the Merger Concept

Proposals for merging regular and special education have not been universally well received. Members of the National Association of State Directors of Special Education, for example, demanded that Will clarify her report on the integration of regular and special education, stating "Will is too quick in promoting an initiative that could be educationally sound but that raises confusing questions and possible legal hurdles" (State officials 1987, 5). In addition, the Stainback and Stainback article (1984) sparked some controversy. Mesinger (1985) describes the proposed merger as the lamb lying down with the lion, and Lieberman (1985) compares it to throwing a wedding and neglecting to invite the bride.

Mesinger (1985) cites the need for improved teacher training and professional practice in regular education as a rationale for *not* merging regular education and special education. According to the *Nation at Risk* report (National Commission on

Excellence in Education 1983), an insufficient number of academically proficient individuals are choosing teaching as a profession. Further, considering the difficulties in teaching violent, recalcitrant, and handicapped youths, and the increasing realization that a good match between specific learning problems and instructional interventions is not likely to be found in the near future, Mesinger urges caution. He calls for even tighter controls over who is recruited into the field of special education, as well as over the specific types of training these individuals are given (Mesinger 1985).

Lieberman (1985), on the other hand, before denouncing the Stainback's proposal for merger, first states that they are, of course, right to advocate their position. However, he contends, "Being right and being real are very different" (Lieberman 1985, 513). He criticizes the Stainbacks' proposal on the grounds that it must come from regular educators in order to be successful. He also challenges the statement that children are not handicapped or deviant, but are simply different from one another along a continuum; according to Lieberman, diminished options clearly represent a handicap, not just a difference.

Lieberman further states that, in regular education, the curricula are dictated by the system, whereas in special education the curriculum is dictated by the child. As a result, the current nationwide push for excellence in education may eventually serve to widen the gap between regular and special education (Lieberman 1985; Shepard 1987). As higher standards are introduced for all students, there may be an ever greater tendency to refer children to special education (Shepard 1987), thereby augmenting the problem of overidentifying students as handicapped.

The federal initiative to integrate regular and special education has also been criticized. Although special education is offering seven million dollars in discretionary grant awards, the level of investment from regular education has been questioned; some officials have stated that the "initiative will be doomed to failure unless the Office of Special Education and Rehabilitative Services and the Office of Elementary and Special Education work together" (State officials 1987, 6). However, staff at these two federal offices are preparing a joint statement on ways schools can effectively synthesize regular and special education programs. This cooperative spirit supported by federal grant money promises a strong start for the integration of regular and special education programs. However, an effective merger will require careful planning, extensive resources, and uncompromising professional commitment. Whether strong enough support exists is unclear. As one doubting state official said, the closely monitored demonstration projects may be successful, but they "don't always work when exported to massive numbers of children" (State Officials 1987, 6). This challenge still lies ahead.

REFERENCES

Chalfant, J., Pysh, M., & Moultrie, R. (1979). Teacher assistance teams: A model for within building problem solving. *Learning Disabilities Quarterly, 2,* 85–86.

Dunn, L. M. (1968). Special education for the mildly retarded—Is much of it justifiable? *Exceptional Children, 35,* 5–24.

Gardner, W. I. (1982). Why do we persist? *Education and Treatment of Children, 5,* 369–378.

Heller, K., Holtzman, W., & Messick, S. (Eds.) (1982). *Placing children in special education: A strategy for equity.* Washington, DC: National Academy Press.

Hobbs, N. (1975). *The futures of children.* San Francisco: Jossey-Bass.

Hobbs, N. (1980). An ecologically oriented service-based system for the classification of handicapped children. In E. Salzinger, J. Antrobus, & D. Glick (Eds.), *The ecosystem of the "risk" child.* New York: Academic Press.

Leinhardt, G., & Pallay, A. (1982). Restrictive educational settings: Exile or haven? *Review of Educational Research, 52,* 557–558.

Lieberman, L. M. (1985). Special education and regular education: A merger made in heaven? *Exceptional Children, 51,* 513–516.

Lilly, S. (1979). *Children with exceptional needs.* New York: Holt, Rinehart and Winston.

Lortie, D. (1978). Some reflections on renegotiation. In M. Reynolds (Ed.), *Futures of education for exceptional students.* Reston, VA: The Council for Exceptional Children.

Madden, N., & Slavin, R. E. (1983). Mainstreaming students with mild handicaps: Academic and social outcomes. *Review of Educational Research, 53,* 519–569.

McLaughlin, M. W. (1982). States and the new federalism. *Harvard Educational Review, 52,* 564–583.

Mesinger, J. F. (1985). Commentary on "A rationale for the merger of special and regular education" or, Is it now time for the lamb to lie down with the lion? *Exceptional Children, 51,* 510–512.

Moran, M. R. (1984). Excellence at the cost of instructional equity? The potential impact of recommended reforms upon low achieving students. *Focus on Exceptional Children, 16,* 1–12.

National Commission on Excellence in Education (1983). *A nation at risk: The imperative for educational reform.* Washington, DC: U.S. Government Printing Office.

Potter, M., Ysseldyke, J., Regan, R., & Algozzine, B. (1983). Eligibility and classification decisions in educational settings: Issuing "passports" in a state of confusion. *Contemporary Educational Psychology, 8,* 146–157.

Reynolds, M. C., & Wang, M. C. (1983). Restructuring "special" school programs: A position paper. *Policy Studies Review, 2,* 189–212.

Reynolds, M. C., Wang, M. C., & Walberg, H. J. (1987). The necessary restructuring of special and regular education. *Exceptional Children, 53,* 391–398.

Shepard, L. (1983). The role of measurement in educational policy: Lessons from the identification of learning disabilities. *Educational Measurement: Issues and Practice, 2,* 4–8.

Shepard, L. A. (1987). The new push for excellence: Widening the schism between regular and special education. *Exceptional Children, 53,* 327–329.

Shepard, L., & Smith, M. L. (1981). *Evaluation of the identification of perceptual-communicative disorders in Colorado.* Boulder, CO: Laboratory of Educational Research.

Stainback, W., & Stainback, S. (1984). A rationale for the merger of special and regular education. *Exceptional Children, 51,* 102–111.

State officials ask Will to clarify her "regular education initiative." (1987, April 1). *Education of the Handicapped,* pp. 5–6.

Tucker, A. (Ed.). (1985). Curriculum-based assessment (Special Issue). *Exceptional Children, 52.*

Wang, M. C., & Birch, J. W. (1984). Effective special education in regular classes. *Exceptional Children, 50,* 391–398.

DISCUSSION QUESTIONS

1. Do you think we are ready for the merger of special and regular education in the United States today? What factors influence your answer?
2. Who do you think would be more receptive to merging, special education teachers or regular education teachers? Why? What concerns do you think each group would have?
3. In recommending a merger, several authors note the need to change teacher preparation. What do you think would have to be changed, and what skills would new teachers need? How would you deal with the many teachers who have been trained under separate systems?
4. Which students do you think would benefit most from integrating regular and special education?
5. Do you think merging should affect all students, regardless of the severity of their handicapping condition? Why?
6. By providing grant funds and support for this merger, the federal government seems to be making a major change in how programs for handicapped children can be supported. Why do you think they are suggesting these changes? What else do they need to do?

Educating All Students in Regular Education

William and Susan Stainback

A small, but growing number of parents and educators are beginning to advocate that students with severe disabilities be integrated into the mainstream of regular education. This would involve full-time placement in chronological age appropriate regular classes in neighborhood schools. Their goal is to move beyond the notion that these students should be placed in segregated "special" classes in regular schools with integration only occurring in carefully selected "regular" education programs or activities (e.g. homeroom, art, music, recess).

As this movement intensifies and progresses, it will be essential to remain cognizant that regular education is not, at the present time, structured or equipped to successfully

Note. Educating All Students in Regular Education by W. Stainback and S. Stainback, 1987, *TASH Newsletter, 13*, pp. 1, 7. Copyright 1987 by the Association for Persons With Severe Handicaps. Reprinted by permission.

meet the needs of all students with severe disabilities. This does not mean, however, the goal of integration is inappropriate or that these students cannot be integrated at the present time into the mainstream of regular education. It only means it is critical to proceed carefully, strongly advocate, and work to have today's regular educational system modified and expanded so that it can successfully meet the needs of all students.

The following are some suggestions for changing regular education so it can better accommodate the needs of students with severe disabilities.

INTEGRATION FACILITATOR

School personnel in Gormley, Ontario have found that employing an integration facilitator can help regular education become more accommodating. The role of an integration facilitator is to build a support circle of teachers, peers and friends around students with severe disabilities, offering them mainstream support for such things as understanding and communicating with their peers and teachers, knowing when the bus leaves school, or finding ways to support and assist their "normal" peers. The primary emphasis is on building a network of supportive people (e.g. peers, friends) who are in the natural environment as opposed to paid professionals. As the regular school environment is adjusted to meet the needs of the student and the student becomes adjusted to that environment, the support provided by the integration facilitator is gradually faded. However, it should be stressed, support is continued as long as it is needed. Annmarie Ruttimann served as one of the first integration facilitators in Canada and believes, "Almost anyone who is open, flexible, willing to take risks, work hard, accept failure and try again, can be an integration facilitator." Integration facilitators come from all walks of life.

RETHINKING THE REGULAR EDUCATION CURRICULUM

All students should be in regular classes and in regular education. However, some students, including those with severe disabilities, sometimes need experiences and/or activities in curriculum areas traditionally not included in regular education. Thus, the curriculum in mainstream education requires expansion if the needs of all students are to be met. Curriculum areas such as daily life and community living skills, competitive and supported employment, sign language, braille, speech, reading, and other similar areas, need to become an inherent part of regular education. In this way, students who require these curriculum areas could gain access to them, rather than having to be assigned to "special" classes to get the training they need.

The expertise to expand the curriculum base in regular education is already available in the schools. The curriculum in regular ed-

ucation could be expanded if these professionals currently working in special education joined regular education and, in effect, became regular educators. As a consequence, tutoring or classes in areas such as mobility training, braille, and community-based instruction could be offered under the guidance of skilled personnel, within the context of the regular educational system. This change would allow students needing instruction in these areas to become a more integral part of the educational mainstream. And, it would do away with some students being classified as special, and assigned to special personnel, in special classrooms, in order to receive an education appropriate to their needs.

PERSONNEL PREPARATION

The importance of modifying personnel preparation practices to facilitate changes in education has been pointed out by Professor Seymour Sarason of Yale University: "School personnel are graduates of our colleges and universities. . . . What we see in our public schools is a mirror image of what exists in colleges and universities." Thus, it is important that colleges and universities set an example for normalized and integrated education. To help this come about, special education professors could join regular education departments in colleges and universities and offer within regular education, instruction in self-care, community based learning and other related skills. As a result, school personnel who have traditionally prepared for special education careers could do as regular educators currently do—specialize or major in instructional areas rather than categories of students with their certification and job assignments being focused on their specific area(s) of instructional expertise such as behavior management, daily-life and community living, alternative communication methods or basic supported and competitive employment. As a consequence, all educators could more easily be viewed and treated as "regular" educators and as "regular" integrated members of "regular" neighborhood public schools. This also would broaden the professional expertise in regular education to more adequately meet the unique instructional needs of all students within the mainstream. Finding an alternative to the current collegiate system for training educators is critical, since preparing some personnel to work with students with handicaps and other personnel to work with students without handicaps impedes the goals of integration. It ultimately leads to the division of school personnel, students and programs along with handicapped and non-handicapped lines in the public schools.

ATTITUDE CHANGE

A current popular attitude about serving the needs of students with severe disabilities is that if their needs cannot be met in regular education, a different or special education option must be developed. If the goal of educational integration is to be attained, a new attitude needs to be adopted. A shift is required to an attitude that recognizes the necessity of modifying, expanding and/or adjusting regular education to meet the needs of all students.

Also requiring change is the current prevailing attitude that it is somehow extraordinary, or special, to educate students with severe disabilities. Because students with severe disabilities were denied an education for many decades, it is now viewed as something special or extraordinary to provide them with an education. But it is neither special nor an act of charity to provide students with severe disabilities an education. All individuals should have a right to receive an education that meets their needs as a normal or standard practice. This attitude change is important if students with severe disabilities are to be treated equitably within the mainstream of regular education, since equality suffers when the education of students with disabilities is viewed as different, special, and charity-like, while the education of others is viewed as regular, normal, and expected. As noted by Douglas Biklen, a leading advocate for the rights of individuals who have severe disabilities, "Until accommodation for children who are disabled is seen as regular, normal and expected, it will be seen instead as special. As long as it is special, it will be, by definition, unequal." Ted Kennedy, Jr., who has a severe disability recently stated: "We are tired of being treated as dependents to be cared for through special and welfare programs."

In summary, while regular education is not at the present time structured to meet the needs of all students, this does not mean that we can not join regular educators, become regular educators and help make regular education more accommodating to the unique needs of all students. It is important that we do so since students with severe disabilities can and should be educated in the mainstream of regular education. This is the only way to realistically prepare them to live in the mainstream of regular community life in their post school years. After all, there is no "special" world. There are not "special" sections of restaurants, grocery stores, banks or churches and similarly there are no special and regular cashiers at grocery stores or tellers at banks. In short, we have created two separate and independent worlds in our public schools that do not exist in the real world of community life—an artificial special world and a regular world.

EDUCATING INDIVIDUALS WITH SEVERE HANDICAPS

Individuals with severe and profound handicaps represent only a small (.05%) segment of the population (Snell 1987), and are at the far end of a continuum of handicapping conditions that range from mild to profound (Van Etten, Arkell, and Van Etten 1980). Until recently, children in this group could generally be found in the back wards of large institutions, often in cribs, scarcely responding to the limited stimuli present (Stainback, Stainback, and Mauer 1976). In fact, this population is often only vaguely defined—through long descriptions, categorical labels, or unclear lists of service needs. When Justen and Brown (1977) surveyed state education departments, they discovered that relatively few states had adopted a generic definition of the term *severely handicapped.* In fact, over half the states in the survey reported that they had no definition of severely handicapped students, although, at the time, 56 percent had legislation mandating services to this group.

While some researchers define this group of students as those who were previously unserved (Van Etten, Arkell, and Van Etten 1980), others provide long, often quite negative, descriptions of the behaviors they perceive as characterizing this population. For example, in 1974, the Bureau of Education for the Handicapped in the United States Office of Education (USOE) defined people with severe handicaps as . . .

> those who, because of the intensity of their physical, mental, or emotional problems or a combination of such problems, need educational, social, psychological, and medical services beyond those which are traditionally offered by regular and special education programs, in order to maximize their full potential for useful and meaningful participation in society and for self-fulfillment. Such children include those classified as seriously emotionally disturbed (schizophrenic and autistic), profoundly and severely mentally retarded, and those with two or more serious handicapping conditions such as the mentally retarded-blind and the cerebral palsied deaf.
>
> Such severely handicapped children may possess severe language and/or perceptual cognitive deprivations and evidence a number of abnormal behaviors including: failure to attend to even the most pronounced social stimuli, self-mutilation, self-stimulation, manifestation of durable and intense temper tantrums, and the absence of even the most rudimentary forms of verbal control, and may also have an extremely fragile physiological condition (USOE 1974, sec. 121.2, cited in Van Etten et al. 1980, 33).

The more severe the handicapping condition, the greater the number of problems individuals and their families incur. As the severity of the disability increases, less incidental learning occurs and specific training is needed to help these individuals acquire even the most basic life skills (Van Etten, Arkell, and Van Etten 1980).

More than any other disability group, people with severe handicaps have suffered the consequences of lowered social status and perceived ineptitude (Walker 1984). As Goldberg and Lippman (1974, 331) point out, "Many special educators never before saw them [severely handicapped students] . . . They were invisible."

The Evolution of Services

For years, schools in the United States served some groups of handicapped children; however, it was rare for schools to serve severely handicapped children (Sontag, Burke, and York 1973). Prior to the mid 1970s, such children were often excluded because they were not toilet trained or were too hard to manage. In fact, during the 1950s, the appropriateness of public education even for trainable mentally retarded children was widely debated (Goldberg and Cruickshank 1958). Children with severe handicaps were educated, if at all, in private programs, often operated out of church basements or other rented space. Only since the 1970s have lawmakers and special educators in the United States begun to recognize the constitutional rights and educational potential of students with severe handicapping conditions. As noted by Walker (1984), this change is the result of many forces, including parental and professional advocacy, litigation, and new legislation.

Notable among these forces was the lawsuit *Pennsylvania Association of Retarded Children (PARC) v. Commonwealth of Pennsylvania* (1972). The judgment in this case stated that free public education should be provided for all mentally retarded persons, regardless of their level of retardation. In 1972, *Mills v. Board of Education* expanded the implications of the *PARC* case to all handicapped children, not just those labeled mentally retarded (Sontag, Burke, and York 1973). The Mills case called for a "free and suitable publicly supported education regardless of the degree of the child's mental, physical or emotional disability or impairment" (Abeson 1973, 3).

Shortly after these landmark court cases, several other events signaled a growing commitment to the education of severely handicapped students. In 1974, the American Association for the Education of the Severely and Profoundly Handicapped was organized, with approximately sixty people attending the first meeting. This organization, later renamed The Association for the Severely Handicapped (TASH), grew rapidly to a membership of nearly twelve hundred by 1975. Five hundred people attended the first national TASH conference. This organization played a major role in shaping public school programs for severely handicapped students (Schmid, Moneypenny, and Johnston 1977). Then in 1975, the National Association for Retarded Citizens (NARC) held a national training meeting on the educational needs of the severely and profoundly handicapped (Stainback, Stainback, and Mauer 1976). Once again the needs of severely handicapped individuals were receiving widespread attention.

The stage was set for the passage of P.L. 94-142, the Education of All Handicapped Children Act of 1975. This legislation echoes earlier court decisions, and mandated that in order to receive federal funds, beginning in September 1978, every school system in the United States would have to provide free, appropriate public education for all children between the ages of three and eighteen (three to twenty-one by 1980) regardless of how seriously handicapped they were. In addition, this legislation required that those students not currently receiving special education be given first priority, with the second priority going to the most severely handicapped students (Hallahan and Kauffman 1982).

Provision of Services

After the passage of P.L. 94-142, as noted by Van Etten, Arkell, and Van Etten (1980), special educators were suddenly faced with the nearly impossible task of educating a group of students for whom there were few valid diagnostic instruments, available curricula, or instructional materials. To make matters more complex, there were few trained teachers, state standards, or teacher training programs preparing teachers to work with severely handicapped individuals. More important, there was little time to prepare for these things before the law was implemented. Less than three decades earlier the professional literature had first hinted that severely handicapped individuals could be trained (Schmid, Moneypenny, and Johnston 1977); now full rights to an appropriate education were mandated by law.

This right to education extended to children and adolescents not previously considered to have the necessary academic potential or capability to acquire even basic life skills (Goldberg and Lippman 1974). This necessitated a new view of education. For example, Roos (1971, 2) redefines education as the "process whereby an individual is helped to develop new behavior or to apply existing behavior, so as to equip him to cope more effectively with his total environment." Roos emphasizes that education is not limited to academics, but includes all the behaviors that make an individual human, including such skills such as toileting, dressing, grooming, and communicating.

Now that the schools no longer have the option of excluding severely handicapped students, administrators and teachers face new programmatic, economic, architectural, and legal concerns (Luckey and Addison 1974). The medical services, transportation, parent-school interactions, scheduling, student-teacher ratios, and coordination with other agencies required by students with severe handicaps are more intensive and more expensive than those encountered by mildly handicapped students (Sontag, Burke, and York 1973).

While it is only within the past decade that educators have emphasized the value of education for severely handicapped students, the benefits of intervention have been outlined by many authors (Jordan and Dailey 1975; Sailor and Guess 1983; Snell 1987; Van Etten, Arkell, and Van Etten 1980; Walker 1984). However, Haring (1982) comments that the typical educational program for severely handicapped students may be as many as ten to twenty years behind the research. Further, lack of extensive knowledge about the abilities of severely handicapped students has resulted in debates as to the best program goals and services (Schmid, Moneypenny, and Johnston 1977).

Programming Issues

In the not too distant past, many people thought that severely handicapped individuals were not capable of learning. Therefore, educational programs designed to serve these people were often seen as futile (Luckey and Addison 1974). However, a decade of experience in teaching severely handicapped students in a variety of settings has modified this view. It has been demonstrated that the use of systematic instruction and behavioral principles can result in learning in many different skill areas. For example, severely handicapped students can make measurable progress in the areas of reading (Browder et al. 1984; Domnie and Brown 1977) and math (Lowe and Cuvo 1976; McClennen and Harrington 1982; Smeets, Lancioni, and Van Lieshout 1985); cooking skills (Johnson and Cuvo 1981); travel skills (Coon, Vogelsburg, and Williams 1981); shopping skills (Gaule, Nietupski, and Certo 1985); vending machine use (Sprague and Horner 1984); housekeeping skills

(Bauman and Iwata 1977; Brueske and Cuvo 1985; Snell 1982); such self-help skills as feeding, toileting and dressing (Azrin and Armstrong 1973; Azrin and Foxx 1971; Young et al. 1986); and communication skills (Browder, Morris, and Snell 1981; Reid and Hurlbut 1977). In addition, the necessity of one-to-one instruction for severely handicapped students has been questioned since some studies (Favell, Favell, and McGimsey 1978; Oliver 1983) have shown group instruction to be effective. However, Reid and Favell (1984) caution that further study is still needed in this area.

Despite extensive research, many questions remain unresolved. Some of the concerns related to assessment, instructional approaches, teacher preparation, and placement in the least restrictive environment will be addressed in this section.

Assessment Practices

Professionals who work with severely handicapped individuals encounter two main difficulties in attempting to evaluate their students' skills. First, many support personnel who would typically be involved in these evaluations—psychologists, speech therapists, and occupational or physical therapists have not been trained to work with this population. As a result, they may be a less useful resource to teachers of severely handicapped students (Sontag, Burke, and York 1973). Using school psychologists as an example, Matey (1985) states that few traditionally trained practitioners have any background in working with children who have sensory handicaps, severe communication or physical disabilities, or severe or profound levels of retardation. He notes that traditional training programs for school psychologists did not provide much experience that would assist their graduates in assessing children functioning at low levels, or helping teachers develop strategies for instructing and otherwise dealing with severely handicapped students. While some university programs are starting to provide students more preparation in this area, currently practicing professionals will not have had this training.

Second, most assessment instruments were not designed for severely handicapped individuals (Sontag, Burke, and York 1973), and generally fail to provide much meaningful information (Brown 1987). Many tests that require students to make motor or verbal responses have been standardized on nonhandicapped learners, and can be viewed as discriminatory when administered to severely handicapped students (Duncan 1981). As stated by Tawney and Smith (1981), the field of special education lacks its own standardized instruments and strategies to measure severely handicapped students' behavioral changes. A traditional evaluation may ask a severely handicapped student to complete such traditional tests as the WISC-R, Stanford-Binet, Wide Range Achievement Test, or Bender (Matey 1985). Since these tests are usually far beyond the abilities of severely handicapped students, the child is often described as untestable, and placed in a special education program with little discussion of appropriate instructional objectives.

In recognition of the importance of linking assessment to classroom instruction, two nontraditional assessment approaches have been proposed. The first is developmental assessment, which is based on the assumption that the normal sequence of development can be used as a guideline for instructional planning for severely handicapped children (Bagnato and Neisworth 1981; Haring and Bricker 1976). This approach, which uses many early childhood assessment tools, is not without criticism, however. Brown et al. (1980) recommend instead that a functional approach be used. Stressing the importance of teaching functional skills, Brown et al. caution that too much instructional time could be spent teaching nonfunctional skills such as stacking blocks.

While the debate continues over which of these two approaches is best, both are clearly improvements over traditional assessment techniques (Matey 1985), and each can be used (with varied success) with different groups of students. However, yet another alternative needs to be considered: interviews with parents or teachers and structured observations in the student's natural environment. In fact, Mullikan and Buckley (1983) state that interviews and observations are the only valid sources of information for severely handicapped students. Many assessment devices now being developed focus on this interview and observation information. As Valletutti (1984) notes, given the lack of appropriate formal assessment devices for severely handicapped students, the use of informal diagnostic tools is essential and is, perhaps, one of the most effective ways to gain the necessary information for program planning.

Instructional Approaches

While educational programs for severely handicapped students have changed markedly over the past decade, there are still areas of debate. For example, in a controversial article, Burton and Hirshoren (1979a) caution against forming expectations that are too high for severely handicapped students; and in an earlier article (Burton and Hirshoren 1978), they state that public school education for severely handicapped students may carry false hope about the extent of learning such students can achieve. In contrast, Sontag, Certo, and Button (1979) reject any limitations on the potential learning levels for this group. Regardless of these differing perspectives, most educators agree that for maximum learning to take place, carefully structured environments and curricula are essential (Snell 1987; Sontag, Burke, and York 1973).

However, getting beyond this basic level of agreement is hard. Appropriate instructional content and strategies are still being debated. The issue of functional, as opposed to developmental programming, is a spillover from the assessment concern mentioned earlier, with Holvoet et al. (1980) stating that a developmentally based curriculum has little impact on a student's ultimate self-sufficiency. The functional approach identifies the skills needed by an independent adult, and teaches them, while the developmental approach starts by teaching skills normally performed by infants, moving on to more advanced skills as the basic ones are mastered (Snell and Grigg 1987).

Regardless of the type of programming used, most teachers use various instructional approaches in their classrooms. And there is still very strong disagreement about which behavioral strategies are most effective and appropriate. For example, some parents and professionals support the use of punishment while both the Association for Persons with Severe Handicaps and the National Association for Retarded Citizens oppose its use. Additional discussion of this practice is presented in *Chapter 7.*

Least Restrictive Environment

Perhaps the most controversial topic at present is the actual location of classes for severely handicapped students. Options vary from a cluster approach with self-contained classes in an all-special-education building, to self-contained classes interspersed throughout a school district, to integrated classes of handicapped and non-handicapped students. While Burton and Hirshoren (1979a, 1979b) state that public school placement is not appropriate for all students and recommend a cluster approach, others provide strong legal and philosophical arguments for integration (Sailor 1982; Sontag, Certo, and Button 1979).

Clustering students in one school offers many practical advantages: greater accessibility, shared teacher and material resources, more efficient therapy services with less travel time, better monitoring of medical problems thanks to higher nurse-student ratios, and functional grouping of students. However, logistics aside, many argue that clustering is philosophically and morally wrong (Biklen 1985; TASH 1987) calling it merely another form of institutionalization and segregation (Sontag, Burke, and York 1973). In a cluster service delivery model, students are not exposed to normalized experiences, teachers and other students do not have the opportunity to interact with handicapped students, and severely handicapped students spend more time traveling to programs (rather than taking part in them). While TASH (1987) calls for the total integration of severely handicapped students into regular educational programs, however, not all schools appear ready for this step.

Teacher Preparation

Recent studies suggest that limited resources, negative attitudes, and a lack of trained teachers are impeding the full implementation of education in the least restrictive environment (Ysseldyke and Algozzine 1982). The need for specially trained teachers has never been more acute. As Sontag, Burke, and York (1973) note, the more severe the student's disability, the more precise and specific the teacher's skills need to be. Teachers need experience applying rapidly advancing technology, skills from many allied disciplines, and behavior management techniques (Snell 1987). TASH (1987) calls for both special and regular education teachers to receive this specialized training. However, once again there is no consensus about how this teacher training should be structured or provided. Sontag, Certo, and Button (1979) recommend that teachers of severely handicapped students be trained at the graduate level and have at least two years of experience with this population before being accepted into teacher training programs. On the other hand, Burton and Hirshoren (1979a) indicate that a two-year training program might be more appropriate for teachers of severely handicapped students, although they later suggest a two-tier system for teachers (1979b). In this model, they specified that the teachers working directly with the clients could be trained in a two-year program, but they would be working under the supervision of professionals with four to five years of preparation. Regardless of these differences in thought, it is important that prospective teachers of severely handicapped students have intensive field experiences so they will know whether or not they have the abilities to teach this population (Drew, Hardman, and Bluhm 1977; Haring 1982).

Tawney and Smith (1981) point out that the field of special education for the severely handicapped has grown so that there are now clearly stated theoretical approaches to instruction, highly structured intervention programs, specialized teacher training programs, and a rapidly growing body of research. In spite of this progress, however, they cite the need to continue documenting the skill acquisition of severely handicapped students.

The rights extended to individuals with severe handicaps as a result of litigation and legislation indicate the tremendous changes in attitudes and public awareness that have occurred during the past twenty-five years (Gearheart 1980; Larsen 1977; Walker 1984). However, this national legislative commitment has not eliminated all resistance. Walker (1984) states that the nonhandicapped segment of society still resists the integration of severely handicapped individuals into less restrictive educational settings and neighborhood residential facilities; as a result, she recommends research to identify and test strategies for encouraging public acceptance of severely handicapped people. Much progress has been made since the passage of P.L. 94-142, but much remains to be done.

REFERENCES

Abeson, A. (Ed.) (1973). *A continuing summary of pending and completed litigation regarding the education of handicapped children.* Arlington, VA: Council for Exceptional Children.

Azrin, N., & Armstrong, P. (1973). The "mini-meal"—A method for teaching eating skills to the profoundly retarded. *Mental Retardation, 11,* 9–11.

Azrin, N., & Foxx, R. (1971). A rapid method of toilet training the institutionalized retarded. *Journal of Applied Behavior Analysis, 4,* 89–99.

Bagnato, S., & Neisworth, J. (1981). *Linking developmental assessment and curricula.* Rockville, Maryland: Aspen Systems Corp.

Bauman, K., & Iwata, B. (1977). Maintenance of independent housekeeping skills using scheduling plus self-recording procedures. *Behavior Therapy, 8,* 554–560.

Biklen, D. (1985). *Achieving the complete school.* NY: Teachers College Press.

Browder, D., Hines, C., McCarthy, L., & Fees, J. (1984). A treatment package for increasing sight word recognition for use in daily living skills. *Education and Training of the Mentally Retarded, 19,* 191–200.

Browder, D., Morris, W., & Snell, M. (1981). Using time delay to teach manual signs to a severely retarded student. *Education and Training of the Mentally Retarded, 16,* 252–258.

Brown, F. (1987). Meaningful assessment of people with severe and profound handicaps. In M. Snell (Ed.) *Systematic instruction of persons with severe handicaps.* Columbus, OH: Charles E. Merrill.

Brown, L., Falvy, M., Vincent, N., Johnson, F., Ferrara-Parrish, P. & Gruenewald, L. (1980). Strategies for generating comprehensive, longitudinal, and chronological-age-appropriate individualized education programs for adolescent and young adult severely handicapped students. *Journal of Special Education, 4,* 199–216.

Brueske, S., & Cuvo, A. (1985). Teaching home cleaning skills to a blind client. *Journal of Visual Impairment and Blindness, 79,* 18–23.

Burton, T., & Hirshoren, A. (1978). The focus of responsibility for education of the severely and profoundly retarded. *Psychology in the Schools, 15,* 52–56.

Burton, T., & Hirshoren, A. (1979a). The education of severely and profoundly handicapped children: Are we sacrificing the child to the concept? *Exceptional Children, 45,* 598–602.

Burton, T., & Hirshoren, A. (1979b). Some further thoughts and clarifications on the education of severely and profoundly handicapped children. *Exceptional Children, 45,* 618–625.

Coon, M., Vogelsburg, T., & Williams, W. (1981). Effects of classroom public transportation instruction on generalization of the natural environment. *Journal of the Association of the Severely Handicapped, 6,* 46–53.

Domnie, M., & Brown, L. (1977). Teaching severely handicapped students reading skills requiring printed answers to who, what, and where questions. *Education and Training of the Mentally Retarded, 12,* 324–331.

Drew, C., Hardman, M., & Bluhm, H. (Eds.) (1977). *Mental retardation: Social and emotional perspectives.* St. Louis: C. V. Mosby.

Duncan, D. (1981). Nondiscriminatory assessment of severely physically handicapped individuals. *Journal of the Association for the Severely Handicapped, 6,* 17–22.

Favell, J., Favell, J., & McGimsey, J. (1978). Relative effectiveness and efficiency of group vs. individualized training of severely retarded groups. *American Journal of Mental Deficiency, 83,* 104–109.

Gaule, K., Nietupski, J., & Certo, N. (1985). Teaching supermarket shopping skills using an adaptive shopping list. *Education and Training of the Mentally Retarded, 20,* 53–59.

Gearheart, B. (1980). *Special education for the 80s.* St. Louis, MO: C. V. Mosby.

Goldberg, I., & Cruickshank, W. (1958). The trainable but noneducable: Whose responsibility? *National Education Association Journal, 47,* 622–623.

Goldberg, I., & Lippman, L. (1974). Plato had a word for it. *Exceptional Children, 40,* 325–334.

Hallahan, D., & Kauffman, J. (1982). *Exceptional children.* Englewood Cliffs. NJ: Prentice Hall.

Haring, N. (Ed.) (1982). *Exceptional children and youth.* Columbus, OH: Charles E. Merrill.

Haring, N., & Bricker, W. (1976). Overview of comprehensive services for the severely and profoundly handicapped. In N. Haring & L. Brown (Eds.), *Teaching the severely handicapped,* Vol. I. NY: Grune and Stratton.

Holvoet, J., Guess, D., Mulligan, M., & Brown, F. (1980). The individualized Curriculum Sequencing model (II): A teaching strategy for severely handicapped students. *Journal of the Association for the Severely Handicapped, 5,* 337–351.

Johnson, B., & Cuvo, A. (1981). Teaching mentally retarded adults to cook. *Behavior Modification, 5,* 187–202.

Jordan, J., & Dailey, R. (1975). *Not all little red wagons are red.* Reston, VA: Council for Exceptional Children.

Justen, J., & Brown, G. (1977). Definitions of severely handicapped: A survey of state departments of education. *AAESPH Review, 2,* 8–14.

Larsen, L. (1977). Community services necessary to program effectively for the severely/ profoundly handicapped. In E. Sontag (Ed.), *Educational programming for the severely and profoundly handicapped*. Reston, VA: Council for Exceptional Children.

Lowe, M., & Cuvo, A. (1976). Teaching coin summation to the mentally retarded. *Journal of Applied Behavior Analysis, 9,* 483–489.

Luckey, R., & Addison, M. (1974). The profoundly retarded: A new challenge for public education. *Education and Training of the Mentally Retarded, 9,* 123–130.

Matey, C. (1985). Best practices in working with severely and profoundly handicapped children. In A. Thomas & J. Grimes (Eds.), *Best practices in school psychology*. Kent, OH: The National Association of School Psychologists.

McClennen, S., & Harrington, L. (1982). A developmentally-based functional mathematics program for retarded and autistic persons. *Journal of Special Education Technology, 5,* 23–30.

Mills v. Board of Education of the District of Columbia. 348 F. Supp. 866 (D.D.C. 1972).

Mullikan, R., & Buckley, J. (1983). *Assessment of multihandicapped and developmentally disabled children*. Rockville, MD: Aspen Systems Co.

Oliver, P. (1983). Effects of teaching different tasks in group versus individual training formats with severely handicapped individuals. *Journal of the Association for the Severely Handicapped, 8,* 79–91.

Pennsylvania Association for Retarded Children v. Commonwealth of Pennsylvania. 343 F. Supp. 279 (E.D. PA. 1972).

Reid, D., & Favell, J. (1984). Group instruction with persons who have severe disabilities: A critical review. *Journal of the Association for Persons with Severe Handicaps, 9,* 167–177.

Reid, D., & Hurlbut, B. (1977). Teaching nonvocal communication skills to multihandicapped adults. *Journal of Applied Behavior Analysis, 10,* 591–603.

Roos, P. (1971). Current issues in the education of mentally retarded persons. In W. Cegelka (Ed.), *Proceedings: Conference on the Education of Mentally Retarded Persons*. Arlington, TX: National Association for Retarded Citizens.

Sailor, W. (1982). *Research institute on transition of severely handicapped students to LRE*. San Francisco: San Francisco University.

Sailor, W., & Guess, D. (1983). *Severely handicapped students and instructional design*. Boston: Houghton-Mifflin.

Schmid, R., Moneypenny, J., & Johnston, R. (1977). *Contemporary issues in special education*. NY: McGraw-Hill Book Co.

Smeets, P., Lancioni, G., & Van Lieshout, R. (1985). Teaching mentally retarded children to use an experimental device for telling time and meeting appointments. *Applied Research in Mental Retardation, 6,* 51–70.

Snell, M. (1982). Teaching bedmaking to severely retarded adults through time delay. *Analysis and Intervention in Developmental Disabilities, 2,* 139–155.

Snell, M. (Ed.) (1987). *Systematic instruction of persons with severe handicaps*. Columbus, OH: Charles E. Merrill.

Snell, M., & Grigg, N. (1987). Instructional assessment and curriculum development. In M. Snell (Ed.). *Systematic instruction of persons with severe handicaps*. Columbus, OH: Charles E. Merrill.

Sontag, E., Burke, P., & York, R. (1973). Considerations for serving the severely handicapped in the public schools. *Education and Training of the Mentally Retarded, 8,* 20–27.

Sontag, E., Certo, N., & Button, J. (1979). On a distinction between the education of the severely and profoundly handicapped and a doctrine of limitations. *Exceptional Children, 45,* 604–616.

Sprague, J., & Horner, R. (1984). The effects of single instance, multiple instance, and general case training on a generalized vending machine use by moderately and severely handicapped students. *Journal of Applied Behavior Analysis, 17,* 273–278.

Stainback, S., Stainback, W., & Maurer, S. (1976). Training teachers for the severely and profoundly handicapped: A new frontier. *Exceptional Children, 42,* 203–210.

TASH: The Association for Persons with Severe Handicaps (1987, February). Resolution on the redefinition of the continuum of services. *Newsletter,* p. 3.

Tawney, J., & Smith, J. (1981). An analysis of the forum: Issues in education of the severely and profoundly retarded. *Exceptional Children, 48,* 5–18.

Valletutti, P. (1984). Introduction and overview. In P. Valletutti & B. Sims-Tucker, *Severely and profoundly handicapped students: Their nature and needs.* Baltimore, MD: Brookes.

Van Etten, G., Arkell, C., & Van Etten, C. (1980). *The severely and profoundly handicapped.* St. Louis, MO: C. V. Mosby.

Walker, S. (1984). Issues and trends in the education of the severely handicapped. In E. Gordon (Ed.), *Review of Research in Education.* Washington, DC: American Educational Research Association.

Young, K., West, R., Howard, V., & Whitney, R. (1986). Acquisition, fluency training generalization, and maintenance of dressing skills of two developmentally disabled children. *Education and Treatment of Children, 9,* 16–29.

Ysseldyke, J., & Algozzine, C. (1982). *Critical issues in special and remedial education.* Boston: Houghton Mifflin.

DISCUSSION QUESTIONS

1. Which approach to providing services to severely handicapped students would you support: a cluster approach or a totally integrated class? Explain your reasoning.
2. How would you begin to change attitudes so that there would be more widespread public acceptance of severely handicapped students? Be specific.
3. Since so many changes have occurred in the past ten years, what do you think the future holds for persons with severe handicapping conditions?
4. Some people believe that the amount of money spent on the education of severely handicapped students could be spent more effectively in other areas of education. What is your reaction to this perspective? Aside from a legal mandate, how would you justify continuing or expanding these services?
5. Do you think teachers who work with severely handicapped students should be prepared at the advanced level, with perhaps a graduate degree required, or do you think a two-year training program would be adequate? Why?

EDUCATIONAL PROGRAMS FOR GIFTED STUDENTS: NECESSITY OR LUXURY?

The history of educational programs for gifted students has been cyclical (Tannenbaum 1983), with the commitment to specialized programming for gifted and talented students shifting according to the national temper (Goldberg 1986a). In the late 1950s, following the launching of Sputnik by the Soviets, Americans recognized the importance of helping children develop those talents seen as essential for military and scientific advancement. Although some increased support for gifted programs resulted, it generally proved insufficient as a motivator for improving gifted education on a large scale (Marland 1972b), and the movement lost momentum (Passow 1986).

The present renaissance of educational programs for gifted students can be traced to the early 1970s, when the U.S. Office of Education issued the Marland Report. Named for the former Commissioner of Education, Dr. Sidney P. Marland, the report stated that the needs of gifted students were not being adequately met (Passow 1986). Only a relatively small percentage of gifted students were benefiting from existing programs (Marland 1972a); services for gifted students were of low priority at all levels of administration; and a lack of trained personnel combined with conflicting funding priorities were contributing to the limited advancement of education for gifted students. As a direct result of this report, the Office of Gifted and Talented was established in Washington, DC. In 1986, this office received its first federal funds under Public Law 93-300, Section 404, and the federal leadership for programs of education for gifted students began to expand (Sisk 1980).

Even with legislative backing for gifted programs, many issues are still unresolved. Recent articles address such topics as egalitarianism and excellence, definition and assessment, content development and delivery, criteria for appropriate programs, staffing problems, self-concept and self-esteem issues, learning styles and preferred instructional techniques, the vulnerabilities of higher level gifted students and the nature of extreme giftedness (Goldberg 1986a; Goldberg 1986b; Janos, Fung, and Robinson 1985; Powell and Hayden 1984; Ricca 1984; Roedell 1984; Stewart 1981). In this section, we will focus on three issues of critical importance: equity versus excellence, assessment and identification, and program planning.

Equal Opportunity versus Elitism

According to Goldberg (1986a), fluctuating attitudes toward special programs for gifted students reflect society's conflict between a belief in egalitarianism and a recognition of the need to develop students' special talents. These conflicting values have inhibited both the initial establishment of programs for gifted students and the wholehearted support of such programs, once established (Gallagher 1986). While the current attitude is generally supportive, opposition to these programs remains strong and vocal. Those opposed to programs for the gifted are concerned that they will slow racial integration, draw resources from educational programs for disadvantaged students, and conflict with efforts to achieve equality in programs for all children (Goldberg 1986a). One frequently raised question is a deceptively simple one: "Isn't what you are doing for the gifted good for all youngsters?" (Renzulli 1980, 3).

Persons who favor special programming for gifted students argue that these students, as a direct result of their giftedness, have different learning requirements than other students (White 1970). Curiosity, ability to concentrate, craving for knowledge, and a capacity for abstract reasoning are said to be present to such a high degree in gifted students that traditional educational programs are inappropriate for meeting their needs (Olstad 1978).

Studies assessing the common characteristics of gifted learners and their preferred instructional techniques support the notion that gifted students would benefit more from specialized educational programs. In an early study, Terman and Oden (1959) identified general intelligence, desire to know, originality, and common sense as four traits which clearly differentiated gifted from average children. Powell and Haden (1984) identified ability to create structure, desire to know, and efficient information processing as intellectual traits which differed significantly among normal ability, moderately gifted, and extremely gifted children. Gifted elementary school students seem to prefer instructional techniques which emphasize independence, while their peers from the general population prefer more structured methods (Stewart 1981). Gifted students also indicate a greater preference for working alone and for independent study (Ricca 1984).

Feldman (1979) suggests that gifted students are often bored and listless in class, and, because of unchallenging work, are more likely to become disturbed or distressed. Not only will an education adapted specifically to their needs result in their leading happier lives (Feldman 1979), but, it is claimed, a lack of such adaptation may actually cause their giftedness to wither (Maeroff 1980).

In a study designed to determine the importance of courses for gifted students, Tremaine (1979) compared high school graduates who had participated in educational programs for gifted students with their gifted peers who had not participated in any special programs. Comparing achievements, accomplishments, and attitudes of the graduates, Tremaine found that the enrolled gifted students had higher grade point averages, had taken more difficult and demanding academic courses, and had obtained significantly higher scholastic aptitude test verbal scores. In addition, the enrolled gifted students had higher regard for their school and teachers, and were more involved in school activities. While such studies do not conclusively demonstrate a direct cause-and-effect relationship between decreased intellectual or social/emotional functioning among gifted students and the absence of appropriate special programs, they do at least lend support for providing such programs.

Gifted individuals are seen by many as a deprived group, a group who former U.S. Commissioner of Education, Sidney P. Marland, Jr., said were among the nation's most neglected students. In reference to his 1971 report, Marland (1972b, 18) concluded that ". . . education of the gifted was of such little official concern to the federal, state, and most local governments and education agencies that it best could be described as nonexistent on the national agenda." Gifted children, Marland reported, were often not being identified in their schools. Moreover, when they are known, ". . . they often suffered hostility or apathy and were afflicted with the same kinds of self-doubts that are recognized in other mistreated minority children" (Marland 1972b, 18). According to Zettel (1980), those students least likely to receive an educational program which would facilitate maximum growth may well be the gifted and talented students.

Our neglect of gifted students' needs is thought to result from pressures on schools to both offer equal educational opportunities and produce equal educational outcomes. The opponents of special programming for the gifted have apparently failed to differentiate between an equal education for all students and an equal opportunity for all students to realize their full potential (Olstad 1978).

Raspberry (1976) cautions that by attempting to democratize education, we may actually be mediocratizing it and downplaying the pursuit of excellence. Proponents of special educational programs for the gifted fear that neglecting the special needs of these students may result in a "strange distortion of the notion of equality" (Drews 1976, 26), and may actually make the pursuit of excellence appear educationally subversive (Olstad 1978).

Opponents of special education programs for gifted children have charged that the programs guarantee special privileges, which could benefit all children, to an elite few who need them least. Opponents see the programs as providing exciting and innovative activities for a select few, while the rest of the students plod along, doing the same old kind of work they have been doing for years (Baer 1980). Those who argue against the development of these special programs are not opposed to the innovative methods of broadening children's knowledge, to the qualitatively different educational experiences, or to the development of new perspectives and ways of looking at the world. Rather, they support these changes, but maintain that they are suitable for *all* children rather than just a select few identified as gifted. Making these programs exclusive, they argue, denies all children an equal opportunity to develop their talents and realize their full potential (Baer 1980). Finkel (1980) presents the following argument against designing special programs which exclude the majority of youngsters:

> It should be apparent that creating a coterie of a specially educated gifted few is certainly questionable and probably stupid. What, after all, could possibly be the social legacy of a system that denies 90 percent of its members opportunities and advantages given to a privileged 10 percent? Noncreative, unthinking, and insensitive behavior will likely be the outcome (93).

This controversy is obviously a heated one, and will not be settled on the basis of research evidence alone. Passow, a past president of the World Council for Gifted and Talented Children and an active researcher in the area of education of gifted students since 1954, suggests that those who favor special programs for the gifted will continually have to justify the need for such programs and to explain why such programs are not elitist (Passow 1986).

Problems Identifying Gifted Students

Among those opposed to special programs for the gifted, many claim that the identification and selection criteria are not adequate to identify all gifted children. Ideally, identifying a child as gifted calls for a thorough analysis of test scores and school records, combined with interviews of teachers, parents, or others, who know the child well. In reality, however, most selection criteria still rely heavily on the results of IQ tests (Alvino, McDonnel, and Richert 1981). Intelligence tests have been shown to discriminate against minorities (Baer 1980), and a reliance on such measures may cause many gifted children, including the learning disabled, the underachieving, minorities and the disadvantaged, to be overlooked in the identification process (Sisk 1980). So, while the proponents of gifted programming fight for equal opportunity, current methods of identifying and selecting gifted students often, in fact, work to undermine equality (Baer 1980).

The problem of defining and assessing giftedness and talent has continually troubled the field (Goldberg 1986a), in some respects becoming even more complex following the adoption of the following definition by the U.S. Office of Education in 1972:

> Gifted and talented children are those identified by professionally qualified persons, who by virtue of outstanding abilities, are capable of high performance. These are children who require differentiated educational programs and/or services beyond those normally provided by "regular school programs" in order to realize their contributions to self and society. Children capable of high performance include those who have demonstrated any of the following abilities or aptitudes, singly or in combination: 1) general intellectual ability, 2) specific academic aptitude, 3) creative or productive thinking, 4) leadership ability, 5) visual and performing arts aptitude, 6) psychomotor ability (Marland 1972b, 10).

This federal definition was intended to expand the definition of giftedness to include nonacademic areas, but it did not clearly differentiate between the terms gifted and talented (Richert 1985). Further, it did not expand upon the various areas that giftedness included, therefore leaving the parameters of such terms as leadership and psychomotor ability vague and unspecified (Goldberg 1986). According to Alvino, McDonnel, and Richert (1981), problems with identification were only intensified with the adoption of this federal definition.

In a national survey of the identification practices used by schools to select students for gifted and talented programs, abuses of standardized testing and a lack of understanding of appropriate identification procedures were found (Alvino, McDonnel, and Richert 1981). General intellectual ability, as expressed by an IQ score, continued to be the basis for identifying most gifted students, despite the broadened definition of giftedness. The reported use of nominations was the second most often used procedure to identify gifted students, with achievement test scores ranked third. As an illustration of how standardized test scores were being misused, achievement tests were reportedly used for identifying general intellectual ability three times as often as they were used for identifying academic aptitude. Conversely, intelligence tests were reportedly used twice as frequently as achievement tests for identifying specific academic aptitude. Neither application, of course, is appropriate. Further, standardized tests were often reportedly used on populations for which they were not normed (Alvino, McDonnel, and Richert 1981).

A more recent survey of identification practices revealed similarly disturbing findings. Richert (1985, 69) reports that "achievement and IQ tests are used almost interchangeably. . . . They are also being inappropriately used to identify creativity and leadership." The identification instruments and procedures reportedly used all but ignore several categories included in the federal definition, with actual selection frequently limited to students who perform well academically (Richert 1985). The use of teachers' nominations has been similarly criticized because children who present management problems in the classroom or who are poor achievers are not likely to be nominated (Goldberg 1986a).

The value of standardized tests in identifying gifted students has been questioned on the basis that test scores are given undue emphasis (Kirschenbaum 1983). Kirschenbaum advocates the use of multi-dimensional selection procedures which are locally designed and normed, and which attempt to balance the importance of test scores with recommendations from teachers and parents, other indicators of school achievement, and performance in problem-solving situations.

Kirschenbaum's inclusion of performance in problem-solving situations is consistent with Renzulli's (1980) notion of identifying "gifted behavior" as opposed to "giftedness"—which resides somewhere within the child. Renzulli's Revolving-Door model requires that students earn the right to obtain special services, and allows them to move in and out of programs, thus making room for more students. His proposed Three-Ring Conception of Giftedness, in which above-average ability, task commitment, and creativity interact, deemphasizes the exclusive importance typically placed on superior abilities (Renzulli 1978). Busse and Mansfield (1980) concur with Renzulli, and suggest that programs for gifted students be open to all who demonstrate a capacity to benefit from them.

However, no matter what instruments or procedures are used, no identification process exists in a vacuum. In order to be maximally effective and predictive of success, Kirschenbaum (1983) states that any identification procedure used should be tied to the program and curriculum model to be implemented. This link between identification and programming is crucial.

Programs for Gifted Students

According to the generally accepted definition, gifted and talented students are those ". . . who require differentiated educational programs and/or services beyond those normally provided by the regular school programs . . ." (Marland 1972b, 10). In other words, any program specifically designed to meet the needs of gifted and talented students must be substantially different from the traditional school program, and must present significantly greater challenges to the enrolled students (Goldberg 1986b). The challenge of developing appropriate curricula for gifted students is perhaps the least advertised, but one of the most troubling aspects of educational programs for gifted students.

Tannenbaum (1983) distinguishes between "provisions" and "programs" for the gifted. Provisions are described as learning experiences lacking long-range goals or a clear direction, while programs are described as being comprehensive in scope and supported as integral components of a district's educational plan. He cautions against ad hoc educational provisions for the gifted student, stressing that programs for them must go beyond simply adding more interesting parts to an existing curriculum. In addressing this same issue, Passow (1986) emphasizes the need for a differentiated curriculum, based upon the needs of individual students.

Renzulli (1978) criticizes many gifted programs for their lack of continuity and limited emphasis on developing the very abilities which led the students to be identified as gifted in the first place. In assessing the adequacy of a program for gifted students, it is important to examine the match between the characteristics of that program and the characteristics of the individual student (Goldberg 1986b). An effective program allows for differences in students' competence, interests, motivations and learning styles (Goldberg 1986b). The need for a match between program and student characteristics brings us back to our earlier discussion of identification procedures. Weber and Battaglia (1985) state that the identification process is critical to program success. When identification procedures are oblivious to program expectations, children placed in the program may fail to perform at anticipated levels. According to Weber and Battaglia, identification must play a prescriptive, as well as descriptive role, thereby promoting the development of individualized programs.

Renzulli and Delcourt (1986) describe several performance-based research designs which emphasize the match between student and program characteristics. One design uses academic mastery in a domain-specific area as the determiner of giftedness. For example, Stanley (1984) defines giftedness as a high level of performance in mathematics, and then uses performance on tests of mathematical aptitude to predict success in an accelerated mathematics program. A second design examines a student's creative productivity in domain-specific or interdisciplinary areas through the use of situational testing (Renzulli and Delcourt 1986). In this design, students are placed in actual learning situations and then evaluated on the basis of their responses to these experiences. As with the previous design, the important feature here is the ". . . logical and direct relationship between the predictor and the criterion" (22). When the emphasis is on identifying *gifted behavior* as opposed to *giftedness,* students are more likely to be placed in programs consistent with their talents and interests, and consequently, are more likely to succeed.

Program options for the gifted student generally fall into the categories of enrichment or acceleration, although special classes are also used in some areas. Enrichment activities are generally considered horizontal in nature, as they involve participation in extra activities without any other changes or advancement in the traditional instructional sequence. The value of enrichment experiences, however, is difficult to assess by any standardized measure, and the appropriateness of enrichment activities for nongifted as well as gifted students remains a question (Goldberg 1986b). Budgetary constraints, the continuing controversy over elitism, and the lack of efficacy data all have served to block proposals for enrichment programs (Christopherson 1981). Acceleration programs or those which can benefit all students are less likely to meet with opposition.

Acceleration helps a child progress through school at a more rapid rate than usual by providing learning experiences that would typically be encountered later. The available research on acceleration suggests that the level of academic challenge presented to gifted students can be significantly raised without substantial expenditures or negative effects on the students (Goldberg 1986b). Christopherson (1981) offers a modified acceleration model, called "developmental placement." This model places gifted students in classrooms with the appropriate intellectual and academic levels for that gifted student. Such individualized placement helps ensure that the child can continue to experience success yet be appropriately challenged in the classroom. However, given the wide variety of skills of gifted children, this may be more difficult to do in practice than it sounds.

Whether they are served through acceleration or pull-out programs, the majority of gifted students spend a considerable portion of their time in the regular classroom (Treffinger 1982). This realization, along with the continuing need to justify special programming for an elite few, has prompted an interest in instructional techniques and programs which can be beneficial to all students. Williams (1980) suggests making the practices used to educate gifted students a part of regular education, since the theories of learning typically applied in gifted education were originally general theories designed for all students. Through the Williams Model for Implementing Cognitive-Affective Behaviors in the Classroom, he proposes that all instruction be differentiated ". . . so that every child in a classroom can work up to capacity" (94). In discussing how instruction should relate to regular students, Treffinger (1982) describes sixty characteristics of effective instruction which can be used by the regular classroom teacher in working with gifted students. Many of these characteristics could also be applied to the instruction of nongifted students.

The multiple-talent approach to teaching, a system designed to help teachers identify and facilitate development of talents in such areas as productive thinking, predicting, communicating, planning and decision-making, can be applied equally well to gifted and nongifted students (Schlichter 1981). In research with heterogeneous groups of students, the multiple-talent approach has been shown to have a positive impact on students' creative thinking abilities, self-concept and academic achievement (Schlichter 1981). The successful application of such models as this in both regular and gifted education ". . . suggests important implications for the more comprehensive services to gifted students, as well as the provision of enriching experiences for all youngsters" (Schlichter 1981).

REFERENCES

Alvino, J., McDonnel, R. C., & Richert, S. (1981). National survey of identification practices in gifted and talented education. *Exceptional Children, 48,* 124–132.

Baer, N. A. (1980). Programs for the gifted: A present or a paradox? *Phi Delta Kappan, 61,* 621–623.

Busse, T. V., & Mansfield, R. S. (1980). Renzulli is right. *Gifted Child Quarterly, 24,* 132.

Christopherson, S. L. (1981). Developmental placement in the regular school program. *G/C/T, 19,* 40–41.

Drews, E. M. (1976). Leading out and letting be. *Today's Education, 65,* 26–28.

Feldman, D. (1979). Toward a nonelitist conception of giftedness. *Phi Delta Kappan, 60,* 660–663.

Finkel, I. F. (1980). Today's gifted education: From questionable to stupid. *Learning, 9,* 93–94.

Gallagher, J. J. (1986). Equity vs. excellence: An educational drama. *Roeper Review, 8,* 233–235.

Goldberg, M. L. (1986a). Issues in the education of gifted and talented children Part I. *Roeper Review, 8,* 226–233.

Goldberg, M. L. (1986b). Issues in the education of gifted and talented children Part II. *Roeper Review, 9,* 43–50.

Janos, P. M., Fung, H. C., & Robinson, N. M. (1985). Self-concept, self-esteem, and peer relations among gifted children who feel "different." *Gifted Child Quarterly, 29,* 78–81.

Kirschenbaum, R. J. (1983). Let's cut out the cut-off score in the identification of the gifted. *Roeper Review, 5,* 6–10.

Maeroff, G. (1980). Programs for gifted pupils stirs dispute in Brooklyn. *The New York Times,* November 24, p. 3.

Marland, S. P. (1972a). *Education of the gifted and talented.* Report to the Congress of the United States by the U.S. Commissioner of Education. Washington, DC: U.S. Government Printing Office.

Marland, S. P. (1972b). Our gifted and talented children—A priceless national resource. *Intellect, 101,* 16–19.

Olstad, D. (1968). The pursuit of excellence is not elitism. *Phi Delta Kappan, 60,* 187–188, 229.

Passow, A. H. (1986). Reflections on three decades of education of the gifted. *Roeper Review, 8,* 223–226.

Powell, P. M., & Haden, T. (1984). The intellectual and psychosocial nature of extreme giftedness. *Roeper Review, 6,* 131–133.

Raspberry, W. (1976). What about elitist high schools? *Today's Education, 65,* 36–39.

Renzulli, J. S. (1978). What makes giftedness? Reexamining a definition. *Phi Delta Kappan, 60,* 180–184, 261.

Renzulli, J. S. (1980). Will the gifted child movement be alive and well in 1990? *Gifted Child Quarterly, 24,* 3–9.

Renzulli, J. S., & Delcourt, M. A. B. (1986). The legacy and logic of research on the identification of gifted persons. *Gifted Child Quarterly, 30,* 20–23.

Ricca, J. (1984). Learning styles and preferred instructional strategies of gifted students. *Gifted Child Quarterly, 28,* 121–126.

Richert, E. S. (1985). Identification of gifted children in the United States: The need for pluralistic assessment. *Roeper Review, 8,* 68–72.

Roedell, W. C. (1984). Vulnerabilities of highly gifted children. *Roeper Review, 6,* 127–130.

Schlichter, C. L. (1981). The multiple talent approach in mainstream and gifted programs. *Exceptional Children, 48,* 144–150.

Sisk, D. (1980). Issues and future directions in gifted education. *Gifted Child Quarterly, 24,* 29–32.

Stanley, J. C. (1984). Use of general ability and specific aptitude measures in identification: Some principles and certain cautions. *Gifted Child Quarterly, 28,* 177–180.

Stewart, E. D. (1981). Learning styles among gifted/talented students: Instructional technique preferences. *Exceptional Children, 48,* 134–138.

Tannenbaum, A. J. (1983). *Gifted Children: Psychological and educational perspectives.* New York: Macmillan Publishing Co.

Terman, L. M., & Oden, M. (1959). *The gifted group at midlife: Vol. V.: Genetic studies of genius.* Stanford, CA: Stanford University Press.

Treffinger, D. J. (1982). Gifted students, regular classrooms: Sixty ingredients for a better blend. *The Elementary School Journal, 82,* 267–273.

Tremaine, C. D. (1979). Do gifted programs make a difference? *The Gifted Child Quarterly, 23*, 500–517.

Weber, P., & Battaglia, C. (1985). Reaching beyond identification through the "Identi-Form" system. *Gifted Child Quarterly, 29*, 35–47.

White, M. J. (1970). The case for specifically designed education for the gifted. *Gifted Child Quarterly 14*, 159–162.

Williams, F. E. (1980). Gifted education offers hope for every child. *Learning, 9*, 94–95.

Zettel, J. J. (1980). *Gifted and talented education from a national perspective.* Reston, VA: Council for Exceptional Children.

DISCUSSION QUESTIONS

1. Since there is still so much controversy on the topic of gifted students, create your own definition of which students you would consider gifted, and explain how you would identify them.
2. In some school districts, parental pressure to place children in programs for gifted students is resulting in remedial tutoring for gifted students who can't keep up. What problems do you see with this situation and how might you prevent them?
3. Should there be separate programs for gifted students? Why?
4. What problems do teachers encounter as a result of having gifted students in a class? What benefits do they get? How might they encourage the benefits and reduce the problems?
5. You are at a parent-teacher association or school board meeting and parents of the "average" children in the schools are complaining about how much money is spent on handicapped and gifted children. They feel that their children are being shortchanged. What might you tell them? What suggestions could you make?

Our Towns: When Classes for Gifted Swell with Ungifted

Michael Winerip

STONY BROOK, L.I., Jan. 13—Kathy Moravick, a fifth-grade honors math teacher, has gifted pupils still stuck on fourth-grade math. She spends lunch hour doing remedial tutoring for the gifted. Recently a dozen of them were slow in catching on to least common denominators.

Mrs. Moravick estimates that a third of her pupils do not belong in honors. Dr. Ben Werner, the administrator who founded the district's elementary honors program, believes that half do not.

And yet the gifted program here grows

and grows. Today there are about three times more gifted elementary-school pupils than there were when the program began in 1979—even though the district's elementary enrollment has dropped 20 percent in that time. "Incredible," said Robert Benanti, a teacher.

A lot of it has to do with parental pressure, now back in vogue after a brief letdown in the 1970s. "I had parents threatening me if I didn't put their children in," said Dr. Werner, who retired last summer. Some threatened to sue him, some threatened to punch him.

Some parents whose youngsters do not score high enough on the school screening tests are paying hundreds of dollars to have testing done by outside experts in hope of getting their child certified as gifted. School officials acknowledge that it gives the rich child an advantage.

Parents of the gifted have formed their own group here, Parents and Teachers of Gifted and Talented. It is a political force, nominating school board candidates. Everyone knows which board members are pro-gifted.

This year, 15 percent of the elementary pupils are in honors, about three times the normal rate. There are those who warn that if it keeps up at this pace, before long the entire district will be gifted.

Last spring, creaking under the pressure of so many ungifted gifted children, all fourteen honors teachers wrote a letter to the school board, saying, basically, "Help." These teachers say they love the program— it has just turned into too much of a good thing.

Even the School Superintendent, Joseph King, who arrived two years ago from Fairfax County, VA.—known as a very gifted area—was startled by the masses of the gifted here. About 2 percent of Fairfax elementary pupils take honors classes.

Officials say the swarms of gifted can be explained in part by the area—many parents are affiliated with the State University at Stony Brook. "It's a good gene pool," said

Mr. Benanti, a music teacher. "But it's not that good."

More basic, officials say, is the behavior of parents who are worrying about how to put their child on track for a top college sooner; youngsters who are tested so much that they have become gifted test takers, though not necessarily gifted thinkers, and teachers who are under pressure to teach what is on standardized tests.

The district, known as Three Village Schools, tests for the first-grade honors program in kindergarten. "The pressure on little kids is horrendous," said Lucrezia Iacomino, whose child missed honors by one point.

Maureen Denzler, the mother of a second-grader in honors, said, "It's a big topic at the supermarket: how your kindergarten kid did on the California Achievement Test." The week kindergartners are tested, the school sends home a note advising parents to be sure the child eats a good breakfast and gets plenty of sleep.

Teachers feel sorry for the children under so much pressure to be gifted. Mrs. Denzler knows one kindergarten teacher who tried to give the pupils little hints during the testing. "She's a lovely person and didn't want the children disappointing their parents," Mrs. Denzler said.

Few districts have an honors program that starts with children so young or that beginning in third grade, segregates the gifted.

Dr. Werner, the designer of the program, thought first and second grades would provide a good trial period. He thought teachers would sort out those who did not belong. "Unfortunately, once a kid got in," said Dr. Werner, "parents assumed they had an Einstein and expected the child to stay until graduate school."

Given the parents' attitude, Dr. Werner admits he was reluctant to remove children, for fear that at home, they would be told they had failed.

When the program was small, there were children who scored poorly on screening tests, but were admitted because teachers felt they had gifted minds. Now, their test scores decide—a combined total of 320 on the California Achievement Test and the IQ test, and they are in. "It's unfortunate," said Dr. Werner, "but if we deviated from the test numbers, we would have had hundreds of parents saying, 'put my kid in.' "

Mr. Benanti said such a large honors program had caused morale problems for nonhonors teachers, who feel they do not receive the same resources. Principals report fights between the gifted and the nongifted. Parents want to know why a child has to be gifted to study philosophy. Honors teachers complain that truly gifted children are not advancing quickly enough because instruc-tion must be slowed to accommodate the semi-gifted.

There has been so much unrest, an independent study is being commissioned. "It could split the district up one side and down the other," Dr. Werner said. Parents of the gifted oppose major changes.

The other side has been quieter. "No one wants to get up and admit they have a regular child," said Frank Marino, the school board president.

Each year, Jim Lakatos tells his honors science pupils that he expects a lot, and they can leave if they want. "They all snicker," he says. They know their parents would kill them.

CHAPTER 2

Teacher Preparation Issues

INTRODUCTION

The status and quality of teaching have become nationwide concerns. Educators and parents alike worry over the growing shortage of qualified teachers and the ever-increasing number of teachers leaving the profession for such reasons as lack of support and burnout.

Chapter two is divided into five sections. Section one, *Teacher Certification and Competencies,* includes a discussion of the issues of categorical versus noncategorical certification, competencies needed by special educators, and the development of professional standards for teachers. A reprint of the article *Characteristics of Superior and Average Special Education Teachers* is included. The authors discuss some factors that may influence teachers' qualifications.

Section two, *Paraprofessionals in Special Education,* focuses on the evolution of the role of paraprofessionals in special education. Included is a reprint of *Paraprofessionals in Special Education* by Richard White, who discusses paraprofessionals and their varied responsibilities—which range from relieving the teacher of noninstructional duties to actually teaching.

The third section, *Teacher Burnout,* deals with the symptoms of and factors contributing to burnout, as well as suggestions for preventing it. The *Stress Profile for Teachers,* developed by Christopher Wilson, is included. The profile is designed to assist the classroom teacher in identifying the areas and frequency of their stress.

The fourth section, *Preservice Preparation of Bilingual Special Educators,* addresses the critical shortage of bilingual special educators and the competencies needed by such teachers. Large numbers of bilingual handicapped children are entering the schools, but because of a lack of qualified teachers, these children are being taught by teachers from white middle class backgrounds who understand very little about the students' backgrounds and experiences.

Section five, *Are Teachers Prepared for Mainstreaming?,* asks whether regular education teachers are trained to work with mainstreamed students. Until the passage of P.L. 94-142, the responsibility for educating handicapped students was left to trained special education teachers. Regular education teachers now face the challenge of educating handicapped children in the educational mainstream, but are they prepared for this responsibility? Attitudes play a significant role in the integration of a handicapped child in the regular education classroom, yet traditionally, special educators have held the belief that regular education teachers did not view mainstreaming favorably. However, the reprinted article, *Special Educator Predictions of Regular Class Teacher Attitudes Concerning Mainstreaming* indicates that special educators tend to underestimate regular educators' positive attitudes concerning mainstreaming.

The teaching profession faces many critical issues that must be examined and eventually resolved before we can consistently recruit and retain quality teachers. This chapter examines some of those issues.

TEACHER CERTIFICATION AND COMPETENCIES

In recent years, the status and quality of teaching has been scrutinized from many perspectives. Since *A Nation at Risk* (National Commission on Excellence in Education 1983) emphasized the need for educational reform, at least half a dozen subsequent reports, including *A Nation Prepared* (Carnegie Task Force 1986) and *Tomorrow's Teachers* (The Holmes Group 1986), have called for dramatic changes in America's classrooms and teacher training programs. While these reports address educational problems in general, the concerns expressed are relevant to special education. For example, some reports call for colleges and universities to upgrade admissions criteria to help ensure that students entering teacher preparation programs are well qualified. Others call for university faculty to help guarantee that their students acquire necessary teaching competencies in their training programs.

While the importance of preparing well-qualified teachers seems obvious, the preparation of teachers remains a relatively unstudied area (Sarason, Davidson, and Blatt 1962), and there is little research on teacher effectiveness in special education settings (Englert 1983; Stevens and Rosenshine 1981). Therefore one may legitimately ask even the most basic question: "Have the qualities and skills required of an outstanding special education teacher been clearly delineated?" Examples of how perceptions of exemplary special educators have changed can be found in the following two examples. Although special education teachers were not certified as such at the time of this description, Ray's (1852) description of the qualifications of an attendant working with the insane matches very closely the qualifications required of a modern special education teacher:

> They must manifest patience under the most trying emergencies, control of temper under the strongest provocations, and a steady perseverance in the performance of duty, disagreeable, and repulsive as it oftentimes is. They must be kind and considerate, ever ready to sacrifice their own comfort to the welfare of their charge, cleanly in all their ways, and unsaving of any pains necessary to render their charge so also. In all respects, their deportment and demeanor must be

precisely such as refined and cultivated persons have indicated as most appropriate to the management of the insane. In short, they are expected to possess a combination of virtues which, in ordinary walks of life, would render their possessor one of the shining ornaments of the race (52–53).

More recently, Hobbs (1966) described the ideal teacher-counselor:

> . . . but most of all a teacher-counselor is a decent adult; educated, well trained; able to give and receive affection, to live relaxed and to be firm; a person with private resources for the nourishment and refreshment of his own life; not an itinerant worker but a professional through and through; a person with a sense of the significance of time, of the usefulness of today and the promise of tomorrow; a person of hope, quiet confidence, and joy; one who has committed himself to children and to the proposition that children who are emotionally disturbed can be helped by the process of re-education (Cited in Payne, Kauffman, Patton, Brown, and DeMott 1979, 133–34).

While these descriptions provide some insight into the more personal characteristics required of teachers in the past, they do not address the skills and competencies needed by today's effective teacher. The issues of teacher certification, competency-based training, and professional standards in special education will be reviewed in this section.

Meisgeier (1965) noted the lack of research on the characteristics of teachers of mentally or physically handicapped students or on how to predict effective teaching of these children. This was in spite of the availability of numerous surveys and descriptions of state certification requirements, competency statements, and special education teacher qualifications (Balow 1966; Council for Exceptional Children 1966; Hewett 1966; Mackie, Williams, and Dunn 1957; Schwartz and Oseroff 1975). During the rapid growth of special education in the 1960s and 1970s, the problem of preparing large numbers of special education teachers was compounded by this lack of research (Jones 1966). Since problems in categorizing teacher competencies continue to exist, much research still needs to be conducted before substantial improvements can be made in teacher education.

Teacher Qualifications

Hawley (1986) warns that the United States is experiencing a severe shortage of qualified teachers together with a shortage of candidates with average or above average abilities in areas where there is an unmet demand. Historically, these shortages have been dealt with by reducing or eliminating requirements for entry into the teaching profession. However, Hawley expresses hope that the current concern for quality education combined with universities' traditional opposition to an easing of requirements, will encourage us to seek other alternatives. Years ago, Kirk (1965) highlighted the problem:

> Under the pressure of extreme shortages of professional personnel, a major issue becomes whether to a) focus on immediate needs in terms of the numbers without

regard to quality; b) concentrate on quality in the preparation of professional personnel, even though it may mean a decrease in the numbers thus prepared, or c) find a radically new method of accomplishing both goals at the same time (102).

At present, it appears that the issue of quantity still may be interfering with the need to improve quality.

While many university training programs follow a competency-based program emphasizing demonstrated skills, in most states, current certification standards and final judgments of competence are based on a review of courses taken or credits completed (Maple 1983). To complicate matters even further, universities and colleges often offer programs which vary so greatly that it is almost impossible to translate coursework into certification standards.

To facilitate graduates' certification, university training programs may develop their curriculum according to state certification standards, not the optimal competencies needed by effective teachers. Unfortunately, these certification standards only establish minimum criteria for teacher qualifications; they may be markedly insufficient for preparing superior teachers. Further, because of the short supply of teachers and the need to fill immediate job openings, many states and local districts offer provisional certifications designed to speed the entry of teachers into the work force in areas of shortages. As Maple (1983) states, standards often reflect only minimum qualifications to begin with, and beginning teachers are often hired before they fulfill even these minimum requirements. As a result, full special education teacher certification has become the maximum (rather than the minimum) standard, and provisional certification has become the new minimum. When standards in one university program are raised by increasing coursework or requiring graduate work, that program, because it is now more expensive and taxing on students, may be at a competitive disadvantage. Rather than complete a more intensive program, students select a less rigorous program that satisfies state certification requirements (Maple 1983). Of course, merely tacking on more courses to the students' programs affords no guarantee of teaching excellence. The course content must enable students to develop the special skills they will need as teachers.

Certification: Categorical or Noncategorical?

As far back as 1934, Laycock recommended that categories of exceptionality be disregarded; rather, special educators should be viewed as educational diagnosticians. Lord (1956) warned that teaching, based on assumed differences between categories of children, was not fruitful, and suggested that special educators view their services as comprehensive for all categories of children.

The theory that categories of handicapping conditions are meaningless for teachers has now been applied to teacher training. Reynolds and Balow (1972) suggest that training programs for teachers be specific to instructional systems and teaching competencies rather than to categories of exceptionalities. This argument is reiterated by Smith and Neisworth (1975), who caution that the categorical training of teachers, as well as the classification of children into categories, encourages a search for categorically unique instructional techniques and materials that simply do not exist (Reger 1972; Ysseldyke and Algozzine 1979). Furthermore, they argue, training teachers and issuing special education teaching certificates by category leads to redundancy in coursework and establishes territorial disagreements in the field of special education.

The Professional Guidelines Project of the Council for Exceptional Children (Hebeler and Reynolds 1976) reported that the trend over the 1970s would be to reduce the number of categories for teacher certification in special education; however, this did not happen as rapidly as expected. For example, Belch (1979) surveyed all states and reported that only eleven had a comprehensive noncategorical teacher certification policy, although twelve others reported being headed in that direction. The other twenty-seven states neither had any comprehensive noncategorical certification, nor expected to have one in the near future. The bottom line, however, was that at the time of Belch's study, approximatley 80 percent of the states were still issuing categorical teaching certificates. A more recent survey showed continued movement toward noncategorical certification, although half of the states still retained categorical requirements (Smith-Davis, Burke, and Noel 1984).

While effective teaching is believed more dependent on the organization of instruction than on the grouping of students (Lilly 1979), current practices are not easily changed, and teacher educators in universities may hold opinions that differ from direct service providers. For example, when responding to a survey that asked if secondary special education programs could serve students with mental retardation, behavior disorders, and learning disabilities in the same program, 83.3 percent of the university faculty compared to only 34.6 percent of the local special education directors responded positively (Miller, Sabatino, and Larsen 1980).

In some states, teachers receive certification endorsements for different categories of students, even though the states or local districts may combine these categories. In other states, teachers receive a noncategorical certificate, even though school programs are based primarily on categorical placements. In these cases, teachers may be certified in one area while working with students from another. Local districts must then rely on their teachers' initiatives and innovative skill to serve students whom they have not been formally prepared or certified to teach (Maple 1983). The most common cross-categorical certification permits teachers to instruct behaviorally disordered, mentally retarded, or learning disabled children (Heller 1982). These certifications were designed to allow for delivery of services to students with handicaps so mild they did not need categorical identification to allow for effective remediation (Vallecorsa 1983). As Carri (1985) notes, in certain states, resource room teachers are being certified as cross-categorical teachers even without preparation in all the areas in which they are expected to teach. The assumption is that the teachers' skills are generalizable to several groups of students. However, when surveyed, teachers of learning disabled and mentally retarded students shared similar views of the skills and competencies that they needed, while teachers of students with behavior disorders differed in their ratings of the necessary skills and competencies (Carri 1985).

Despite perceived differences regarding needed skills and competencies, however, the type of training received by teachers may have little real impact on their effectiveness. In one study, Myers (1981) compared the competencies of two groups of first-year special education teachers. One group consisted of 109 teachers with primarily categorical training, the second of 99 graduates with noncategorical training. The results revealed no significant differences between the two groups of teachers. More recently, Marston (1987) explored the effects of teacher certification on students' reading achievement by examining whether students identified as having learning disabilities or mild retardation made better progress in reading when taught by teachers certified in the students' disability category. The results indicated that students taught by teachers with matching certification did not make significantly greater gains than did those taught by teachers whose certification did not match the students' handicapping conditions. Since teacher certification within the categorical model does not seem to relate to student progress, at least with reading instruction for mildly handicapped students, a revision in certification requirements and teacher training programs may be needed, although it may already be in progress in some areas. In addition, Maple (1983) recommends the following four specific actions: identifying important teacher competencies, implementing professional growth plans, increasing the supply of special education teachers through effective recruiting, and developing a code of professional ethics.

Teacher Competencies

The quality of teaching seems to vary from teacher to teacher, regardless of how closely integrated certification and training may be. Evidently other strategies are needed to ensure teaching excellence. One attempt has been the emphasis on the development of specific teacher competencies needed by special education teachers (Maple 1983)—even though Lilly (1979) cautions that while competency-based training has its benefits, it is not a panacea for assuring teacher quality.

In the past, teacher education has often been based on an embarrassing assumption: that verbalized knowledge was a condition for effective teaching (Schwartz and Oseroff 1975). However, the movement to competency-based teacher education (CBTE) has led educators away from dependence on paper-and-pencil testing of knowledge. Currently, CBTE provides a way to specify and define teacher competencies in teacher education programs, as well as to study the relationship of the competencies to student achievement (Gagne 1970). This model of teacher education requires that teacher education programs define explicit competencies or teaching behaviors in relation to student growth, and that teachers in training demonstrate these competencies in a school or clinical setting as evidence of mastery (Turner 1972).

Several educators (Chalfant and Scheffelin 1969; Connor and Cohen 1973) point out the need for professionals from many disciplines and different training institutions to pool their ideas on competency specifications and to jointly analyze the tasks needed to be accomplished by teachers. While competency statements alone cannot define teaching effectiveness, they can serve as important, observable indicators of probable competence.

It is important to note that despite some common elements, competency statements will likely vary from college to college because of differences in philosophy or emphasis. At best, even field-tested competencies must be considered tentative since they may be affected by changing social issues, new research findings, and population changes (Connor and Cohen 1973).

CBTE also leads to questions regarding the relationship of teacher preparation to teacher certification. Should performance criteria be the sole basis for certification? Or even after competencies are demonstrated, should coursework still be required? Is it logical to require a college degree for teachers, or is certification based on demonstrated competencies sufficient? Obviously answers to these questions could have tremendous impact on university programs and certification agencies (Connor and Cohen 1973). As noted earlier, many states, while requiring competency-based teacher education, ignore it for certification and rely on course credit hour counts.

While many educators believe competency-based education necessary to improving teacher effectiveness, it's far from receiving universal support. For example, Blatt, Biklen, and Bogdan (1977) state that competency-based strategies and new approaches to certification (or noncertification) are making things worse rather than better. In an attempt to raise the quality of education, most states now require that new teachers take paper-and-pencil teacher examinations as a requirement for initial certification, although this seems to be a step backward toward testing knowledge rather than the skills so carefully defined during the competency-based teacher education movement. In addition to this entry level testing, Pipno (1986) notes that more states are beginning to require competency testing for already practicing teachers.

Professional Standards

With so many changes occurring in schools, university training programs, and state certification requirements, trainers and practitioners in the field of special education face a growing challenge in controlling the quality of programs through systematic and conscientious monitoring of their own practices and members (Heller and Ridenhour 1983). No group is better qualified to exercise this control than special educators themselves. Because of the inconsistencies in requirements among accrediting agencies, university programs, and state certification offices, Parker (1980) concludes that national professional standards be developed and adopted for special education teachers. This constitutes a massive undertaking, but it's one that cannot be avoided. Birch and Reynolds (1982), applying criteria from other professions, concluded that special education did not meet all the criteria of a profession, and was still being regarded as a "semi-profession."

Though the field of special education initially evolved without benefit of written standards or a formal code of ethics, there have been several efforts to change that situation. In 1966, the delegate assembly of the Council for Exceptional Children (CEC) adopted a report, *Professional Standards for Personnel in the Education of Exceptional Children,* which served as a guide for the profession until it was replaced in 1976 by *Guidelines for Personnel in the Education of Exceptional Children* (Heller and

Ridenhour, 1983). However, these guidelines, though generally accepted by special education professionals, consisted primarily of suggestions, rather than requirements or mandates.

Since 1976, several other milestones have been attained enroute to formulating professional standards. First, the National Council for Accreditation of Teach Education (NCATE) implemented new standards for special education (Heller and Ridenhour 1983). Unfortunately, NCATE is a voluntary accreditation agency and not all institutions of higher education involved in teacher education follow these guidelines (Heller 1983). In April 1983, the delegate assembly of CEC unanimously adopted three new documents: a *Code of Ethics, Standards for Professional Practice,* and *Standards for the Preparation of Special Education Personnel.* These three documents represent the cornerstone for building special education into a strong profession. However, even the best cornerstone provides only a beginning. Heller (1983) stresses that the adoption of standards does not mean that anything in special education will change, nor does it suggest change, if it did occur, would take place. Stephens (1985) also emphasizes the need for *enforceable* professional standards and high professional ethics for special educators.

In Heller's opinion (1983), recognition of poor practices and ineffective instruction in the field of special education was the impetus behind CEC delegates' acceptance of the three "cornerstone" documents in 1983. Acknowledging the need for special educators to govern the quality of programs and personnel serving exceptional children, The Professional Standards Committee of CEC, along with CEC members, were charged with the task of developing implementation procedures for these standards. The task has not been a simple one. Though information on professional ethics should be presented to students before they enter the teaching field (Stephens 1985), at present this is rarely done.

The field of special education, if it is to gain status as a profession, must take responsibility for examining the quality of special education teachers, and improving instruction as needed. Setting and enforcing standards is a start, but it does not provide all the answers. The question remains as to whether the field can control its own professional destiny from within, or whether it must depend on pressure from external forces such as accreditation agencies or state certification offices.

REFERENCES

Balow, B. (1966). A program of preparation for teachers of disturbed children. *Exceptional Children, 32,* 455–460.

Belch, P. (1979). Toward noncategorical teacher certification in special education—myth or reality? *Exceptional Children, 46,* 129–131.

Birch, J., & Reynolds, M. (1982). Special education as a profession. *Exceptional Education Quarterly, 2,* 1–13.

Blatt, B., Biklen, D., & Bogdan, R. (1977). *An alternative textbook in special education.* Denver, CO: Love Publishing Co.

Carnegie Task Force on Teaching as a Profession (1986). *A nation prepared: Teachers for the 21st century.* Washington, D.C.: Carnegie Forum on Education and the Economy.

Carri, L. (1985). Inservice teachers' assessed needs in behavioral disorders, mental retardation, and learning disabilities: Are they similar? *Exceptional Children, 51,* 411–416.

Chalfant, J., & Scheffelin, M. (1969). *Central processing dysfunctions in children: A review of research.* (NINDS Monograph No. 9). Washington, DC: U.S. Government Printing Office.

Connor, F., & Cohen, M. (1973). *Leadership preparation.* New York: Teachers College, Columbia University.

Council for Exceptional Children (1966). *Professional standards for personnel in the education of exceptional children.* Washington, D.C.: Council for Exceptional Children.

Englert, C. (1983). Measuring special education teacher effectiveness. *Exceptional Children, 50,* 247–254.

Gagne, R. (1970). Policy implications and future research: A response. In *Do teachers make a difference: A report on recent research on pupil achievement.* Washington, D.C.: U.S. Government Printing Office.

Hawley, W. (1986). Toward a comprehensive strategy for addressing the teacher shortage. *Phi Delta Kappan, 67,* 712–718.

Hebeler, J., & Reynolds, M. (1976). *Guidelines for personnel in the education of exceptional children.* Reston, VA: The Council for Exceptional Children.

Heller, W. (1982). Preparing special educators: Status and prospectives. *Exceptional Education Quarterly, 2,* 77–86.

Heller, H. (1983). Special education professional standards: Need, value, and use. *Exceptional Children, 50,* 199–204.

Heller, H., & Ridenhour, N. (1983). Professional standards: Foundation for the future. *Exceptional Children, 49,* 294–298.

Hewett, F. (1966). A heirarchy of competencies for teachers of emotionally handicapped children. *Exceptional Children, 33,* 7–11.

Jones, R. (1966). Research on the special education teacher and special education teaching. *Exceptional Children, 33,* 251–257.

Kirk, S. (1965). *Educating the handicapped* (U.S. Office of Education Bulletin No. 3, consultants' papers prepared for use at the White House Conference on Education). Washington, DC: U.S. Government Printing Office.

Laycock, S. (1934). Every teacher a diagnostician. *Exceptional Child Review, 2,* 47.

Lilly, S. (1979). Competency-based training. *Teacher Education and Special Education, 2,* 20–25.

Lord, F. (1956). A realistic look at special classes. *Exceptional Children, 22,* 321–325.

Mackie, R., Williams, H., & Dunn, L. (1957). *Teachers of children who are mentally retarded* (U.S. Office of Education Bulletin No. 3). Washington, D.C.: U.S. Government Printing Office.

Maple, C. (1983). Is special education certification a guarantee of teaching excellence? *Exceptional Children, 49,* 308–313.

Marston, D. (1987). Does categorical teacher certification benefit the mildly handicapped child? *Exceptional Children, 53,* 423–431.

Meisgeier, C. (1965). The identification of successful teachers of mentally or physically handicapped children. *Exceptional Children, 32,* 229–235.

Miller, S., Sabatino, D., & Larsen, R. (1980). Issues in the professional preparation of secondary school special educators. *Exceptional Children, 46,* 344–349.

Myers, R. (1981). *Employer and graduate ratings of competencies of first year special education teachers.* (ERIC Document Reproduction Service No. ED 215 489).

National Commission on Excellence in Education. (1983). *A nation at risk: The imperative for educational reform.* Washington, D.C.: U.S. Department of Education.

Parker, L. (1980). Teacher competencies or certification competencies. *Behavioral disorders: Posture on issues and programs for children with behavioral problems, 5,* 163–168.

Payne, J., Kauffman, J., Patton, J., Brown, G., & DeMott, R. (1979). *Exceptional Children in Focus.* Columbus, OH: Charles E. Merrill Publishing Co.

Pipno, C. (1986). Kappan special report: States move reform closer to reality. *Phi Delta Kappan, 68,* K1–K8.

Ray, I. (1852). On the best methods of saving our hospital for the insane from the odium and scandal to which institutions are liable, and maintaining their place in the popular estimation; including the consideration of the question, How far is the community to be allowed access to such hospitals? *American Journal of Insanity, 9,* 36–65.

Reger, R. (1972). Resource rooms: Change agents or guardians of status quo? *Journal of Special Education, 6,* 355–359.

Reynolds, M., & Balow, B. (1972). Categories and labels in special education. *Exceptional Children, 38,* 357–376.

Sarason, S., Davidson, K., & Blatt, B. (1962). *The preparation of teachers: An unstudied problem in education.* New York: John Wiley and Sons, Inc.

Schwartz, L., & Oseroff, A. (1975). *The clinical teacher for special education.* (Final report volume two—Grant No. OEG-O-71-1668 (603) Division of Personnel Preparation, Bureau of Education for the Handicapped, U.S. Department of Health, Education, and Welfare).

Smith-Davis, J., Burke, P., & Noel, M. (1984). *Personnel to educate the handicapped in America: Supply and demand from a programmatic viewpoint.* College Park, MD: University of Maryland, Institute for the Study of Exceptional Children and Youth.

Smith, R., & Neisworth, J. (1975). *The exceptional child—A functional approach.* NY: McGraw-Hill.

Stephens, T. (1985). Personal behavior and professional ethics: Implications for special educators. *Journal of Learning Disabilities, 18,* 187–192.

Stevens, R., & Rosenshine, B. (1981). Advances in research on teaching. *Exceptional Education Quarterly, 2,* 1–9.

The Holmes Group (1986). *Tomorrow's teachers: A report of the Holmes Group.* East Lansing MI: The Holmes Group.

Turner, R. (1972). Levels of criteria. In B. Rosner (Ed.), *The power of competency-based teacher education: A report.* Boston: Allyn and Bacon.

Vallecorsa, A. (1983). Cross-categorical resource programs: An emerging trend in special education. *Education, 104,* 131–136.

Ysseldyke, J., & Algozzine, B. (1979). Perspectives on assessment of learning disabled students. *Learning Disabilities Quarterly, 2,* 3–13.

DISCUSSION QUESTIONS

1. After reading the early descriptions of the qualifications teachers and other personnel needed to work with special populations, write a list of the qualifications that you think a special education teacher needs today.
2. What are the major problems in controlling teacher quality? What would you recommend doing about these problems?
3. If you are in a special education teacher preparation program, is it categorical or noncategorical? Discuss what you see as the strengths and weaknesses of its orientation. If you are not in a program, select one orientation and discuss it in the same way.

4. For years we have been talking about the need to determine what makes a teacher effective. What makes it so hard to get an answer to this question? What factors do you think make a teacher effective?
5. Many of you may have to take and pass the National Teacher Examination or a similar test in order to be certified in any area of teaching. Investigate what is tested on these exams and react to them as a way of measuring teaching ability. Do you think these exams will improve the quality of teachers? Why?

Characteristics of Superior and Average Special Education Teachers

David L. Westling
Mark A. Koorland
Terry L. Rose

With the current trend in the field of special education to improve the quality of services for exceptional children, there has been a focus on the development of teacher competencies. Recent literature has included some discussion of competencies that should be demonstrated by teachers serving different severity levels and/or categories of exceptional children.

REVIEW OF RESEARCH

One problem regarding the development of such competencies is that they often lack empirical validity (Shores, Cegelka, & Nelson 1973). Relatively few studies have been conducted within special education to identify specific characteristics, strategies, tactics or other teaching variables that are more desirable than others.

Some of the studies conducted have investigated the relationship between the

teacher's effectiveness and various personal variables not amenable to programmatic change. Meisgeier (1965), for example, analyzed the relationship between the quality of teaching mentally or physically handicapped children and the teacher's scholastic aptitude, scholastic achievement, vocational interest, personality, and attitudes. As might be expected, the better teachers had favorable scores in each of these areas. Such information, however, is not very useful for identifying areas to be developed in order to improve the quality of special education through preservice or inservice training.

In a study similar to Meisgeier's, Scheuer (1971) examined the relationship among certain personality variables of teachers of emotionally disturbed students, their competence as teachers, and student academic gains. The only substantial finding was that student gains correlated significantly with student evaluations of the teacher-pupil relationship. As with Meisgeier's results, Scheuer's study presented little information that could provide direction for improving the skills of special educators.

In another study, Blackwell (1972) investigated the differences between good and poor teachers of trainable mentally retarded

Note. Characteristics of Superior and Average Special Education Teachers, 1981, *Exceptional Children, 47,* pp. 357–363. Copyright 1981 by the Council for Exceptional Children. Reprinted by permission.

children. The teachers were ranked according to their supervisors' evaluations. Independent variables included personal data, personality traits, and attitudes toward children. Blackwell found that having more positive attitudes, being a woman, and teaching at the preschool level were related to better teachers.

The studies by Meisgeier, Scheuer, and Blackwell derived their dependent measures (i.e., teacher competence or effectiveness) from ratings by the teachers' supervisors. While this tactic is viable, a more empirical procedure was used by Fredericks, Anderson and Baldwin (1977) in differentiating the quality of teachers of severely handicapped students. They distinguished between good and poor teachers based on the gains made by their pupils during the previous year. Through questioning and observing the teachers, it was determined that four variables accounted for 90 percent of the variance in student gains: length of the instructional day, percentage of programs task analyzed, positive consequence delivery by volunteers, and the consequence delivery of teacher and aide. While such variables are not as specific as might be needed to translate them directly to teacher competencies, they do provide a significant departure from earlier studies in specifying the nature of tasks required to improve teaching performance.

PURPOSE OF THE STUDY

Like earlier studies, the present investigation used teacher responses to determine appropriate characteristics, strategies, and tactics that might serve as a basis for preservice and inservice training that would result in better qualified special educators. The study differed from earlier studies in two ways. First, instead of focusing on a specific categorical group of teachers, special educators teaching a variety of children with various exceptional learning conditions were included. The second difference was the nature of the

independent variables studied. In attempting to determine predominant characteristics of superior teachers and differences between superior and average special educators, variables were analyzed that traditionally have been directly associated with special education teaching practices such as the classroom teaching arrangements used, reinforcement tactics, and testing procedures. High inference variables and variables that generally are not considered to be susceptible to change (e.g., sex, personality) were not investigated. Basically, the research sought to answer two questions:

1. What characteristics, strategies, and tactics describing current classroom activities and related experiences would be identified by a majority of superior special educators in the sample?
2. What characteristics, strategies, tactics, and related experiences would be identified by superior special educators that would differ significantly ($p<.05$) from those identified by a contrast group of average special educators?

METHOD

Subjects

Initially, a letter was sent to all sixty-seven district directors of special education in the state of Florida. The letter stated that the researchers were attempting to identify characteristics of superior special educators. Directors were asked to submit the names of three of their best special education teachers or at least three names of those considered to be among the best. In selecting the names, directors were asked to disregard degree level, certification status, number of years teaching experience, and area of exceptionality taught. Of the letters returned by the directors, fifty-three (80 percent) were usable. Each letter listed the name and school address of three special education teachers. Fifty of these lists were selected, and one teacher was randomly selected from each list. These fifty individuals were sent a letter explaining the purpose of the study, how they were selected to participate, a questionnaire, and a return envelope. Forty-five questionnaires (90 percent) were returned. These individuals were then designated as the group of "superior" special educators.

The three districts whose responses had been removed from the original fifty-three were used to provide the contrast data from an "average" group of special educators. In order to develop a contrast group of average special educators, it was thought that a heterogeneous sample would have to be questioned. The most feasible approach to achieve this was to select an intact group of educators from a given source. Therefore, directors from the three districts were asked to present the questionnaire to all of their teachers and return those completed. The total number of teachers in the contrast districts was seventy-nine. None of the superior special educators indicated in the original responses from the contrast district directors had been sent an individual letter and questionnaire. Instead, the directors were to ask all of their special education instructional personnel to fill out the forms. In doing so, the directors were requested to assure their teachers of anonymity and not to coerce them in any way to complete the forms. They were simply to inform them that the data were to be used as part of a study on characteristics and behaviors of special educators. A total of sixty responses (76 percent) were returned from the contrast districts. These individuals comprised the average group.

Questionnaire

The questionnaire used in the study was designed to reflect the status and behaviors of the teachers in several areas. A total of one hundred questions were asked. The majority (eighty-eight) were yes-no questions. The remaining questions were answered by selecting an answer from three or more choices. No question required the teacher to express

an attitude, opinion, or idea: instead the teacher was asked to indicate the answer to the question according to his or her current or past experiences. The questionnaire was referred to as the Special Education Teacher Profile (Westling, Koorland, & Rose 1978).

The questions were divided into seven categories: personal/professional data; professional preparation; classroom teaching activities; classroom management; evaluation; professional interaction; and parental interaction. Personal/professional data included questions about the exceptionality being taught, the administrative arrangement, experience, and certification status. Professional preparation questions requested information about preservice and inservice training including practicum experiences and the number of journals currently received and read. The classroom teaching activities section allowed the teachers to respond in regard to the sources of their curricula and materials. In this section teachers were also asked about student-teacher ratios and the use of instructional media.

In the classroom management section, teachers were asked about the use of reinforcement, punishment, and various counseling techniques. They were also questioned about keeping systematic records of changes in students' behavior. Questions on evaluation focused on the manner and frequency of use of different kinds of pupil assessment techniques.

The final two sections presented questions regarding the teachers' interactions with other professionals and with parents. They were asked about types of interactions that occurred and the frequency of their occurrence.

RESULTS

The data analyzed from the first section of the questionnaire (personal/professional) indicated only one significant difference ($p < .05$) between the two groups: 45 percent of the average teachers were in their first or second year of teaching their current exceptionality, whereas only 22 percent of the superior teachers indicated such limited experience. All other response frequencies within this section showed no significant differences when analyzed using the chi square test statistic.

The responses to questions in the remaining sections of the questionnaire were analyzed in two ways to answer the questions of the study. The first analysis found those items that were answered positively by a majority (>50 percent) of the superior group of special educators. Thirty items were found that met this criterion. They are indicated in Table 1 along with the percentage of superior teachers who answered "yes" to the question.

TABLE 1 ITEMS ANSWERED POSITIVELY BY THE MAJORITY (>50%) OF SUPERIOR SPECIAL EDUCATORS

Section	Item (percent answering yes)
Personal professional	Certified in present area of teaching (96%)
Professional preparation	Holds BA/BS in area of exceptionality currently teaching (76%)
	Had voluntary experiences with exceptional children prior to entering training program (56%)
Classroom teaching activity	Develops own curriculum for at least 50% of instructional activities (83%)
	Uses commercial materials for at least 50% of learning activities (82%)
	Uses teacher-made materials for at least 50% of learning activities (82%)
	Uses instructional media at least once a week (91%)
	Uses a one-to-one instructional ratio for at least one-third of the day (82%)
	Uses small group (3–5 students) instructional arrangements for at least one-third of the day (88%)
Classroom management	Commonly uses the following reinforcement tactics: smiles and gestures (91%), verbal praise (98%), physical contact (91%), verbal (71%), games and toys (62%), notes to parents (60%).
	Commonly uses the following punishment tactics: time-out (53%), verbal reprimand (83%), facial gestures (71%), loss of free time (51%), loss of special privileges (62%), ignores inappropriate behavior and reinforces appropriate behavior (51%)
	Uses value clarification activities (51%)
Evaluation	Uses standardized tests at the beginning of the year (84%)
	Tests are individually administered (84%)
	Uses the same tests at the end of the year (80%)
	Uses informal testing techniques with a majority of students (93%)
	Keeps records or graphs of individual student performance (69%)
Professional interaction	Consults with regular class teachers as part of regular teaching duty (58%)
	Assists guidance counselor in planning and/or conducting counseling sessions for exceptional students (58%)
	Keeps the principal informed of students' progress (73%)

The second analysis compared differences in responses to individual items between the superior teachers and the contrast group of teachers. Each item was analyzed in a contingency table that was divided by groups and the number of yes and no or multiple choice responses. The chi square test statistic was used to determine significant (p<.05) differences in responses (Roscoe 1975). In this analysis the objective was to determine whether or not a significant difference existed between the two groups in terms of the frequency of types of responses. Significant differences (p<.05) in frequency of responses were found on eleven items.

These items are indicated in Table 2 along with the percentage of both groups of teachers providing affirmative answers.

DISCUSSION

As seen in Tables 1 and 2, a number of noteworthy items were found either to be indicated by the majority of the superior teachers or to differentiate the superior and average teachers. Before discussing the results and their implications, some consideration should be given to the limitations of the study.

TABLE 2 ITEMS HAVING SIGNIFICANTLY DIFFERENT (p<.05) "YES" RESPONSE FREQUENCIES BETWEEN SUPERIOR AND AVERAGE SPECIAL EDUCATORS

Section	Item	Superior teachers answering "yes"	Average teachers answering "yes"
Professional preparation	Holds MA/MS in present area of teaching	31%	15%
	Number of courses taken that included practicum experience:		
	0	4%	23%
	1–2	22%	18%
	3–4	24%	8%
	5–6	11%	18%
	more than 6	38%	32%
	Had voluntary experiences with exceptional children prior to entering training program	56%	75%
Classroom teaching activity	Uses instructional media at least once a week	91%	73%
	Uses large-group (more than 5) instructional arrangements for at least one-third of the day	29%	50%
Classroom management	Commonly uses facial gestures as a punishment tactic	71%	87%
Evaluation	Tests students at the end of the year (using same tests as at the beginning of the year)	80%	58%
	Uses informal testing techniques at least once a week	36%	55%
Professional interaction	Provides inservice training for non-special education personnel in the school or district	44%	12%
Parental interaction	Meets regularly with most students' parents	40%	18%
	Meets with most students' parents once a year	20%	38%

Limitations of Study

In a study of this nature, certain limitations must be recognized. The first limitation of the present study was the manner of selecting the superior teachers. While it was assumed here that supervisors could accurately identify their best teachers, a more empirical approach (e.g., one based on student gains) may be desirable. Even when such an approach is used, however, there will also be limitations, though perhaps of a different nature. For example the variance in student gains may be due to sources other than teacher behaviors. In the present study, several selection procedures were considered. Given the variety of limitations that may affect any such process, it was felt that the most efficacious method was used.

A second limitation resulted from the manner in which the superior teachers were addressed. Their responses may have been influenced by their knowledge that they had been selected as superior teachers. Due to the nature of the questionnaire, however, this was considered by the authors to be a minimal threat. Because the teachers were asked to indicate facts, there was little leeway allowed to express what one thought should be the situation, which is often the case with attitudinal or other high inference scales.

A final limitation that must be considered is that even if the indicated responses correlate highly with actual classroom and related practices, this does not necessarily mean that the practices indicated by the superior teachers result in optimal student gains.

Factors Affecting Teacher Quality

Notwithstanding the recognized limitations of the study, there are various specific findings indicated in Tables 1 and 2 that could provide for extensive discussion. Also important is the lack of expected positive and/or differential responses to many of the items contained on the questionnaire. Due to space limitations, the present discussion can only highlight some of the more relevant results.

Years of Experience

As mentioned earlier, there were significantly fewer superior teachers in their first year or two of teaching than there were average teachers. In addition, as seen in Table 1, significantly more superior teachers held master's degrees. Despite the fact that district directors were asked not to select the superior teachers based on experience or degrees, they may have ignored this request. On the other hand, one could conclude that experience and graduate training is more typical of the superior teacher.

Practicum Experience

Perhaps a more important finding in the area of professional preparation is the extent of practicum experience differentiating the two groups. Since it is highly doubtful that the directors were aware of the particulars of their teachers' preservice training, it could be assumed that this finding is valid in its own right. Thus, it could be concluded that more extensive preservice practicum experiences are associated with a greater number of superior teachers.

Instructional Arrangements

One of the more interesting findings in the classroom teaching activity section regarded the use of instructional arrangements. A majority of the superior teachers provided individual and small group instruction, and significantly fewer of the superior teachers used large group instruction. Since one of the features of special education is to provide individualized instruction, it might have been expected that superior teachers would arrange for instructions to be delivered to smaller groups. The implication of this finding is not so much the obvious need to use small group instruction, but the need to train teachers in ways of managing instruction of children who, at a given time, are not receiving individual or small group instruction. It is possible that average teachers use so much large group instruction because they have difficulty managing the behavior of children not in the targeted instructional group. This may imply a need to provide teachers with better management techniques.

Use of Postyear Evaluations

Preyear and postyear evaluations of students using standardized tests (including achievement tests and adaptive behaviors tests) were reported by a majority of the superior teachers. When contrasted with the average group, significantly more of the superior teachers conducted postyear evaluations. This would indicate that an effort was being made by the superior teachers to document student gains during the year. This procedure, along with the common use of informal testing and record keeping, would indicate that the majority of superior special educators are attempting to comply with the spirit of legislative mandates. It is the responsibility of training programs to present this evaluation format to all preservice teachers, not only to encourage satisfying the requirements of law but also to enhance superior teaching performance.

Interaction with Parents and other Professionals

The final point to be made is that the data depict most superior teachers as being extensively involved with other school personnel and with parents. Most superior teachers are working with regular educators. Additionally, more superior teachers are providing inservice training for non-special education personnel and are meeting regularly with parents. Since a majority of the superior teachers did not indicate consistently a significant frequency of meeting with parents, these data were not indicated in Table 1. However it was found, in combination, that a majority of the superior special educators met at least twice a year with their students' parents.

CONCLUSIONS

Two general impressions are relatively clear. First, as a group, special education teachers perceived by their district directors as being superior tend to have had more formal educational experience, particularly at the graduate level. The data also point out that as a group superior teachers have had more practicum experience in their preparatory coursework and more teaching experience with exceptional children. While the latter finding cannot be controlled at the preservice stage of training, the former certainly can.

The second general conclusion that may be inferred is that, by and large, the superior teachers are fulfilling the intent of current legislation affecting special education. This is clearly seen from the results in the sections on evaluation, professional interaction, and parental interaction. Other data that may also support this inference are in the section on classroom teaching activity, wherein a majority of the superior teachers reported developing their own curriculum. It may be reasoned that state and/or commercial curriculum guides simply do not allow for enough individualized planning. This hypothesis is somewhat supported by the extent of preyear and postyear evaluation conducted by superior teachers.

As in any profession, special education will always have members who range from superior to average to below average. It cannot be expected that this range, whatever may cause it, will ever be overcome entirely. It is felt, however, that by pointing out some of the characteristics and tactics that are common to superior teachers and differentiate them from average teachers, preservice and inservice training programs may be designed that will improve the overall quality of all special education teachers.

REFERENCES

Blackwell, R. Study of effective and ineffective teachers of the trainable mentally retarded. *Exceptional Children*, 1972, *39*, 139–143.

Fredericks, H., Anderson, R., & Baldwin, V. The identification of competencies in teachers of the severely handicapped. In P. Mittler (Ed.), *Research to practice in mental retardation* (Vol. II: Education and training). Baltimore: University Park Press, 1977.

Meisgeier, C. The identification of successful teachers of mentally or physically handicapped children. *Exceptional Children*, 1965, *32*, 229–235.

Roscoe, J. Fundamental research statistics for the behavioral sciences. New York: Holt, Rinehart, & Winston, 1975.

Scheuer, A. The relationship between personal attributes and effectiveness in teachers of the emotionally disturbed. *Exceptional Children*, 1971, *37*, 723–731.

Shores, R., Cegelka, P., & Nelson, C. Competency based special education teacher training. *Exceptional Children*, 1973, *40*, 192–197.

Westling, D., Koorland, M., & Rose, T. *Special education teacher profile*. Tallahassee: Department of Childhood, Reading, and Special Education, Florida State University, 1978.

PARAPROFESSIONALS IN SPECIAL EDUCATION

While paraprofessionals have been used in special education classrooms for years, one of the first documented uses of special education paraprofessionals occurred nearly twenty years ago in a demonstration project at Syracuse University where it was shown that paraprofessionals could be used effectively in special and regular education classes (Cruickshank and Haring 1957). However, shortly thereafter in 1965, as a result of Title I of the Elementary and Secondary Education Act, salaried paraprofessionals entered the workforce to assist professionals with noninstructional duties (Greer 1980).

By the 1970s, the number of paraprofessionals began to grow dramatically. In 1973, there were an estimated twenty-seven thousand special education paraprofessionals employed in the public schools with nine states reporting certification procedures for all paraprofessionals, and one state having established criteria for special education paraprofessionals. By 1979, eight states had established certification procedures for all paraprofessionals, while two others had developed certification procedures for paraprofessionals in special education programs (Fimian, Fafard, and Howell 1984). Recognizing the rapidly growing number of paraprofessionals in special education programs, the Bureau for the Education of the Handicapped (BEH) awarded funds to the New Careers Training Laboratory to establish the National Resource Center for Paraprofessionals. The goal of this center was to address the needs and improve the quality of training for special education paraprofessionals (New Careers Training Laboratory 1979–1981).

By 1980, the estimated number of employed special education paraprofessionals reached 125,000 (Pickett 1979, 1980). During this same year three states defined or at least made reference to paraprofessionals in their state laws (Pickett 1979; New Careers Training Laboratory 1979–1981).

Paraprofessionals Defined

The term *paraprofessional*, although widely used in special education, generates confusion. Part of this confusion results from the interchangeable use of the terms *paraprofessional, teacher aide, teacher assistant,* and *teacher associate* in the special education literature. There is no consensus about an appropriate term to describe the career levels of the skilled assistant (Reid and Johnston 1978). However, in some school districts, a distinct career hierarchy based upon the type and degree of training a person has received is used. Therefore, a person may be promoted from aide to assistant to associate (Fimian, Fafard, and Howell 1984).

For the purpose of our discussion, we will use the definition of *paraprofessional* suggested by Fimian, Fafard, and Howell (1984):

> Paraprofessionals are working-aged adults who directly assist special education teachers in the delivery of instruction, are credited for their assistance through title, and are employed by the school. Usually, paraprofessionals have pursued additional training for their position or are seeking a career in special education. Depending on state requirements, paraprofessionals may or may not be certified. They frequently have designated responsibilities in the classroom and are expected to have more numerous and diverse skills in a variety of subject areas in comparison to volunteers and peer tutors. Paraprofessionals often include teacher associates, technicians, assistants, and teacher aides (7).

Responsibilities of Paraprofessionals

Historically, the paraprofessional's position in special education was characterized by high job turnover rates, low pay, low status, and a minimum of education or training (Shotwell, Dingman, and Tarjan 1960; Taylor 1964). In many cases there was much friction between professional and paraprofessional regarding the latter's duties (Blessing 1967; Fredericks, Baldwin, Hanson, and Fontana 1972). Reid and Reid (1974) classified the duties of this group as clerical, housekeeping, noninstructional, and instructional. The implication of these categories is that teachers teach while paraprofessionals prepare materials and manage the children.

With the passage and implementation of Public Law 94-142, the demands for individualized instruction increased (Greer 1978; New Careers Training Laboratory 1974a, 1974b). Since most school districts have budgetary limitations on the number of certified teaching staff they can hire, the use of paraprofessionals in the special education classroom was viewed as one way of providing an optimal student-teacher ratio (Green 1977).

Frith and Lindsey (1980) identified eight areas in which paraprofessionals should have expertise when working with multiply handicapped students: administration of screening and informal assessment instruments; planning learning activities; obtaining special materials and equipment; adapting curricula, materials, and equipment; supporting team efforts; providing individualized instruction; providing mobility training; and coordinating home-school programming. May and Marozas (1981) examined the roles and characteristics of paraprofessionals and found that they were assuming a wide array of responsibilities in special education classrooms, including instructional planning, report writing, and testing. Many of these responsibilities require formal training, and were once considered the teacher's responsibility. It is apparent, therefore, that the role of the paraprofessional has changed over the years. This shift in roles and responsibilities may be due, in part, to more effective use of paraprofessionals in special education programs. Paraprofessionals have successfully provided educational services to learning disabled (Jones 1969); mentally retarded (Budner, Arnold, and Goodman 1971); severely handicapped (Tucker and Horner 1977); emotionally disturbed (Terrel et al. 1972); and preschool handicapped children (Karnes, Teska, and Hodgins 1970).

If paraprofessionals are to function as well-prepared and cooperative team members, they must be given appropriate training relevant to their future responsibilities, and preferred duties (McKenzie and Houk 1986). Variations in their backgrounds and responsibilities must be examined and taken into account by program teachers and administrators in designing the most effective programs to serve handicapped individuals (May and Marozas 1981). Many college programs are preparing special education paraprofessionals at the preservice level (New Careers Training Laboratory 1974b). In addition, a large number of inservice training programs are reaching paraprofessionals who are already employed in programs serving handicapped individuals, but who wish to upgrade their skills (Fafard 1975).

Are Teachers Prepared to Work with Paraprofessionals?

While the growth of paraprofessional training programs has been impressive (Whorton and Reid 1978), many paraprofessionals must still be trained by the teachers with whom they work. In her Update Report on Paraprofessionals in Special Education, Fafard (1975) emphasizes the need for preparation courses in effectively developing and managing paraprofessional training in the classroom. Strengthening of preservice programs was a stated priority of the Division of Personnel Preparation in the Special Education Programs Office (Sontag 1982). In order to deliver the most effective educational programs to handicapped individuals, paraprofessionals and professionals must work together as a team. However, little attention has been placed on preparing teachers to work with paraprofessionals (Marozas 1984). To achieve the desired teamwork and effectiveness, the new teacher must be trained to coordinate, manage, and supervise paraprofessionals.

Over the years, many complaints from both professionals and paraprofessionals reflect problems in their working relationship. For example, Fredericks, Baldwin, Hanson, and Fontane (1972) report the following comments made by professionals about paraprofessionals: "I don't know what to do with them," "They're more trouble than they are worth." Conversely, one paraprofessional had this to say about a professional: "The teacher didn't give me adequate instructions on how to do the task she wanted me to do and became annoyed when I didn't do it properly." These comments, while perhaps being more severe than we would find in many programs today, do point out the necessity of a good paraprofessional/professional relationship.

To assure maximum cooperation with paraprofessionals, teachers need new skills in three main areas: supervision, training, and evaluation (Whorton and Reid

1978). Effective supervision is crucial. The teacher is responsible for the day-to-day supervision of the paraprofessional and the delineation of their respective roles. If the teacher is able to structure the classroom in such a way as to make the paraprofessional a team member, not just an extra body, a much more successful relationship can develop. In addition, good personal interaction skills during supervision can make the paraprofessional feel like a welcome team member rather than an outsider. Criticisms should be given constructively, so that the paraprofessional is not so fearful of failing to live up to expectations that anxiety negatively influences his performance.

Teachers also need competence in training. Paraprofessionals have widely varied backgrounds and responsibilities. The teacher must be able to determine the paraprofessional's strengths, weaknesses, and preferences, and use this information to help the paraprofessional capitalize on strengths and overcome weaknesses.

Finally, teachers need to know how to effectively evaluate a paraprofessional's performance. This information can be used by both team members in making future decisions about job responsibilities, future employment, and salary raises.

For many beginning teachers, these are difficult skills to acquire. They are still working hard to develop their own teaching abilities and may be overwhelmed by the additional responsibilities. However, the opportunity to build skills during their teacher preparation programs—before they find themselves in the classroom—may help them to feel more comfortable in this role.

In an attempt to remedy this apparent lack of content on paraprofessionals in preservice special education programs, a U.S. Department of Education training grant was awarded to establish a National RETOOL Center. This Center would develop training modules to assist special educators in using paraprofessionals more effectively (Humm 1982). While this approach might assist some teachers who have already graduated from college, many preservice students in university programs could benefit more from coursework on dealing with paraprofessionals.

REFERENCES

Blessing, K. (1967). Use of teacher aides in special education: A review and possible implications. *Exceptional Children, 34,* 107–113.

Budner, S., Arnold, I., & Goodman, L. (1971). The plan and reality: Training and utilization of paraprofessionals for service to the retarded. *American Journal of Public Health, 61,* 297–307.

Cruickshank, W., & Haring, N. (1957). *Assistants for teachers of exceptional children.* Syracuse: Syracuse University Press.

Fafard, M. (1975). *Paraprofessionals in special education: Update report.* New York: New Careers Training Laboratory. (ERIC Document Reproduction Service No. ED 112 591).

Fimian, M., Fafard, M. B., & Howell, K. (1984). *A teacher's guide to human resources in special education: Paraprofessionals, volunteers, and peer tutors.* Boston: Allyn & Bacon, Inc.

Fredericks, H., Baldwin, V., Hanson, W., & Fontana, P. (1972). Structure your volunteers. *Education and Training of the Mentally Retarded, 7,* 26–30.

Frith, G., & Lindsey, J. (1980). Paraprofessional roles in mainstreaming multihandicapped students. *Education Unlimited, 2,* 17–21.

Green, W. A. (1977). *Paraprofessional training manual: An inservice approach for training staff working with the severely-to-profoundly handicapped.* New York: City University of New York. (ERIC Document Reproduction Service No. ED 013371).

Greer, J. (1978). Utilizing paraprofessionals and volunteers in special education. *Focus on Exceptional Children, 10,* 1–15.

Humm, A. (Ed.). (1982). *New Directions, 3,* 1.

Jones, J. (1969). Dyslexia: Identification and remediation in a public school setting. *Journal of Learning Disabilities, 2,* 533–538.

Karnes, M., Teska, J., & Hodgins, A. (1970). The successful implementation of a highly specific preschool instructional program by paraprofessional teachers. *Journal of Special Education, 4,* 69–80.

Marozas, D. (1984). Preservice preparation of teachers to work with paraprofessionals. *CEC FORUM, 10,* 9–10.

May, D., & Marozas, D. (1981). The role of the paraprofessional in educational programs for the severely handicapped. *Education and Training of the Mentally Retarded, 16,* 228–231.

McKenzie, R. G., & Houk, C. S. (1986). Use of paraprofessionals in the resource room. *Exceptional Children, 53,* 41–45.

New Careers Training Laboratory (1974a). *Directory of college programs for paraprofessionals.* New York: Behavioral Publications.

New Careers Training Laboratory (1974b). *The utilization of paraprofessionals in special education: Present status and future prospects.* New York: Queens College.

New Careers Training Laboratory (1979–1981). *New Directions: The Newsletter of the national resource center for paraprofessionals in Special Education.* CASE/CUNY, 33 West 42nd St., New York, N.Y. 10036. Volumes 1 (1–3) and 2 (1–3).

Pickett, A. L. (1979). *Paraprofessionals in special education: The state of the art—1979.* Unpublished manuscript. New York: New Careers Training Laboratory.

Pickett, A. L. (1980). *National state of the art regarding state of paraprofessionals in special education.* Paper presented at the 58th Annual International Convention of the Council for Exceptional Children, Philadelphia, PA.

Reid, B., & Johnston, M. (1978). Paraprofessionals in education for the severely/profoundly handicapped. In N. G. Haring and D. D. Bricker (Eds.). *Teaching the severely handicapped, Vol. 3.* (pp. 77–93). Seattle: American Association for the Education of the Severely/ Profoundly Handicapped.

Reid, B., A., & Reid, W. R. (1974). Role expectations on paraprofessional staff in special education. *Focus on Exceptional Children, 6,* 1–14.

Shotwell, A., Dingman, F., & Tarjan, G. (1960). Need for improved criteria in evaluating job performance of state hospital employees. *American Journal on Mental Deficiency, 65,* 208–213.

Sontag, E. (1982, December 9). Quality and leadership in special education personnel preparation. Paper presented at the Invitational Meeting for Personnel Preparation. Washington, D. C.

Taylor, H. (1964). Attendants: Assessment and application. *Mental Retardation, 2,* 83–88.

Terrel, D., Spencer, A., McWilliams, S., & Cowen, E. (1972). Description and evaluation of group-work training for nonprofessional aides in a school mental health program. *Psychology in the Schools, 9,* 70–75.

Tucker, D., & Horner, D. (1977). Competency-based training of paraprofessional teaching associates for education of the severely and profoundly handicapped. In E. Sontag and N. Certo (Eds.). *Educational programming for the severely and profoundly handicapped.* Reston, Va.: Council for Exceptional Children.

Whorton, J., & Reid, B. (1978). The implications of paraprofessional training for upper division programs of teacher preparation. *Education and Training of the Mentally Retarded, 13,* 93–95.

DISCUSSION QUESTIONS

1. It is apparent that the role of the paraprofessional has expanded significantly over the past two decades to include such instructional responsibilities as planning, writing reports, and testing. Do you feel the special education paraprofessional should be assuming such responsibilities? Why?
2. The Director of Special Education has selected you to develop an inservice training program for all the paraprofessionals in the district. What general skills and/or competencies will you emphasize in your program? Why?
3. Do you feel that states should establish certification procedures for paraprofessionals? Why?
4. Do you feel that colleges and universities are adequately preparing professionals to work with paraprofessionals? Why?

Paraprofessionals in Special Education

Richard White

The recent *Nation at Risk* report by the Commission on Excellence in Education (1983) has focused considerable public attention on the role, competence, and performance of all educational professionals. The commission concluded that too many of the less academically able are recruited into education and that teacher preparation programs need substantial improvement. To overcome the slide toward mediocrity in education, the commission urged higher standards of recruitment, higher expectations for performance, and additional incentives for meritorious service. The message of the study is clear and simple—to enhance education, improvement in the quality and preparation of persons entering teaching is paramount.

Though the report mentions exploring alternative classroom options, there is no discussion of restructuring educational services, nor of altering the roles of practitioners. The traditional role of the classroom teacher is essentially assumed and unchallenged. The study lacks any examination of the implications of profound changes in the role of teachers within the last several decades, particularly in the provision of services to students with special needs.

The professional/consumer relationship is a major facet of the teacher role that has been redefined. Historically, human-service professionals were imbued with an almost mystical or omniscient capacity to unilaterally prescribe a plan of treatment or service to the recipient (Tracy, et al. 1976). Professional training and certification justified the dominance of the service provider and the submissiveness of the consumer. Today, however, the false authority and autonomy

Note. Paraprofessionals in Special Education by R. White, 1984, *Social Policy*, pp. 44–47. Copyright 1984 by Social Policy Corporation. Reprinted by permission.

associated with this role have significantly eroded. Parents and professional educators are struggling to restructure education so that the knowledge of the professional and the experience of the consumer are blended into a coordinated program of service.

In contrast to antiquated professional practices that attempted to "keep the client in his/her place" and punished "bad" clients who dared question professional decisions, knowledgeable professionals recognize that effective services are dependent upon the activation of consumers in their own learning (Gartner 1979). "Parents as partners" is becoming a common phrase among special educators. This change in relationships is formally recognized in recent legislation regarding services to citizens with special needs. The Education for All Handicapped Children Act (P.L. 94-142), the Vocational Rehabilitation Act (P.L. 93-516), and the Developmentally Disabled Assistance Bill of Rights Act (P.L. 95-605) all require that service recipients be involved in the development of the individual's program of service. The legislation requires equal protection, due process, and informed consent safeguards to insure that consumers fully understand the proposals of professionals and have full opportunity to amend these proposals.

Changes in roles among professionals prescribe service programs in isolation from other points of view. All human services, particularly services to special citizens, are shifting to multidisciplinary or interdisciplinary forms. The major pieces of legislation mentioned previously all require that individualized plans of service must be developed by consensus of all relevant professional personnel in conjunction with the consumer advocate. One professional or one discipline may not decree diagnosis or prescriptions without cross-examination from other disciplines.

As a result of these changes, public-school teaching involves more adult-to-adult interaction. Special educators, regular-grade educators, school psychologists, school nurses, and others must communicate effectively and coordinate programs jointly to a degree greater than ever before. These activities require new sets of skills. Coursework in positive team communications, interdisciplinary team building, consensus building, and conflict resolution is becoming more prominent in the offerings of personnel preparation programs.

However, while these developments have led to a definite decrease in the isolation of professionals in the instructional stages of diagnosis and service planning, too many professionals remain isolated during the actual provision of services. Once a special-needs child is referred, a team of professionals is sanctioned to complete their respective diagnosis, and another team, in concert with the consumer or consumer advocate, determines an appropriate placement and education plan. Then, however, the bulk of the responsibility for implementing the program typically falls on a single teacher in a single classroom. The teacher in isolation may be a regular-grade educator depending on the particular placement. There may be occasional clinical support services provided by other professionals who were involved in the planning of the program, but the hour-to-hour daily instruction generally remains in the hands of a teacher. Even when a regular-grade educator and a special educator are given joint responsibility for delivering a child's program, the services are generally provided in separate classrooms at separate times.

At the point of service provision, special education in many public schools is not so special. The "egg crate school" (classroom compartments off hallways), the closed-door syndrome, and the lonely teacher still characterize most schooling for special children. Apter (1977) charges that an environment in which a single adult rarely sees or communicates with another adult can hardly be termed supportive. He associates the isolation with the prevalence of dull, listless, and burned-out teacher performance that was implicitly critiqued by the Commission on Excellence.

FROM ISOLATION TO SUPPORT

The paraprofessional movement in the human services and special education has been in the forefront of those proponents of support systems for professionals. For some time, advocates for paraprofessional utilization have argued that the capacity of professionals to perform effectively in isolation is limited (Calvin 1975; Fafard 1975). Proposals for differentiated staffing, team teaching, volunteer support, and peer tutoring systems from other sources reflect a similar recognition that additional human resources are necessary. Ellson (1975) argues that the teacher-in-isolation model in education is analagous to the one-man-band model in music. While one marvels at the flexibility and versatility of the performer, the quality of music is not exceptional. In contrast to this model, he argues that educators ought to be conductors of the orchestra, coordinating multiple performers to improve the quality of education.

The conceptualization of the teacher as program manager (Boomer 1980; Brown, et al. 1977) is consistent with this perspective. In this role, teachers administer and direct the contribution of paraprofessionals, interns, volunteers, and other helpers to meet the needs of students. While direct student instruction remains the predominant role of teachers, it is not the only role.

The shift in role from sole provider of instruction to program manager has the following commonly cited advantages:

1. The overall teacher-to-student ratio is decreased, allowing for more individualized attention. The instructional time each child receives is greater (Fimian, et al., in press).
2. The presence of paraprofessional support enables the teacher to organize the classroom differently and more ef-

fectively. Small subgroup and one-to-one instruction are facilitated by paraprofessional support (Boomer 1980; Harrison, et al. 1980).
3. Paraprofessionals may contribute strengths and talents to the classroom that teachers may not have.
4. Paraprofessionals may help teachers develop a more complete and accurate assessment of the student (Boomer 1982). The ongoing feedback and mutual problem-solving between paraprofessional and professional improve decision-making and enhance instructional creativity.
5. The professional-paraprofessional relationship entails mutual emotional support. The quick and cursory exchanges among educators coming and going in school hallways are replaced by meaningful dialogue.
6. Paraprofessionals may act as liaisons between the teacher and other programs. If a certain child leaves the classroom for an alternative service, the paraprofessional may follow the child, thus linking the programs (Boomer 1982). Paraprofessionals may be a vital link in desegregating special-needs children from educational services "for handicapped only."
7. Paraprofessionals may provide partial relief from time-consuming noninstructional chores required of teachers, such as attendance-taking and lunch money collection.
8. Paraprofessionals may improve the credibility of professionals in the community since most paraprofessionals are indigenous to the locale. Paraprofessional advocates have claimed this benefit for some time (Pearl and Riessman 1965).

This additional human support for professionals does require new skills, new roles, and new attitudes. Austin (1978) differentiates between instructional theories and practices of andragogy (adult education) and pedagogy (child education). Since the role of the school professional is evolving from an exclusively pedagogical to a combined pedagogical-andragogical role, teachers must learn to be effective instructors of adult partners. In addition to the consumer relations and interdisciplinary teaming skills discussed previously, the program manager role requires competence in adult personnel management and instruction, and the elimination of self-defeating pseudo-professional posturing behaviors.

FROM HOUSEKEEPER TO INSTRUCTOR

Originally, paraprofessionals in education were hired as teacher aides for the sole purpose of freeing the teacher from noninstructional duties. By increasing the time teachers spent on instruction rather than clerical tasks, it was believed that the quality of instruction would be improved. This type of job description was soon deemed unsatisfactory. Classroom maids, housekeepers, and clerks were roles ascribed to the meaningless and unrewarding nature of this work. It was questionable whether there was sufficient noninstructional work to keep a full-time person busy and, therefore, questionable whether expending resources for hiring classroom housekeepers was justifiable. Many educators began to view this type of role as an unacceptable underutilization of a potentially valuable resource and recommended an instructional role for paraprofessionals (Reid and Reid 1974).

While there was some debate over this change, the transformation of the paraprofessional role from predominantly noninstructional to instructional was relatively quick. The change was given impetus by the burgeoning development of associate degree programs for paraprofessionals at two-year or community colleges, and by federal support for special paraprofessional programs. The question for educators switched from

"Should paraprofessionals be instructors?" to "To what degree should paraprofessionals be instructors?"

Once that question was posed, educators concerned about the respective roles of professionals and paraprofessionals attempted to delineate tasks that were the province of each. Teare (1978) refers to this effort as job factoring. The general trend associated with these efforts was that drill and practice types of instructional tasks were assigned to the paraprofessional, and the design and presentation of instruction remained the sole responsibility of the teacher. However, depending on the particular program, there was much variance concerning the tasks paraprofessionals were permitted to do. Some programs precluded paraprofessionals from grading tests or communicating with parents. Others were established for the primary purpose of having paraprofessionals communicate with parents (e.g., Project SEARCH; see Kaplan 1978).

The role of the special education paraprofessional in the development of individual education plans required by federal law (P.L. 94-142) is a clear example of differential paraprofessional utilization. Fafard (1979) discusses varying levels of paraprofessional involvement. At the less involved end of the continuum, the role of paraprofessionals is to monitor the classroom while the teacher attends the formal planning meeting attended by all relevant professionals (commonly known as the case conference). In other locales, paraprofessionals attend the case conference and contribute as full team members.

As paraprofessionals have gained access to more comprehensive and systematic training opportunities, they have demonstrated ability to do many things that were supposedly only within the jurisdiction of professionals. In fact, many of the ceilings placed on the role and responsibilities of paraprofessionals has had more to do with easing administrative concerns and protecting "turf" than with paraprofessional competence. Fears that paraprofessionals would take over teachers' jobs or become under-paid teachers were the apparent motivation of some job factoring schemes. However, many job factoring attempts were probably done with the good intentions of protecting the paraprofessional from administrative abuse and to eliminate difficult delegation of authority decisions for classroom teachers.

While it is still appropriate to develop job descriptions that protect paraprofessionals from inappropriate administrative placement (e.g., assigning sole responsibility for a classroom program to a paraprofessional and using paraprofessionals as substitute teachers), task-specific job descriptions tend to be too limiting and are an unjustifiable constraint on the program-management responsibility of teachers. Job factored employment descriptions are static. Individual differences among paraprofessionals and paraprofessional growth and development are not taken into account.

In sum, the paraprofessional role ought to be dynamic and constantly expanding as the paraprofessional develops professionally. Progressive educators will see their role as encouraging and assisting in the growth of paraprofessionals. The limits of paraprofessional involvement ought to be based on the competence and motivation of the paraprofessional. In essence, the paraprofessional role needs to be continually redefined and negotiated with the teacher. If paraprofessionals, after negotiations with teachers, feel abused by underutilization or inappropriately used, they should have recourse to due process grievance procedures rather than reliance on a constrained job description.

One of the crackerbarrel sessions at the Second Annual Conference on the Utilization and Training of Paraprofessionals in Special Education featured a panel of teacher-paraprofessional teams discussing their various roles and responsibilities. One teacher stated rather matter-of-factly, and with no trace of defensiveness, that her paraprofessional partner had learned "most of what I know," and that "we actually have a team teaching relationship . . . if you observe our classroom you couldn't tell who was the teacher and who was the paraprofessional." It was a lesson in changed roles and responsibilities.

REFERENCES

S. Apter, "The Public Schools." In B. Blatt, P. B. Klen, and R. Bogdan (eds.), *An Alternative Textbook in Special Education* (Denver: Love Publishing, 1977).

M. Austin (ed.), *Professionals and Paraprofessionals* (New York: Human Sciences Press, 1978).

L. Boomer, "Special Education Paraprofessionals: A Guide for Teachers," *Teaching Exceptional Children*, vol. 12 (1980), pp. 146–149.

L. Boomer, "The Paraprofessional: A Valued Resource for Special Children and Their Teachers," *Teaching Exceptional Children*, vol. 14 (1982), pp. 194–197.

E. Brown, D. Elliott, R. White, *ASSIST: Associate Instructional Support for Teachers* (Bloomington, Indiana: Indiana University Developmental Training Center, 1977).

R. Calvin, "Preservice and Inservice Education: A Case for Teacher Aides," *Teacher Education Forum*, vol. 3 (1975).

D. Ellson, personnel communication, November, 1975.

TEACHER BURNOUT

Howard, a teacher of junior high learning disabled students, was well prepared for his job, perhaps better trained than most teachers. He had received his undergraduate degree in special education with honors from a local state university and a Master's Degree from a prestigious Ivy League college. In his third year of teaching, Howard received an Excellence in Teaching award from the state education department; one of the highest honors that could be bestowed upon a teacher in the state's public school system. Comments from students, colleagues, and administrators indicated that Howard was an exceptionally gifted teacher noted for his thoroughness, organization, knowledge of subject matter, and compassion and helpfulness to students. By the beginning of his fifth year of teaching, Howard began to show signs of irritability. He limited his social interactions with peers, appeared less interested in his work, quit as the girls softball team coach, and at times seemed cynical. Colleagues attributed his behavior to "problems at home." By the end of his fifth year of teaching, Howard left the profession to become a carpenter's assistant, too emotionally and physically exhausted to continue. Howard could no longer cope with the demands of his "chosen profession"; he had burned out on the job.

While Weiskopf (1980) states that no data exist on exactly how many teachers burn out each year, or how many continue to teach while "burned out," Kyriacou and Sutcliffe (1975) report that one-quarter of all teachers feel burned out at any given time, and Wilson (1979) states that 90 percent of all teachers feel some stress, and 95 percent indicate the need for stress management courses. The tragic result of burnout is that education is continually losing qualified professionals (Cook and Leffingwell 1982)—professionals like Howard.

What is Burnout?

Burnout can be defined as the result of unsuccessful attempts to deal with stress (Shaw, Bensky, Dixon, and Bonneau 1980). Freudenberger (1977) defines burnout as physical and emotional exhaustion from excessive demands on energy, strength, or resources. The most often cited definition of burnout is "emotional exhaustion resulting from the stress of interpersonal contact" (Maslach 1976, 56). Burnout has become the term associated with job-related stress.

Symptoms of Burnout

Burnout manifests itself in many different ways. As the degree of burnout increases so do its symptoms (Weiskopf 1980). Freudenberger (1975) discusses the symptoms of burnout from two perspectives: physical and behavioral signs.

Physical signs include exhaustion, loss of weight, sleeplessness, frequent headaches, increases in smoking or drinking, and problems in interpersonal relationships. Behavioral indicators include absenteeism, excessive time spent at work with less productivity, cynicism, complaints of overwork, quickness to anger, and a reduction in social interactions with students and other teachers (Freudenberger 1975, 1977; Maslach 1976; Mattingly 1977; McBride 1983; Weiskopf 1980; Zabel and Zabel 1980). This list is not all-inclusive. Further, these symptoms vary from person to person (Freudenberger 1975). Therefore, the intial signs of burnout may sometimes go unrecognized.

Factors Contributing to Burnout

The major factor contributing to burnout is the teacher's inability to cope with stress (Shaw, Bensky, and Dixon 1981). Although everyone reacts differently to stress, certain factors precipitating stress are well documented in the literature (Cooper and Marshall 1976; Fimian and Blanton 1986; Fimian, Pierson, and McHardy 1986; Freudenberger 1977; Mattingly 1977; Weiskopf 1980).

In addition to planning and implementing educational programs, teachers have a number of additional responsibilities: serving on curriculum committees, meeting with parents, attending fund raisers and chaperoning student events. Although many of these responsibilities are above and beyond a teacher's normal teaching load, they often go unrewarded or unrecognized. Weiskopf (1980) states that as a teacher's workload increases, job tension rises considerably and the result is a decrease in job satisfaction.

Another factor which may lead to feelings of burnout is a lack of observable progress among students. Working with persons who have developmental disabilities is no easy task. Teachers often see limited progress in students and as a result become disenchanted. What they perceive as their own lack of success on the job contributes to lowered self-esteem and eventually to burnout (Collins 1977; Daley 1979; Freudenberger 1977; Mattingly 1977; Pines and Kafry 1978; Proctor 1979).

Increasing the amount of direct contact with children often increases the risk of burnout. Special educators spend several hours each day interacting with students. Often their day is so filled with student interaction that they have very little time alone with colleagues. Maslach and Pines (1977) cite a direct correlation between the number of hours staff members in a day-care center spent with children and their attitudes toward those children. They concluded that "longer working hours were associated with more stress and negative attitudes . . ." (107).

Teacher training may be an underlying causative factor in teacher burnout. Many beginning teachers become disillusioned with the field of education after accepting their first teaching position. Their initial goal is to change society or at least make it a little bit better; their idealism is evident. But new teachers quickly learn the realities of the situation: limited budgets, problems ordering supplies, numerous meetings that place many demands on already limited time. Many of these realities seem far removed from what they had been taught in school to expect. Sarason, Davidson, and Blatt (1962) report that "teachers are more painfully aware than any other professional group about the inadequacies and irrelevancies of their training" (12). This disillusionment with the real world may contribute to stress and eventually lead to burnout.

Lack of program structure may also contribute to teacher burnout. Maslach and Pines (1977) report that the more flexible and less structured a program, the more demanding it is on the teacher. Even when programs are fairly structured, there are demands on the classroom teacher who must implement and manage that structure (Weiskopf 1980). "The prevailing tone of certain structure and moderate control is necessary to alleviate excessive emotional stress" (Weiskopf 1980, 20).

Finally, having responsibility for others in the classroom may be stress-provoking. Special educators are members of a helping profession which attends to the needs of another person, often with limited or no reinforcement from students. In addition, some teachers don't have the luxury of support services from ancillary personnel. This lack of reinforcement and assistance places greater demands on teachers and in turn, diminishes the care and concern they can provide, resulting in burnout.

A Model for Preventing Burnout

Because of the stress special educators experience in their day-to-day encounters with students, parents, and other professionals, qualified teachers such as Howard (described in this chapter's opening scenario) are either leaving the profession or continuing to teach while "burned out." Special educators must learn to identify and cope with personal stressors before burnout occurs. McBride (1983) describes a five-step procedure for preventing burnout (See Figure 2.1).

The first step in preventing burnout is to recognize the symptoms in their earliest stages. As discussed earlier, these symptoms may be physical or behavioral. Unfortunately, the burnout process can be very gradual and symptoms often go unnoticed until a serious problem exists. Early recognition of the symptoms reduces the likelihood that burnout will occur.

A second step involves identifying the causes of burnout. Many social, emotional and political factors cause stress; the key to preventing burnout is identifying these factors. Self-assessment questionnaires such as the Wilson Stress Profile for Teachers are particularly useful for identifying the sources of stress. (See Figure 2.2.)

The third step is prioritizing needs. McBride (1983) indicates that it is impossible to resolve all stressors at once. Therefore, it is most efficient to begin with those causes of stress that have the greatest impact on the individual.

The adoption of intervention strategies such as physical exercise is the fourth step. Exercise is only one alternative. Strategies for coping with stress are as diverse as the symptoms underlying it, and may vary from developing support systems to taking time off from the job. Specific intervention strategies for dealing with stress will be discussed in more detail in the next section of this chapter.

The final step in McBride's model is the evaluation of intervention strategies employed in step four. The evaluation should be ongoing and flexible because no one strategy can be guaranteed to reduce stress for all people in all situations (McBride 1983).

Strategies for Preventing Burnout

Preventing burnout is not easy, nor is it the sole responsibility of the teacher. Administrative personnel, parents, and other professionals must all play a role in stress reduction (Weiskopf 1980). In addition, coping effectively with stress requires the knowledge of and ability to choose good remediation techniques. Following is a

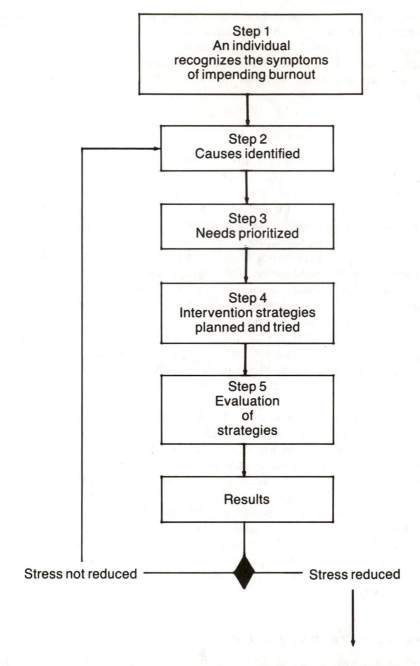

Figure 2.1 A procedure for preventing burnout. *(From* Contemporary Issues in Special Education *(2nd ed.) (p. 227) by R. E. Schmid and L. M. Nagata, 1983, New York: McGraw-Hill, Inc. Copyright 1983 by McGraw-Hill, Inc. Reprinted by permission.)*

Name _____ Date _____

School _____ District _____

STRESS PROFILE FOR TEACHERS

Instructions

The Wilson Stress Profile for Teachers is designed to help you more clearly define, on a self-scoring basis, the areas and frequency of your stress. As you read each item, evaluate the statement in terms of a period of time rather than a specific day you remember. Indicate how often the source of stress occurs by circling the number that corresponds to the frequency of occurrence. Do not read the stress profile scoring sheet until after you have completed items 1-36.

		Never	Seldom	Sometimes	Often	Very Often

Student Behavior

1. I have difficulty controlling my class. 1 2 3 4 5

2. I become impatient/angry when my students do not do what I ask them to do 1 2 3 4 5

3. Lack of student motivation to learn affects the progress of my students negatively 1 2 3 4 5

4. My students make my job stressful 1 2 3 4 5

Total Items 1 - 4 _____

Employee/Administrator Relations

5. I have difficulty in my working relationship with my administrator(s). 1 2 3 4 5

6. My administrator makes demands of me that I cannot meet 1 2 3 4 5

7. I feel I cannot be myself when I am interacting with my administrator. 1 2 3 4 5

8. I feel my administrator does not approve of the job I do. 1 2 3 4 5

Total Items 5 8 _____

Figure 2.2 Stress Profile for Teachers. *(C. Wilson. Copyright 1979. Reprinted by permission.)*

Teacher/Teacher Relations

		Never	Seldom	Sometimes	Often	Very Often
9.	I feel isolated in my job (and its problems) . .	1	2	3	4	5
10.	I feel my fellow teachers think I am not doing a good job	1	2	3	4	5
11.	Disagreements with my fellow teachers are a problem for me	1	2	3	4	5
12.	I get too little support from the teachers with whom I work	1	2	3	4	5

Total Items 9 - 12 _____

Parent/Teacher Relations

13.	Parents of my students are a source of concern for me	1	2	3	4	5
14.	Parent's disinterest in their child's performance at school concerns me	1	2	3	4	5
15.	I feel my students' parents think I am not doing a satisfactory job of teaching their children	1	2	3	4	5
16.	The home environment of my students concerns me	1	2	3	4	5

Total Items 13 - 16 _____

Time Management

17.	I have too much to do and not enough time to do it	1	2	3	4	5
18.	I have to take work home to complete it	1	2	3	4	5
19.	I am unable to keep up with correcting papers and other school work	1	2	3	4	5
20.	I have difficulty organizing my time in order to complete tasks	1	2	3	4	5

Total Items 17 - 20 _____

Intrapersonal Conflicts

21.	I put self-imposed demands on myself to meet scheduled deadlines	1	2	3	4	5
22.	I think badly of myself for not meeting the demands of my job	1	2	3	4	5
23.	I am unable to express my stress to those who place demands on me	1	2	3	4	5
24.	Teaching is stressful for me	1	2	3	4	5

Total Items 21 - 24 _____

Figure 2.2 (Continued)

Physical Symptoms of Stress

		Never	Seldom	Sometimes	Often	Very Often
25.	The frequency I experience one or more of these symptoms is: stomachaches, backaches, elevated blood pressure, stiff necks and shoulders...	1	2	3	4	5
26.	I find my job tires me out..	1	2	3	4	5
27.	I am tense by the end of the day...................................	1	2	3	4	5
28.	I experience headaches	1	2	3	4	5

Total Items 25 - 28 _____

Psychological/Emotional Symptoms of Stress

		Never	Seldom	Sometimes	Often	Very Often
29.	I find myself complaining to others................................	1	2	3	4	5
30.	I am frustrated and/or feel angry..................................	1	2	3	4	5
31.	I worry about my job	1	2	3	4	5
32.	I feel depressed about my job	1	2	3	4	5

Total Items 29 - 32 _____

Stress Management Techniques

		Never	Seldom	Sometimes	Often	Very Often
33.	I am unable to use an effective method to manage my stress (such as exercise, relaxation techniques, etc.)	1	2	3	4	5
34.	Stress management techniques would be useful in helping me cope with the demands of my job........................	1	2	3	4	5
35.	I am now using one or more of the following to relieve my stress: alcohol, drugs, yelling, blaming, withdrawing, eating, smoking............	1	2	3	4	5
36.	I feel powerless to solve my difficulties............................	1	2	3	4	5

Total Items 33 - 36 _____

Figure 2.2 *(Continued)*

Name _____ Date _____

School _____ District _____

SCORING SHEET
STRESS PROFILE FOR TEACHERS

Instructions for Scoring

1. After you have completed items 1-36, total the scores in each category and enter it in the corresponding box on this page.

2. Plot your score on the dotted line with an "X" and draw a line between your scoring "X's" so that a clear profile of your stress evaluation is visible.

3. Add up all your category scores and enter the number in the box after Total Overall Score. A score of 36-72 is low, 73-108 is moderate, and 109-180 is high.

4. Check your level on the same line as either low, moderate, or high.

STRESS PROFILE SCORES

	Score	Low	Moderate	High
		1 2 3 4 5 6 7 8	9 10 11 12 13 14 15	16 17 18 19 20
Student Behavior				
Employee/Administrator Relations				
Teacher/Teacher Relations				
Parent/Teacher Relations				
Time Management				
Intrapersonal Conflicts				
Physical Symptoms of Stress				
Psychological/Emotional Symptoms of Stress				
Stress Management Techniques				
Total Overall Score		Low _____ 36 - 72	Moderate _____ 73 - 108	High _____ 109 - 180

Figure 2.2 (*Continued*)

list of strategies special educators might use to reduce stress and in turn prevent burnout (Crane and Iwanicki 1986; Freundenberger 1975; Gray 1979; McBride 1983; Shaw, Bensky, Dixon, and Bonneau 1980; Zabel and Zabel 1980).

1. Set realistic goals for yourself. As you meet each of your established goals you will achieve a sense of accomplishment.
2. Establish a support network. Interact with persons who recognize and respect your skills and competencies as a professional and who are interested in you as a person, not just a worker.
3. Manage time effectively. Prioritize what needs to be done and do things in your order of priority.
4. Delegate responsibility. Avoid doing everything yourself; use the skills of paraprofessionals, ancillary personnel, and volunteers.
5. Attend conferences, workshops and meetings with other professionals. Sharing experiences and learning what others are doing at their work sites may alleviate stress.
6. Find time for yourself. Consider taking a vacation, participate in relaxing activities, or simply learn to say no to things which are beyond your realm of responsibility. When on your "own time," avoid discussing school-related problems.
7. Maintain a sense of humor. Avoid taking all work-related problems seriously and personally.

Conclusion

The issue of burnout must be addressed before it reaches epidemic proportions resulting in many competent teachers leaving their chosen profession. Learning to deal with stress, thereby preventing burnout, is possible when symptoms are recognizable and remediation techniques available. Teachers, administrators, and parents must all work together, however, to develop a positive yet professional environment that addresses the needs of both teachers and students. Without such an environment, teachers' classroom effectiveness will suffer and students' learning will be inhibited.

REFERENCES

Collins, G. (1977). Burnout: The hazard of professional people-helpers. *Christianity Today, 21,* 12–14.

Cook, J., & Leffingwell, R. (1982). Stressors and remediation techniques for special edcuators. *Exceptional Children, 49,* 54–59.

Cooper, C. L., & Marshall, J. (1976). Occupational sources of stress: A review of the literature relating to coronary heart disease and mental ill health. *Journal of Occupational Psychology, 49,* 11–28.

Crane, S. J., & Iwanicki, E. F. (1986). Perceived role conflict, role ambiguity, and burnout among special education teachers. *Remedial and Special Education, 7,* 24–31.

Daley, M. R. (1979). Preventing worker burnout in child welfare. *Child Welfare, 7,* 443–450.

Fimian, M. J., & Blanton, L. P. (1986). Variables related to stress and burnout in special education teacher trainees and first year teachers. *Teacher Education and Special Education, 9,* 9–21.

Fimian, M. J., Pierson, D., & McHardy, R. (1986). Occupational stress reported by teachers of learning disabled and nonlearning disabled handicapped students. *Journal of Learning Disabilities, 19,* 154–158.

Freudenberger, H. (1975). The staff-burnout syndrome in alternative institutions. *Psychotherapy, Theory, Research and Practice, 12,* 73–83.

Freudenberger, H. (1977). Burn-out: Occupational hazard of the child care worker. *Child Care Quarterly, 6,* 90–99.

Gray, L. (1979). Slow down: You move too fast. *Teacher, 96,* 52–53.

Kyriacou, C., & Sutcliffe, J. (1975). Teacher stress and satisfaction. *Educational Research, 21,* 89–96.

Maslach, C. (1976). Burned-out. *Human Behavior, 5,* 16–22.

Maslach, C., & Pines, A. (1977). The burnout syndrome in the day care setting. *Child Care Quarterly, 6,* 100–113.

Mattingly, M. (1977). Sources of stress and burnout in professional child care work. *Child Care Quarterly, 6,* 127–137.

McBride, G. (1983). Teachers, stress, and burnout. In R. Schmid, & L. Nagata (Eds.). *Contemporary issues in special education* (2nd ed.). New York: McGraw-Hill.

Pines, A., & Kafry, D. (1978). Occupational tedium in the social services. *Social Work, 23,* 499–507.

Proctor, P. (1979, June 17). How to survive today's stressful jobs. *Parade Magazine,* 4–5.

Sarason, S. B., Davidson, K., & Blatt, B. (1962). *The preparation of teachers: An unstudied problem in education.* New York: John Wiley.

Shaw, S., Bensky, J. M., Dixon, B., & Bonneau, R. (1980). Strategies for dealing with burnout among special educators. *Education Unlimited, 2,* 21–23.

Shaw, S. F., Bensky, J. M., & Dixon, B. (1981). *Stress and burnout: A primer for special education and special services personnel.* Reston, VA: Council for Exceptional Children.

Weiskopf, P. (1980). Burnout among teachers of exceptional children. *Exceptional Children, 47,* 18–23.

Wilson, C. (1979). *Survey conducted in San Diego county.* San Diego, California: California Department of Education.

Zabel, R. H., & Zabel, M. K. (1980). Burnout: A critical issue for educators. *Education Unlimited, 2,* 23–25.

DISCUSSION QUESTIONS

1. Are special educators more prone to burnout than regular educators? Why?
2. Symptoms of burnout may be physical and/or behavioral. These symptoms must be identified as soon as possible to prevent burnout from occurring.
   a. What physical signs do you exhibit when under stress?
   b. What behavioral signs do you exhibit when under stress?
   c. In what ways do you handle the physical and/or behavioral signs you have identified?
3. What types of situations and/or events do you find stressful? Why?
4. You are a learning disabilities teacher in a small rural school district. The Director of Special Education keeps giving you additional responsibilities (e.g. additional students in

your class, responsibility for coordinating parent meetings) because of your knowledge and expertise. You find that you are devoting more time to your work and less time to yourself. How would you cope with this stressful situation?

PRESERVICE PREPARATION OF BILINGUAL SPECIAL EDUCATORS

Providing an appropriate public education for children who are handicapped and raised in culturally and/or linguistically diverse backgrounds is one of the greatest challenges facing special educators today (Baca 1980). It has been estimated that there are approximately 420,000 limited-English-proficient (LEP) handicapped children in the United States (Baca and Bransford 1981). Over 30 percent of the children returning to regular classrooms for the majority of the school day are bilingual handicapped children (Fuchigami 1980). Most of these children can be found in large urban areas, but they also reside in suburban and rural communities (Baca 1980). Although progress has been made in providing an appropriate education for this population (Fuchigami 1980; Plata and Santos 1981), the lack of qualified teachers to work with bilingual special education students remains a persistent dilemma (Ortiz and Yates 1983; Poplin and Wright 1983).

The purpose of this section is to discuss the emergence of bilingual special education, the reasons behind the lack of teacher preparation programs in bilingual special education, the competencies needed by teachers to work with bilingual special education students, and the types of personnel preparation program models currently being used to train teachers.

Emergence of Bilingual Special Education

The emergence of bilingual special education can be traced back to the Civil Rights Act of 1964, which prohibited discrimination on the basis of a person's race, color, creed or national origin. This piece of legislation was followed by the passage and implementation of the Bilingual Education Act in 1968 (P.L. 90-247), which set aside federal monies for the establishment and operation of bilingual education programs. These programs were to incorporate bilingual instructional practices, models, and teaching techniques. The law was amended in 1974 (P.L. 93-380) and again in 1978 (P.L. 95-561) to expand the population of eligible participants. Once limited to children from low-income families whose dominant language was other than English, the law now includes children classified as limited-English-proficient (LEP). LEP children are those who have problems reading, writing, speaking and understanding English (Baca and Cervantes 1984). In addition to this legislation, the courts have affirmed the rights of minority children. Cases such as *Lau v. Nichols* (1971), *Rios v. Read* (1977) and *Aspira v. New York Board of Education* (1974) have assured minority children the right to appropriate educational programs.

The 1972 meeting of the Montal Education Association in California marked the first time that professionals from various disciplines had come together to discuss the exceptional bilingual child (Bernal 1983). In 1974, the Council for Exceptional Children (CEC) hosted its first conference on the culturally diverse exceptional child. Bilingual handicapped children were finally being recognized as a population with unique needs.

The eventual passage of P.L. 94-142 mandated that public schools provide free and appropriate educational services to a large number of bilingual special education students in the least restrictive environment possible. Unfortunately, teachers were not prepared to deal with this new population of children. The United States General Accounting Office (1981) reports that the need to recruit and train teachers of bilingual special education students still exists.

Lack of Training Programs

Salend and Fradd (1985) note that one of the major barriers to providing appropriate special education services to bilingual handicapped children is the lack of qualified teachers. As a result of this lack, teachers from white middle-class backgrounds are often placed in classrooms for bilingual handicapped students (Preston et al. 1984). This is problematic in that most regular and special education personnel are monolingual and fail to understand the cultural backgrounds and experiences of these students (Bernal 1983; Milne 1982).

Yates (1982) identifies several constraining forces which continue to inhibit the development of training programs for bilingual special educators: the national trend toward reducing the number of categories of teacher preparation in special education; the difficulty in recruiting preservice teachers interested in bilingual special education students; the constraint on universities to limit the number of credit hours they can offer; and the difficulty of integrating special education curricular content into regular education programs. Salend and Fradd (1985) note, however, that qualified personnel will only become available when certification and training requirements are mandated by the states.

In a survey of the fifty states and the District of Columbia, Salend and Fradd found that sixteen states offered training for bilingual special educators, twenty-six states provided inservice training in bilingual special education, and only the state of California had established a certification program for bilingual special educators. They concluded that states need to identify certification requirements for teachers working with bilingual special education students to assure that they had demonstrated the necessary competencies in special education, bilingual education and dual language proficiency.

Competencies Needed by Teachers

In 1978, the Council for Exceptional Children (CEC) issued a set of policy statements regarding minorities in special education. One policy statement adopted at the general assembly meeting indicated potential areas of competence needed by teachers of bilingual handicapped students. The statement read (in part) as follows:

. . . an appropriate public education that meets the unique needs of minority children must include careful consideration of cultural and ethnic influences which might affect student performances in areas such as pupil assessment, pupil placement, teaching strategies, curriculum adaptation and development of instructional materials (57).

One year later, the National Council for Accreditation of Teacher Education (NCATE) adopted standards requiring all teacher education programs to include a multicultural education component. With the impetus from CEC, NCATE and various litigation and legislation, professionals began taking a closer look at the competencies needed by teachers of bilingual handicapped children.

In 1981, the Association for Cross-Cultural Education and Social Studies (ACCESS) developed a comprehensive list of competencies for bilingual special education teachers. This competency listing is commonly used in the development and implementation of preservice training programs. A similar competency list was developed by Yates (1982) based on a thorough review of the literature (See Table 2.1). Like that of ACCESS, this list was designed to serve as a resource for the development and implementation of personnel preparation programs.

TABLE 2.1 SUGGESTED COMPETENCIES FOR TEACHERS OF BILINGUAL EXCEPTIONAL CHILDREN

Language Skills. The bilingual/bicultural special education teacher will demonstrate skills in the following areas:
1. Ability to understand the language as spoken by native speakers.
2. Ability to speak with fluency in both formal and informal settings, beyond the limitations of the memorized structures and vocabulary of textbooks or language training programs.
3. Ability to read with thorough comprehension at various levels of expository prose, as found in books, newspapers, and magazines, as well as in professional journals which include specialized vocabulary.
4. Ability to write the native language, including correct spelling or word formation, diacritical markings, punctuation, and syntactical order.
5. Ability to present lessons, describing, comparing, contrasting, giving examples, and making relationships in the target language as well as in English.
6. Ability to translate administrative memos, instructions, and letters to parents and the community.
7. Ability to understand dialects encountered in teaching and in casual conversation with students and parents.
8. Ability to provide instruction, in English and the target language, using the language appropriate to instructional areas.
9. Ability to communicate on professional topics in the native language.
10. Ability to communicate in all areas of the curriculum, relative to both regular and special education, including interpersonal areas and the affective domain.

Linguistics. The teacher will demonstrate the following skills:
1. Understanding of basic concepts regarding the nature of language.
2. Recognition and acceptance of the language of the home and a "standard" language as valid systems of communication, each with its own legitimate functions.
3. Understanding of the basic concepts regarding the effects of contracts between languages.

TABLE 2.1 (Continued)

4. Understanding of the theories of first and second language acquisition:
   (a) Discern and compare phonemic differences in both languages;
   (b) Understand precepts of structural differences between the two languages such as morphemic and grammatical patterns which transfer from one language to the other.
5. Ability to identify local dialects and relate them to the "standard" language for the purpose of building graduated levels of proficiency and language styles.
6. Ability to identify and understand regional, social, and developmental varieties in the child's language(s) at the phonological, grammatical, syntactical, and semantic levels.

Social Foundations. The teacher will demonstrate an ability to:
1. Identify the structure of the local community and the interrelationships of the target groups within it.
2. Identify key elements in the contemporary lifestyles of the target community.
3. Understand the importance of parental and community involvement in the school environment.
4. Identify patterns of migration and social mobility of various cultures and their implications for the learner.
5. Identify the socioeconomic factors of the ethnic community and their effects on the learner.

Cultural Foundations. The teacher will demonstrate the ability to:
1. Identify the universals of culture as they relate to the target student population.
2. Understand cultural variables and their effects upon student learning.
3. Discern similarities and differences between interacting cultures and recognize the potential conflicts and opportunities they may create for children.
4. Identify the patterns of familial structures and individual role definitions in the community culture.
5. Respond positively to the diversity of behavior involved in crossculture environments.
6. Assist children in maintaining pride in their culture.
7. Describe the historical origins of the local bilingual/bicultural community.
8. Identify contributions of the target group to the development of society and incorporate these contributions into educational programming.

Educational Foundations. The teacher will demonstrate:
1. Knowledge of the basic philosophy of education in a pluralistic society.
2. Knowledge and understanding of the philosophies of bilingual education and special education.
3. Knowledge and understanding of the areas of special education and related programs such as bilingual education including:
   (a) Handicapping conditions;
   (b) Legislation;
   (c) Litigation;
   (d) Legal foundations;
   (e) Funding;
   (f) Current research relative to ethnic-linguistic minorities in the areas of special education and bilingual education.
4. Skill in applying educational theory and research to instructional programming for non-English-speaking, limited-English-speaking, and bilingual children with special education needs.
5. Ability to explain to students, community, colleges, administrators, etc., a rationale for programs designed to meet the unique needs of handicapped non-English speakers, limited-English speakers, and bilingual children.

Human Development and Learning. The teacher will demonstrate:
1. Awareness of crossculture patterns, practices, or attitudes and their effect on the cognitive, affective, behavioral, and motivational development of the child. This awareness incorporates knowledge of:

TABLE 2.1 (Continued)

(a) Child-rearing practices;

(b) Socialization systems (familial, cultural, religious, economical, political, educational); and

(c) Sociocultural differences in attitudes toward educational attainment, gratification patterns, motivation, success objectives, etc.

2. Comprehension of inter- and intragroup conflict dynamics and the effects of such conflicts on the development of culturally and linguistically diverse children. This comprehension requires knowledge and understanding of variables such as generational differences leading to conflict, assimilation patterns and consequences, coping techniques or defense mechanisms, motivation, and achievement models.

Psychopersonal. The teacher will demonstrate:

1. Knowledge of the basic theories and/or models in human development and learning related to special education in the areas of behavior, affect, cognition, and motivation.

2. Knowledge of:

(a) Behavior modification through culturally relevant reinforcement processes;

(b) Gestalt or holistic perspectives and approaches;

(c) Transactional communication skills;

(d) Cognitive and bicognitive functioning and learning styles;

(e) Approaches focusing on the intrinsic motivational modes and personal needs of the linguistically and culturally different child.

3. Knowledge and understanding of empirical research in human development and learning related to special education and bilingual education by describing basic methods, findings, and assumptions.

4. Skill in relating methods, findings, and assumptions as they apply to non-English-speaking, limited-English-speaking, or bilingual handicapped children.

Interpersonal relations. The teacher will demonstrate:

1. Awareness of his or her personal beliefs, value systems, attitudes, and the effect of these variables on personal behavior and decision making in working with handicapped non-English-speaking, limited-English-speaking, or bilingual children.

2. Knowledge and understanding of the relationship between teacher expectations and the school achievement of linguistically and culturally different children.

3. Behavior conducive to the establishment of a positive emotional climate in the classroom.

4. Understanding of the importance of continued professional and personal growth by developing strategies for self-assessment and identifying opportunities for continuous personal and professional improvement.

5. Ability to affect communication between regular and special education personnel, parents, guardians, child advocates, and other personnel involved in the handicapped child's instructional program.

6. Ability to work effectively as a member of interdisciplinary teams responsible for the design and implementation of children's individual educational plans.

Educational Programming. The teacher will demonstrate:

1. Ability to use assessment data to plan instructional programs appropriate for handicapped non-English-speaking, limited-English-speaking, and bilingual children.

2. Ability to determine instructional goals based on the identified needs of the handicapped non-English-speaking, limited-English-speaking, or bilingual child.

3. Ability to write clear statements of instructional ideals and goals that define learning outcomes at different levels of complexity, which are appropriate to the handicapped linguistically and culturally different child.

4. Ability to specify performance objectives, instructional sequences, a variety of appropriate teaching/learning activities, materials, and evaluative procedures which can be used with linguistically and culturally different children with special education needs.

5. Ability to select and describe a rationale for the strategy upon which an instructional unit

TABLE 2.1 *(Continued)*

is developed and why that unit is appropriate for a handicapped student or group of students.
6. Ability to implement instructional interventions including monitoring systems to insure progress toward identified goals and objectives.
7. Ability to evaluate whether objectives have been accomplished and to make necessary revisions or modifications or to develop new instructional plans based on the data gathered in the evaluation process.

Developing and Adapting Curricula. The teacher will demonstrate:
1. Ability to adapt curricula to meet the needs of handicapped non-English-speaking, limited-English-speaking, and bilingual children.
2. Ability to edit and review activities to make them more linguistically and culturally appropriate to non-English-speaking, limited-English-speaking, and bilingual children with special education needs.
3. Ability to design tests, work sheets, and illustrations to supplement or substitute materials in order to better meet the needs of linguistically and culturally diverse children with special education needs.

Evaluating and Selecting Learning Materials. The teacher will demonstrate:
1. Ability to develop a set of evaluative criteria and procedures to determine the quality, utility, availability, and appropriateness of learning materials for handicapped non-English-speaking, limited-English-speaking, and bilingual children.
2. Ability to apply the criteria for new materials and to select materials for acquisition in needed areas.
3. Ability to apply criteria to teacher-made materials.

Producing Learning Materials. The teacher will demonstrate:
1. Ability to produce learning materials to complement, fulfill, or enhance curriculum for handicapped linguistic minorities.
2. Ability to secure and adapt or produce learning materials that stimulate active, meaningful, purposeful involvement of students in attaining specific learning.
3. Ability to produce written material for use by pupils which are appropriate to the linguistic and cultural characteristics of these handicapped pupils; i.e., programmed materials, work sheets, etc.

School-Community Relations. The teacher will demonstrate:
1. Understanding of the importance of parental and community involvement in facilitating the successful integration into school environments of non-English-speaking, limited-English-speaking, and bilingual handicapped children.
2. Skill in facilitating contacts and interaction between the handicapped child's family and school personnel.
3. Knowledge of the patterns of child rearing represented in the families of handicapped children so as to better understand children's behavior in the classroom.
4. Ability to plan and provide the direct participation of the families of handicapped non-English-speaking, limited-English-speaking or bilingual children in the instructional program and related activities.
5. Knowledge of local community resources for handicapped.
6. Skills in collecting culturally relevant information and materials characteristic of both the historical and current lifestyles of the child's culture.
7. Ability to incorporate linguistically and culturally relevant information into the curriculum and instructional activities designed for the handicapped child.
8. Ability to involve parents or child advocates in the formulation of the child's individual Educational Plan.
9. Ability to advise parents of their due process rights relative to the delivery of special education.
10. Ability to explain to parents their child's learning needs in a manner which is understandable to the parent.

TABLE 2.1 (*Continued*)

11. Ability to solicit parental support and participation in the child's special education program.
12. Ability to counsel parents regarding their child's handicapping condition(s) including areas such as understanding, acceptance, parent participation in development of child's potential, and effects on family.

Assessment.   The teacher will demonstrate:
1. Ability to define the purpose and functions of assessment.
2. Knowledge of existing assessment procedures and instruments, both formal and informal, in the following areas:
    (a) Language dominance:
    (b) Language development and proficiency;
    (c) Cognitive development;
    (d) Perceptual-motor development;
    (e) Social-emotional behavior;
    (f) Adaptive behavior;
    (g) Achievement;
    (h) Culture-fair assessment.
3. Recognition of potential linguistic and cultural biases of existing assessment instruments and procedures.
4. Ability to select assessment strategies appropriate to ethnic/linguistic minorities.
5. Ability to administer standardized and informal assessment procedures as appropriate, including the use of:
    (a) Task analysis;
    (b) Anecdotal records;
    (c) Observation procedures.

Note. Teacher Training Associated With Serving Bilingual Exceptional Students by J. R. Yates, 1982, *Teacher Education and Special Education, 5,* pp. 64–66. Copyright 1982 by the Teacher Education Division, The Council for Exceptional Children. Reprinted by permission.

Prieto, Rueda and Rodriguiez (1981) conducted a needs assessment survey of seventy-seven public school teachers serving bilingual/multicultural exceptional children. The competencies found to be most important were skills in criterion-referenced assessment, teaching methodology and parental involvement. Familiarity with language, definitions and cultural background were viewed as somewhat less important. Identified as least important were knowledge of legal issues, and competencies in reviewing and implementing research projects and studying related programs. These competencies were similar to those identified by ACCESS (1981).

Individuals responsible for the development, implementation and evaluation of preservice programs should carefully consider the competencies needed by teachers of bilingual handicapped students. Well-thought-out competencies can only assist in providing the best possible services to these children.

Program Models

Based on a survey of thirty universities offering bilingual special education programs in the western United States, the Multicultural Special Education Project

(MUSEP) identified three models used to prepare preservice bilingual special education teachers. The first model recruits bilingual minority students for enrollment in traditional special education programs. The students have no formal training in the education of bilingual children; rather, they are simply students who are themselves bilingual. The second model integrates bilingual content within existing courses. It is assumed in this model that skills outside of what is taught will be obtained independently by the teachers. The third model is a bilingual special education program, separate from the traditional special education program, and offering bilingual special education coursework and related field experiences (Baca 1980).

Figueira-Valero (1986) describes an interdisciplinary model that incorporates aspects of the three models identified by MUSEP. Located at George Mason University in Virginia, the program combines elements of regular, bilingual and special education teacher training, thereby forming a unique working relationship. Two categories of professionals are trained in the program: bilingual special education teachers who have expertise in language development and second language acquisition; and special education teachers who are knowledgeable about bilingual issues and practices. Although the program is new and has no graduates to date, it appears to have a great deal of built-in flexibility and high potential for success (Figueria-Valero 1986).

With increasing numbers of bilingual handicapped students entering the mainstream of public education, universities must identify the competencies required by bilingual special education teachers if they are to provide useful, effective training programs. In addition, states must develop certification requirements to ensure that bilingual handicapped students receive an appropriate education based on this population's unique needs. Until these personnel preparation issues are resolved, one can only question the efficacy of service delivery systems for bilingual handicapped students. "Respecting cultural diversity is not a benevolent act but a prerequisite for science and valid professional practice" (Hilliard 1980, 587).

REFERENCES

Aspira v. Board of Education of the City of New York, C.A. No. 72 Cir. 4002 (MEF), S.D.N.Y., August 29, 1974.

Association for Cross-Cultural Education and Social Studies, Inc. (1981). *Bilingual special education personnel preparation national task-oriented seminar.* Washington, D.C.: Author. (ERIC Document Reproduction Service No. ED 229 893).

Baca, L. (1980). Issues in the education of culturally diverse exceptional children. *Exceptional Children, 46,* 583.

Baca, L., & Bransford, J. (1981). Meeting the needs of the bilingual handicapped child. *Momentum, 12,* 26–29, 49–51.

Baca, L. M., & Cervantes, H. T. (1984). *The bilingual special education interface.* St. Louis: Times Mirror/Mosby.

Bernal, E. M. (1983). Trends in bilingual special education. *Learning Disability Quarterly, 6,* 424–431.

Bilingual Education Act, P.L. 90-247, 81 Stat. 7833816 (Jan. 2, 1968).

Bilingual Education Act, as amended by the Elementary and Secondary Education Amendments of 1978, P.L. 95-561, 92 Stat. 2268 (Nov. 1, 1978).

Figueira-Valero, E. (1986). Bilingual special education personnel preparation: An integrated model. *Teacher Education and Special Education, 9,* 82–88.

Fuchigami, R. Y. (1980). Teacher education for culturally diverse exceptional children. *Exceptional Children, 46,* 634–641.

Hilliard, A. G. (1980). Cultural diversity and special education. *Exceptional Children, 46,* 584–588.

Lau v. Nichols, 414 U.S. 563; 39 L. Ed 2d 1, 94S. Ct. 786, 1971.

Milne, N. M. (1982). Issues and concerns related to the education of exceptional bilingual students. In C. H. Thomas and J. L. Thomas (Eds.), *Bilingual special education resource guide.* Phoenix, AZ: Oryx.

National Council for Accreditation of Teacher Education (1979). *Standards for accreditation of teacher education.* Washington, D.C.: Author.

Ortiz, A. A., & Yates, J. R. (1983). Incidence of exceptionality among Hispanics: Implications for manpower planning. *National Association for Bilingual Education Journal, 7,* 41–53.

Plata, M., & Santos, S. L. (1981). Bilingual special education: A Challenge for the future. *Teaching Exceptional Children, 14,* 99–100.

Poplin, M. S., & Wright, P. (1983). The concept of cultural pluralism: Issues in special education. *Learning Disability Quarterly, 6,* 367–371.

Preston, D., Greenwood, C. R., Hughes, V., Yuen, P., Thibadeau, S., Critchlow, W., & Harris, J. (1984). Minority issues in special education: A principal-mediated inservice program for teachers. *Exceptional Children, 51,* 112–121.

Prieto, A. G., Rueda, R. S., & Rodriguez, R. F. (1981). Teaching competencies for bilingual/multicultural exceptional children. *Teacher Education and Special Education, 4,* 35–39.

Rios v. Read, 75 C. 296 (E.D.N.Y. Jan. 14, 1977).

Salend, S. J., & Fradd, S. (1985). Certification and training programs for bilingual special education. *Teacher Education and Special Education, 8,* 198–202.

The Council for Exceptional Children (1978). Minorities position policy statements. *Exceptional Children, 45,* 57–64.

United States General Accounting Office (1981). *Disparities still exist in who gets special education.* Gaithersburg, MD: U.S.G.A.O.

Yates, J. R. (1982). Teaching training associated with serving bilingual exceptional students. *Teacher Education and Special Education, 5,* 61–68.

DISCUSSION QUESTIONS

1. What major problems are involved in training bilingual special education teachers? How might we alleviate some of these problems?
2. What do you feel are the most important competencies for a bilingual special educator to possess? Why?
3. Of the program models presented in this section, which do you feel would be most effective in preparing bilingual special education teachers? Why?
4. Do you feel that a teacher from a white middle-class background with no coursework in bilingual special education could successfully teach a class of limited-English-proficiency students? Why?
5. You are a student intern in a fourth grade classroom. Four weeks into your experience a non-English-speaking Spanish girl is placed in your class. How will you handle this situation?

ARE TEACHERS PREPARED
FOR MAINSTREAMING?

Public Law 94-142 mandates that all handicapped children receive a free and appropriate public education in the Least Restrictive Environment (LRE). As a result of this landmark legislation, significant numbers of handicapped children have been mainstreamed into regular education programs with their nonhandicapped peers. While some professionals view mainstreaming as a necessity for some handicapped children (Christopolos 1973; Deno 1970; Dunn 1968; Lilly 1970), others have expressed their resistance to integration (Kolstoe 1972; Roos 1970; Smith and Arkans 1974). This resistance evolves, in part, from confusion over terminology, and also in part from awareness of problems that can occur when handicapped children are placed in classrooms with regular education teachers who have limited knowledge and expertise regarding their problems (Dixon, Shaw, and Bensky 1980; Paul and Warnock 1980). The purpose of this section is to discuss misconceptions about LRE and mainstreaming, as well as the attitudes of the regular educator regarding the integration of handicapped children into the mainstream.

Mainstreaming vs. Least Restrictive Environment

The misconception that mainstreaming and the Least Restrictive Environment are synonymous has sparked considerable controversy (Dybwad 1980). In a report to Congress, the United States Office of Education (1979) suggests that referring to the Least Restrictive Environment (LRE) as *mainstreaming* leads to the misinterpretation that all handicapped children, regardless of the severity of their handicap, will be mainstreamed into regular education classes. The National Education Association (1978) also expressed concern over the damage the term *mainstreaming* had done to the precise meaning of the LRE.

Public Law 94-142 requires that "to the maximum extent appropriate, handicapped children . . . are educated with children who are not handicapped" (Section 612 (5) (B): 14). This does not imply that every handicapped child will be placed in a regular education program. Rather, the LRE concept suggests that alternative placements will be made available to meet the varying needs of handicapped children. Resource rooms, self-contained classes, developmental centers, and homebound instruction may all qualify as possibilities. The intent of P.L. 94-142 is to assure a program placement that is "as normal as possible" (Anderson, Martinez, and Rich 1980). For severely handicapped children, "as normal as possible" may mean a developmental center or homebound instruction. The LRE should be whatever environment offers the highest probability of alleviating a child's academic deficits (Meyen and Lehr 1980). It should offer the best match between a person's current level of performance and the kind of support that provides for optimum growth (Johnson and Johnson 1980).

Mainstreaming, on the other hand, is one placement alternative within a continuum of services. Turnbull and Schulz (1979) refer to mainstreaming as placing handicapped students in regular classes with their nonhandicapped peers to the maximum extent possible. Anderson, Martinez, and Rich (1980) define mainstreaming as an educational placement which accommodates children with mild to moderate handicapping conditions provided modifications are made. Others (Meyers, MacMillan, and Yoshida 1980) view mainstreaming as an application of the normalization principle. An often-cited definition of mainstreaming suggests that it involves

> . . . the temporal, instructional, and social integration of eligible exceptional children with normal peers based on an ongoing, individually determined, educational planning and programming process and requires clarification of responsibility among regular and special education administrative, instructional, and supportive personnel (Kauffman et al. 1975, 41).

Viewing the terms mainstreaming and LRE as synonymous has elicited many problems for regular educators. Teachers have often believed that handicapped children could return to regular education classes without benefit of support services or special preparation of regular teachers (Sapon-Shevin 1979). As a result, there has been some concern raised by special educators regarding the regular educator's attitude toward mainstreaming (Hoben 1980).

Regular Education Teachers' Attitudes toward Mainstreaming

Many researchers have cited the importance of the teacher's attitude in an integration program (Goodspeed and Celotta 1982; Hudson, Reisberg, and Wolf 1983; Stevens and Braun 1980; Wynne, Ulfelder, and Dakof 1975). As early as 1958, Haring, Stern, and Cruickshank reported that the extent to which a teacher understood and accepted the handicapped child was critical to the success of mainstreaming. In fact, a teacher's attitude, more than any other single variable, can influence the effectiveness of a mainstreaming program (Raver 1980). Baker and Gottlieb (1980) state that a teacher's attitude is expected to influence the extent to which a handicapped child becomes not only physically integrated, but more important, an accepted member of the regular education program. In short, importance of teachers' attitudes toward mainstreaming is well-documented. Unfortunately, many studies show that negative attitudes prevail.

Barngrover (1971), who interviewed regular education personnel prior to the passage and implementation of P.L. 94-142, found that over half of those interviewed felt that even mildly handicapped students should be retained in special classes. In an often-cited study, Shotel, Iano, and McGettigan (1972) examined regular education teachers' attitudes concerning the appropriateness of integrating educably mentally retarded, learning disabled, and emotionally disturbed children into regular education programs with supportive resource room services. The experimental group consisted of regular education teachers who taught in a resource room program; and the control group consisted of regular education teachers who taught in schools with at least two self-contained special education classes. A thirteen-item yes-no questionnaire was administered at the beginning and end of the school year to elicit teachers' responses. The results of the study showed that the experimental group of regular education teachers in the resource room program felt that mainstreaming, even with special education support, was not the most appropriate placement for many mildly retarded children.

Gickling and Theobold (1975) asked regular education teachers and supervisors what type of special education service delivery model they favored for the future. Fifty percent of those surveyed reported that they endorsed the use of self-contained classes for mildly handicapped children. Similar results were found by Hudson, Graham, and Warner (1979) who reported that 49 percent of the regular education teachers they surveyed did not support the concept of mainstreaming.

More recent studies have shown similar results. Horne (1983) indicates that elementary education teachers question the efficacy of classroom instruction for handicapped children. Ammer (1984), who surveyed regular educators regarding mainstreaming, reports that most have negative attitudes. Their concerns include a lack of communication with resource room teachers and lack of available resources to facilitate their work with special education students.

Although it appears evident that negative attitudes exist, it's important to ask why. Guerin (1979) asked regular education teachers who had mainstreamed educably mentally retarded and emotionally disturbed children in their classes how much comfort or discomfort they experienced in working with these children. The results of the study indicate that teachers were most comfortable with nonacademic activities such as supervising lunch and play activities. They were less comfortable with academic planning, and least comfortable in teaching the students verbal, social, and academic skills.

In a study by Ringlablen and Price (1981), regular education teachers in grades K-12 expressed their concerns about mainstreaming. Of those surveyed, 75 percent agreed with the philosophy of mainstreaming; however, 50 percent did not feel prepared for mainstreaming; 25 percent felt mainstreamed students had a negative effect on their teaching performance, and 23 percent felt mainstreaming had a negative effect on their attitudes toward teaching. In a similar study of primary through high school regular education teachers who had mainstreamed mildly retarded students in their classes, Childs (1981) found that 50 percent of the teachers surveyed felt inadequately prepared to teach handicapped students.

Schultz (1982) used an open-ended survey to examine the concerns regular educators had toward educating handicapped students in the mainstream. Concerns expressed included not knowing how to plan for individual differences, wondering about their role in educating a handicapped student in their classroom, working with ancillary personnel, implementing behavior change programs, personally accepting the students, and dealing with the nonhandicapped students' acceptance of the mainstreamed student. Horne (1983) reports that over 80 percent of elementary education teachers she surveyed felt they did not have adequate training to handle mainstreamed children effectively, and approximately 70 percent felt that having handicapped students in their classes would require significant changes in their classroom procedures.

Taken as a whole, findings from the aforementioned studies indicate the need for preservice and/or inservice training for regular education teachers so that they may deal as effectively as possible with mainstreamed handicapped students. Stewart (1983) recommends coursework that includes training in adaptive academics and behavior management, as well as direct experience with handicapped students at the preservice level. Indeed, such training may make a real difference. In a study of the educational curriculum taken by college students, Hoover and Cessna (1984) conclude that college students who have taken courses related to mainstreaming, and who have had field-related practical experience with handicapped children, tend to exhibit more positive attitudes toward mainstreaming. At the inservice level, Stewart (1983) recommends training that includes a description of the nature and needs of handicapped children, classroom management practices, and assessment and instructional strategies. Leyser, Abrams, and Lipscomb (1982) suggest that teachers, as well as other regular education school personnel, receive training in the form of courses, workshops, seminars and practical experience in working with handicapped students. Increased knowledge and contact have been related more often than not to positive attitudes concerning mainstreaming programs (Schmelkin and Lieberman 1984). Unless teachers have the opportunity to gain that knowledge and personal contact, the mainstreamed handicapped child may eventually have to be returned to the self-contained special class (Cavin and Platu 1984).

Until a decade ago, regular educators did not teach handicapped students in the mainstream; this responsibility was left to trained special education teachers (Sabornie 1985). Most regular educators have had little or no training in special education, though some may want to teach and understand handicapped students. When questioned about mainstreaming, most regular educators offer negative responses. But these attitudes, in part, appear related to teachers' lack of training and experience in working with handicapped children.

If handicapped students are to receive the best possible education in a mainstreamed environment, regular educators must develop more positive attitudes toward these children and their capabilities. Perhaps this can best be accomplished through a systematic inservice training program, supported by knowledgeable special education personnel, that offers teachers a chance to learn more about handicapped students and about the extent of their own abilities through firsthand experience.

REFERENCES

Ammer, J. J. (1984). The mechanics of mainstreaming: Considering the regular educators' perspective. *Remedial and Special Education, 5/6,* 15–20.

Anderson, R., Martinez, D., & Rich, H. (1980). Perspectives for change. In J. Schifani, R. Anderson, & S. Odle (Eds.), *Implementing learning in the least restrictive environment: Handicapped children in the mainstream.* Baltimore: University Park Press.

Baker, J. L., & Gottlieb, J. (1980). Attitudes of teachers towards mainstreaming retarded children. In J. Gottlieb (Ed.). *Educating mentally retarded persons in the mainstream.* Baltimore: University Park Press.

Barngrover, E. D. (1971). A study of educators' preferences in special education programs. *Exceptional Children, 37,* 754–755.

Cavin, J., & Platu, M. (1984). Number skill development in mainstreamed handicapped students. *Teaching Exceptional Children, 12–16,* 131.

Christopolos, F. (1973). Keeping exceptional children in regular classes. *Exceptional Children, 39,* 569–572.

Childs, R. E. (1981). Perceptions of mainstreaming by regular classroom teachers who teach mainstreamed educable mentally retarded students in the public schools. *Education and Training of the Mentally Retarded, 16,* 225–227.

Deno, E. (1970). Special education as developmental capital. *Exceptional Children, 37,* 229–237.

Dixon, B., Shaw, S. F., & Bensky, J. M. (1980). Administrator's role in fostering the mental health of special services personnel. *Exceptional Children, 47,* 30–36.

Dunn, L. (1968). Special education for the mildly retarded: Is much of it justifiable? *Exceptional Children, 35,* 5–22.

Dybwad, G. (1980). Avoiding misconceptions of mainstreaming, the least restrictive environment, and normalization. *Exceptional Children, 47,* 85–88.

Gickling, E. R., & Theobold, J. T. (1975). Mainstreaming: Affect or effect. *Journal of Special Education, 9,* 317–328.

Goodspeed, M. T., & Celotta, B. K. (1982). Changing teacher's perceptions of mainstreaming. *Teacher Education and Special Education, 6,* 18–24.

Guerin, G. R. (1979). Regular teacher concerns with mainstreamed learning handicapped children. *Psychology in the Schools, 16,* 543–545.

Haring, N. G., Stern, G. G., & Cruickshank, W. M. (1958). *Attitudes of educators toward exceptional children.* Syracuse, N.Y.: Syracuse University Press.

Hoben, M. (1980). Integration in the mainstream. *Exceptional Children, 47,* 100–105.

Hoover, J., & Cessna, K. (1984). Preservice teachers' attitudes towards mainstreaming prior to student education. *Journal of Teacher Education, 35,* 49–51.

Horne, M. D. (1983). Elementary classroom teachers attitudes toward mainstreaming. *The Exceptional Child, 30,* 93–98.

Hudson, F., Graham, S., & Warner, M. (1979). Mainstreaming: An examination of the needs of regular classroom teachers. *Learning Disability Quarterly, 2,* 58–62.

Hudson, F., Reisberg, T. E., & Wolf, R. (1983). Changing teacher's perceptions of mainstreaming. *Teacher Education and Special Education, 6,* 18–24.

Johnson, D., & Johnson, R. (1980). Integrating handicapped students into the mainstream. *Exceptional Children, 47,* 90–98.

Kauffman, M. J., Gottlieb, J., Agard, J., & Kukic, M. D. (1975). Mainstreaming: Toward an explication of the construct. In E. L. Meyen, G. A. Vergason, & R. J. Whelan (Eds.), *Alternatives for teaching exceptional children.* Denver, CO: Love Publishing Co.

Kolstoe, O. P. (1972). Programs for the mildly retarded: A reply to critics. *Exceptional Children, 39,* 51–56.

Leyser, J., Abrams, P., & Lipscomb, E. (1982). Modifying attitudes of prospective elementary school teachers toward mainstreaming. *Journal for Special Educators, 18,* 1–10.

Lilly, M. S. (1970). Special education: A teapot in a tempest. *Exceptional Children, 37,* 43–48.

Meyen, E. L., & Lehr, D. H. (1980). Least restrictive environments: Instructional implications. *Focus on Exceptional Children, 12,* 1–8.

Meyers, C. E., MacMillan, D. L., & Yoshida, R. K. (1980). Regular class education of EMR students, from efficacy to mainstreaming: A review of issues and research. In J. Gottlieb (Ed.), *Educating mentally retarded persons in the mainstream.* Baltimore: University Park Press.

National Education Association (1978). *Education for all handicapped children: Consensus, conflict and challenge, a study report.* Washington, DC: NEA.

Paul, J. L., & Warnock, N. J. (1980). Special education: A changing field. *The Exceptional Child, 27,* 3–28.

Public Law 94-142, Education for All Handicapped Children Act of 1975, Section 612(5)(B), 1–38.

Raver, S. A. (1980). Ten rules for success in preschool mainstreaming. *Education Unlimited, 2,* 47–52.

Ringlaben, R. P., & Price, J. R. (1981). Regular classroom teachers' perceptions of mainstreaming effects. *Exceptional Children, 47,* 302–304.

Roos, P. (1970). Trends and issues in special education for the mentally retarded. *Education and Training of the Mentally Retarded, 5,* 51–61.

Sabornie, E. (1985). Social mainstreaming of handicapped students: Facing an unpleasant reality. *Remedial and Special Education, 6,* 12–15.

Sapon-Shevin, M. (1979). Mainstreaming: Implementing the spirit of the law. *The Journal of Negro Education, 48,* 364–381.

Schmelkin, L., & Lieberman, L. (1984). Education students' awareness of mainstreaming concerns: Implications for improving training programs. *Education, 104,* 258–263.

Schultz, L. R. (1982). Educating the special needs student in the regular classroom. *Exceptional Children, 48,* 366–368.

Shotel, J. R., Iano, R. P., & McGettigan, J. R. (1972). Teacher attitudes associated with the integration of handicapped children. *Exceptional Children, 38,* 677–683.

Smith, J. O., & Arkans, J. R. (1974). Now more than ever: A case for the special class. *Exceptional Children, 40,* 497–502.

Stevens, T. M., & Braun, B. L. (1980). Measures of regular classroom teachers' attitudes toward handicapped children. *Exceptional Children, 46,* 292–294.

Stewart, F. K. (1983). Teacher attitudes and expectations regarding mainstreaming of handicapped children. *Teacher Education and Special Education, 6,* 39–45.

Turnbull, A., & Schulz, J. (1979). *Mainstreaming handicapped students: A guide for the classroom teacher.* Boston: Allyn and Bacon, Inc.

U.S. Office of Education (1979). *Progress toward a free, appropriate education.* Washington, DC: U.S. Department of Health, Education, and Welfare.

Wynne, S., Ulfelder, L., & Dakof, G. (1975). *Mainstreaming and early childhood for handicapped children: Review and implications of research.* Washington, DC: Wynne Associates.

DISCUSSION QUESTIONS

1. Do you feel regular education teachers are prepared for mainstreaming? Explain why or why not.
2. What do you feel the role of the special educator should be in facilitating the mainstreaming process?
3. You are a principal of an elementary school that does not mainstream handicapped students. Discuss what you will say in a presentation to parents and teachers to justify your school's mainstreaming philosophy or practices.
4. You have been given the responsibility of conducting an inservice program for the regular education teachers in your building. Discuss what you will include in your curriculum.
5. What variables would you consider in determining whether a handicapped student should be mainstreamed or not?
6. A teacher has stated that he does not want handicapped students in his classroom since he

is not adequately prepared to teach them. Should he be required to accept them in his class? In what ways is either decision fair or unfair to the students and/or the other teachers?

Special Educator Predictions of Regular Class Teacher Attitudes Concerning Mainstreaming

Martin H. Diebold
Landa L. Trentham

ABSTRACT

The purpose of this investigation was to determine whether special educator predictions of regular class teacher attitudes toward mainstreaming were significantly different from actual attitudes expressed by regular educators. To that end, a group of special educators was asked to predict regular educator colleague responses to a questionnaire designed to elicit attitudes about several aspects of the mainstreaming concept and process. Resulting data were submitted to factor and discriminative analysis. Results indicated that nearly half of the special educator group was unable to predict regular educator responses. Special educator prediction consistently underestimated the positiveness of regular education colleagues concerning several aspects of the mainstreaming process. Implications for further research and for carrying out consultation services effectively are presented.

The least restrictive environment mandates of PL 94–142 have necessitated close working relationships between regular and special educators (Carpenter 1980; Diebold

1980; Morsink 1979; Ringlaben & Weller 1981). As a result, there has been an increase in preservice and inservice education programs designed to develop consultation skills of special educators (Curtis & Anderson 1976; Egloff & Lederer 1980; Fleming & Fleming 1983; Haight 1984; Salend & Salend 1984). These programs typically emphasize development of communication and problem-solving skills. The anticipated result of this training is that special educators will be able to provide consultation services that are both effective and more sensitive to the feelings and needs of regular class colleagues. Empathy for and accurate understanding of regular class teachers' attitudes toward problems related to integration of exceptional children have been cited as critical to appropriate consultant—consultee communication and accurate identification of solution alternatives (Bond & Dietrich 1981; Candler & Sowell 1980; Curtis & Anderson 1976; Diebold 1980; Gans 1985; Hauptman 1983). Empathy and understanding of the consultee's attitudes may, however, depend on the degree to which the consultant's perceptions of the consultee's attitude agree with the actual attitude of the consultee. Development of accurate perceptions of attitude takes time. However, because of administrative constraints, contact between special education teacher consultants and regular class colleagues is typically brief. The consultant is often forced to present solutions stemming either from past experience with other teachers or from hurriedly obtained perceptions of both the problem and the attitude of the regular class teacher (Gans 1985; Morsink 1979; Triandis 1971). These constraints may, in turn, lead to the commission of serious judgment errors by consultants. Gans (1985), for example, has stated:

> The consultant, depending upon topic identification procedures or solely upon self-perceptions of the problem is in danger of committing one of three errors. He or she may incorrectly diagnose the problem, as well as misidentify the solution. The consultant may correctly diagnose the problem, but misunderstand the event or situations leading to the problem. Third, the consultant may correctly diagnose the problem, but emphasize the wrong priorities in the steps leading to the solution. In each of these cases there is an increased chance that either the consultant, the teacher, or both will leave the meeting feeling that time was wasted and that he or she was not understood. (pp. 194–195)

There have been several studies investigating attitudes of regular educators about mainstreaming (Biklen 1985; Buttery 1979; Feldman & Altman 1985; Winzer 1985) and comparing regular and special educators' attitudes (Aloia & Aloia 1982; Gans 1985; Knof 1984). There is, however, a dearth of reported research concerning the degree to which special educators can predict regular class teacher attitudes toward integration of exceptional students. Knowledge about the accuracy of such predictions could lead to the development of preservice and inservice education programs designed to prevent consultant errors such as those discussed by Gans (1985).

The purpose of this investigation was to determine whether special educator predictions of regular class teacher attitudes toward integration of exceptional students are significantly different from actual attitudes expressed by regular educators.

METHOD

Instrumentation

The questionnaire developed by Gans (1985) was used to obtain perceptions of both regular and special educators concerning integration of exceptional students into regular classes. The items on the questionnaire were originally selected from (a) a needs assessment questionnaire administered to 127 regular and 17 special education teachers, (b) interviews with school personnel, and (c) a review of the literature (Gans 1985). The questionnaire has three sections. The demographic and attitude section contains items designed to collect information about each teacher's personal characteristics, professional background and experience, and role characteristics associated with integration of exceptional students.

The second section contains items designed to measure the teacher's experience with and attitude toward students with selected handicapping conditions (e.g., hearing impairment, communication disorders). This section uses a 6-point, forced-choice Likert scale. Extremes on the scale range from 1 ("strongly agree") to 6 ("strongly disagree").

The third section, the opinion portion of the questionnaire, also employs a Likert scale. Items in this section are designed to collect teacher information regarding contact with handicapped people and attitude about roles, expertise, confidence, appropriate placement, classroom management, and perceptions of support in the integration process. This section represented the focus for this study.

Gans (1985) administered this instrument to 278 regular class educators and 218 special educators in 21 school districts in northeastern Ohio. The resulting data were submitted to factor analysis. Four identifiable and internally consistent factors were identified: *Confidence, Effect on the Classroom, Time,* and *Appropriate Placement.*

Subjects

Subjects for this study were special education resource/itinerant teachers and regular education teachers employed in 31 schools within four school systems in eastern Alabama. Teachers were selected from the roster of teachers at each of the 31 schools to insure adequate representation of both regular and special education teachers at elementary, middle/junior high, and high school levels.

During the last three weeks of the 1985–86 school year, each selected teacher received a cover letter, a questionnaire, and a return-addressed, stamped envelope. Questionnaire instructions for regular class teachers (Group II) asked that, for each item, they circle the scale response corresponding most closely with their feelings about the statement contained in the item. Special educators (Group I) were instructed to respond to the same set of questionnaire items, but they were to respond to each statement *as they believed regular class colleagues in their respective school systems would respond.*

The cover letter specified a target date for return of the questionnaire directly to the investigators. Follow-up phone calls were made reminding those teachers who failed to return the questionnaire by the target date. An overall return rate of 80.6 percent (216 of 268 questionnaires sent out) was thus obtained. Of 120 special educators, 85 responded, for a return rate of 70.8 percent, while 131 of 148 regular educators, or 88.5 percent, responded.

Of the teachers returning questionnaires, 40.1 percent of those in special education and 39.7 percent of those in regular education were employed in elementary schools (grades K through 4), 29.5 percent of special education teachers and 30.7 percent of regular education teachers in middle/junior high schools (grades 5 through 8), and 30.4 percent of special education teachers and 29.6 percent of regular education teachers in high schools (grades 9 through 12). The investigators were pleased that rela-

tive group representation remained as even as these percentages indicate.

Special educators represented the following specialty areas at all grade levels: mental retardation, learning disabilities, emotional disturbance, speech-language pathology, and hearing impairment. Regular educators represented all grade levels (K through 12) and curriculum categories.

Eleven regular educators were male and 120 were female, while 7 special educators were male and 78 female. The mean number of years of teacher experience for regular educators was 10.66 (SD = 5.74), compared with 8.42 years (SD = 4.59) for special educators. Regular educators reported that they consulted with special educators an average of 1.67 times per week (SD = 1.69; range = 0 to 5). Special educators reported consulting with regular class teachers an average of 5.60 times per week (SD = 6.41; range = 0 to 50). One hundred of the 131 regular educators (76.3 percent) reported that they had participated in at least one course or in-service workshop on mainstreaming.

RESULTS

A data reduction technique involving principal components factor analysis (varimax rotation) and subsequent discriminant analysis was used to analyze the data. This approach was used for two reasons. First, the number of items on the opinionnaire section of the instrument (N = 54) made use of traditional analysis of variance techniques unwise. Second, the data reduction technique permitted analysis of interactions.

A principal components factor analysis (varimax rotation) was performed using scores for all items in the opinionnaire section of the instrument (N = 54). This analysis identified 10 factors composed of three or more items having factor loadings of 0.40 or higher. These 10 factors accounted for a total of 71.3 percent of the variance associated with all opinionnaire responses. Because there were items that loaded on no factor,

TABLE 1 VARIANCE ASSOCIATED WITH EACH OF SIX FACTORS

Factor	Eigenvalue	% of Variance	Cumulative %
1. Willingness to teach handicapped children	9.54375	29.8	29.8
2. Knowledge of where to get information about students with handicaps	3.18853	10.0	39.8
3. Feelings of confidence about specific skills in carrying out the mainstreaming program in the regular class	2.63139	8.2	48.0
4. Effects of mainstreaming on the regular class program	2.26475	7.1	55.1
5. Sufficiency of instruction, planning, and consultation time to carry out the mainstreaming program	1.66461	5.2	60.3
6. Effects of teacher input into eductional program and special education consultant knowledge of the regular class on current opinion about the mainstreaming process	1.35007	4.2	64.5

additional factor analyses were calculated eliminating those items. The final analysis identified six factors (and 32 items) that accounted for 64.5 percent of the variance. These factors and the variance associated with each are identified in Table 1. A total of 22 of the original 54 items did not meet the factor loading criteria at all. These 22 items included three that focused on attitudes concerning mental retardation (i.e., willingness to teach mentally retarded students, knowledge of where to obtain help or information about students with mental retardation, and knowledge of successful or productive adults with mental retardation).

Next, a discriminant analyis was performed using factor loadings of these six factors as independent variables. The purpose of this analysis was to determine the degree to which these factor scores predicted group membership (i.e., special educator vs. regular educator). A total of 187 subjects met the criterion for inclusion in this analysis (i.e., had responded to every pertinent item on the opinionnaire section of the instrument). Group means and standard deviations for each factor by group membership are presented in Table 2. Inspection of factor group means indicates that special educators rather consistently underestimated the positiveness

TABLE 2 GROUP MEANS AND STANDARD DEVIATIONS FOR EACH FACTOR

Groups	Factors					
	1	2	3	4	5	6
Special Educators $N = 78$						
Mean	−0.29	−0.19	−0.22	−0.10	−0.23	0.10
SD	0.93	1.07	0.94	1.04	0.89	0.88
Regular Educators $N = 109$						
Mean	0.20	0.14	0.16	0.07	0.16	−0.07
SD	1.00	0.93	1.02	0.97	1.05	1.08

of regular education colleague responses to various aspects of mainstreaming on opinionnaire items included in five of the six factors identified.

The discriminating power of the predictor variables was determined by computation of Wilks' lambda. The effectiveness of this discrimination for four of the factor variables was significant (see Table 3).

Further analysis identified one canonical discriminant function significant beyond the .0001 level, indicating that the linear combination of four of the six factor scores was significant in discriminating between regular and special educator groups (r = 0.40; x^2 = 31.56; df = 4; p < .0001). Special educators were able to predict the responses of regular educators on two of the six factors. Factor 4—*Effects of placement on the regular class program* (i.e., effect on handicapped and nonhandicapped students, teaching behavior and procedures, and classroom size)—and Factor 6—*Effects of teacher input into the educational program and special education knowledge of the regular class on current opinion about the mainstreaming process.*

Group classifications resulting from the use of the four factor variables identified in the discriminative analysis revealed that, even on the four factors that significantly differentiated responses of special and regular educators, 43 of 78 special educators (55.1 percent) were able to predict regular education colleague responses accurately. However, a substantial number of special educators (35 of 78, or 44.9 percent) were not able to do so. The four factors that appeared to account for most of the errors made by special educators were Factor 1—*Willingness to teach handicapped children;* Factor 2—*Knowledge of where to obtain help or information about skills in carrying out the mainstreaming program in the regular classroom* (i.e., setting goals and objectives, measuring achievement, behavior management, adapting materials and activities, and developing IEPs); and Factor 5—*Sufficiency of time for carrying out the mainstreaming program.*

An effort was made to establish the reliability of the instrument using a computerized item ALPHA reliability model. The ALPHA model computes Cronbach's alpha and item alpha (Cronbach 1951). Subject responses to the 32 opinionnaire items included in the six factors described above represented the targets of this analysis. Results of this analysis yielded a reliability coefficient of 0.92 (standardized item alpha = 0.92). These results indicate that the modified instrument was internally consistent. The questionnaire items identified by discriminative analysis for each factor are presented as Table 4.

DISCUSSION

As in the case with any opinion study, it cannot be said with any degree of certainty whether subjects expressed their true feelings. However, if their responses did reflect true feelings this study indicates that nearly half of the special educators in this investigation had considerable difficulty predicting regular class colleague opinions about 22 of the 32 items (68.7 percent) identified by factor analysis. Special educator predictions consistently underestimated the positiveness of regular class colleagues on matters associated with these items (see Table 4 for a complete list of these items). These results appear to run counter to beliefs frequently put forward by special educators that regular class teachers are negative about the concept and process of mainstreaming. Therefore, it appears that preservice and inservice programs focusing on consulting skillls should stress the need for consultants to find the necessary time needed to obtain accurate perceptions about the regular class teacher's opinions and attitudes about mainstreaming before offering facilitating suggestions. To do otherwise may perpetuate a spuriously negative view of regular class teachers' opinions about mainstreaming. This view, in turn, may have the potential for becoming a self-fulfilling prophecy. Results of this study appear to suggest that special educators may

TABLE 3 WILKS' LAMBDA FOR EACH FACTOR

Variable	Wilks' lambda	F	Significance
Factor 1	0.94112	11.57	.0008*
Factor 2	0.97308	5.12	.0248*
Factor 3	0.96563	6.58	.0111*
Factor 4	0.99277	1.35	.2471
Factor 5	0.96177	7.35	.0073*
Factor 6	0.99299	1.31	.2544

*$p < .05$

be pleasantly surprised by the optimism and willingness of their regular class colleagues to facilitate the integration of exceptional children into the regular school program. This optimism may be the result of several interacting factors, including (a) the effects of comprehensive system of personnel development mandates of PL94–142 (100 of the 131 regular educators—76.3 percent—reported that they had participated in at least one course or inservice workshop on mainstreaming) and (b) successful experience over time with handicapped students in the regular school program (124 of 131 regular educators—94.7 percent—reported that they had taught or were currently teaching students with diagnosed handicaps; 67.2 percent reported that they had personally experienced success in mainstreaming handicapped youngsters; 83.2 percent reported that they knew of other regular educators who had successfully mainstreamed handicapped youngsters).

Special educators in this study were asked to predict responses of regular class teacher colleagues in their school system. Therefore, predictions were determined at a systemwide level. It is recommended that this study be replicated with pairs of regular and special educators within school buildings to determine if predictions improve or worsen as a result of direct and ongoing working relationships at the school building level.

Further research might also focus on the validity of the instrument used in this study as an ecological assessment instrument to help in identifying topical foci for regular educator inservice education programs and to assess the impact of such programs on attitudes of participants.

REFERENCES

Aloia, G. F., & Aloia, S. D. (1982). Variations in expectations of the mainstreamed handicapped child by regular and special education teachers. *Journal for Special Educators*, 19(1), 13–19.

Biklen, D. P. (1985). Mainstreaming: From compliance to quality. *Journal of Learning Disabilities*, 18(1), 58–61.

Bond, C. L., & Dietrich, A. (1981, November). Survey of teacher attitudes toward the role of the resource program. Paper presented at the annual meeting of the Mid-South Educational Research Association, Lexington, KY.

Buttery, T. J. (1979). Pre-service teachers' affective responses to exceptional children. *Southern Journal of Educational Research*, 13(2), 65–70.

Candler, A., & Sowell, V. (1980, April). *Mainstreaming special educators: Interface between regular and special education*. Paper presented at the annual international convention of The Council for Exceptional Children, Philadelphia.

Carpenter, R. L. (1980). Information consultation and special education teachers. *Education Unlimited*, 2(2), 14–17.

Cronbach, L. J. (1951). Coefficient alpha and the internal structure of tests. *Psychometrika*, 16, 297–334.

Curtis, M. J., & Anderson, T. E. (1976). *Consulting in educational settings: A collaborative approach*. Cincinnati, OH: University of Cincinnati, Faculty Resource Center.

Diebold, M. H. (1980). The Education for All Handicapped Children Act: Accent on communication. *The Professional Educator*, 1(1), 50–51.

Egioff, L. J., & Lederer, C. M. (1980). Teacher consultation for mainstreaming: A packet for special educators. *Pointer*, 24(3), 56–66.

TABLE 4 OPINIONNAIRE ITEMS IDENTIFIED BY DISCRIMINATIVE ANALYSIS

Factor	Factor Loading	Opinionnaire Item Description
*1		*Willingness to Teach Handicapped Students*
		I am willing to teach. . . .
	.828	hearing impaired students.
	.803	visually impaired students.
	.753	students with communication disorders.
	.639	learning disabled students.
	.638	emotionally disturbed students.
	.828	orthopedically handicapped students.
	.824	health impaired students.
*2		*Knowledge of Where to Obtain Help or Information About Students with Handicaps*
		I know where to get help or information regarding students with. . . .
	.854	visual impairments.
	.797	hearing impairments.
	.796	communication disorders.
	.775	health impairments.
	.765	orthopedic impairments.
	.614	learning disabilities.
	.591	emotional disturbance.
*3		*Feelings of Confidence About Skills in Carrying out the Mainstreaming Program in the Regular Classroom*
		I feel confident with my skills in. . . .
	.839	adapting materials and activities for handicapped students.
	.818	setting goals and objectives for handicapped students.
	.810	measuring achievement of handicapped students.
	.771	developing IEPs for handicapped students.
	.732	behavior management of handicapped students.
4		*Effects of Placement on the Regular Class Program*
	.795	Placement in the regular classroom means the regular educator must devote most of his or her attention to the handicapped student.
	.758	Placement in the regular classroom would be disruptive to the other students.
	.755	Placement in the regular classroom will hurt the educational progress of the handicapped student.
	.558	When a handicapped child is placed in my room, the size of the class should be reduced.
	.543	The mainstreaming of handicapped students into the regular classroom can be beneficial to regular students.
	.496	The mainstreaming of handicapped students requires significant changes in regular classroom procedures.
*5		*Sufficiency of Time for Carrying out the Mainstreaming Program*
		As it pertains to the mainstreaming program, I have enough. . . .
	.876	planning/preparation time.
	.853	consultation time.
	.734	instructional time.
6		*Effects of Teacher Input into the Educational Program and Special Educator Knowledge of the Regular Class on Current Opinion about the Mainstreaming Process*
	.633	My opinion toward the mainstreaming process is more positive now than when it first started.
	.624	I have input into the program and schedule of handicapped students who are placed in the regular classroom.

90

TABLE 4 *(Continued)*

Factor	Factor Loading	Opinionnaire Item Description
	.516	Special educators acting as consultants have sufficient knowledge of regular classroom to give valuable help.
	.476	Handicapped students are being placed in the educational setting most appropriate to their needs.

* Regular class teacher opinions expressed on all items were difficult for special educators to predict.

Feidman, D., & Altman, R. (1985). Conceptual systems and teacher attitudes toward placement of mildly mentally retarded students. *American Journal of Mental Deficiency, 9,* 345–351.

Fleming, D. C., & Fleming, E. R. (1983). Consultation with multidisciplinary teams: A program of development and improvement of team functioning. *Journal of School Psychology, 21,* 367–376.

Gans, K. D. (1985). Regular and special educators: Handicap integration attitudes and implications. *Teacher Education and Special Education, 8,* 188–197.

Haight, S. L. (1984). Special education teacher consultant: Idealism versus realism. *Exceptional Children, 50,* 507–515.

Hauptman, E. (1983, April). *Communication between special educators and the mainstream teacher.* Paper presented at the annual international convention of The Council for Exceptional Children. Detroit.

Knof, H. M. (1984). Mainstreaming attitudes and special placement knowledge in labeling versus nonlabeling states. *Remedial and Special Education, 5*(6), 7–14.

Morsink, C. (1979). Implementing PL94–142. The challenge of the 80's. *Education Unlimited, 1*(4), 20–22.

Ringlaben, R. P., & Weller, C. (1981). Mainstreaming the special educator, *Education Unlimited, 3*(4), 19–22.

Salend, S. J., & Salend, S. (1984). Consulting with the regular teacher: Guidelines for special educators, *Pointer, 28*(3), 25–28.

Triandis, H. C. (1971). *Attitude and attitude change,* New York: Wiley.

Winzer, M. (1985). Teacher attitudes toward mainstreaming: An appraisal of the research. *British Columbia Journal of Special Education, 9,* 149–161.

CHAPTER 3

Efficacy Issues

Public Law 94-142 mandates the education of handicapped children in the least restrictive environment. As a direct result of this legislation, programs have been developed to provide educational and therapeutic services to children who were either not receiving an education and/or who were being underserved. As special education expanded, concern rose over the efficacy and cost effectiveness of such services. Questions about cost, the effectiveness of early intervention, and self-contained special education classes are natural in an era which stresses accountability.

Chapter three, which seeks to answer some questions relating to accountability, is divided into three sections. Section one, *Early Intervention: How Effective Is It?*, focuses on the validity of early intervention programs. This section includes catalysts for the evolution of early intervention programs, a history of early intervention, results of studies concerning the effects of early intervention and programming, and a discussion of future directions. Nicholas Anastasiow's article entitled *The Research Base for Early Intervention* is included. Dr. Anastasiow stresses that research on the efficacy of early intervention is sufficient to warrant expansion; and the recent passage of P.L. 99-457 seems to add credence to his belief.

Section two, *Efficacy of Special Classes: What Have We Learned?*, reviews the history of the mainstreaming movement, focusing on the debate over the efficiency of special classes, as well as the difficulties involved in interpreting and applying results of this research.

Section three, *Cost Effectiveness of Special Education*, deals with the question of whether special education programs are worth their cost, especially given the large number of children receiving special education services, and the monetary support provided by federal, state, and local governments over the years. This section covers the costs of special education, discusses cost effectiveness as an investment return, and compares the cost effectiveness of different service delivery models.

With the increasing emphasis on accountability and the decline in federal support of special education programs, we can anticipate that concern over efficacy will continue. While some professionals may view these concerns as an albatross, others will see them as an impetus for improving our special education service delivery system.

EARLY INTERVENTION: HOW EFFECTIVE IS IT?

Improved diagnostic techniques now enable us to identify many children with handicapping conditions well before they reach school age. As a result, we are able to provide early intervention, or the delivery of therapeutic and/or educational services to infants and preschool children with a wide variety of handicapping conditions.

Early intervention programs are designed to provide optimum learning experiences during the crucial early childhood developmental period. The importance of the preschool years to future success has been documented by many child development authorities, who emphasize that the first five or six years of a child's life are periods of the highest potential growth in physical, perceptual, linguistic, cognitive, and affective areas (Lerner, Mardell-Czudnowski, and Goldenberg 1981). These early periods of development are particularly important to the handicapped child since it is assumed that the earlier these children are identified and their education begun, the greater the chances of lessening the impact of the handicapping condition on the child and society.

Catalysts for the Development of Early Intervention Programs

In 1968, Congress recognized the need for models of effective preschool special education programs, and began supporting them through the enactment of P.L. 90-583, the Handicapped Children's Early Education Assistance Act (HCEEP). This act, sometimes referred to as the First Chance Program, provided monies for the development and implementation of experimental projects for young handicapped children and their families. These projects were required to include parents, to provide inservice training, to evaluate the progress of both the children and the programs, to coordinate activities with the public schools and other agencies, and to disseminate information on project activities (DeWeerd 1977). The HCEEP continues to support new early intervention programs, and many of the materials and models used in programs across the country were originally developed with HCEEP support.

The Head Start movement, which began in 1964 as part of the War on Poverty, and was funded by the Office of Economic Opportunity, also played an important role in the growth of preschool special education. The goal of Head Start was to offer preschool children from economically deprived homes a comprehensive program that would help compensate for their deprivation. Through Head Start, children received medical care, nutrition, parent involvement, socialization, and education. The Head Start legislation was amended in 1972 and 1974 by P.L. 92-924 and P.L. 93-644, which required that all Head Start programs include a minimum of ten percent handicapped children in their enrollments (Hayden and Gotts 1977).

A further influence on early intervention was the passage and implementation of P.L. 94-142, the Education for All Handicapped Children Act of 1975, which mandated services for all handicapped children from three to five years of age unless contrary to state law. This legislation provided two sources of funds for handicapped preschool children: state entitlement money, which depends on the number of handicapped children counted by the state in its child find activities; and incentive grants, which are available to states with approved state plans that offer services for three-to-five-year-old handicapped children (Lerner et al. 1981).

Despite these federal initiatives, commitment to early intervention varies from state to state, depending on mandatory and permissive legislation, rules, regulations, and practice (Swan 1981). Many states are still not providing adequate preschool special education. As of 1979, twenty-seven had mandated legislation for preschool special education for handicapped children from ages three to five, while only ten had enacted legislation covering the education of handicapped children from birth (Hayden 1979). In 1986, in order to remedy this lack of services, Congress passed P.L. 99-457, which extended all the rights and protections of P.L. 94-142 to all handicapped three-to-five-year-olds by 1990, and made services available to all two-year-olds and younger on a discretionary basis.

Historical Base for Early Intervention

The idea of providing early intervention services to young handicapped or disadvantaged children is supported by the work of Hunt (1961) and Bloom (1964). Hunt (1961) challenges the notion of fixed intelligence and proposes that a faster rate of development might be achieved if children's experiences with the environment could be structured. This viewpoint is reinforced by Bloom (1964), who concludes that environmental experiences have a major impact on children's later development, particularly those experiences that occur during infancy and early childhood.

Several early research studies attempted to measure how changing the early environment might affect children (Kirk 1958; Skeels 1966; Skeels and Dye 1939). Although the methodology of these studies was often criticized, they did demonstrate that early intervention substantially influenced children's functioning. Skeels and Dye (1939) removed thirteen children under the age of three with an average IQ of 64 from an orphanage, and placed them in an institution for people with mental retardation where they were cared for by the institution's attendants and residents. They left twelve children with an average IQ of 67.6 in the orphanage. The children in the institution for the mentally retarded received a great deal of stimulation from the retarded residents, while those who remained in the orphanage received only basic care from the staff. After eighteen months, the children in the institution gained an average of 27.5 IQ points, while those children in the orphanage dropped an average of 26.2 IQ points. Twenty-one years later, in a followup study, Skeels (1966) found that all thirteen of the experimental children were self-supporting. Four of the people who had remained in the orphanage were in institutions for mentally retarded individuals, and a fifth who had been institutionalized had died. The group raised in the institution with stimulation had completed a median of twelve grades in school, while the orphanage control group had only completed a median of three grades. The results of these studies support the concept that early stimulation can increase development, and that, conversely, lack of appropriate stimulation can decrease the rate of development. In addition, the study suggests that these rates remain relatively constant over time.

An Era of Doubt

Despite the promise of these early studies, the Head Start program, which was introduced in the 1960s, produced mixed results. At first, IQ gains were noted among children who participated in the original summer program (Payne et al. 1979). However, to everyone's disappointment, when the Head Start children were compared to a control group at midsemester, the previously noted gains of Head Start children had disappeared. When the results of the Westinghouse study became public (Cicirelli 1969), they were discouraging. Although the Head Start children did score somewhat higher on cognitive measures than children who had not attended Head Start, the differences were smaller than anticipated.

While the nation was concerned about the apparent failure of Head Start to produce the desired effects on disadvantaged children, other programs were demonstrating that early intervention *could* have positive effects on children's IQ, cognitive, and other skill development (Bereiter and Engelmann 1966; Weikart 1970). However, because these gains were often smaller than anticipated and were seldom maintained after the preschool years, the studies also tended to raise new questions about the long-term effectiveness of early intervention.

The pessimism voiced by some research analysts was reinforced by Bronfenbrenner (1975), who reviewed twelve studies of skills children gained through preschool programs. He concluded that neither early entry nor longer enrollment produced lasting gains. However, this perspective was later questioned by many researchers. In a review of studies originally thought to have nonlasting gains, Lazar et al. (1977) noted that gains reported diminished by second grade were present again by fifth grade. Of the five studies reviewed by Lazar et al., four reported from 50 to 90 percent fewer special class placements for children who had had preschool interventions. In other words, although many of the early studies had reported an absence of lasting effects resulting from early childhood programs, more recent research indicates that early intervention programs are successful in producing lasting gains among disadvantaged and handicapped children (Hanson 1985).

An Era of Proof

While data on the efficacy of early intervention programs and maintenance of long-term gains has been available for more than two decades, questions about the effectiveness of these programs persist (Karnes et al. 1981). Continued research is therefore vital, particularly as the need for funding grows. Programs for young handicapped children are currently in an era of fiscal austerity (Jelinek 1981). And Lazar (1979,7) warns educators not to "count on sentiment to keep your program supported. We must be able to show that early intervention for all children pays off in tangible ways."

The need to document program effectiveness has generated a large body of research. While it is impossible to review all relevant articles, we can summarize the results of some major studies. Palmer (1977) reported that children with preschool experience had significantly higher IQ and arithmetic achievement scores than the children without preschool experience. The average preschool attendee was six months more advanced than the control children, and 45 percent of the control group (as compared to only 22 percent of the experimental children) were one or more years behind grade level in academics. In another study, Hayden and Haring (1976) stated that Down's syndrome children who had been enrolled in a structured preschool demonstrated more advanced skills across several school years than similar children not exposed to preschool.

In a systematic study of those children who had attended High/Scope's Ypsilanti Perry Preschool Project, Schweinhart and Weikart (1981) followed 123 children, ages three to nineteen. When the study began, the children were randomly assigned to either a preschool program or no preschool. Those children who were in the preschool program showed lasting improvement in their commitment to school and achievement. Thirty-nine percent of the students who did not attend preschool were later placed in special education classes, compared to only 19 percent of those who had attended preschool. The scholastic achievement of the preschool children was consistently higher even ten years later, and they had higher motivation, did more homework, and had less delinquent behavior. In 1979 dollars, the cost per child of the two-year preschool program was $5,984. And in 1979 dollars, the estimated benefits were these: $3,353 per child saved by the public schools because the children needed fewer years of special education; $10,798 per child in projected lifetime earnings resulting from their improved educational status; and $668 per child estimated as the value of each mother's released time while the child attended preschool. These benefits amount to a 248 percent return on the original investment. While few studies have been as thorough as the Perry Preschool Project, the overwhelming number of studies (Bricker and Sheehan 1981; Karnes et al. 1981; Simmons-Martin 1981; Zeitlin 1981) indicate that, at least with mildly handicapped and disadvantaged high-risk children, preschool programs result in immediate gains that are likely to last into the public school years.

It must be acknowledged, however, that initial studies did not focus on the gains of more severely handicapped children enrolled in preschool programs (Moore, Fredericks, and Baldwin 1981); these studies came later. Hanson (1985), who studied the effects of early intervention on children with moderate to severe disabilities and on their parents, reported significant positive behavioral changes for both. Moore et al. (1981) studied 151 nine-, ten-, and eleven-year-old children who had been in preschool programs for the trainable mentally retarded, and reported significant differences in language skills, academic performance, self-help, and motor skill performance between those with two or more years of preschool and those with only one year or less.

Yet, while many programs conduct self-evaluation, it is difficult and often unwise to generalize from these highly individualistic studies to all early intervention programs. Before drawing any broad conclusions, it is important to examine research based on multiple studies. Lazar & Darlington (1982), in the Consortium for Longitudinal Studies, reanalyzed follow-up data on more than one thousand children from fifteen early intervention programs, and reported that the preschool programs did indeed have lasting impact. Graduates of these preschool programs, as compared to control students who had not attended preschool, had higher reading and arithmetic achievement scores, were less likely to be placed in special or remedial classes, had higher self-esteem, and demonstrated increased participation in the work force in late adolescence and early adulthood.

Casto and Mastropieri (1986) cite a summary in which 94 percent out of a sample of fifty-two previous reviewers had concluded that early intervention was beneficial for disadvantaged, handicapped, and at-risk children, and that it resulted in improved cognitive, motor, and language skills, as well as increased social-emotional growth for both the children and their families. However, Casto and Mastropieri express concern about interpreting these results since the conclusions were based mainly on studies of disadvantaged or at-risk children, rather than handicapped children. In an effort to obtain more generalizable data, Casto and Mastropieri (1986) conducted a meta-analysis of seventy-four studies that had reported interventions with handicapped preschoolers. While the results of this meta-analysis did suggest that early intervention was beneficial, it also led the researchers to question several assumptions from previous studies. For example, data from the meta-analysis did not support the ideas that parent involvement leads to more benefits, that programs should start as early as possible, or that highly structured programs are more effective than less structured programs. Although Casto and Mastropieri's conclusions were criticized by Dunst and Snyder (1986) and by Strain and Smith (1986), they do point out problems in interpreting the early intervention literature.

Difficulties in Interpreting the Efficacy Studies

In 1985, Meisels asked, "Why are we still asking questions about the efficacy of early intervention?" and proposed that it was because too many people involved with early intervention failed to ask critical questions. Meisels stressed that questions about the design of the studies had to be addressed before the effects of those studies could be meaningfully evaluated, and recommended that critical questions about the theoretical rationale of intervention programs, their specific intervention strategies, measurement criteria, and subject selection criteria needed to be examined.

Jelinek (1985) stresses how difficult it can be to document the impact of early intervention programs since traditional research designs are difficult to implement with early intervention research. For example, randomly assigning children to control groups creates ethical and legal problems if the treatment is believed potentially effective, since P.L. 94-142 forbids withholding treatment from individuals. In addition, Jelinek notes that children are often heterogeneously mixed in programs; this can confound results by intermingling data on the progress of mildly and severely handicapped children, thereby making precise documentation of progress difficult with standard analysis techniques.

Another difficulty in evaluating early intervention programs arises because so many different outcome measures are used (Casto and Lewis 1985; Jelinek 1985). Unfortunately, these various outcome measures are often limited in scope and may not relate closely to program content. Future research studies need to use broader based outcome measures and more stringent design requirements if the results are to be truly useful in improving the quality of early intervention efficacy studies (Casto and Mastropieri 1986).

Directions for the Future

Anastasiow (1986) states that the efficacy of early intervention programs should be less a research question than a social and moral issue. In his view, it should not be necessary to defend the continuation of early intervention but only to demonstrate how to deliver services more effectively, using what materials, and in which settings.

Researchers still need to examine which kinds of early intervention models produce the best results. Up to this point, research has failed to indicate any clear superiority of one model over another (Miller and Dyer 1975; Moore et al. 1981; Weikart 1971). For example, although Ramey et al. (1985) demonstrated that gains were superior for the more intensely treated group of children in their study, this effect was questioned by Castro and Mastropieri (1986).

In addition, conclusive data is still needed regarding the cost effectiveness of early intervention programs. Conflicting results persist. For instance, in a cost-benefit analysis, the Perry Preschool Project reported that two years of a high quality preschool program returned three and a half times the initial investment. But other programs have reported widespread variations in costs. The House of Representatives (Select Committee on Children, 1985) reported that in Colorado, even after subtracting the cost of the preschool special education programs, school districts saved $1560 per handicapped pupil and $1050 per at-risk pupil when the children were enrolled in preschool programs. In addition, the House report cautioned that if intervention for handicapped infants were delayed until age six, the educational costs per child would rise to an estimated $53,350, while intervention from birth could potentially lower educational costs to $37,272. One of the problems with this type of cost analysis, however, is that these cost-per-child figures fail to account for the variability in services and the differences in costs across programs (Macy and Schafer 1985).

In general, existing evidence does support the efficacy of early intervention programs. Nevertheless, because many programs have not been carefully evaluated, some questions are still unanswered. Well-designed research is needed before this issue can be resolved.

REFERENCES

Anastasiow, N. (1986). The research base for early intervention. *Journal of the Division for Early Childhood, 10,* 99–105.

Bereiter, C., & Engelmann, S. (1966). *Teaching disadvantaged children in the preschool.* Englewood Cliffs, NJ: Prentice Hall.

Bloom, B. (1964). *Stability and change in human characteristics.* NY: John Wiley.

Bricker, D., & Sheehan, R. (1981). Effectiveness of an early intervention program as indexed by measures of child change. *Journal of the Division for Early Childhood, 4,* 11–27.

Bronfenbrenner, U. (1975). Is early intervention effective? In M. Guttenlag and E. Struening (Eds.), *Handbook of evaluation research,* (Vol. 2). Beverly Hills, CA: Sage Publications.

Casto, G., & Lewis, A. (1985). Selecting outcome measures in early intervention. *Journal of the Division for Early Childhood, 10,* 118–123.

Casto, G., & Mastropieri, M. (1986). The efficacy of early intervention programs: A meta-analysis. *Exceptional Children, 52,* 417–424.

Cicirelli, V. (1969). *The impact of Head Start: An evaluation of the effects of Head Start on children's cognitive and affective development.* Springfield, VA: U.S. Department of Commerce Clearinghouse, PB 184 328

Deweerd, J. (1977). Introduction. In J. Jordan, A. Hayden, M. Karnes, & M. Wood (Eds.), *Early childhood education for exceptional children.* Reston, VA: Council for Exceptional Children.

Dunst, C., & Snyder, S. (1986). A critique of the Utah State University early intervention meta-analysis research. *Exceptional Children, 53,* 269–276.

Hanson, M. (1985). An analysis of the effects of early intervention services for infants and toddlers with moderate and severe handicaps. *Topics in Early Childhood Special Education, 5,* 36–51.

Hayden, A. (1979). Handicapped children, birth to age three. *Exceptional Children, 45,* 510–517.

Hayden, A., & Gotts, E. (1977). Multiple staffing patterns. In J. Jordan, A. Hayden, M. Karnes, & M. Wood (Eds.), *Early childhood education for exceptional children.* Reston, VA: Council for Exceptional Children.

Hayden, A., & Haring, N. (1976). *A preliminary report on a study of the acceleration and maintenance of developmental gains in school-aged Down's syndrome children.* Paper presented at the Fourth International Congress of the International Association for the Scientific Study of Mental Deficiency, Washington, DC, 22–27.

Hunt, J. (1961). *Intelligence and experience.* NY: Ronald.

Jelinek, J. (1981). *The Wyoming infant stimulation program.* Paper presented at the American Speech-Language-Hearing Association Convention, Los Angeles, CA.

Jelinek, J. (1985). Documentation of child progress revisited: An analysis method for outreach or local programs. *Journal of the Division for Early Childhood, 9,* 175–182.

Karnes, M., Schwedel, A., Lewis, G., Ratts, D. & Esry, R. (1981). Impact of early programming for the handicapped: A follow-up study into the elementary school. *Journal of the Division for Early Childhood, 4,* 62–79.

Kirk, S. (1958). *Early education of the mentally retarded.* Urbana, IL: University of Illinois Press.

Lazar, I. (1979). Does prevention pay off? *DEC Communicator, 6,* 1–7.

Lazar, I., & Darlington, R. (Eds.). (1982). Lasting effects of early intervention: A report from the Consortium for Longitudinal Studies. *Monographs of the Society for Research in Child Development, 47,* (2–3, Serial No. 195).

Lazar, I., Hubbell, R., Murray, H., Rosche, M. & Royce, J. (1977). *Preliminary findings of the developmental continuity longitudinal study*. Paper presented at the Office of Child Development's "Parents, Children, and Continuity" Conference, El Paso, Texas, May 23.

Lerner, J., Mardell-Czudnowski, C., & Goldenberg, D. (1981). *Special education for the early childhood years*. Englewood Cliffs, NJ: Prentice Hall, Inc.

Macy, D., & Schafer, D. (1985). Real-time cost analysis: Application in early intervention. *Journal of the Division for Early Childhood, 9,* 98–104.

Meisels, S. (1985). The efficacy of early intervention: Why are we still asking this question? *Topics in Early Childhood Special Education, 5,* 1–11.

Miller, L., & Dyer, J. (1975). Four preschool programs: Their dimensions and effects. *Monograph of the Society for Research in Child Development, 40.*

Moore, M., Fredericks, B., & Baldwin, V. (1981). The long-range effects of early childhood education on a trainable mentally retarded population. *Journal of the Division for Early Childhood, 4,* 94–110.

Palmer, F. (1977). *The effects of early childhood intervention*. Paper presented at the Annual Meeting of the American Association for the Advancement of Science, Denver. CO.

Payne, J., Kauffman, J., Patton, J., Brown, G., & DeMott, R. (1979). *Exceptional children in focus*. Columbus, OH: Charles E. Merrill.

Ramey, C., Bryant, D., Sparling, J., & Wasik, B. (1985). Project CARE: A comparison of two early intervention strategies to prevent retarded development. *Topics in Early Childhood Special Education, 5,* 12–25.

Schweinhart, L. & Weikart, D. (1981). Effects of the Perry Preschool Program on youths through age 15. *Journal of the Division for Early Childhood, 4,* 29–39.

Select Committee on Children, Youth, and Families (House of Representatives). (1985). *Opportunities for success: Cost-effective programs for children*. Washington, DC: U.S. Government Printing Office.

Simmons-Martin, A. (1981). Efficacy report: Early Education Project. *Journal of the Division for Early Childhood, 4,* 5–10.

Skeels, H. (1966). Adult status of children with contrasting early life experiences. *Monograph of the Society for Research in Child Development, 31.*

Skeels, H., & Dye, H. (1939). A study of differential stimulation of children. *Proceedings of the American Association on Mental Deficiency, 44,* 114–136.

Strain, P., & Smith, B. (1986) A counter-interpretation of early intervention effects: A response to Casto and Mastropieri. *Exceptional Children, 53,* 260–265.

Swan, W. (1981). Efficacy studies in early childhood special education: An overview. *Journal of the Division for Early Childhood, 4,* 1–4.

Weikart, D. (1970). A comparative study of three preschool curricula. In J. Forest (Ed.), *Disadvantaged child*. New York: Houghton Mifflin.

Zeitlin, S. (1981). Learning through coping: An effective preschool program. *Journal of the Division for Early Childhood, 4,* 53–61.

DISCUSSION QUESTIONS

1. Your school district is getting ready to begin an early intervention program for handicapped preschoolers, and you have been asked to make a brief presentation on possible problems and benefits. Outline your presentation.
2. All states have mandates to provide early intervention programs to handicapped children, ages three to five, by 1990. Do you think this provision should be extended to younger children? Why?

3. At present some states have separate teacher certification for preschool special education; however, many states do not offer a separate license. What skills would you consider essential for a teacher of young handicapped children? Do you think there should be special certification for this? Why?
4. You know a family that does not seem to give their young children the type of attention and experiences that would help them to develop. What procedures might you follow to help, and what might you tell the family?
5. As the director of a preschool program that serves handicapped children, you recognize the need for good program evaluation. What things do you think are important to measure, and how would you structure your program to facilitate the evaluation?

The Research Base for Early Intervention

Nicholas J. Anastasiow

My talk will summarize what I perceive to be the three major themes developed during the conference. First, ample data were presented in the various sessions to substantiate that the effort to improve the lives of impaired children and their families is effective. If there were any doubts before the conference began about the positive results of early intervention programs, these doubts should have been forevermore laid to rest.

Two, in spite of these data, questions continue to be asked about the efficacy studies, about the research design and the appropriateness of the research and evaluation strategies used to claim effectiveness. These questions create a general atmosphere of distrust regarding the efficacy data, particularly casting doubts on the validity of clinically arrived-at insights. Among some researchers, there appears to be a general suspicion of data arrived at through inductive-intuitive modes of research. Whereas these critiques have some intellectual interest, they are of limited value in guiding clinical and educational practice. Critics of the inductive method of research fail to recognize the problems of the more highly prized deductive method. Philosophers of science currently hold that the deductive method is more suited for technology than it is for education (Phillips 1985), a point that will be returned to later in the paper.

Three, in addition to the evaluation data available from the efficacy studies, there are data supporting the logic of early intervention programs. These data are found in the human development literature, in data derived from experimental studies with animals, and in the pioneering works of Howard Skeels, Sam Kirk, and J. McVicker Hunt and a host of other research social science investigators who have studied the effects of environments on the development of humans. It might be good to pause here and remind ourselves of the major social concern that generated the national interest in providing services to young handicapped children toward the purpose of enabling them to function as competent and autonomous adults.

Recent efforts to ameliorate the negative effects of at-risk biological and environmental factors arose out of observations made in 1930–1960 that children who re-

Note. The Research Base for Early Intervention by N. J. Anastasiow, 1986, *Journal of the Division for Early Childhood, 10,* pp. 99–105. Copyright 1986 by the Division for Early Childhood, The Council for Exceptional Children. Reprinted by permission.

sided in orphanages, Indian pueblos, canal boats in England, the hollows of Appalachia, the barrios of the Southwest, the back seats of cars of migrant workers, and the ghettos of the inner city were not only overly populated in special education classes, if any existed, but were at high risk for school failure, school drop out, and lower status occupations. As adults, the products of these environments tended to live erratic and disorganized lives. The initial societal concern was not for impaired children. In fact, many physicians felt it was best to institutionalize handicapped infants at birth. If in the 1940s and 1950s you were to have visited a state hospital for the retarded or insane, you would have found large groups of listless, atrophied emotionally and mentally retarded men and women. The initial societal concern was for the children of the economically poor, who tended not to fare well in society. The thread that united the concern for children of the economically poor and the institutionalized child was the fact that many infants appeared at birth to be fairly normal, but as they grew and developed, whether in institutions or slums, they declined in IQ. For the orphanage-reared infant, the decline was in the early years of life, and at times death intervened. For the poverty child, the decline in IQ was noted in the first to third grades (although it may have occurred earlier, as these children were not seen in school until age six), with their IQs leveling off in the retarded range. A commonly held assumption to account for these low IQ scores was that poor genes and inadequate nutrition contributed to low levels of functioning. The thrust of *Intelligence and Experience* (Hunt, 1961) was that IQ is not fixed at birth but is a product of genes and environment and that declines in measured IQ are due to environmental inadequacies, not to genes. The message of hope from Hunt's book was that declines in IQ can be prevented by providing enriched environmental experiences for children who do not naturally have them in their economically impoverished environments. Regardless of

rhetoric to the contrary, the basic intent of the first poverty programs of the late 1960s was to prevent the decline of IQ and the seven-hour retarded child—that is, the child who was retarded only during school hours. It has been Hunt's contention that all but a small percentage of the world's children are genetically capable of achieving a normal life if given appropriate environmental conditions (Hunt, 1979). In addition, in the late fifties, Sam Kirk, another giant at the University of Illinois and a colleague of Hunt, demonstrated that impaired children can function at much higher levels, given training and educational intervention (Kirk 1958).

Both Kirk's and Hunt's work influenced the establishment of early childhood handicapped programs. The issue of early intervention for the handicapped and early education for children who reside in poverty became dominant societal efforts. The career of Merle Karnes is an example of someone who has achieved excellence in working both with children who reside in poverty and with populations of handicapped children. It is also important to be aware that the decline in IQ has been elegantly demonstrated by a number of investigators to be preventable with Down's Syndrome children as reported by Guralnick and Bricker (in press) and with poverty children by Berrueta-Clement, Schweinhart, Barnett, Epstein and Weikart (1984), Garber and Heber (1976), and Ramey and colleagues (1979). There is enough solid research data to support the claim that prevention of IQ declines can be achieved with significant numbers of normal and handicapped children who are vulnerable for an IQ decline. A national policy to establish intervention programs for all children at-risk for IQ decline would do much to ensure optimal functioning of children from poverty groups, particularly the children of the very poor. The very poor have been labeled *The Underclass* (Auletta, 1983). The Underclass is mainly composed of women and children (70% of the total 9 million). These children are reared in settings and conditions which lead many of them to develop behavior patterns perceived as inappropriate. These behaviors of children of the underclass make them prime candidates for classes for the emotionally disturbed once they reach school age. It should be noted that there are currently more poor children than adults who reside in poverty (Moynihan 1985).

No band-aid services such as "Job Corps" or "summer camps" will resolve the real needs of the underclass, who subsist on excessively low incomes surrounded by public displays of wealth. Special educators need to be concerned with the underclass, for unlike most poverty groups of the past, this group is not upwardly mobile and is producing children who overpopulate classes for the emotionally disturbed and the retarded and, as adults, the prisons (Auletta 1983).

EFFICACY RESULTS

The papers presented at the conference cover a variety of types of programs for handicapped children and their families. For example, papers were presented which described home-based programs, programs in centers and programs that combined both approaches. The papers described programs which contained children displaying a range of handicapping conditions. Uniformly, the presenters provided data to substantiate that the outcomes of these intervention programs have improved the lives of the vulnerable, the at-risk and the handicapped children and their families. Clearly, the question of whether programs for at-risk children should be continued is not a research question. It is a social-moral issue. The question of "should" or "whether" the programs be continued need no longer be asked. As a profession, we must guard against defending the wrong question; that is, we need not respond defensively to the *should* question. Nor need we defend *why* handicapped infants and children need be served. The research question to be asked is: *How* to deliver

services better, with *what* materials, and in *what* settings. In essence the overall efficacy question has been answered, which allows us now to face the more definitive questions as to what kinds of approaches work and with what kinds of children and with what kinds of effects.

The conference members have addressed public policy issues in some of their sessions. I would suggest that educators would do well to learn from those who do know how to influence public policy to insure that prevention programs are maintained and that intervention becomes a part of the fabric of our society. Just as 99 percent of babies in the United States are being born in hospitals, we should be assured that 99 percent of at-risk infants and children receive the services they require. If we need research, we need research that will help us understand how to affect those who set priorities. We must learn how to influence priorities. We must not give sanction to distorted priorities that waste valuable human resources in the search for the perfect means of destruction. Greenspan and White speak to this issue (1985), when they quote Shore (1981):

> You Americans have a funny way of looking at evaluation. First you confuse research and politics. There are some things that are not research questions; that is, issues such as should there be equity in health care? There are basic questions of social philosophy that the country must answer. Research can determine if this equity is taking place. But one does not research whether or not people should have a place to live or food to eat. In addition, in the United States you evaluate programs to decide whether or not to withdraw financial support. This differs from the attitude in much of Europe, where the basic thrust of a program is assumed to be correct and the evaluation is used to improve it, or to determine why it did not accomplish what it set out to do. (p. 401)

It was ironic to observe at this conference the need to defend what has been the most successful federal program of our generation—

The Handicapped Children Early Education Program, fought for and obtained by Sam Kirk and James J. Gallagher, brilliantly maintained by Edwin Martin, Jr., led by Jane DeWeerd, and implemented by hundreds of our colleagues, among whom are Louise Phillips, Setsa Furuno, Alice Hayden, Mary Woods, Ann Sanford, Bud Fredericks, Sam Meisels, Diane Bricker, Mike Guralnick, all the named and unnamed heroines and heroes of our times.

Do we need to ask:

- Should we reduce high risk infants from being high risk?
- Develop ways to help high risk infants survive?

Should we not be concerned that we lead The Netherlands, France, England, Sweden, and Wales in:

- infant mortality
- death in children under four
- increases in infant mortality, particularly among the poor?

We have sufficient knowledge, technology, and personnel to prevent many handicapping conditions and to improve many of them that cannot be prevented. Should we not recall, as Carl Sandburg wrote, "There is only one child in the world and that child's name is all children"?

INDUCTIVE-DEDUCTIVE RESEARCH ISSUE

The second theme is the issue of the legitimacy of the research strategies used to collect efficacy data. There is not high agreement among educators on philosophy, methods of instruction, or evaluation data. In the summer of 1984, I shared a panel with a special educator in Athens who conducts sophisticated research on language development in children who reside in economic poverty. I shared with her my enthusiasm for Shirley Heath's book *Way With Words* (1983). Heath, an ethnographer and linguist, lived, taught, and studied in an Appalachian community for several years. Heath's work, to me, was a landmark study, documenting her insights into the sources of low academic achievements among children of the economically poor, both white and black. My colleague's response surprised me, although it shouldn't have. She maintained that Heath had interesting ideas, maybe some hypotheses, but definitely *no data.* Upon return to the United States, I was delighted to read in the *New York Times* that Heath had been awarded a MacArthur Fellowship. Gloating, I shared the details of my Athens encounter with a New York colleague and ended with my learning of Heath's award of the MacArthur. Again to my surprise, my new colleague saw no irony in the two events. She also claimed that Heath had no data and that, afterall, the MacArthur fellows aren't necessarily researchers, since awards are also given to novelists, such as Leslie Sitko for *Ceremony,* Maxine Kingman for *Warrior Women* and *China Man,* and William Gaddis for *J.R.* Clearly my two colleagues had not found what Freud found in Tolstoy—that is, the richness of artists' insights into human behavior in all of its complexities, insights that usually escape the laboratory. The artist trusts his or her inductive reasoning and intuitively arrives at insights in a way researchers tend to shy away from.

Critiques of current efficacy studies often focus on the argument between the use of inductive research and the more highly prized deductive model. Both models have weaknesses. However, the deductive model, although very useful to technology, is not as applicable to complex human ecological and transactional settings. As Phillips (1985) states: "Physics involves constructs which are not sentient." We explain nature but we understand mental life. This means that the methods of studying mental life and history and society should vary greatly from those used to acquire knowledge of nature. Both deductive and inductive methods give us insights into human functioning, as does clinical practice. Major insights have been made by careful observers of the world who invent theories to give us meanings. Later, after long, hard work, scientists confirm or reject fragments of the theory (Sarr 1985). Artists have much to offer us. As Lewis Thomas, a scientist and author suggests: "The poets, on whose shoulders the future rests, might late nights, thinking things over, begin to see meanings that elude the rest of us."

RESEARCH BASE

The third theme raised at the conference was the research base for early intervention theory. Sam Meisels (1985) suggests in a provocative article that we still respond to the efficacy issue as if it were one question and still a question we are moved to defend. At the heart of the issue, Meisels suggests, is the failure to realize that programs operate out of theories of human development and that these theories influence the intervention strategies and program evaluations. I believe strong data to support our efforts are found in developmental theory and research with animals and humans. These studies fall into what is referred to as a psycho-biological view, which perceives development as the reciprocal interaction of genes and environment (Sameroff 1979).

Two developmental principles are well established: The first is that normal humans are born genetically programmed to act upon the environment, particularly the social one. In this respect, children contribute to their own development. The second principle is that the manner in which basic caregivers interact with infants and children influences the course of development so as to be facilitating or debilitating. Facilitating child-rearing strategies assist both normal and handicapped children toward developing positive attachment and autonomy and competence by age three. Debilitating practices are more lethal than breech birth or anoxia and lead to insecure or anxious attachment, with a variety of environmentally produced pathologies such as:

- nongenetic autistic-like behavior
- excessive aggression
- passive withdrawal
- failure to thrive
- failure to achieve

Personality is not a function of genes but a product developed in environments. Normal and handicapped children appear to need moderate psychological warmth, responsiveness to their requests, low physical punishment, a push or encouragement to make developmental progress, verbal interaction, and freedom to explore and act on objects in their environments (Werner & Smith 1982). When caregivers implement these facilitating practices, their infants and children maintain and fulfill their genetic potential whether they have been reared in orphanages (Hunt 1979) or in poverty (Bradley & Caldwell 1984; Ramey, Parron, & Campbell 1979; Garber & Heber 1976). Facilitating practices assist in the development of positive social skills and in the avoidance of being labeled handicapped (Berrueta-Clemment, Schwienhart, Barnett, Epstein, & Weikart 1984; Lazar & Darlington 1982). Given cognitive ability, facilitative practices can assist a severely and profoundly handicapped person such as a deaf-blind individual to achieve normal adult status. For example, when Edwin Martin, then Associate Commissioner of Education, headed a delegation to observe the work of the Institute of Defectology in the U.S.S.R., we observed four young adults, candidates for B.A. degrees in psychology, whose sole communication with adults was through finger spelling in the palms of their hands and through braille. These young people went on to complete their degrees, and when I commented on the marvelous success those who worked with these young adults had achieved, one professional turned to me and said, "But of course anyone would do this work, otherwise they would be animals." The work and theory are beautifully described in a book whose title suggests the moral intent of those special educators' work—*Awakening to Life* (Meschereyakow 1979). The research base for the need for early environmental intervention is found in evidence from animal research on the impact of environmental experience on the brain. I will not take the time to report these data in as full, as I have dealt with them extensively in publications elsewhere (Anastasiow 1986), but I will briefly summarize the major findings. Although only one third of the human brain is mature at birth, it undergoes rapid proliferation of connections among neurons. The impact of environmental events on brain development is clear in research with animals, which has been summarized by Greenough (1976) and by Rosenzweig (1984). Compared with animals raised in isolated environments, those raised in enriched environments have more connections among neurons, heavier brains, and thicker cortexes, can restore brain functioning after insult, learn mazes faster, have better memories, have healthy attachment, peer relationships, and adult relationships, are less aggressive, are less withdrawn, display less stress, sleep more, and have better appetites. Further, if perceptual systems are normal at birth but are not used, they fail to function. For example, if an animal is raised in the dark until the visual system is fully mature, the animal behaves as if it were blind. Greenough (1975) notes that neuron changes are relatively enduring processes that occur in conjunction with environmental events. Experience during development brings about rapid and profound alternatives in the functioning of the central nervous system. Once established, these environmental effects may be relatively permanent.

There is not as much direct data on the impact of experience on the human brain, but one recent study draws a close parallel to the animal research reported above. In a recent study, Purpura (1983) looked at the brains of two groups of babies who had died due to physiological disorders such as lung and/or heart abnormalities in the first weeks of life. One group of babies had been placed in the hospital's intensive care unit; the other had not. A computer study of branch points to 20 neurons showed development in the intensive care babies whereas there was no similar development in those babies who

had not received the intensive care. Menolascino (1983) concludes that the critical importance of early and *ongoing sets* of developmental experiences and transactions with the environment for maturation of the central nervous system, and the orderly development of intelligence and personality in normal individuals has been clearly documented (p. 89).

In closing, I believe that these research data and the data from the efficacy studies are sufficient to pursue vigorously the continuation and expansion of service to all children. I recently read what Einstein wrote for the time capsule in the 1930s. "Dear Posterity, If you have not become more just, peaceful, and generally more rational than we are (or were)—why then, the devil take you" (Seyen 1985). If Einstein had been a special educator, he might have written: "Dear Posterity, If you have not continued and increased service to impaired infants, children, and their families and reduced the numbers of high-risk infants due to the intensity of poverty and not become more rational and loving then we are, then the devil take you." I believe we should follow John Dewey's advice when he wrote: "What the best and wisest parent wants for his own child, that must be what the community wants for all its children. Any other ideal for our society is narrow and unlovely; acted upon it destroys our democracy" (Grubb & Lazerson 1982, 43).

REFERENCES

Anastasiow, N. J. (1986). *Development and Disability: A psychobiological analysis for special educators*. Baltimore, MD: Paul H. Brookes Publishing Co.

Auletta, K. (1983). *The Underclass*. New York: Vintage Books.

Berrueta-Clement, J. R., Schweinhart, L. J., Barnett, W. S., Epstein, A. S., & Weikart, D. P. (1984). Changed Lives. *Monographs of the High/Scope Educational Research Foundation, 8*. Ypsilanti, Mich.: The High Scope Press.

Bradley, R. H., & Caldwell, B. W. (1984). 174 children. In A. Gottfried (Ed.), *Home environ-*

ment and early cognitive development. Orlando, FL: Academic Press.

Garber, H., & Heber, H. (1976). The Milwaukee Project: Indications of the effectiveness of early intervention to prevent mental retardation. In P. Mittler (Ed.), *Research to practice in mental retardation: Vol. 1. Care and intervention.* Baltimore: University Park Press.

Greenough, W. T. (1975, January-February). Experimental modifications of the developing brain. *American Scientist, 63,* 37–46.

Greenspan, S. I., & White, K. R. (1985). The efficacy of preventive intervention: A glass half full? *Bulletin of the National Center for Clinical Infant Programs: Zero To Three, 5*(4), April.

Grubb, W. N., & Lazerson, M. (1982). *Broken Promises.* New York: Basic Books.

Guralnick, M. J., & Bricker, D. D. (in Press). The effectiveness of early intervention with children with cognitive and general developmental delays. In M. J. Guralnick and F. C. Bennett (Eds.), *The effectiveness of early intervention for at-risk and handicapped children.* New York: Academic Press.

Heath, S. (1983). *Way with words.* Cambridge: Cambridge University Press.

Hunt, J. (1961). *Intelligence and Experience.* New York: The Ronald Press.

Hunt, J. M. (1979). Psychological development: Early experience. In M. R. Rosenzweig and L. W. Porter (Eds.), *Annual review of psychology* (pp. 103–143). Palo Alto, CA: Annual Review Inc.

Kirk, S. A. (1958). *Early education of the mentally retarded.* Urbana: University of Illinois Press.

Lazar, I., Darlington, R. B. (1982). Lasting effects of early education. *Monographs of the Society for Research Child Development, Serial No. 195.*

Meisels, S. J. (1985). Why are we still asking this question? In S. Gray Garwood, John T. Neisworth, Allen A. Mori, & Rebecca R. Fe-

well (Eds.), *Topics in Early Childhood Special Education, 5*(2), 1–11.

Menolascino, F. J. (1983). Development interactions of brain impairment and experience. In F. J. Menolascino, R. Newman, and J. A. Stark (Eds.), *Curative aspects of mental retardation.* Baltimore, MD: Paul H. Brookes.

Meshchereyakow, A. (1979). *Awakening to life.* Moscow Press.

Moynihan, D. P. (1985, October 20). New generation of poor youths emerges in U.S. *New York Times,* p. 1.

Papura, D. (1983). Cellular neurology of mental retardation in F. Menolascino, R. Newman, and J. A. Stark (Eds.), *Curative aspects of mental retardation* (pp. 57–68). Baltimore, MD: Paul H. Brookes.

Phillips, D. C. (1985). On what scientists know, and how they know it. In Elliot Eisner (Ed.), *Learning and teaching the ways of knowing* (pp. 37–59). Chicago, IL: The National Society for The Study of Education.

Ramey, C. T., Parron, D. C. & Campbell, F. A. (1979). Predicting IQ from mother infant interactions. *Child Development, 50,* 804–814.

Rosenzweig, M. (1984, April). Experience, memory, and the brain. *American Psychologist, 39,* 365–376.

Sameroff, A. J. (1979). The etiology of cognitive competence: A systems perspective. In R. B. Kearsley and I. E. Sigel (Eds.), *Infants at risk: Assessment of cognitive functioning* (pp. 115–151). Hillsdale: NJ: Erlbaum.

Seyen, J. (1985). *Einstein in America.* New York: Growth Publisher.

Shore, M. F. (1981). Marking time in the land of plenty: Reflections on mental health in the United States. *American Journal of Orthopsychiatry, 51,* 391–402.

Werner, E. E., & Smith, R. S. (1982). *Vulnerable, but invincible: A longitudinal study of resilient children and youth.* New York: McGraw-Hill.

EFFICACY OF SPECIAL CLASSES: WHAT HAVE WE LEARNED?

Because Public Law 94-142 calls for the education of handicapped children in the "least restrictive environment," many handicapped children have been taken out of special classes and placed in regular classes or resource rooms. Are these the best places for the education of these children? In an effort to answer this question, this section will review the history of mainstreaming, focusing on the debate over the efficacy of special classes, as well as the difficulties inherent in interpreting and applying research results.

History of the Efficacy Question

When first introduced in the early 1900s, the self-contained special education class marked a radical development in the way educational services were provided to handicapped learners. The number of special classes grew rapidly during the 1940s and 1950s—for several compelling reasons (Jenkins and Mayhall 1976): First, special classes permitted children with comparable ability to be grouped together thereby assuring that demands on the children were appropriate, and allowing the special class teachers to focus instruction within a more limited ability range. Second, with special classes, the number of children per class could be restricted, resulting in more favorable student-teacher ratios. Finally, it was argued that the special class teachers would have special training and experience and would therefore be able to employ curricula designed especially for children with special needs.

While these classes proliferated, however, they were not without critics. Shortly after their implementation, a series of efficacy studies suggested that special classes might be inappropriate for the education of exceptional children. Ten of the early efficacy studies conducted between 1932 and 1965 showed either no achievement differences between children in regular and special classes (Ainsworth 1959; Blatt 1958; Goldstein, Moss, and Jordan 1965; Thurstone 1959; Wrightstone et al. 1959), or better achievement among the children with mild retardation in the regular classes (Bennett 1932; Cassidy and Stanton 1959; Elenbogen 1957; Mullen and Itkin 1961; Pertsch 1936). None of these researchers reported achievement data favorable to the segregated class (Gottlieb 1981). As a result, the prevailing view in the 1960s held that there seemed little reason to continue a segregated educational system that, in addition to being more expensive, did not seem to produce superior results.

Arguments Against Self-Contained Classes

In the 1960s, several major reviews of the effectiveness of special class and regular class placements for mildly retarded students were published (Dunn 1968; Johnson 1962; Kirk 1964). These reviews fueled the mainstreaming movement by presenting four major arguments supporting the movement to disband special classes. First, it was pointed out that children with mild retardation did not achieve any better in self-contained classes than they did in regular education settings. Second, many professionals were concerned about the stigma and social rejection that might result from children being labeled mentally retarded and placed in special classes. To avoid this, they recommended education in regular classes. Third, it was argued that integration of handicapped and nonhandicapped children would help overcome the racially segregated nature of special classes. (This issue of the disproportionate number of minority children placed in special classes was later addressed in the courts [Dunn 1968; Smith and Polloway 1983].) Finally, the last argument behind the suggestion to abolish special classes was based on the advances made in the ability of regular educators to individualize the curriculum. While there were theoretical reasons to believe this would happen, little research actually examined this teacher ability question. These four arguments have all been supported by more recent data (Carlberg and Kavale 1980; Semmel, Gottlieb, and Robinson 1979) and, in spite of efforts by dissenters (Smith and Arkans 1974) have led to a marked decline in the growth of special classes in the 1970s.

Results of the Studies

It is impossible here to review the vast number of studies that have examined the effectiveness of special class versus regular class placements. As part of the procedures for their study, Carlberg and Kavale (1980) searched the literature and located approximately 860 documents addressing this issue. While not all of these were actual research studies, the sheer number of available documents on this topic is overwhelming and underscores the controversy in the field regarding special education classes.

As noted earlier, early efficacy studies failed to demonstrate significant differences in achievement between students from regular and special classes (Smith and Polloway 1983). Using both academic and social criteria, Carlberg and Kavale (1980) found no evidence that either special education or regular class placement was clearly superior for mildly retarded students. As they pointed out, while many researchers (Goldstein, Moss, and Jordan 1965; Mayer 1966; Myers 1976) discovered either negligible differences in performance or inferior academic performance among mildly retarded children educated in segregated classes, other researchers failed to replicate these findings (Budoff, Meskin and Kemler 1968; Wrightstone et al. 1959). Their review also highlighted the inconclusive results in studies that examined the social adjustment and personality traits of children with mild retardation who were placed in either integrated or segregated classes. While Baldwin (1958), Gottlieb and Budoff (1973), and Walker (1974) suggested that children in special classes made better gains in social and emotional adjustment, other studies found either no difference (Iano et al. 1974; Mayer 1966) or better adjustment in integrated settings (Budoff and Gottlieb 1976; Goldstein, Moss, and Jordan 1965; Haring and Krug 1975).

Similar results were reported in studies of both behavior disordered and learning disabled children (Carlberg and Kavale 1980). For example, no significant differences were reported between integrated and segregated placements for behavior disordered children on achievement, behavioral, and sociometric variables (Glavin 1974; Vacc 1972), or for learning disabled children on achievement or perceptual motor functioning measures (Bernsoff et al. 1972; Sabatino 1971). Conversely, however, Quay et al. (1972) reported better results in integrated settings, while Vacc (1968) found positive effects in segregated settings.

Since it became evident that no firm conclusions on the relative merits of different educational placements could be drawn from a review of individual studies, and since reviews which attempted to integrate studies were also inconclusive, Carlberg and Kavale (1980) conducted a meta-analysis of studies comparing regular and special class placements. For inclusion in their analysis, studies were required to have 1) an identifiable category of exceptional children; 2) examined special class placement; 3) a comparison group; and 4) results reported in a way that could be used in the meta-analysis. Out of hundreds of documented studies on the topic, fifty met these criteria.

When data from all fifty studies were aggregated (representing approximately 27,000 special and regular class students with a mean IQ of 74 and an average of sixty-nine weeks of educational intervention) they provided some interesting insights regarding the effects of special class placement. Carlberg & Kavale (1980) reported that special class placement reduced the relative standing of average special class students by five percentile ranks—the grade equivalent of one to two months on most tests used in the elementary schools. The data were also analyzed according to the type of outcome measures, and special class placement was found inferior to regular class placement regardless of the outcome measure used; the special class students dropped six percentile ranks on achievement measures, four percentile ranks on personality or social scales, and one percentile rank on various other measures. However, slightly different results were reported when the data were analyzed according to category of exceptionality; that approach showed different effects for different categories of children. For example, special class placement was least effective for those children with lower IQ's; when compared to their regular class counterparts, slow learners (IQ 75–90) lost thirteen percentile ranks and mildly retarded children (IQ 50–75) declined by six percentile ranks. Conversely, learning disabled and emotionally disturbed/behavior disordered children improved eleven percentile ranks when placed in special classes. This indicated that the average learning disabled or emotionally disturbed/behavior disordered child in a special class was more successful than 61 percent of his or her peer group in regular classes. As a result of their analysis, Carlberg and Kavale (1980) stated that special class placement was not uniformly detrimental, but that the effects were related to other variables, such as the handicapping condition of the students. The investigators thus cautioned against unconditional generalizations about mainstreaming.

Criticisms of the Research

Many previously discussed studies have been criticized on the basis of methodological and design flaws. As early as 1964, Kirk, in his review of the efficacy issue, noted difficulties in interpreting relevant studies due to problems in sampling (using intact groups for comparison), lack of control over the length of special education placement before the studies, lack of control over the special class curriculum and teachers' qualifications, and inadequate measurement instruments (often improvised with unknown validity or reliability). He concluded, "Until we obtain well-controlled studies of a longitudinal nature, our opinions about the benefits or detriments of special classes will remain partly in the realm of conjecture" (Kirk 1964, 63).

Despite such concerns, however, inadequacies in methodology continued, and in 1971, MacMillan restated the need to look at the design of many efficacy studies. He noted that sampling biases often made results uninterpretable. Since many studies used intact classes and did not randomly assign subjects to either the special or the regular class, it was impossible to know whether those children left in the regular class were there because they were academically superior before the studies even began. MacMillan (1971) also criticized the assessment instruments used to measure social status since teachers and students in regular and special classes had variable frames of reference. In addition, he emphasized the difficulty in comparing different sociometric ratings since social acceptance in a special class may not be the same as acceptance in a class with children of higher abilities.

The other often criticized methodological flaws are lack of control over the confounding variables of teacher and method (Carlberg and Kavale 1980; MacMillan 1971). As a result, it is difficult to determine to what extent failures of the special class can be attributed to the type of educational placement, and to what extent they result from teachers' inadequacies. This question, in fact, has defied researchers since the beginning of educational research. As stated by Warren (1979), one might make a case for placement in either a regular or special class on the basis of the teacher's characteristics. She cautions that the skills of a child's teacher may be more important than the type of classroom; a good teacher of a regular class may be far better for a mildly retarded child than an average or less than average teacher of a special class—and vice versa.

A final criticism of the efficacy research lies in the fact that when it was originally conducted, researchers and teachers were only addressing children labeled *educable mentally retarded*. In addition to the fact that these studies are now being cited as justification for eliminating all special classes, even those for low functioning children, the early studies were also considering a different population, comprising primarily mildly retarded children. When much of the original research was conducted, the definition of *mental retardation* included children with IQ's as high as 85; however, as a result of a change in the American Association on Mental Deficiency's definition of mental retardation, the IQ cutoff for mental retardation was lowered to 70 (Smith and Polloway 1983). Therefore, Gottlieb (1982) states that early research on the effectiveness of special classes has little relevance today since the current group of mildly retarded students represents only the lower level of the past group. In some respects, this change may make the mainstreaming debate less critical since the students about whom Dunn (1968) was originally concerned when he raised the issue are, in many cases, no longer placed in self-contained classes. Dunn himself (1973) acknowledges that:

> . . . accompanying the trend to integrate so-called educable retardates into general education has come the realization that most children from standard English speaking homes with IQ's in the 50s cannot function in an academically oriented class. Thus more and more of these students are likely to be reclassified as moderately retarded and placed in self-contained special education facilities. (101)

Arguments for Special Classes

Empirical evidence on the effectiveness of special classes has not settled the debate on the best educational placement for exceptional children; there are still those who support use of the special class. In 1971, MacMillan maintained that the total abolition of special classes for mildly retarded students seemed premature, since the classes were still useful for some low-IQ children. In fact, he contended that a self-contained special class might well be the best place for some students. In support of this theory, he cited a study (Goldstein, Moss, and Jordan 1965) in which EMR pupils were randomly assigned to either special or regular classes. At the end of a two-year treatment period, students in the regular class were found to achieve at higher levels in reading. However, by the end of four years, children in the self-contained class had caught up. Further analysis showed that low-IQ children in the special classes had significantly higher reading levels than children from the low-IQ subsample who had remained in the regular class.

At the time of MacMillan's article (1971), he noted that most proponents of integration had not advocated the integration of trainable mentally retarded (TMR) children into regular classes, since it was felt that such children deviated too markedly on many variables for that type of integration to succeed. However, some authors were calling for the elimination of all special classes (Christopolos and Renz 1969; Hammons 1972), although the research on the efficacy of special classes for the TMR child was less than adequate (Cain and Levine 1963; Hottel 1958; Smith and Arkans 1974). Smith and Arkans (1974) stated that there were no data supporting improved development among trainable level children in regular classes. Rather, they concluded that special classes offered the most appropriate public school environment for this population.

After most of the efficacy studies were completed, the student population in most public schools changed dramatically. With the passage and implementation of P.L. 94–142, all children, no matter how severely handicapped, became the educational responsibility of the schools. This influx of more severely handicapped children (than had previously been served by the schools) might have affected how integration was perceived. However, The Association for Persons with Severe Handicaps (TASH) recently proposed a resolution that opposes the segregation of any students. A portion of that resolution is presented here:

> TASH calls for a new continuum of services which emphasizes . . . the provision of specialized staff, resources, and services to meet individual needs without removal from the regular classroom, neighborhood school, home and family, and community program and setting . . .
> . . . the systematic shifting of service delivery design and services away from a categorical, homogeneously grouped, and separate model to one which requires integration and thrives on a variety of grouping arrangements . . .
> . . . the philosophical and administrative merger of special and regular education and specialized and generic services into one service delivery system (TASH 1986, 2).

It is clear from this statement that questions of special class placement now extend much beyond concerns for only mildly handicapped students. Yet what evidence is there for this position?

Many educators question whether the social, personal, and emotional needs of students with moderate or severe mental retardation can be met in a class where the teacher is also responsible for twenty to forty other children. Smith and Arkans (1974) ask whether we need to rediscover that a low functioning child will become a social isolate in the regular class. In addition, regular education teachers and administrators question their abilities to meet the very special needs of more severely handicapped students, or to effectively use the specialized equipment this population may require. Once again, practical logistics and idealistic philosophy seem at odds.

Alternatives to the Regular vs. Special Class Debate

Though not addressed in many efficacy studies, other placement alternatives may fit the concept of *least restrictive environment* without requiring integration as an all-or-nothing phenomenon. For example, resource rooms can provide special services to children who are mainstreamed in some curricular areas. While resource rooms usually include more mildly handicapped children, and only rarely include more severely handicapped learners, such placement is another option in a continuum of services model. In a recent review of research on mainstreaming programs, Madden and Slavin (1983) conclude that regular class placement of mildly handicapped students, using individualized instructional programs and cooperative learning supplemented by well-designed resource room programs, improves achievement, self-esteem, and behavior among handicapped students. However, as discussed by Jenkins and Mayhall (1976), despite a strong rationale for the adoption of resource room programs and widespread interest in both practice and in the literature, there is conflicting evidence on whether resource rooms are any more effective than the alternatives of regular or special class placements.

MacMillan (1971) cautions that special educators must not allow the issue to become one of special class versus regular class placement lest they find themselves in an unresolvable debate; yet, this polarization seems to be what is happening. As one group condemns special classes, another feels compelled to defend them. And despite many years of debate and research, we still lack adequate evidence on the effectiveness of special classes—a fact which, by itself, further divides opinions on how to proceed.

For example, Warren (1979) states that since the most effective type of placement for exceptional children is still unknown, good research is critical in determining the effects of special classes and other alternatives. But "good" research implies that both schools and researchers may need to endure inconveniences in order to assure that such variables as teachers and curriculum can be controlled. MacMillan (1971) cautions that unless the quality of the research is high, results will not support informed educational decisions regarding the appropriate placement of children.

Warren (1979) also notes that in the absence of an empirical base, decisions about the education of children are instead based on legal, philosophical, and ethical grounds. Blatt (1979) demonstrates this clearly by stating that research has nothing to do with whether we should continue the practice of segregating people with mental retardation. He argues that research cannot tell us how to better live our lives; but rather, America needs to pledge itself to integrate its mentally retarded, crippled, blind, deaf, and elderly citizens. This philosophical and ethical perspective is also evident in the studies of mainstreaming presented by Biklen (1985). In his book, *Achieving the Complete School,* Biklen suggests that such questions as "Does mainstreaming work?" are inappropriate because they're ultimately unanswerable through scientific research. Rather, Biklen suggests, we must actively challenge society's stereotypes of disabled students.

Whichever perspective we accept, it is crucial that we remember the children in need of education. We must be sure not to let our debates interfere with the best education we can provide. It may be that better placement depends on variables not addressed in this efficacy research—such as the teacher, the child's previous experiences, and the support of the school staff and parents. It is important to find the best placement, but many more factors need to be examined before we can fully clarify what "best" means.

REFERENCES

Ainsworth, S. (1959). *An exploratory study of education, social, and emotional factors in the education of educable mentally retarded children in Georgia public schools.* (U.S. Office of Education Cooperative Research Program, Project No. 171). Athens: University of Georgia.

Baldwin, W. (1958). The social position of the educable mentally retarded in the regular grades in the public schools. *Exceptional Children, 25,* 106–108.

Bennett, A. (1932). *A comparative study of subnormal children in the elementary grades.* New York: Teachers College, Bureau of Publications.

Bersoff, D., Kabler, M., Fiscus, F., & Ankney, R. (1972). Effectiveness of special class placement for children labeled neurologically handicapped. *Journal of School Psychology, 10,* 157–163.

Biklen, D. (1985). *Achieving the complete school.* New York: Teachers College Press.

Blatt, B. (1958). The physical, personality, and academic status of children who are mentally retarded attending special classes as compared with children who are mentally retarded attending regular classes. *American Journal of Mental Deficiency, 62,* 810–818.

Blatt, B. (1979). A drastically different analysis. *Mental Retardation, 17,* 303–306.

Budoff, M., & Gottlieb, J. (1976). Special-class EMR children mainstreamed: A study of an aptitude (learning potential) X treatment interaction. *American Journal of Mental Deficiency, 81,* 1–11.

Budoff, M., Meskin, J., & Kemler, D. (1968). Training productive thinking of EMR's: A failure to replicate. *American Journal of Mental Deficiency, 73,* 195–199.

Cain, L., & Levine, S. (1963). *Effects of community and institutional school programs on trainable mentally retarded children.* (CEC Research Monograph, Series B., No. B–1). Washington, D.C.: The Council for Exceptional Children.

Carlberg, C., & Kavale, K. (1980). The efficacy of special versus regular class placement for exceptional children: A meta-analysis. *The Journal of Special Education, 14,* 295–309.

Cassidy, V., & Stanton, J. (1959). *An investigation of factors involved in the educational placement of mentally retarded children* (U.S. Office of Education Cooperative Research Program, Project No. 43). Columbus: Ohio State University.

Christopolos, F., & Renz, P. (1969). A critical examination of special education programs. *Journal of Special Education, 3,* 371–379.

Dunn, L. (1968). Special education for the mildly retarded—Is much of it justifiable? *Exceptional Children, 35,* 5–22.

Dunn, L. (1973). Children with mild general learning disabilities. In L. Dunn (Ed.), *Exceptional children in the schools.* New York: Holt, Reinhart, and Winston.

Elenbogen, M. (1957). A comparative study of some aspects of academic and social adjustment of two groups of mentally retarded children in special classes and regular classes. *Dissertation Abstracts, 17,* 2496.

Glavin, J. (1974). Behaviorally oriented resource rooms: A followup. *Journal of Special Education, 8,* 337–347.

Goldstein, H., Moss, J., & Jordan, L. (1965). *The efficacy of special class training on the development of mentally retarded children* (U.S. Office of Education Cooperative Project No. 619). Urbana: University of Illinois.

Gottlieb, J. (1981). Mainstreaming: Fulfilling the promise? *American Journal of Mental Deficiency, 86,* 115–126.

Gottlieb, J. (1982). Mainstreaming. *Education and Training of the Mentally Retarded, 17,* 79–82.

Gottlieb, J., & Budoff, M. (1973). Social acceptability of retarded children in nongraded schools differing in architecture. *American Journal of Mental Deficiency, 78,* 15–19.

Hammons, G. (1972). Educating the mildly retarded: A review. *Exceptional Children, 38,* 565–570.

Haring, N., & Krug, D. (1975). Placement in regular programs: Procedures and results. *Exceptional Children, 41,* 413–417.

Hottel, J. (1958). Report of a study of the effectiveness of special day classes for trainable children. *Peabody College Research Series in Mental Retardation.* Nashville: Peabody College.

Iano, R., Ayers, D., Heller, H., McGettigan, J., & Walker, V. (1974). Sociometric status of retarded children in an integrative program. *Exceptional Children, 40,* 267–271.

Jenkins, J., & Mayhall, W. (1976). Development and evaluation of a resource teacher program. *Exceptional Children, 42,* 21–29.

Johnson, G. (1962). Special education for the mentally handicapped: A paradox. *Exceptional Children, 29,* 62–69.

Kirk, S. (1964). Research in education. In H. Stevens & R. Heber (Eds.). *Mental retardation.* Chicago: University of Chicago Press.

MacMillan, D. (1971). Special education for the mildly retarded: Servant or savant? *Focus on Exceptional Children, 2,* 1–11.

Madden, N., & Slavin, R. (1983). Mainstreaming students with mild handicaps: Academic and social outcomes. *Review of Educational Research, 53,* 519–569.

Mayer, C. (1966). The relationship of early special class placement and the self-concepts of mentally handicapped children. *Exceptional Children, 33,* 77–81.

Mullen, F., & Itkin, W. (1961). The value of special classes for the mentally handicapped. *Chicago Schools Journal, 42,* 353–363.

Myers, J. (1976). The efficacy of the special day school for EMR pupils. *Mental Retardation, 14,* 3–11.

Pertsch, C. (1936). *A comparative study of the progress of subnormal pupils in the grades and in special classes.* New York: Teachers College, Columbia University.

Quay, H., Glavin, J., Annesley, F., & Werry, J. (1972). The modification of problem behavior and academic achievement in a resource room. *Journal of School Psychology, 10,* 187–197.

Sabatino, D. (1971). An evaluation of resource rooms for children with learning disabilities. *Journal of Learning Disabilities, 4,* 27–35.

Semmel, M., Gottlieb, J., & Robinson, N. (1979). Mainstreaming: Perspectives on educating handicapped children in the public schools. In D. Berliner (Ed.), *Review of research in education* (Vol. 7). Washington, DC: American Educational Research Association.

Smith, J., & Arkans, J. (1974). Now more than ever: A case for the special class. *Exceptional Children, 40,* 497–502.

Smith, J. D., & Polloway, E. (1983). Changes in mild mental retardation: Population, programs and perspectives. *Exceptional Children, 50,* 149–159.

TASH: The Association for Persons with Severe Handicaps (1986). Proposed resolution on continuum of services. *Newsletter, 12,* 2.

Thurstone, T. (1959). *An evaluation of educating mentally handicapped children in special classes and in regular grades* (U.S. Office of Education Cooperative Research Program, Project No. OE–SAE 6452). Chapel Hill: University of North Carolina.

Vacc, N. (1968). A study of emotionally disturbed children in regular and special classes. *Exceptional Children, 35,* 197–204.

Vacc, N. (1972). Long-term effects of special class intervention for emotionally disturbed children. *Exceptional Children, 39,* 15–22.

Walker, V. (1974). The efficacy of the resource room for educating retarded children. *Exceptional Children, 40,* 288–289.

Warren, S. (1979). What is wrong with mainstreaming? A comment on drastic change. *Mental Retardation, 17,* 301–303.

Wrightstone, J., Forlano, G., Lepkowski, J., Sontag, M., & Edelstein, J. (1959). *A comparison of educational outcomes under single track and two track plans for educable mentally retarded children* (U.S. Office of Education Cooperative Research Program, Project No. 144). New York: New York City Board of Education.

DISCUSSION QUESTIONS

1. Consider your feelings about placing handicapped students in either regular or special classes. Are your reactions based more on the philosophical or research perspective? Why?

2. When the TASH resolution was first presented, they asked people to respond to it. Write your response to this resolution that appeared on page 112.

3. One common criticism of efficacy studies is lack of control over the teacher variable. How might a study be constructed to avoid this problem? How important do you think this teacher issue is, and how can it be dealt with?

4. Do you think the results of early efficacy studies can be applied today given that the student population served by special education has changed so much? Why?

5. Since some research indicates that special class placement affects some groups of children in different ways, what criteria would you use to place students?

6. One reason proposed for abolishing special classes was that regular teachers were better able to meet the needs of handicapped students by individualizing the regular class curriculum. Do you agree with this rationale? Why?

COST EFFECTIVENESS OF SPECIAL EDUCATION PROGRAMS

The number of children receiving special education services has rapidly increased since the passage of P.L. 94–142 in 1975. In fact, in recent years, over four million handicapped students have received special education services supported by federal, state, and local monies (Algozzine and Korinek 1985). In introducing the 1984 Annual Report to Congress (U.S. Department of Education 1984), Madeleine Will, Assistant Secretary for Special Education and Rehabilitation Services, U.S. Department of Education, noted a shift from the initial procedural activities in implementing P.L. 94–142 to a strengthened concern for the quality of special education programs. However, few studies have examined this shift.

While evaluation studies were first mandated and supported by P.L. 94–142 in 1976, thus far evaluations have focused on the progress and effects of implementing the act itself, rather than on how the programs affect handicapped children. However, the 98th Congress enacted amendments that shifted the emphasis from implementation to program effectiveness and cost effectiveness (Select Committee on Children, Youth, and Families 1985).

Though published evaluation results are still pending, several studies conducted before P.L. 94–142 examined cost factors relating to special education services. In addition, researchers who have reviewed early childhood special education programs have provided some information on their cost effectiveness. This section examines their findings.

Kim and Harris (1980) divide cost analysis approaches into three categories: a unit cost analysis that yields an average cost-per-child figure; a cost differential analysis, which gives different costs for different categories of students; and a cost benefit analysis that examines the relationship of costs to the benefits resulting from the educational program. Examples of each can be found in the studies reviewed.

The Costs of Special Education

It is clear that special education, with its lower student-teacher ratios, therapies, and specialized materials and equipment costs more than regular education services. However, these costs vary considerably depending on the type and severity of students' handicapping conditions. In 1976, Marinelli reported that the cost of special education programs varied from 1.18 times the cost of educating an average child to 4.18 times the cost. Children with speech and language problems had the lowest special education cost and physically handicapped children the highest. In a study of twenty-four school districts in five states, Rossmiller, Hale, and Froehreich (1970) found that the cost index for all areas of special education averaged about twice that spent for regular education. While their sample was much larger than that involved in other studies, and may present a more accurate picture of the national cost, it is important to remember that these costs were incurred before P.L. 94–142 was enacted, and may therefore not include the costs of educating more severely handicapped students or all now-mandated related services. In these studies, higher costs resulted directly from instruction, public service expenses, capital equipment investments, specialized personnel costs, and extra transportation.

Cost Effectiveness As an Investment Return

Another way to view cost effectiveness is to explore the education of handicapped children and youth as an income-generating form of human capital (Braddock 1976). In other words, to ask, Do the costs alloted for educational and training programs for handicapped individuals produce a positive or negative return on this investment? Braddock asks whether handicapped students, educated towards self-sufficiency at public expense, pay the investment back through taxes on earned income. Unfortunately, answers to these questions are not clear. Policy researchers at the Rand Corporation (Kakalik et al. 1973) noted that while a growing literature on this topic existed in general education, special education had generally neglected cost analyses due to the difficulty and high cost of conducting the studies and the lack of available data.

Nevertheless, cost effectiveness studies in this area do exist. For example, Conley (1973) constructed a ratio of mentally retarded workers' future earnings to the costs of their public education. He reported that the lifetime earnings of mildly retarded adults was approximately six times (6 : 1) the costs of their education. Therefore, from this perspective, educational services for individuals with mild retardation can be justified on the basis of their earnings alone. However, the cost-benefit outlook for moderately retarded people was much less favorable, with the ratio of earnings to educational costs ranging from .1 : 1 to 1 : 1.

Braddock (1976) introduced an alternative way to analyze the benefits of special education services by examining the number of years benefits have to accumulate before the educational costs spent on special education programs are matched by the estimated annual tax recouped. Using this educational payback analysis, he found that the payback period varied from only 2.3 years for a speech impaired child, to 11.2 years for a mildly mentally retarded child and 162.7 years for a severely retarded child. Most other special education categories had a payback period of about 25 years. This analysis was based on recovery of excess educational costs rather than total educational costs since all children have some educational costs; the average cost of educating a nonhandicapped child in a regular program was subtracted from the overall average cost of educating a handicapped child to determine the excess cost.

Results of this analysis indicate that for mildly handicapped students, the projected taxes recouped directly and indirectly by avoiding welfare and other types of income supplements exceed the total cost of a twelve-year education. Only in the case of severe intellectual retardation or emotional disturbance does the educational payback period exceed the handicapped individual's normal working lifetime. Even then, if institutional custodial costs are considered in this computation—costs that would likely be incurred if the individual were not educated—the long-term payback shows positive results even for those with severe handicaps (Braddock 1976).

Cost Effectiveness of Different Levels of Services

Since studies indicate that special education costs may exceed regular education costs by as much as one and one-half to four times (Rossmiller 1971; Wilkerson and Jones 1976), it is important to determine if the most expensive programs are also the most effective. By examining the cost effectiveness of the self-contained learning disabilities classroom with that of resource room or learning center, Franklin and Sparkman (1978) linked two important issues in special education: cost effectiveness and program delivery systems. Their cost effectiveness analysis examined the input of the educational program (costs) related to its output (academic gain), and defined cost effectiveness as the per pupil academic gain divided by the total per pupil cost.

Results of their analysis indicated that the resource room program was more cost effective than the self-contained classroom. Although the students in the self-contained class gained more in achievement than those in the resource room, this gain was not significant, and the self-contained class was significantly more expensive. The resource room program cost was $1321 per child, the self-contained class cost $2830—over twice as much. While Franklin and Sparkman (1978) made cost effectiveness distinctions between two different types of programs, caution must be used in interpreting this data since it is based on only two classrooms. While it might be assumed that changes in students' achievement resulted from the educational services associated with the type of class involved, many other factors (such as teachers, parents, principals, and the curriculum itself) may also have influenced that achievement.

Similar cautions are needed in reviewing DeWitt's 1976 dissertation, which analyzed the two major types of special education service delivery systems, resource room and self-contained classroom, to determine which was more cost effective for the education of educable mentally handicapped children. DeWitt found that the educably mentally handicapped children placed in resource rooms performed better on the Wide Range Achievement Test post-test than a comparable group of students enrolled in self-contained classes. Since there appeared to be a difference in the relative costs per grade level gain, DeWitt concluded that the resource room programs appeared to be more cost effective for the subjects.

Hayes (1976) investigated the costs of special education in relation to quality at Pennsylvania elementary and secondary schools. Within a random sample of classes for five categories of handicapped children, special education pupils demonstrated significant progress in both basic skills and social maturity and the quality of special education instruction was generally rated good as measured by a specially developed list of quality indicators. In addition, Hayes reported that the costs of special education varied considerably within categories, and that the costs did not consistently correlate with achievement gains. Further, costs did not correlate consistently with the quality indicators. This analysis underscored the need for better comparisons between high- and low-cost programs; clearly if no clear relationship existed between cost and achievement or cost and quality, then some modification of high-cost programs seemed to be called for.

Cost Effectiveness of Early Childhood Special Education

Many early childhood special education programs have had to justify their existence on the basis of preventing or reducing future expenditures within special education. As a result, there appear to be more studies examining cost effectiveness in this area. In its report on the cost effectiveness of preschool education, the Select Committee on Children, Youth, and Families (1985) reported that a $1 investment in preschool education returned $4.75 in savings. This savings was calculated from the High/Scope Perry Preschool Project in the following way: For each dollar invested in one year of high quality preschool for economically disadvantaged children, $1 was saved by reduced public school education costs, $.50 by reduced crime costs, and $.25 by reduced welfare administration costs. Further, $3 were gained in lifetime earnings, along with $.75 in increased tax revenues. Overall, the cost benefit analysis for this project showed that two years of quality preschool returned three and a half times the initial investment.

Reporting on an early intervention program in Colorado, the Select Committee (1985) also found that even after subtracting the costs of a preschool special education program, school districts that had such programs saved $1560 per handicapped child and $1050 per at-risk child. After analyzing all this data, the Select Committee concluded that if intervention for handicapped infants is delayed until age six, education costs until age eighteen are estimated to be $53,350 per child; starting intervention at birth was estimated to lower the total education costs to $37,272 per child—a savings of $16,078.

These calculations, as well as the demonstrated academic and social benefits of early intervention, clearly indicate the cost effectiveness of early intervention programs. However, Macy and Schafer (1985) suggest an additional type of cost analysis. They recommend real-time cost analyses that provide a way of determining the absolute dollar cost of any service or group of services. The major advantage to this method is the potential for conducting cost analyses across projects, thereby allowing for the study of cost efficiency among alternative service models. Since most of the studies conducted have not done this to date, it seems that this should be the direction of future research.

REFERENCES

Algozzine, B., & Korinek, L. (1985). Where is special education for students with high prevalence handicaps going? *Exceptional Children, 51,* 388–394.

Braddock, D. (1976). *Dollars and sense in special education.* Reston, VA: Council for Exceptional Children. (ERIC Document Reproduction Service No. ED 136 544).

Conley, R. (1973). *The economics of mental retardation.* Baltimore, MD: The Johns Hopkins Press.

DeWitt, D. (1976). A comparison of self-contained and resource room programs by per capita expenditures, student achievement and district size in South Carolina. *Dissertation Abstracts International, 38,* 199A. (University Microfilms No. 77–13, 901).

Franklin, G., & Sparkman, W. (1978). The cost effectiveness of two program delivery systems for exceptional children. *Journal of Education Finance, 3,* 305–314.

Hayes, R. (1976). *Special education quality cost-effectiveness study.* Harrisburg, PA: Pennsylvania State Department of Education. (ERIC Document Reproduction Service No. ED 132 770).

Kakalik, J., Brewer, G., Dougharty, L., Fleischauer, P., & Genensky, S. (1973). *Services for handicapped youth: A program overview.* Santa Monica, CA: Rand Corporation.

Kim, J., & Harris, R. (1980). *Computing cost-benefit measures as criteria for social investment in education.* Paper presented at the annual meeting of the American Educational Research Association, Boston, MA.

Macy, D., & Schafer, D. S. (1985). Real time cost analysis: Application in early intervention. *Journal of the Division for Early Childhood, 9,* 98–104.

Marinelli, J. (1976). Financing the education of exceptional children. In F. Weintraub, A. Abeson, J. Ballard, & M. LaVor (Eds.), *Public policy and the education of exceptional children.* Reston, VA: The Council for Exceptional Children.

Rossmiller, R. (1971). Resource configurations and costs in educational programs for exceptional children. In R. Johns, K. Alexander, & K. F. Jordan (Eds.), *Planning to finance education.* Gainesville, FL: National Educational Finance Project.

Rossmiller, R., Hale, J., & Froehreich, L. (1970). *Educational programs for exceptional children: Resource configurations and costs.* Madison, WI: Department of Educational Administration, University of Wisconsin.

Select Committee on Children, Youth and Families (House of Representatives). (1985). *Opportunities for success: Cost-effective programs for children.* Washington, DC: U.S. Government Printing Office.

U.S. Department of Education. (1984). Executive summary—Sixth annual report to Congress on the implementation of Public Law 94–142: The Education for All Handicapped Children Act. *Exceptional Children, 51,* 199–202.

Wilkerson, W., & Jones, P. (1976). *Review of special education cost studies: CEC institute on finance.* Reston, VA: Council for Exceptional Children.

DISCUSSION QUESTIONS

1. Many people have expressed some concern over the general movement towards examining the costs of special education programs. Why might someone oppose evaluation of special program costs?

2. What problems would likely be encountered in comparing the costs and benefits of two different types of delivery systems (for example, a resource room program and a self-contained special education class)? What factors would you have to consider?

3. One of the questions often asked when looking at cost effectiveness as a return on money invested is whether handicapped students pay back the extra money spent on them through taxes on later income. Can you think of any other group of people about whom this question is asked? Do we ask if food stamp recipients pay back society's investment in them? What societal factors might influence this attitude?

4. The cost effectiveness of early intervention programs seems to have been more closely studied than the cost effectiveness of other types of special education programs. Why do you think this is? Do you think this type of evaluation will continue?

CHAPTER 4

Mainstreaming

INTRODUCTION

As early as 1968, with the publication of the classic article *Special Education For the Mildly Retarded—Is Much Of It Justifiable?* by Lloyd Dunn, there was growing concern that too many mildly handicapped children were being labeled *handicapped* and placed in special education programs. As a result of such concern and the passage and eventual implementation of P.L. 94-142, mainstreaming, or the integration of exceptional children with their nonhandicapped peers, became a reality. Now, even after a decade of debate there is still little agreement about the effectiveness or even the proper definition of mainstreaming.

Chapter four presents the evolution of mainstreaming, discusses problems incurred in implementing this approach, and explores efficacy studies assessing the effects of mainstreaming on the social and academic performance of handicapped students. A reprint of the article *Avoiding Misconceptions of Mainstreaming, The Least Restrictive Environment, and Normalization* is included. In this article Gunnar Dybwad clarifies the often misunderstood principles inherent within these three concepts.

MAINSTREAMING: PROBLEMS AND SOLUTIONS?

The Education for All Handicapped Children Act of 1975, P.L. 94-142, provided a federal mandate for the placement of handicapped students in the least restrictive environment. This concept of *least restrictive environment* has in many cases, perhaps erroneously, been interpreted to mean that handicapped students should be mainstreamed into regular education classes (Gresham 1982). The purpose of this section is to present a brief historical perspective on the practice of mainstreaming, discuss some of the difficulties encountered in its implementation, review research assessing the effects of mainstreaming on the academic and social development of handicapped students, and present the most promising practices and techniques for mainstreaming.

Historical Perspective

The Goldberg and Cruickshank debate (1958) brought the issue of public school responsibility for the education of trainable mentally retarded children into the public forum. While Cruickshank held that these children were neither entitled to nor capable of benefiting from education, Goldberg held that placement in the best educational environment was their right. Ten years later in a landmark article, Dunn addressed the issue of service delivery to mildly handicapped students, asserting that, "A better education than special class placement is needed for socioculturally deprived children with mild learning problems who have been labeled educable mentally retarded" (Dunn 1968, 5).

Litigation in the early 1970s also provided impetus to the mainstreaming movement. The *PARC v. Commonwealth of Pennsylvania* (1972) case established the right to education for all mentally retarded children in Pennsylvania, and the court ruling in *Mills v. Board of Education of the District of Columbia* (1972) supported the right to education for all children considered mentally retarded, physically handicapped, emotionally disturbed, or incorrigible. Moreover, the Mills case established the mandate for a hearing prior to classification or exclusion from an educational program (MacMillan 1982). These court cases and others (MacMillan 1982), in combination with the arguments of Goldberg and Dunn and the writings of Wolfensberger (1972) on the concept of normalization, served as the springboard for Public Law 94-142.

Problems Implementing Mainstreaming

One reason implementing and evaluating the effectiveness of mainstreaming has proven so difficult is that the process has seldom been operationally defined (Warren 1979). The term *mainstreaming*, in fact, never appears in P.L. 94-142. What is stated is that

> . . . to the maximum extent appropriate, handicapped children, including children in public or private institutions or other care facilities, are educated with children who are not handicapped, and that special classes, separate schooling, or other removal of children from the regular educational environment occurs only when the nature or severity of the handicap is such that education in regular classes with the use of supplementary aids and services cannot be achieved satisfactorily. (Sec. 612, 5B)

Phrases such as "maximum extent appropriate," "nature or severity of the handicap," and "education in regular classes . . . achieved satisfactorily" are not further defined, thus leaving the responsibility for interpretation to local school districts. It is unlikely that the terms *mainstreaming* or *least restrictive environment* connote a singular concept or unified course of action for those responsible for implementing it (Switzky and Miller 1978).

Zigler and Muenchow (1979) reported that some school districts considered time students spent in the halls or in the cafeteria as mainstreaming. In a more recent study of mainstreamed elementary school students' schedules, Sansone and Zigmond (1986) found that very few of the 844 students studied had "appropriate" schedules. While there was evidence of mainstreaming in all of the schools studied, for the majority of students, mainstreaming was reserved for special subject classes that were often not appropriate for the students. Other scheduling difficulties included being assigned to regular classes that were not grade-appropriate; being assigned to attend regular classes with more than one group of students; and being assigned to instruction in the regular class for only some portion of the instructional sequence in a given academic area. It is this third point, the inclusion of mainstreamed students for only part of the full instructional sequence, which seems most potentially limiting to the success of mainstreaming programs.

Logistical problems in mainstreaming abound. For instance, handicapped students may come and go from classes at inappropriate times. Or, regular classroom teachers and special education teachers may use different materials (Martin 1974). The concept of *opportunity* has received much attention recently as a critical variable in achievement, on the premise that "learning is more likely to take place if students are given opportunities to engage in learning-specific tasks" (Sansone and Zigmond 1986, 453). To the extent that handicapped students are not scheduled for the full instructional sequence in a given subject area, their opportunity for learning may be limited. Obviously, limited opportunity can negatively affect a student's achievement.

Scheduling handicapped students for instruction in the mainstream is only one of the difficulties in implementing mainstreaming. Another problem involves the instructional practices followed in the regular classroom and the degree to which regular classroom teachers modify the way they teach. In studying the accommodations of mainstream secondary school teachers, Zigmond, Levin, and Laurie (1985) found that the majority of teachers made few modifications when learning disabled students were placed in their classrooms. While they believed these students' problems warranted special attention, the teacher interviewed used the same lesson plans for handicapped and nonhandicapped students. However, nearly half of the 132 teachers who responded to the survey said that they modified their grading practices for learning disabled students, enabling those students to pass.

In another survey of elementary and junior/senior high school teachers, nearly 85 percent of the regular education teachers indicated that they made limited modifications in instruction for the handicapped students mainstreamed into their classrooms (Ammer 1984). Similar practices have been described by other researchers as well (Adams 1971; Johnson and Johnson 1980). Such problems make it difficult to analyze the effects of mainstreaming on students since mainstreaming may mean so many different things.

While the placement of handicapped children in regular education classes may be largely an administrative function, it is the role of the regular classroom teacher which may be most critical in determining the success or failure of mainstreaming for a particular student. As Warren (1979, 302) states, "It is quite possible the skills of the child's teacher are more important than either the classroom in which the child sits or the label on the door of the classroom to which children report each morning." Semmel and Snell (1979) conclude that the type of placement alone has little to do with effectiveness; but the teacher, who creates the classroom conditions, is crucial. Given the importance of the teacher's role, many students have been undertaken to assess teachers' attitudes toward mainstreaming and their perceptions of its effectiveness. These studies are discussed in the section entitled *Are Teachers Prepared for Mainstreaming?* found in Chapter 12.

Effects of Mainstreaming

While teachers' attitudes, curriculum, and opportunity all strongly influence the outcomes of mainstreaming, studies assessing the academic and social outcomes of mainstreaming versus special class placement indicate few benefits are derived from full-time special education programs for academically handicapped students. A meta-analysis of such studies (Carlberg and Kavale 1980) and a recent review of the literature (Madden and Slavin 1983) provides comprehensive analyses of the efficacy of special class placement. The literature is too extensive to present in its entirety in this context; therefore, the reader is encouraged to read Carlberg and Kavale (1980) and Madden and Slavin (1983) for a more comprehensive description.

In their meta-analysis, Carlberg and Kavale (1980) assessed the posttreatment differences between regular and special class placement. Fifty studies, which met their criteria (investigating an identifiable exceptionality group, examining special class placement, including a comparison group, and reporting results in a way that could be translated for meta-analysis) were included. When the outcome measures of academic achievement and social/personality variables were used, posttreatment differences were nonsignificant. When compared to regular class placement, Carlberg and Kavale (1980) suggested that neither academic status nor social/personality condition was improved by special class placement. When data was grouped by category of exceptionality, however, differential posttreatment effects did emerge. Special class placement based primarily on low IQ was determined to be disadvantageous, while special class placement based on learning disabilities and/or behavioral or emotional difficulties showed some positive posttreatment results on both academic and social/personality measures. Carlberg and Kavale concluded their article with the assertion that special class placement is an inferior alternative to regular class placement, but they qualify this statement by saying that some justification exists for the special class placement of children with learning disabilities or behavioral/emotional difficulties.

In an extensive review of what they define as methodologically adequate research, Madden and Slavin (1983) suggest that full-time special education placement of students with mild academic handicaps offers few advantages over regular class placement. In contrast to Carlberg and Kavale (1980), however, these authors believe low-IQ students to be the one group that might benefit from special placement. Madden and Slavin describe the research on social-emotional outcomes as reasonably consistent, and state that mild academically handicapped students " . . . who are mainstreamed in regular classes with appropriate supports (such as individualized instruction or well-designed resource programs) have better self-esteem, more appropriate behavior, and are less self-deprecating than are students in special classes" (1983, 557). The studies reviewed by Madden and Slavin also support the conclusion that ". . . in general, it is regular class placement with appropriate supports that is better for the achievement of these students" (1983, 555).

Factors that Influence Effectiveness

Madden and Slavin (1983) discuss appropriate supports as important to the success of mainstreaming programs. In this section, a variety of appropriate supports will be presented, ranging from preplacement practices to instructional techniques which are equally appropriate for both handicapped and nonhandicapped students.

Successful implementation of a mainstreaming program does not begin with placement. Prior to any placement decision, a student must be properly assessed. Palmer (1980) suggests that for a handicapped student, assessment must consist of more than the traditional battery of standardized tests; it must also examine the characteristics of the instructional setting in which the child is to be placed to ensure a good match between student and classroom. "Specifically," notes Palmer, "instructional tasks, conditions, and consequences operating in regular classrooms, and willingness of teachers to modify their instructional practices in order to meet handicapped pupils' educational needs should be considered before making any placement decision" (1980, 169).

Collaboration between regular and special educators is also crucial for the successful implementation of mainstreaming programs. The quality of communication and the support between what have previously been separate educational delivery systems may be determining factors in the success of mainstreaming efforts (Salend 1984) and regular teachers may not always feel they have the support they need. In response to a questionnaire regarding their roles and responsibilities in the education of handicapped students, regular education teachers cited a lack of communication with special educators and a need to develop cooperative sharing of responsibility for the handicapped students' educational programs as primary concerns (Ammer 1984).

Ottman (1981) offers a number of suggestions to help special educators facilitate the mainstreaming process. These suggestions included helping classroom teachers define and assess potential problems; inviting the classroom teachers to an individualized education program (IEP) meeting so that they may take part in the development of goals for the student; assisting classroom teachers in developing strategies which might ease the handicapped student's transition into the mainsteam; and providing ongoing assistance to classroom teachers in developing and implementing behavior management programs.

A useful three-stage model for preparing secondary level special subject teachers for mainstreaming has been developed by Rocha and Smith (1985). This collaborative model emphasizes continual consultation between special and regular educators. In the formative stage, the special education teacher acquires information about the special subject course being considered and discusses handicapped students who may be appropriately mainstreamed into that course. Stage two, the process stage, focuses on identifying the learning characteristics of the handicapped student and developing the IEP. Stage three, the summative stage, involves monitoring which helps ensure communication because it is continual throughout the mainstreaming process. Whatever the specific steps, the critical feature is communication. As Johnson and Johnson (1980, 97–98), state, "It is just as important that the regular and special education teachers work together as a collaborative team as it is that handicapped and nonhandicapped students cooperate together in learning situations."

The cooperation of handicapped and nonhandicapped students in learning situations is an area of research which has seen considerable expansion in recent years. Johnson and Johnson (1980) recommend the structuring of cooperative learning activities as a means of promoting such cooperation. In cooperative learning situations, handicapped and nonhandicapped students work together in groups, typically earning rewards on the basis of group performance (Slavin 1984). Cooperative learning methods have been demonstrated to increase student achievement (Slavin 1984) and to promote positive interactions between handicapped and nonhandicapped classmates (Johnson and Johnson 1980).

Individualized instruction, characteristically associated with special education, is another instructional method which can be successfully implemented in the regular classroom. Teachers who use individualized instruction in mainstream classrooms can appropriately meet the needs of both handicapped and nonhandicapped students by treating all of their students as special (Slavin 1984). Like cooperative learning, individualized instruction can improve both the academic and social functioning of mainstreamed students (Madden and Slavin 1983; Slavin 1984; Wang, Peverly, and Randolph 1984).

Madden and Slavin (1983) suggest that three conditions facilitate the development of positive interactions between handicapped and nonhandicapped classmates: opportunities for nonsuperficial, cooperative contact; lack of identification of mainstreamed students as members of a "special" group; and noncompetitive classroom organization. It has been suggested that a combination of individualized instruction and cooperative learning, because it meets all three conditions, may be the best strategy for successful mainstreaming of handicapped students (Madden and Slavin 1983).

Importantly, Slavin (1984) reports that meeting the instructional needs of academically handicapped students in the mainstream does not seem to preclude meeting the needs of their nonhandicapped classmates. In fact, it has been shown that, with proper instruction, academic, social, and behavioral gains can be achieved by both handicapped and nonhandicapped students (Madden and Slavin 1983). The most effective instruction for handicapped students, suggests Slavin (1984), may be the most effective instruction for *all* students. Perhaps educators must realize that before mainstreaming can be optimally successful, the unique instructional and social needs of all students must be considered.

REFERENCES

Adams, R. (1971). A sociological approach to classroom research. In I. Westbury & A. Bellack (Eds.), *Research into classroom processes: Recent developments and next steps.* New York: Columbia University, Teachers College Bureau of Publications.

Ammer, J. J. (1984). The mechanics of mainstreaming: Considering the regular educators' perspective. *Remedial and Special Education, 5,* 15–20.

Carlberg, C., & Kavale, K. (1980). The efficacy of special versus regular class placement for exceptional children: A meta-analysis. *The Journal of Special Education, 14,* 295–309.

Dunn, L. M. (1968). Special education for the mildly retarded—Is much of it justifiable? *Exceptional Children, 35,* 5–22.

Goldberg, I. I., & Cruickshank, W. M. (1958). The trainable . . . Are they the public school's responsibility? *National Education Association Journal, 47,* 622.

Gresham, F. M. (1982). Misguided mainstreaming: The case for social skills training with handicapped children. *Exceptional Children, 48,* 422–433.

Johnson, D. W., & Johnson, R. T. (1980). Integrating handicapped students into the mainstream. *Exceptional Children, 47,* 90–98.

MacMillan, D. L. (1982). *Mental retardation in school and society.* Boston: Little, Brown and Company.

Madden, N. A., & Slavin, R. E. (1983). Mainstreaming students with mild handicaps: Academic and social outcome. *Review of Educational Research, 53* 519–569.

Martin, E. W. (1974). Some thoughts on mainstreaming. *Exceptional Children, 41,* 150–153.

Ottman, R. A. (1981). Before a handicapped student enters the classroom: What the special educator can do. *Teaching Exceptional Children, 14,* 41–43.

Palmer, D. J. (1980). Factors to be considered in placing handicapped children in regular classes. *Journal of School Psychology, 18,* 163–171.

Rocha, R., & Smith, E. (1985). Business education teachers assess mainstreaming experiences. *The Balance Sheet, 66,* 31–34.

Salend, S. J. (1984). Factors contributing to the development of successful mainstreaming programs. *Exceptional Children, 50,* 409–416.

Sansone, J., & Zigmond, N. (1986). Evaluating mainstreaming through an analysis of students' schedules. *Exceptional Children, 52,* 452–458.

Semmel, M., & Snell, M. (1979). Social acceptance and self-concept for handicapped pupils in mainstreamed environments. *Education Unlimited, 1,* 65–68.

Slavin, R. E. (1984). Team assisted individualization: Cooperative learning and individualized instruction in the mainstreamed classroom. *Remedial and Special Education, 5,* 33–42.

Switzky, H. N., & Miller, T. L. (1978). The least restrictive alternative. *Mental Retardation, 16,* 52–54.

Wang, M. C., Peverly, S., & Randolph, R. (1984). An investigation of the implementation and effects of a full-time mainstreaming program. *Remedial and Special Education, 5,* 21–32.

Warren, S. A. (1979). What is wrong with mainstreaming? A comment on drastic change. *Mental Retardation, 17,* 301–303.

Wolfensberger, W. (1972). *Normalization: The principle of normalization in human services.* Toronto: National Institute on Mental Retardation.

Zigler, E., & Muenchow, S. (1979). Mainstreaming: The proof is in the implementation. *American Psychologist, 34,* 993–996.

Zigmond, N., Levin, E., & Laurie, T. E. (1985). Managing the mainstream: An analysis of teacher attitudes and student performance in mainstream high school programs. *Remedial and Special Education, 18,* 535–541.

DISCUSSION QUESTIONS

1. How would you define *mainstreaming?* Talk to other people—teachers, principals, or parents—and see how they would define it.
2. One of the criticisms of mainstreaming is that many students are mainstreamed into inappropriate classes. If you have access to a school, try to find out what classes handicapped children are mainstreamed in. What classes do you think would be best and why? How should this decision be made?
3. If, as some studies report, teachers are not modifying their teaching, but rather are modifying their grading policies for handicapped students, what implications does this have for the students? How do you think this will affect them in the future?
4. There seems to be some difference of opinion on the benefits of mainstreaming for mentally retarded, learning disabled, and emotionally disturbed children. What factors do you think might lead to these variations?
5. Describe a program you think would help teachers better serve mainstreamed children. What would be its essential components?

Avoiding Misconceptions of Mainstreaming, the Least Restrictive Environment, and Normalization

Gunnar Dybwad

In the field of special education hardly anything provokes heated controversy as surely as the use of the new catchwords: mainstreaming, normalization, and the least restrictive environment. Ensuing conversation reveals that these terms are seen as representative of an intrusion or even an attack on well-established philosophy and practices in the field of special education through court actions initiated by a coalition of meddlesome civil rights lawyers and discontented parents.

HISTORICAL DEVELOPMENT

This line of argument is an oversimplification, if not a distortion, that ignores significant historical development. Notwithstanding some pioneering efforts early in the 19th century that led to a growing public responsibility for the teaching of children who were blind, deaf, or mildly retarded, these programs were administered as separate categorical entities. In the first half of this century, they grew in numbers and achieved

Note. Avoiding Misconceptions of Mainstreaming, the Least Restrictive Environment, and Normalization by G. Dybwad, 1980, *Exceptional Children, 47,* pp. 85–88. Copyright 1980 by the Council for Exceptional Children. Reprinted by permission.

significant advances in the training of teachers and the development of instructional methodology. Yet it was not until after World War II that there developed a general recognition of the field of special education, a generic approach to education in all areas of disability reflected in the structure of both the local public school systems and the teacher training institutions.

Largely as a result of the genetic scare, the field of mental retardation generally ranked very low in terms of public programs and public recognition during the first half of this century. Nonetheless, because of the sheer numbers affected by mental retardation, it gained a place of importance. This was underlined when, through the intervention of Representative John Fogarty, then Chairman of the House Appropriations Subcommittee on Labor and Health, Education, and Welfare, the US Office of Education received in 1957 an appropriation earmarked for research in the problems of educating mentally retarded children. In like fashion, in 1958, states were allocated federal monies for the training of teachers in mental retardation, a major breakthrough considering the widespread fear of federal intrusion into the field of education. Three years later, President John F. Kennedy established the President's Panel on Mental Retardation, which led to further federal programs and appropriations, including the elevation of special education to a more significant level within the US Office of Education.

These particular historical data are given here not to minimize in any way the considerable achievements that were taking place in educational programing for other exceptionalities, but rather to explain the striking impact on the field of special education of a series of court actions—largely in behalf of children categorized as mentally retarded—beginning with the PARC right to education case: Pennsylvania Association for Retarded Children, Nancy Beth Bowman et al. versus Commonwealth of Pennsylvania, David M. Kurtzman et al. (1972).

The heightened awareness of the human potential for rehabilitation and re-education demonstrated in World War II and the ensuing recognition of the dignity of the human person helped point the way to the establishment in 1950 of the National Association for Retarded Children (now Citizens) (NARC) the first of a series of protest organizations or consumer action groups organized by parents on behalf of their handicapped children.

A main effort of NARC right from the start was directed at improving the educational opportunities for children with mental retardation. Thus, NARC came early to confront the issue of a group of children denied admission to the public school altogether, the so called "trainable" children. Fortuitously, a foundation grant from the American Legion enabled the Association in 1956 to engage Dr. Ignacy Goldberg as education consultant to work specifically in this area. Dr. Goldberg's pioneering efforts culminated in a brief but pointed debate in the pages of the National Education Association (NEA) journal with Dr. William Cruickshank, widely recognized authority in special education. Cruickshank held that such children were neither able to benefit from education (as distinguished from training), nor entitled to an education since they were incapable of returning anything of value to the community. Goldberg took the opposite view, that such children had the right to be placed in the best educational environment (Goldberg & Cruickshank 1958). This debate in NEA's own journal was a significant milestone toward mainstreaming.

Another early concern of NARC was the question of rights. In a submission to the 1960 White House Conference on Children and Youth, the Association stated, "Insufficient attention has been given in the past to the legal status of the mentally retarded child and adult, particularly with reference to the degree of legal protection required as related to the degree of the mental handicap" (Dybwad 1964, 210).

This theme was taken up in 1967 by an

international symposium organized in Stockholm by the International League of Societies for the Mentally Handicapped. From the symposium conclusions (International League 1967) the League fashioned a declaration on the rights of mentally retarded persons. Adopted by the General Assembly of the United Nations four years later by unanimous vote, the declaration was endorsed by the President's Committee on Mental Retardation and also was cited by Judge Frank Johnson of the Federal Court in Montgomery, Alabama in the leading right to treatment case (*Wyatt* v. *Stickney*, 1972).

The emphasis by NARC on the rights and legal status of persons with mental retardation contributed significantly to the decision by the Pennsylvania Association for Retarded Children in January 1971 to initiate legal action against the state government for the purpose of securing the right of retarded children to a public education, all other avenues of redress having been exhausted.

While the decision to take the Commissioners of Education and of Public Welfare to court was an unprecedented step, the substance of the lawsuit did not come as a surprise to the professional leadership in special education. As a matter of fact, three months later at their annual convention, the membership of The Council for Exceptional Children adopted a significant position paper titled "Basic Commitments and Responsibilities to Exceptional Children" (CEC 1971), which had been under review for more than a year. This position paper put CEC squarely behind the philosophy of a universal right to education regardless of degree of handicap; the principal of mainstreaming (although the word was not used); elimination of the labeling-categorizing of children; and similar issues. To a remarkable extent, the citizens (parents), the judiciary, and the professional community had arrived at a significant confluence of goals and objectives, although this confluence remained to be translated into the daily realities of

methodology, administration, and enforcement.

The PARC case was followed almost immediately by the *Mills* case in Washington, D.C. and both ended with a strong affirmation of the right to education and the right to a least restrictive environment.

These progressive happenings take on additional significance when placed into a broader frame of reference. In 1970, Congress passed the Developmental Disabilities Act, which, for the first time, allocated an action priority to cases of severe disability. A 1975 amendment added to it a Bill of Rights for persons with developmental disabilities and required the establishment of a Protection and Advocacy system in each state. In the related area of rehabilitation, Congress enacted revised rehabilitation legislation, which, for the first time, gave priority to rehabilitation services for the most severely disabled persons.

Seen in this broader perspective, Public Law 94–142, the Education for All Handicapped Children Act of 1975, is enhanced by the fact that it is paralleled by other legislation of benefit to persons with disabilities. Together, these various enactments support each other and are a tangible expression of new societal concerns.

INTERPRETATION OF TERMS

In a report to Congress on the implementation of P.L. 94–142 submitted in January 1979, three and a half years after the enactment of the law, the Office of Education suggested that referring to the least restrictive environment provision in the act and its regulations as "mainstreaming" left much room for misinterpretation as did the implication that all handicapped children, regardless of the severity of their handicap, must be mainstreamed into regular education classes (US Office of Education 1979). Indeed, mainstreaming has often been so misinterpreted and oversimplified in statements such as "Mainstreaming is a form of educational programming that integrates special needs and nonspecial needs children in regular classrooms" (Meisels 1978).

There is no justification for such a narrow interpretation of the term. Sociologically speaking, the mainstream of society covers a wide range of positions and opportunities economically, socially, and vocationally. For example, it should include the recently arrived immigrant from Southeast Asia living in the inner city as much as the resident of a suburban community. In any case, in 1975 The Council for Exceptional Children (CEC 1975) had already published a very concise statement as to what mainstreaming is and is not, making clear that this includes a range of alternative provisions for those needing a more specialized program than the regular class offers.

In like manner, the term *least restrictive environment* (or placement, or alternative) has given rise to many questions and objections in the professional literature. Most of the critics (e.g. Cruickshank 1977; Switzky & Miller 1978) imply that the problem with this concept is that it was devised by attorneys and brought to the field of special education by judicial edict; thus, small wonder that it does not "fit." The facts are quite to the contrary. The concept can be found clearly enunciated in *Exceptional Children* as far back as 1962, in an article by Maynard C. Reynolds, "A Framework for Considering Some Issues in Special Education." Two citations from it will suffice:

The prevailing view is that normal home and school life should be preserved if at all possible. When a special placement is necessary to provide suitable care or education, it should be no more "special" than necessary. (368)
. . . having a broad range of services is important, and . . . children should be placed in programs of no more special character than absolutely necessary. There should be continuing assessment of children in special programs with a view toward returning them to more ordinary environments as soon as feasible. (370)

Thus, Reynolds established a clear line from the least restrictive alternative to the normalization principle. Although reference is frequently made to the principle of normalization as the philosophical basis for mainstreaming and the least restrictive alternative (McDevitt 1979), it was not until 1969 that the normalization principle, under that name, was introduced to the United States in a volume prepared for the President's Committee on Mental Retardation (Kugel & Wolfensberger 1969). Whatever their sequential origin, it is obvious that these three concepts are interlocking, and that each of them can be utilized properly only on the basis of an individual assessment. Far from being rigid mandates, they call for flexibility and personalization. It is normal to be different is the message of Public Law 94–142.

Granted, the implementation of this legislation is proceeding all too slowly on the local, state, and federal levels (Education Advocates Coalition 1980); and granted also that misuse of this new legislation by unscrupulous school authorities can work to the detriment of classroom teachers as well as students (National Education Association 1978); still there can be no question that the United States has indeed moved a giant step forward in meeting the educational needs of children with handicaps.

The major articles that follow in this issue on Free Appropriate Public Education describe procedures that work. They have been tried, tested, and proved effective in various localities around the country.

REFERENCES

Cruickshank, W. M. Least restrictive placement: Administrative wishful thinking. *Journal of Learning Disabilities*, 1977, 10, 193–194.

Council for Exceptional Children. Basic commitments and responsibilities to exceptional children. *Exceptional Children*, 1971, 38, 181–187.

Council for Exceptional Children. What is mainstreaming? *Exceptional Children*, 1975, 43, 174.

Dybwad, G. Trends and issues in mental retardation. In *Challenges in Mental Retardation.* New York: Columbia University Press, 1964.

Education Advocates Coalition. Report on federal compliance activities and implementation of the Education for All Handicapped Children Act, Washington DC: Author, 1980.

Goldberg, I. I., & Cruickshank, W. M. The trainables . . . Are they the public schools' responsibility? *National Education Association Journal,* 1958, 47, 622.

International League of Societies for the Mentally Handicapped. Conclusions. *Stockholm symposium on legislative aspects of mental retardation.* Brussels: ILSMH, 1967.

Kugel, R., & Wolfensberger, W. *Changing Patterns in residential services for the mentally retarded.* Washington DC: President's Committee on Mental Retardation, 1969.

McDevitt, G. M. (Ed.), *The handicapped experience: Some humanistic perspectives.* Baltimore: The University of Baltimore, 1979.

Meisels, S. J. First steps in mainstreaming. *Early Childhood,* 1978, 4, 1–2.

National Education Association. *Education for all handicapped children: Consensus, conflict and challenge, A study report.* Washington DC: NEA, 1978.

Pennsylvania Association for Retarded Children. Nancy Beth Bowman et al. v. Commonwealth of Pennsylvania. David M. Kurtzman et al. 343 F. Supp. 279 (E.D. Pa. 1972).

Reynolds, M. C. A framework for considering some issues in special education. *Exceptional Children.* 1962, 28, 367–370.

Switzky, H. N., & Miller, T. L. The least restrictive alternative. *Mental Retardation,* 1978, 16, 52–54.

US Office of Education. *Progress toward a free, appropriate education.* Washington DC: US Department of Health, Education, and Welfare, 1979.

Wyatt v. *Stickney.* 344 F. Supp. 390 (Mid. Ala. 1972).

CHAPTER **5**

Residential Alternatives

INTRODUCTION

With the growing acceptance of the principle of normalization, the passage and implementation of P. L. 94-142, and the deinstitutionalization movement, persons with mental retardation began to be placed in community-based programs in significant numbers. The impetus of deinstitutionalization and the resultant development of community residence programs has raised a number of issues. Lack of community support, fear, concern over property values, zoning regulations, and funding remain obstacles to the effective integration of individuals with mental retardation into community-based programs.

The first section of this chapter, *Deinstitutionalization: An Era of Change,* addresses the issue of deinstitutionalization from the perspectives of the efficacy studies, the individual with mental retardation, the family and the community, and future directions. The second section, *Community Residences: One Option,* discusses the principles of normalization and least restrictive environment, with particular emphasis on the development of community residence programs and the opposition often incurred by them.

Two article reprints have been included in this chapter. In their article *Setting Free the Captives: The Power of Community Integration in Liberating Institutionalized Adults From the Bonds of Their Past,* Baker and Salon (1986) demonstrate that integration can have positive effects on staff and residents alike. They argue that institutions by their very nature limit the growth potential of persons with mental retardation and should be eliminated. Margolis and Charitonidis (1981), in their article *Public Reactions to Housing For the Mentally Retarded,* report that most of the people in their study were willing to accept mentally retarded people as tenants. However, stereotypic attitudes were still demonstrated by those landlords who would not accept mentally retarded people as tenants.

Progress has undoubtedly been made in deinstitutionalization and the development of community residence programs. Continued efforts are needed, however, to assure and maintain optional living arrangements for individuals with mental retardation.

134

DEINSTITUTIONALIZATION: AN ERA OF CHANGE

The deinstitutionalization of mentally retarded citizens has been a national goal in the United States for more than twenty years (Bock and Joiner 1982). In 1963, in a statement to Congress, President John F. Kennedy challenged the people of the United States to ". . . promote to the best of our ability and by all possible and appropriate means the mental and physical health of all our citizens" (Kennedy 1963, 14). Included in this statement were goals for improving the level of care given to mentally retarded citizens, reducing the number of persons confined to institutions, returning mentally retarded and mentally ill individuals to the community, and improving community-based educational and rehabilitative services.

The deinstitutionalization movement in the United States was strengthened by the introduction of the Scandinavian concept of normalization. This concept, originated by Bank-Mikkelson and written into Danish law in 1959, was not formally introduced into the United States until 1969 (Wolfensberger 1972). At that time, Nirje defined normalization as "making available to the mentally retarded patterns and conditions of everyday life which are as close as possible to the norms and patterns of the mainstream of society" (1969, 181). This definition was expanded by Wolfensberger (1972) to describe the use of culturally normative means to establish and/or maintain personal behavior and characteristics which are as culturally normative as possible.

Deinstitutionalization has been seen as a natural outgrowth of the normalization principle; since institutions are not normal environments, their residents have been denied opportunities to develop normally (de Silva and Faflak 1976). Sproger (1980) defined deinstitutionalization as moving individuals from large, distant, impersonal, segregated (generally public) institutions to small, local, humane, integrated residences in the community. Others have given the process of deinstitutionalization the broader meaning of promoting practices which aim not only to reduce the number of residents currently living in institutions, but also to promote the development of normal living environments in the community and prevent the need for residential placement in large institutions (Larkin and Bruininks 1985). The major assumption underlying deinstitutionalization is that the quality of life for mentally retarded individuals will be significantly improved with placement in a community setting (Butler and Bjaanes 1977).

Reported trends in residential services for mentally retarded and developmentally disabled individuals over the past twenty-five years indicate that deinstitutionalization is being implemented on a widescale basis. Between 1960 and 1969 alone, thirty thousand residents were moved from long-term care institutions to community residential facilities (CRFs) (Bock and Joiner 1982). An even greater shift was seen between the 1966–67 and 1980–81 periods, when occupancy in public residential facilities decreased by sixty-nine thousand persons (Scheerenberger 1982). Hill, Lakin, and Bruininks (1984) reported that this depopulation of large residential public institutions was continuing at a rate of approximately six thousand residents a year. As a result, there has been rapid development of community residential facilities (Bruininks, Hauber, and Kudla 1980). One-eighth of the state institutions which operated in 1965 have now been closed; seventeen closures have been completed or scheduled since 1982, while at least five additional closures were planned for the 1985–87 period (Braddock and Heller 1985a).

Although no institution has as yet been mandated to close as a result of litigation, closure has provided an alternative to continued litigation in some cases (Braddock and Heller 1985a). One such example is the impending closure of the Staten Island Developmental Center (previously known as Willowbrook State School) in New York (Braddock and Heller 1985a). In 1972, a media exposé led to a lawsuit charging that conditions at Willowbrook were inhumane and destructive, with overcrowding, understaffing and a virtual absence of therapeutic care (MacMillan 1982). In 1975, the Willowbrook Consent Decree was signed, which ordered a reduction in the number of residents from 2,761 to 250 by April of 1981 (McDonald 1985). After more than a decade of litigation and extensive community placements, New York State is anticipated to close Staten Island Developmental Center in 1987 (Braddock and Heller 1985a).

The movement of mentally retarded individuals from large institutions to smaller community-based settings, along with an increasing trend for initial placement in CRFs, has resulted in the need for research to determine the efficacy of such placements. The remainder of this section will present examples of this efficacy research, discussion of the factors that influence the successes and failures surrounding deinstitutionalization, as well as predictions of future trends.

Outcome Studies

When compared to institutions, CRFs generally differ in two important ways: they are smaller than institutions and they tend to be located in residential areas. Like institutions, however, CRFs may be more different from one another than they are alike. They differ in size, location, staff qualifications and attitudes, and rehabilitative efforts. All of these characteristics have impact on the quality of life experienced by residents of the community facilities (MacMillan 1982). When reviewing outcome studies, therefore, it is difficult to make generalizations about the success or failure of deinstitutionalization efforts because of the variety of factors which must be considered. A sampling of the available outcome studies will nevertheless be presented here.

One way of evaluating the success of community-based placements is to study readmission records of individuals who have been discharged from institutions. In a study of the readmission of 117 mentally retarded individuals to a state hospital in California, Pagel and Whitling (1978) identified maladaptive behaviors as a primary source of failure. Maladaptive behaviors were found to be a source of failure for individuals across all levels of intellectual functioning and community placement options. When medical problems resulted in readmission, the individuals were most likely to be profoundly retarded and residing in convalescent hospitals. Keys, Boroskin, and Ross (1973) similarly described behavior and medical problems as the reasons for the institutional readmission of 126 individuals placed in family care and home leave. While characteristics such as IQ, sex, age, and functional skill level are inconsistently related to community success or failure, maladaptive behavior appears to consistently predict a return to institutional living (Crawford, Aiello, and Thompson 1979; Gottesfeld 1977). For mildly retarded individuals, lack of skills in such areas as money management, apartment cleanliness, social behavior, and meal preparation have also resulted in the return from independent living situations to more restrictive settings (Schalock and Harper 1978).

Despite the problem of readmission, a number of outcome studies support deinstitutionalization as a means of promoting positive change for mentally retarded individuals at all functioning levels. O'Neill et al. (1985), for example, evaluated the change in skills and activity patterns of twenty-seven severely/profoundly retarded individuals who moved from total care institutions to community-based settings. Within three months of discharge from the institutions, residents demonstrated improved skills in four areas: expressive communication; eating; serving meals and washing dishes; and meal preparation. Moreover, they reported that the residents showed significant movement toward a nondisabled pattern of daily living. Kleinberg and Galligan (1983) studied twenty mentally retarded individuals as they moved from a large developmental center to small community residences and found consistent improvement in the areas of language development, domestic activity, responsibility, and social interaction.

In another study, Walsh and Walsh (1982) evaluated the behavior changes of forty adults after they had been deinstitutionalized. Two assessment instruments, developed to measure specific skills and dimensions of behavior related to success in group and institutional living environments, were used. Although the authors stated that while noted changes could not unequivocally be attributed to movement from the institutions, consistent patterns of positive change on the two instruments favored deinstitutionalization.

While the complexities involved in measuring important residential variables have made it difficult to ascertain the relationship between residential arrangements and individual change following deinstitutionalization, efforts have been made to determine these relationships (MacMillan 1982). Eyman, Demaine, and Lei (1979), for example, conducted a three-year study in which they measured changes in personal and community self-sufficiency and in personal and social responsibility among retarded individuals living in institutions and in a variety of community-based settings. Their findings suggest that environmental characteristics were responsible for the variations in growth observed. The most positive changes were promoted by foster care homes and by board-and-care facilities. Residential characteristics based upon the normalization principle have also been studied by examining such variables as administrative policies, location and proximity of services, and appearance of the residence. These factors were found to be related to the development of retarded persons living in the community (Eyman et al. 1977).

Preparing the Individual for a Change in Placement

According to Coffman and Harris (1980), one reason for the occurrence of maladaptive behavior patterns following deinstitutionalization may be transition shock.

Comparing the deinstitutionalization of mentally retarded individuals to the experiences of ex-prisoners, recently divorced persons, and visitors to a foreign land, Coffman and Harris suggest that many of the difficulties encountered by mentally retarded persons following relocation are, under the circumstances, widely shared and normal. During the transition period, new residents may display maladaptive behaviors that have not been observed or reported by institutional staff; this may create a situation in which the CRF and the institutional staff distrust and question one another. Responses to the new resident's adjustment symptoms may result in unnecessary medication, inappropriate job assignments or training opportunities, or, in some cases, a return to the institution (Coffman and Harris 1980).

Karan and Gardner (1984) suggest that the stress of relocation could be significantly reduced by carefully planning the move from the institution. Suggested activities prior to transfer include involving community and institutional staff, arranging visits to the new setting prior to relocation, involving both the resident and the family in planning the move, and involving a personal advocate. Karan and Gardner provide an extensive list of references and resources to help ease the transition process.

In examining the decision process used to deinstitutionalize mentally retarded individuals, Vitello, Atthowe, and Cadwell (1983) report that institutional review teams employ specific criteria when making placement decisions. Typically, these criteria result in the highest functioning residents being recommended for community placement, and the lowest functioning residents remaining institutionalized. The authors suggest that retarded individuals are not likely to be deinstitutionalized until they have attained higher levels of cognitive and adaptive functioning, and they emphasize the role of the institution in preparing residents for community placement.

The effectiveness of institutionally based training programs in preparing residents for community life has, however, been questioned (Martin, Rusch, and Heal 1982). While virtually all institutions have such training programs, surprisingly little evidence exists to support these programs as facilitating community adjustment (Sigelman et al. 1980). In a review of the literature on community placement of institutionalized individuals, McCarver and Craig (1974) found only one study in which community success was related to training received in the institution, and even then, the relationship between the two was nonsignificant. Since the available research indicates that institutional training programs are of questionable value, Martin, Rusch, and Heal (1982) suggest that community-based training programs should be used whenever possible. In a review of training procedures for ten community survival skills, Martin, Rusch, and Heal (1982) also provide evidence that mentally retarded adults can acquire appropriate skills and behaviors when systematic real life training is provided.

Community-based training is further supported by research which suggests that the institutional environment may actually suppress the emergence of certain skills (O'Neill et al. 1985). Kleinberg and Galligan (1983), studying changes in the adaptive behavior of mentally retarded adults following deinstitutionalization, found a pattern of rapid initial improvement followed by stabilization, rather than gradual and continual improvement over time. Based on the shape of the learning curve and the types of behavior which showed the greatest improvement, Kleinberg and Galligan suggested that "deinstitutionalized individuals show changes that primarily represent the manifestation of skills already in their repertoire" (1983, 25). With respect to self-care skills, Walsh and Walsh (1982) indicate that residents in an institution may have little need to care for themselves, since what they do *not* do will be done for them by institutional staff. As they suggest, "It may be that the primary requirement for an increase in independent living skills among the developmentally disabled is an environment with room for those skills to be developed and exhibited" (1982, 66).

As part of their guidelines for community program planners, Karan and Gardner (1984) note that the way an individual behaves in an institutional setting may not be an accurate predictor of how he or she will behave in the community. In addition, assessments completed in the institution may be of little use in predicting adjustment to community settings since participation in community experiences may be a prerequisite to the demonstration of community skills. Karan and Gardner (1984) caution against making assumptions about an individual's competence until he or she demonstrates that competence under natural conditions and, like O'Neill et al. (1985), suggest that the institutional environment itself may perpetuate the very difficulties which preclude consideration for discharge.

Preparing the Family and Community

The decision to deinstitutionalize a mentally retarded child or adult must take into account not only the individual's readiness to return to community life, but also the readiness and the ability of the community to accept and meet the individual's needs. In a study of families of mentally retarded individuals two years after deinstitutionalization, Willer, Intagliata, and Atkinson (1981) report that approximately 50 percent of the families experienced crisis as a result of the family member's return to community life. Further, crisis occurred whether or not the individual was actually returned to the family's home. Families of individuals returned to their own homes experienced intense anxiety associated with anticipated difficulties in managing behavior; families of individuals placed in alternate settings within the community more typically experienced guilt as a result of not allowing the family member to return home. Family structure was also found to be related to crisis, with more highly structured families more likely to experience crisis as a result of deinstitutionalization (Willer, Intagliata, and Atkinson 1981).

The move toward community placement has generated a backlash of support for institutions from parents (Payne 1976); in some cases, families have sued the state to prevent the closure of institutions (Braddock and Heller 1985b). In a survey among parents of residents of state facilities for the mentally retarded in Texas, the institution was seen as providing better care, a more experienced staff, and greater security (Payne 1976). Interestingly, studies of families' attitudes following deinstitutionalization have generally found that their views change dramatically over time, with most families reporting satisfaction with community placement outcomes

(Conroy and Latik 1982; Heller, Bond, and Braddock 1983). Rudie and Riedl (1984) suggest it is simply the status quo that parents want most to maintain. Whether an individual is institutionalized or has been moved to a community placement, parents tend to want their children to remain where they are.

In a 1984 study of 761 children who were deinstitutionalized, Seltzer and Krauss reported that a surprisingly low number, 6.6 percent, were returned to their natural families. Those children who did return home were found to have the fewest medical problems and to need the least amount of community support and specialized services.

The availability of specialized community services is a critical factor to assess prior to deinstitutionalization. Intagliata, Kraus, and Willer (1980) report that increased numbers of deinstitutionalized individuals are seeking support services in the community, and that the needs of this population are often different and more intensive than those traditionally served. The importance of adequate support services has been demonstrated by research which shows that individuals not provided with the necessary support services are more likely to return to the institution (Bollay et al. 1978).

In a study of the impact of deinstitutionalization on a community-based service system, Intagliata, Kraus, and Willer (1980) found that most community agencies were providing services for severely mentally retarded or multiply handicapped individuals who in the past would have been served in an institutional setting. While agency directors report that deinstitutionalized individuals often need the same kinds of services as other clients, they also note the need for more intensive services, particularly during the early period of adjustment to community life. Agency directors also report that deinstitutionalized individuals need more assistance in using community services, and that, in some cases, new programs have had to be developed to meet the needs of some severely retarded or multiply handicapped individuals.

When appropriate programs are not available in the community, individuals are often returned to the institution (Karan and Gardner 1984). Karan and Gardner describe the discrepancies between community options and individual characteristics as a "lack of fit," and offer a set of guidelines for community program planners which focus on maximizing the fit between individuals and their environments. In his model for successful deinstitutionalization, Scheerenberger (1974) lists a number of community services which either *must* be or *should* be available. According to his model, community services which are essential for successful deinstitutionalization are adequate homelike environments (including natural homes, foster homes, group homes, nursing homes, and independent living facilities); health services; education and training; employment (open or sheltered); and mobility. Recreational and religious services, as well as other services available to any citizen, should also be available (Scheerenberger 1974).

Trends and Future Directions

Two national surveys—in 1977 and 1982—of all state facilities for mentally retarded individuals indicated a number of trends toward deinstitutionalization for individuals across all skill and ability levels. Comparisons of the two surveys suggested that the number of children being served in out-of-home placements was decreasing; the proportion of severely/profoundly handicapped individuals being served in community placements was increasing; and the number of smaller residential services in the community was increasing substantially (Hill, Lakin, and Bruininks 1984). These results were consistent with 1978 predictions (Girardeau et al. 1978; Roos 1978) that normalization rates would continue to increase.

More recent predictions, based on a Delphi study (Putnam and Bruininks 1986), noted a similar trend. This survey predicted that the deinstitutionalization movement would continue at its present pace and that institutions would eventually be used only for those individuals who posed a serious physical threat to others. Other expectations of those surveyed were that handicapped children would remain with their own families or in foster families until they were adults, and that community-based services would become increasingly available to individuals across all handicapping conditions (Putnam and Bruininks 1986). According to Hill, Lakin, and Bruininks (1984), there is a growing perception that community-based care is appropriate for severely/profoundly retarded individuals. While they concede that a national policy of totally eliminating institutions does not seem imminent, longitudinal evidence suggests that a continued development of programs established over the past few years may result in an elimination of institutions by the turn of the century (Hill, Lakin, and Bruininks 1984).

REFERENCES

Bock, W. H., & Joiner, L. M. (1982). From institution to community residence: Behavior competencies for admission and discharge. *Mental Retardation, 20,* 153–158.

Bollay, E., Freedman, R., Wyngaarden, M., & Kurtz, N. R. (1978). *Coming back.* Cambridge, MA: Abt Books.

Braddock, D., & Heller, T. (1985a). The closure of mental retardation institutions I: Trends in the United States. *Mental Retardation, 23,* 168–176.

Braddock, D., & Heller, T. (1985b). The closure of mental retardation institutions II: Implications. *Mental Retardation, 23,* 222–229.

Bruininks, R. H., Hauber, F. A., & Kudla, M. J. (1980). National survey of community residential facilities: A profile of facilities and residents in 1977. *American Journal of Mental Deficiency, 84,* 470–478.

Butler, E. W., & Bjaanes, A. T. (1977). A typology of community care facilities and differential normalization outcomes. In P. Mittler (Ed.), *Research in practice in mental retardation: Care and intervention* (Vol. 1). Baltimore: University Park Press.

Coffman, T. L., & Harris, M. C. (1980). Transition shock and adjustments of mentally retarded persons. *Mental Retardation, 18,* 3–7.

Conroy, J. W., & Latik, A. (1982). Family impact: Pre-post attitudes of 65 families of clients deinstitutionalized. *Pennhurst Longitudinal Study.* Philadelphia: Temple University Developmental Disabilities Center.

Crawford, J. L., Aiello, J. R., & Thompson, D. E. (1979). Deinstitutionalization and community placement: Clinical and environmental factors. *Mental Retardation, 17,* 59–63.

deSilva, R. M., & Faflak, P. (1976). From institution to community—A new process? *Mental Retardation, 14,* 25–28.

Eyman, R. K., Demaine, G. C., & Lei, T. (1979). Relationship between community environ-
    ments and resident changes in adaptive behavior: A path model. *American Journal of
    Mental Deficiency, 83,* 330–338.
Eyman, R. K., Silverstein, A. B., McLain, R., & Miller, C. (1977). Effects of residential
    settings on development. In P. Mittler (Ed.), *Research to practice in mental retardation.* Vol.
    1, Care and intervention. Baltimore: University Park Press.
Girardeau, F. L., Cairns, G. F., Rogers, B., & Weidenhofer, L. (1978). *Deinstitutionalization in
    HEW region VII: The past and the future.* Kansas City, KS: Department of Community
    Health and Kansas Center for Mental Retardation and Human Development.
Gottesfeld, H. (1977). *Alternatives to psychiatric hospitalization.* New York: Gardner Press.
Heller, T., Bond, M., & Braddock, D. (1983). *Family reactions to institutional closures.* Paper
    presented at the American Psychological Association, Anaheim, CA.
Hill, B. K., Lakin, C., & Bruininks, R. H. (1984). Trends in residential services for people
    who are mentally retarded: 1977–1982. *The Journal of the Association for Persons with
    Severe Handicaps, 9,* 243–250.
Intalgliata, J., Kraus, S., & Willer, B. (1980). The impact of deinstitutionalization on a
    community based service system. *Mental Retardation, 18,* 305–307.
Karan, O. C. (1981). Deinstitutionalization in the 80's—When the bucks are thin cooperation
    is in. *Select papers of the National Association of Developmentally Disabled Managers,* No. 5.
Karan, O. C., & Gardner, W. I. (1984). Planning community services using the Title XIX
    waiver as a catalyst for change. *Mental Retardation, 22,* 240–247.
Kennedy, J. (1963). *Message from the president of the United States.* Washington, DC: House of
    Representatives (88th Congress), Document No. 58.
Keys, V., Boroskin, A., & Ross, R. T. (1973). The revolving door in an MR hospital: A study
    of returns from leave. *Mental Retardation, 11,* 55–56.
Kleinberg, J., & Galligan, B. (1983). Effects of deinstitutionalization on adaptive behavior of
    mentally retarded adults. *American Journal of Mental Deficiency, 88,* 21–27.
Larkin, K. C., & Bruininks, R. (1985). Contemporary services for handicapped children and
    youth. In R. H. Bruininks & K. C. Larkin (Eds.), *Living and learning in the least restrictive
    environment.* Baltimore: Paul H. Brookes.
MacMillan, D. L. (1982). *Mental retardation in school and society.* Boston: Little, Brown and
    Company.
Martin, J. E., Rusch, F. R., & Heal, L. W. (1982). Teaching community survival skills to
    mentally retarded adults: A review and analysis. *Journal of Special Education, 16,* 243–
    267.
McCarver, R. B., & Craig, E. M. (1974). Placement of the retarded in the community:
    Prognosis and outcome. In N. R. Ellis (Ed.), *International review of research in mental
    retardation* (Vol. 7). New York: Academic Press.
McDonald, E. P. (1985). Medical needs of severely developmentally disabled persons resid-
    ing in the community. *American Journal of Mental Deficiency, 90,* 171–176.
Nirje, B. (1969). The normalization principle and its management implications. In R. Kugel
    & W. Wolfensberger (Eds.), *Changing patterns in residential services for the mentally retarded.*
    President's Committee on Mental Retardation, Washington, DC.
O'Neill, J., Brown, M., Gordon, W., & Schonhorn, R. (1985). The impact of deinstitutionali-
    zation on activities and skills of severely/profoundly mentally retarded multiply-handi-
    capped adults. *Applied Research in Mental Retardation, 6,* 361–371.
Pagel, S., & Whitling, C. (1978). Readmissions to a state hospital for mentally retarded
    persons. *Mental Retardation, 16,* 164–166.
Payne, J. E. (1976). The deinstitutional backlash. *Mental Retardation, 14,* 43–45.

Putnam, J. W., & Bruininks, R. H. (1986). Future directions in deinstitutionalization and education: A Delphi investigation. *Exceptional Children, 53,* 55–62.

Roos, S. (1978). The future of residential services for the mentally retarded in the United States: A Delphi study. *Mental Retardation, 16,* 355–356.

Rudie, F., & Riedl, G. (1984). Attitudes of parents/guardians of mentally retarded former state hospital residents toward current community placement. *American Journal of Mental Deficiency, 89,* 295–297.

Schalock, R. L., & Harper, R. S. (1978). Placement from community-based MR programs: How well do clients do? *American Journal of Mental Deficiency, 83,* 240–247.

Scheerenberger, R. C. (1974). A model for deinstitutionalization. *Mental Retardation, 12,* 3–7.

Scheerenberger, R. C. (1982). *Public residential services for the mentally retarded.* Madison, WI: National Association of Supervisors of Public Residential Facilities for the Mentally Retarded.

Seltzer, M. M., & Krauss, M. W. (1984). Family, community residence, and institutional placements of a sample of mentally retarded children. *American Journal of Mental Deficiency, 89,* 257–266.

Sigelman, C. K., Novak, A. R., Heal, L. W., & Switzky, H. N. (1980). In A. R. Novak & L. W. Heal (Eds.), *Integration of developmentally disabled individuals into the community.* Baltimore: Paul Brookes.

Sproger, S. R. (1980). Misunderstanding deinstitutionalization: A response to a recent article. *Mental Retardation, 18,* 199–201.

Vitello, S. J., Atthowe, J. M., & Cadwell, J. (1983). Determinants of community placement of institutionalized mentally retarded persons. *American Journal of Mental Deficiency, 87,* 539–545.

Walsh, J. A., & Walsh, R. A. (1982). Behavioral evaluation of a state program of deinstitutionalization of the developmentally disabled. *Evaluation and Program Planning, 5,* 59–67.

Willer, B. S., Intagliata, J. C., & Atkinson, A. C. (1981). Deinstitutionalization as a crisis event for families of mentally retarded persons. *Mental Retardation, 19,* 28–29.

Wolfensberger, W. (1972). *The principle of normalization in human services.* Toronto: National Institute on Mental Retardation.

DISCUSSION QUESTIONS

1. Many families made the decision to institutionalize their children years ago. Now, as institutions close, they are faced with the return of their children to the community. What feelings do you think they are having, and how would you suggest they deal with their reactions? How would you advise them?
2. A lack of preparation for community living seems to increase the probability of someone's returning to an institution, yet institutional training is of questionable value. How could you solve this dilemma? Outline your training solutions.
3. Make a list of community services that might be needed by previously institutionalized individuals when they move to the community. Which of these services might be difficult to obtain in the community and why?
4. Who might be positively affected by the deinstitutionalization movement? Negatively affected?
5. Do you think deinstitutionalization is moving too fast, too slowly, or at about the right speed? Why? Do you think the rate of deinstitutionalization affects various groups differently? Explain.

Setting Free the Captives: The Power of Community Integration in Liberating Institutionalized Adults from the Bonds of their Past

Milton J. Baker
Rebecca S. Salon

This article demonstrates the power that integration can have in bringing out the positive potential within people with handicaps and in positively altering stereotypes and expectancies of staff. The experiences of nine people who had the opportunity to leave their institutional environment for a week-long vacation are described herein. During these vacations, all of which were in popular vacation spots in New York State, dramatic behavior changes were witnessed in the men and women from the institution. Staff were transformed as well. Their expectations and perceptions changed markedly. It became clear that a person's behavior and demonstrated abilities in an institutional setting cannot be used to predict his or her readiness for, or behavior in, a typical community setting. Other lessons which can be learned from community integrative experiences are included in these nine vignettes.

What is now called the Syracuse Developmental Center (SDC), a residential institution for people labeled mentally retarded, was opened in 1854 as the New York Idiot Asylum. It is the oldest state institution for people with mental retardation in the United States on the same site, even though all the old buildings have been replaced with modern ones. Several of SDC's living units for adults are clustered into an administrative unit called Team B. In recent years, the staff of Team B have engineered activities and experiences in the community for the ninety-one people who reside there, including a variety of educational, social, vocational, recreational, and religious involvements.

The people who live on these units are generally quite handicapped—all with labels of severe or profound mental retardation. Many of the people are elderly, many have multiple handicapping conditions, and all have been in various institutions for most of their lives. Their lives have been seriously lacking in regular experiences outside in the community. They have spent their years interacting primarily with other people with handicaps and with paid institutional staff, within an institutional environment. Additionally, many of these people have facial or other physical stigmata; others have physically disabling conditions. Still others exhibit aggressive or otherwise offensive behaviors. Despite all of these disadvantages, remarkable progress has been achieved by many of these individuals. We believe strongly that these achievements stem from the beliefs, attitudes, and philosophical orientation of the team's staff and leadership—that is, from their commitment to community integration and to the basic human needs of the people living on Team B.

Ten years ago, the staff of Team B began to take some of the people who live on the unit on summer vacations. For the past five years, *all* of the people living on Team B take an annual vacation, away from the institution. The staff have selected the following vignettes to demonstrate the value of this type of community integrative activity. These vignettes reflect one particular summer a few years ago, during which small groups of people took week-long vacations, primarily in New York State.

In putting this material together, we were emotionally moved by the obvious power that integration has in lifting the human spirit and calling forth the positive potential within people with disabilities. We cannot offer "measurability" per se. However, we can demonstrate positive growth and movement for people whom our society (and our field) has always considered the least capable—people who have had overwhelmingly negative experiences during their long-term institutionalization and due to the severity of their handicap(s).

Social validation procedures (Kazdin 1977; Wolf 1978) were utilized in compiling and interpreting these vignettes. That is, combining social comparison and subjective evaluation methods (Kazdin 1977), (a) behavior before and after community integrative experiences was contrasted with the typical expectancies in the contexts described, and (b) judgments were made regarding qualitative aspects of an individual's behavior by people who knew an individual well and who knew him or her in a variety of contexts. Such procedures, therefore, allow research to address the social significance of goals, the social appropriateness of procedures, and the social importance of the effects (Wolf 1978).

Much has been written on the effects of institutional living on an individual's behavior. Balla and Zigler (1982), Blatt (1970, 1973), Blatt and Kaplan (1966), Goffman (1961), and Vail (1967) provide comprehensive reviews of the issues and/or of the extensive research on the impact of institutionalization. However, relatively little has been written that relates the experiences of people labeled mentally retarded in the community (Bogdan & Taylor 1982; Edgerton 1967; Edgerton & Bercovici 1976; Edgerton, Bollinger, and Herr 1984), especially as it compares to institutional experiences and behaviors (Sigelman et al. 1980).

It is not our intent to offer programmatic descriptions, training regimens, or technical "how-to" suggestions. The techniques themselves and the program content are (and were) less important than the program context. That is, the "success" of this "program" can be attributed to the staff's positive, growth-promoting expectancies: their attention to the needs of the people who live on Team B (specifically, the needs for acceptance; to be challenged and engaged by their environment activities, and relationships; to have choices, options, and therefore a degree of control; for security and predictability in their relationships, activities, and even in a new environment; to be involved in activities that are typical and valued); and their attention to the "details" which promote and foster successful community integration and the successful development of relationships (small groupings; dispersed locations; attention to personal hygiene, grooming, dress, mannerisms, and overall appearances; provision of positive role models; and the opportunities to model and rehearse positive social interactions).

In many ways, the vignettes that follow speak for themselves. Each story has its own lessons to teach. Each vignette will be followed by a statement of what we learned from these community integration opportunities. A summary of these "lessons" will then follow.

SUMMER OF 1983

Mr. R spent a week away from the institution at Lake George. Mr. R, who is forty-one years old, has been institutionalized for nineteen years of his life. In the institution, Mr. R is frequently aggressive and periodically assaultive to other people, regardless of whether he knows them or not. He is consistently resistant to following directions and frequently refuses to care for his clothing and his room. He walks around with a frown on his face and clearly is not happy. When Mr. R is expected to participate in routine activities in the institution, the "programming" frequently becomes a confrontation, with Mr. R at the least talking in aggressive, loud, objecting tones.

Upon arrival at Lake George, after a four-hour ride from the institution, Mr. R became very helpful. He helped others put supplies away, went to look for his room at the motel, and put his own clothing away. Throughout the vacation, he was open to suggestions about trips and activities. One day, while a group was sitting around the pool, Mr. R sat down in a lounge chair next to a couple he had never met before. He very appropriately started a conversation with them and, for over a half hour, the three of them talked about radios and stereos. Not once during the vacation was Mr. R aggressive or assaultive.

When he returned to the institutional parking lot, he did not want to get out of the van. He verbally expressed how well he liked the vacation and how much he disliked coming back. He actually physically resisted going back into the building.

Ms. B is twenty-eight years old and has been institutionalized for twenty-three years of her life. She has no speech, is hyperactive, and is self-abusive—digging at her face until it bleeds. Before the vacation, Ms. B was so agitated and self-abusive that staff questioned whether or not she should go on the trip. However, believing that perhaps the institutional environment was contributing to her upsetness, she was included in the trip. While on vacation at Cooperstown, her agitation was significantly reduced and there was a dramatic reduction in her self-abusiveness. She also did not take other people's food and her table manners were good—a marked contrast to her behavior in the institution.

Mr. K has been institutionalized for twenty-three years of his life; he is thirty-one years old. In the institution Mr. K exhibits a variety of ritualistic and repetitive behaviors. When one of his "routines" is interrupted, he becomes assaultive and very uncooperative. Some of these behaviors and reactions have been so "deviant" that Mr. K has had to have special staff assigned to him, to prevent him from injuring himself or others.

While on vacation at Old Forge, Mr. K exhibited no problem behaviors. He showered independently and retired at night at an appropriate hour, along with the other vacationers. A number of times during the vacation, Mr. K noticed things that needed to be done and spontaneously began helping without being asked. Mr. K did not have additional staff working with him on the vacation. People were amazed at the dramatic change in his behavior during this week away from the institution.

Institutional behavior cannot predict a person's adjustment to a more typical environment—especially one in which there are positive, valuing, stimulating expectations. In these instances one could not even have accurately predicted staffing needs, based on institutional expectations.

If the unit's staff had waited for Mr. R, Ms. B, or Mr K to demonstrate that they were "ready" for experiences in the community, based on their behavior in the institution, they clearly never would have had any community experiences. In the institution, once a person acts aggressively, we assume that the behavior must be addressed in the institutional setting, when and if it decreases, the person may then be considered to be "ready" and able to cope with the community. We offer these vignettes as "evidence" that integration itself is often the most effective way of addressing troublesome behaviors—especially when compared to traditional approaches such as isolation, time-out, psychotropic or tranquilizing drugs, and so on.

Also, as was the case with many others, people who had always been recipients of the assistance and efforts of others became active, contributing members of their community environment—with-

out the addition of extra staff or of formal, technical training techniques.

Mr. M is multiply handicapped, using an electric wheelchair for mobility. He is fifty-seven years old and has been institutionalized for forty-nine years of his life. In the institution, Mr. M is very sullen and is not at all outgoing. Although he has fairly good command of language, he talks infrequently. When he does talk, he usually complains and his speech is difficult to understand. In the institution, Mr. M spills food, is not neat in his appearance, and frequently slides down in his chair, in spite of mechanical adaptations to the chair to help him sit upright. He requires a great deal of staff time.

Mr. M went to Lake George on vacation for a week. The first two days on vacation, Mr. M's behavior was much like that in the institution. However, on the third day, he was much more outgoing, talking with people clearly and pleasantly. After going on a sightseeing boatride around Lake George, Mr. M spent the following day talking about how much he enjoyed the experience. Throughout the vacation, Mr. M was concerned about his appearance. He sat straight in his chair, and his eating skills were excellent. When he went shopping, he picked out everything by himself, and it was apparent that he was happy and very proud.

Mr. S has been institutionalized for twenty-six of his thirty-three years. In the institution, Mr. S frequently talks in aggressive, threatening tones. He has often broken his own possessions and those of others when he cannot have his own way. His behavior in the institution has been so troublesome that he has had to have one-to-one staffing provided. There have been occasions when the institutional security officers had to be called for assistance in handling his aggressive behaviors, and instances of injections of thorazine being administered to "calm him down."

In contrast Mr. S exhibited no behavioral difficulties while on vacation. The people accompanying him expressed their amazement at his change in behavior, commenting on what a pleasure he was to be around for the entire period of time. His vacation, which was in Cooperstown, included the Baseball Hall of Fame. He was obviously excited and interested in this experience, asking many questions about baseball, the players, and the exhibits.

Mr. S is an individual who becomes extremely impatient when he has to wait for something. However, he remained patient and cooperative even after a two-hour wait at a restaurant in Cooperstown.

Mr. S also developed a friendship with a fisherman during this trip. They had many discussions about fishing, the types of fish caught, and what types of tackle produced the best catch. The fisherman so enjoyed their talks that he came by the campsite daily to talk with Mr. S.

Mr. W, who is forty-five, has lived in institutions for thirty-five years. He often keeps to himself and needs many reminders to follow through on personal hygiene tasks.

While vacationing at Eagle Bay, he enthusiastically participated in all the community events, including hiking, fishing, dining in restaurants, and going on a boat trip. He interacted socially with other people who vacationed with him, spontaneously sharing his possessions with others. He also attended to his personal hygiene needs without reminders. Staff were truly surprised to see the tremendous amount of energy Mr. W had, especially contrasted with his low energy level and lack of involvement in the institution.

The change in setting, removal of restrictions, and availability of opportunities for new, interesting, valued experiences provided these men with a motivation and energy that could never be generated within an institutional environment, which by its very nature is routinized and low intensity.

These vacation experiences not only provided liberating experiences for the people who live at SDC, these events also liberated staff from the confines of very narrow perceptions and expectations of the people with whom they worked on a daily basis. *That is, staff learned that people have much more potential and ability than they are given credit for in the institution. The very nature of integrative settings causes expectancies—and therefore behaviors—to change drastically.*

Ms. A is severely handicapped. She is forty-two years old and has been institutionalized since the age of five. She cannot speak and has very, limited self-help abilities. In the institution, she sits by herself, while on vacation, she actually sought out the company of others.

Ms. A particpates in self-stimulating behavior placing her hand in her mouth and producing large quantities of saliva. Although this behavior did occur during the vacation, the frequency was drastically decreased—accomplishing what years of highly structured behavior modification programs were never able to achieve.

Although she exhibited some inappropriate behaviors, staff attempted to compensate by being diligent in attending to her personal appearance, hygiene, and grooming. These efforts significantly minimized the attention she called to herself in public places during the vacation.

She went on her first boat trip, sitting quietly and appropriately, watching people and observing the scenery. At mealtimes, she independently came to the table, which she has never done in the institution.

Another woman, Ms. H, has been institutionalized for thirty-four years. She is thirty-seven years old. She has epilepsy and has had periodic seizures while in the institution. On occasion, there have been series of seizures which have necessitated her hospitalization. Professional assessment has determined that her seizure disorder may be influenced by the institutional environment in which there is a large number of people and much confusion and noise. In planning for Ms. H's vacation away from the institution, there was some concern that the excitement of participating in the activities of the trip and the interactions with new people might induce seizures. However, during her one-week vacation at Lake George, she had no seizures.

Ms. H went on a boat tour while on vacation. On the tour, she was thrilled about the trip and the scenery. She also socialized appropriately with the people sitting next to her. Although Ms. H has always been an outgoing person, she has had few opportunities to interact with people who are nonhandicapped. She was able to socialize with her typical peers while on vacation with acceptance, even though her many years of institutionalization deprived her of such interactive social experiences.

Neither woman was denied the opportunity to participate in community integrative activities due to medical/physical conditions or due to lack of training and experience in socially appropriate interactions in the community. Their actions and experiences in the institution would have been poor predictors of their behavior and abilities in a stimulating, positive, motivating community setting. Also, new experiences were instrumental in eliciting new behavior patterns. Finally, we need to remember that every effort needs to be taken to accentuate positives and minimize negatives.

Ms. E is severely impaired and has lived in the institution for thirty-six of her forty-three years. In the institution, Ms. E typically engages in run-on conversations and does not stop talking when it is time for the other person to respond. She will often speak incoherently, saying many words that are not linked logically and ending with phrases about people not liking her and about how much she dislikes the institution, expressing her desire to move into a group home. She will also interrupt other people's conversations and will walk in on meetings, talk in loud, disruptive tones, and often start to cry. While on vacation, these behaviors did not occur once. She did not impose herself inappropriately on the people in adjoining campsites, nor did she interrupt conversations, become tearful, or talk in loud tones. She thoroughly enjoyed her vacation. Throughout the week of vacation, Ms. E carried on appropriate conversations, not only with people who were vacationing with her, but also with the people who were administering the campsite.

She made a number of trips into the

community, acting acceptably each time. While dining out, she was able to order her meal correctly. Ms. E generally needs many reminders to sit quietly at mealtimes and to chew with her mouth closed. In the community restaurants, her table manners were excellent and she needed no reminders about what was expected of her.

During the vacation, Ms. E also assisted in the shopping for and the preparation of meals. This is something that she does not do in the institution, in spite of the fact that her living area has a stove and that cooking is an integral part of the institutional "program" for her. She kept her room neat and orderly, including her closet and dresser. This too was not typical of her behavior in the institution.

In no way did she call attention to herself in these integrated community settings. Staff were astounded at the dramatic changes in her behavior in the community, as contrasted with what they were used to in the institution. Upon returning to the institution from vacation, Ms. E's inappropriate behaviors immediately returned. In the weeks that followed, she asked over and over about when she would be going on vacation again.

This is one of many vignettes we could have offered in which someone was so engaged by their integrative experiences that he or she did not need to seek negative attention. Instead this person was reinforced by positive, typical social interactions, including interactions with nonhandicapped people. Also, all of the positive, adaptive social and communication skills she demonstrated on vacation serve as excellent examples of the power of learning through modeling, observation, and imitation—given the presence of strong positive expectations for growth and typical behavior. Removal from the community removed the motivation, and her institutional repertoire reemerged.

CONCLUSIONS

To summarize the lessons these vignettes have to teach, we offer the following ten points *and* words of caution.

1. A person's behavior in an institutional setting cannot be used to predict his or her behavior in a community environment, especially when that person is involved in experiences with "typical" nonhandicapped people and there is diligence in organizing the particular community experience.

2. Medical diagnoses, even severe ones, cannot and should not be used to predict someone's behavior or as a justification for segregation.

3. Our expectancies of someone, based on his or her behavior in an institutional setting (or on his or her appearance or diagnosis), should never be used as reasons to limit that person's experiences or opportunities, since institutional expectancies can be assumed to be limiting and frequently inaccurate.

4. The expectations we convey to others, regardless of the severity of their handicaps and limitations, will surely be self-fulfilling. Unless we take conscious, positive actions to liberate ourselves from our expectancies and/or from the environments which produce and reinforce them, we will not promote and support growth and development in persons who have disabilities.

5. Even in situations in which a person is severely limited, both in abilities and experiences, we should never underestimate the powerful effects that modeling and "observational learning" experiences can have.

6. A person's lack of "readiness" should not be used as an excuse to limit his or her opportunities or experiences. It is impossible to predict a person's readiness for a new experience or to predict his or her reactions or receptivity to a new experience, especially based on our knowledge of that person in the segregated, restrictive, unstimulating, nonengaging, abnormal environment of the institution.

7. Regardless of the severity or number

of handicapping conditions and/or differences in behavior or appearance that a person may exhibit, it is critical that we make every effort to minimize the impact of a person's physical and behavioral differences and that we minimize a person's need to seek negative attention.

8. People who have always been dependent and have been recipients can become contributing and helpful, given the motivation that can be provided by a secure, predictable, valuing environment. (Note too that security and predictability are not necessarily linked to familiarity. The people discussed below found security and predictability in settings which were new to them and while involved in activities which represented new experiences for them. The routine and familiarity of the institution cannot provide the stimulation or the expectations for typical valued behavior and involvement. Neither can the institution provide a controlled manageable, secure learning environment where there are consistent expectations and where a person can feel safe.)

9. In typical community settings, people become motivated to belong, to establish relationships, to act in accordance with the expectations of the environment, and to become actively engaged, at some level. Therefore, again, one cannot predict the degree to which people will be able to establish relationships or become involved in community activities based on their behavior, their energy level, or their interests in the institution.

10. We need to acknowledge that institutional environments create circumstances in which people learn deviant behaviors and have them reinforced. Because these behaviors are viewed as unacceptable in our society, their presence is then used as a rationale

for the perpetuation of the institutional model and for segregation. Billions of dollars have been, and are being invested in holding people captive in institutional settings. Until we are truly committed to ending all institutionalization, we will continue to limit and, in fact, waste the human potential of the people we purport to serve.

In all of the vignettes, a contrast between behaviors in the institution and those in an integrated setting has been drawn. In many of our examples, the differences from a person's typical responses have been nothing less than dramatic. We offer caution, lest the reader conclude that with the right goals, strategies, techniques, staffing pattern, technology, or any other system or regimen, the institutional environment can yield lasting, consistently positive results. We must emphatically point out that the institution, by its very nature, is atypical, deindividualizing, routinized, and devaluing, and therefore can only convey expectancies which are consistent with its atypical nature—both for its staff and for its clientele with disabilities. We also believe that no amount of "programming," money, reorganizational strategies, or even good intentions can make an institutional environment yield the positive results that can be gained naturally and often almost spontaneously within positive, socially integrative experiences. Neither can positive short-term gains in the community be internalized, so that the learning is permanent, if a person lives in an institutional setting. For the people who live on Team B, without exception, their institutional behaviors invariably reappeared upon return to the institution.

The history of human services has been replete with institutional settings used as the "treatment of choice" in addressing deviant behavior. It was plain to see, however, that during these brief vacations from the institution, people showed abilities and potential in areas that never would have been evidenced within the institutional setting. There was improvement in medical conditions, increases in activity levels, greater ranges of physical activity, greater behavioral control, enhanced personal appearance, improved communication skills and abilities, improved social skills, the development of social relationships and an overall increase in learning—all without the "benefit" of interdisciplinary teams: speech, physical, and occupational therapists; time-out rooms, drugs, IEPs, IHPs, or IPPs, psychologists and psychiatrists, extra money, extra staffing, and so on.

Therefore, the greatest lesson that these vignettes, and countless others we could have included, have to offer is that we all are in a position to limit or expand other people's potential with our expectations. Institutional environments, as well as other types of congregate living arrangements, by their very nature foster deviant behaviors and limit growth potential. We must not limit a person's options or deny someone the opportunity for community involvement (or, more important, for community living) based on his or her behavior within an institutional setting.

(We should note that, although we have been using the term *institution* literally, institutional environments can unfortunately be created anywhere. The same circumstances can be found wherever a living, work, or recreational environment promotes restrictiveness, regimentation, dehumanization, and deindividualization.)

These vignettes teach us what visionaries in the field have been saying for years. In the words of Burton Blatt (Blatt, Ozolins, and McNally 1979, 143):

We must evacuate the institutions for the mentally retarded. We need to empty the institutions. The quicker we accomplish that goal the quicker we will be able to repair the damage done to generations of innocent inmates. The quicker we get about converting our ideologies and resources to a community model, the quicker we will learn how to forget what we perpetrated in the name of humanity.

REFERENCES

Balla, D., & Zigler, E. (1982). Impact of institutional experience on the behavior and development of retarded persons. In E. Zigler & D. Balla (Eds.). *Mental retardation: The developmental difference controversy.* Hillsdale, NJ: Lawrence Erlbaum Associates.

Blatt, B. (1970). *Exodus from pandemonium.* Boston: Allyn & Bacon.

Blatt, B. (1973). *Souls in extremis.* Boston: Allyn & Bacon.

Blatt, B., & Kaplan, F. (1966). *Christmas in purgatory.* Boston: Allyn & Bacon.

Blatt, B., Ozolins, A., & McNally, J. (1979). *The family papers: A return to purgatory.* New York: Longman.

Bogdan, R., & Taylor, S. J. (1982). *Inside out.* Toronto: University of Toronto Press.

Edgerton, R. B. (1967). *The cloak of competence: Stigma in the lives of the mentally retarded.* Berkeley: University of California Press.

Edgerton, R. B., & Bercovici, S. M. (1976). The cloak of competence: Years later. *American Journal of Mental Deficiency, 80,* 485–497.

Edgerton, R. B., Bollinger, M., & Herr, B. (1984). The cloak of competence: After two decades. *American Journal of Mental Deficiency, 88*(4), 345–351.

Goffman, E. (1961). *Asylums.* New York: Doubleday.

Kazdin, A. E. (1977). Assessing the clinical or applied importance of behavior change through social validation. *Behavior Modification, 1*(4), 427–451.

Sigelman, C. K., Novak, A. R., Heal, L. W., & Switzky, H. N. (1980). Factors that affect the success of community placement. In A. R. Novak & L. W. Heal (Eds.), *Integration of developmentally disabled individuals into the community* (pp. 57–74). Baltimore: Paul H. Brookes.

Vail, D. J. (1967). *Dehumanization and the institutional career.* Springfield, IL: Charles C. Thomas.

Wolf, M. M. (1978). Social validity: The case for subjective measurement or how applied behavior analysis is finding its heart. *Journal of Applied Behavior Analysis, 11*(2), 203–214.

COMMUNITY RESIDENCES: ONE OPTION

The dehumanizing conditions of large residential facilities for people with mental retardation are well-documented in the literature (Blatt 1970, 1973; Blatt and Kapln 1966; Wolfensberger 1974). However, in the past, the family of a child with severe or profound mental retardation often had to decide whether to keep that child at home or to place him or her elsewhere, and in most cases, the only alternative was placement in a residential institution (MacMillan 1982). More recently, other placement alternatives have become available. There has been a dramatic shift away from large centralized institutions toward smaller community-based programs (Janicki, Mayeda, and Epple 1983). This movement was sparked by litigation (*Wyatt v. Stickney* 1971; *New York State Association for Retarded Children v. Carey* 1975) and legislation (Rehabilitation Comprehensive Services and Developmental Disabilities Act of 1978; Section 504 of the Rehabilitation Act of 1973). Coupled with the evolution of social policy in the field of mental retardation, and using the principle of normalization as its basis, the deinstitutionalization movement gained momentum. This section examines the problems and issues involved in the establishment and operation of community residence programs as one alternative to institutionalization.

Principle of Normalization

Normalization means "making available to the mentally retarded patterns and conditions of everyday life which are as close as possible to the norms and patterns of mainstream society" (Nirje 1969, 181). The normalization principle originated in 1959 when Bank-Mikkelson, head of the Danish Mental Retardation Service, wrote into Danish Law that individuls with mental retardation should live a life as close to normal as possible. However, it wasn't until 1969, when Nirje wrote the monograph *Changing Patterns in Residential Services for the Mentally Retarded* (Kugel and Wolfensberger 1969), that the principle of normalization was systematically addressed in the literature. Although the concept was later expanded and supported by Wolfensberger (1969) in the United States, the best efforts at providing normalized environments for persons with mental retardation have been in Sweden and Denmark (Bank-Mikkelson 1968; Dybwad 1970; Nirje 1969).

Normalization means more than merely placing a person with mental retardation in a normalized environment; in addition, systematic support services must be provided (Drew, Logan, and Hardman 1984). It is possible for a person with mental retardation to be part of a community in the physical sense, but not necessarily in the social and psychological sense (Edgerton, Eyman, and Silverstein 1975). Deinstitutionalization should be a gradual process where the person with mental retardation is prepared for community living (Turnbull and Turnbull 1975), and the community is prepared for the individual. Activities that we often take for granted—such as shopping, washing clothes, and crossing streets—must be taught to individuals with mental retardation who are being placed in a community living situation. Life in the community should provide the mentally retarded person with identity, dignity, and the motivation for community involvement (Shapiro 1973).

Community Residences

Community residence programs have become the most widely used placement alternative to institutionalization for adults who are mentally retarded (Heward and Orlansky 1984). As of 1982, for example, the institutional population had decreased from 190,000 to 130,000 in a ten-year period (NYSOMRDD 1982). It is clear that if this trend continues, the need for community residence programs will increase (Janicki, Mayeda, and Epple 1983). Bruininks, Hauber, and Kudla (1980) reported that in 1977, a total of 23,500 mentally retarded persons were residing in community-based programs. And Janicki, Mayeda, and Epple (1983) indicated that in 1982, there were more than 5,700 small-community residences (6,300 if larger community residences were considered) in the United States—an increase of over 900 percent since 1972. In addition, they found that almost 43,000 (58,000 if larger community residences were counted) persons now lived in community residences, an increase of 183 percent over the 1977 survey figures compiled by Bruininks et al. (1980). Although the number of community residences varies from state to state, O'Connor (1976) stated that nearly one-half of all community residences were located in only six states. In a Delphi Survey, Putnam and Bruininks (1986) forecasted that this trend toward community-based programs would not lose momentum, although others (Bruininks 1981; Conroy 1977; Thorsheim and Bruininks 1978) have predicted that institutional readmissions would continue to increase or remain at a very high rate.

Community residence programs vary in size, purpose, location, staff and philosophy. As a result, definitions of community residences vary considerably. O'Connor and Sitkei (1975, 35) define a community residence as a "facility that operates twenty-four hours a day to provide services to a small group of disabled people who are presently or potentially capable of functioning in a community setting with some degree of independence." The key point to note in this definition is the fact that persons who are disabled must be able to function in the community with some degree of independence; not everyone is qualified for community residence placement. Studies by O'Connor (1976) and by Bruininks, Hauber, and Kudla (1980) indicate that mildly mentally retarded individuals predominate in community-based programs. Eymann and Borthwick (1980) found that residents of community-based programs had an average IQ of 48, whereas those persons residing in institutions had an average IQ of 25. In addition, persons in community residence programs demonstrated better self-help skills and fewer behavior problems. However, this does not necessarily limit community residences to mildly mentally retarded people, although it does indicate the need to prepare people for the experience before they are moved to the community.

Community Residences and Normalization

As stated earlier in this section, normalization means more than merely placing a mentally retarded person in the community. Poorly managed community residences can have environments just as impersonal and debilitating as those of institutions (MacMillan 1982). Roos (1970) describes normalized environments as homelike. This, in contrast to institutional placement, means that residents would be provided with private bathroom facilities, small dining areas and smaller living units. In explaining what makes community residences more normalized than institutions, Wolfensberger (1972) describes them as integrated, small, separated from day programming, designed for various age groups with various levels of supervision available, and part of a continuum of services.

In an attempt to evaluate the degree to which a service system is providing a normalized environment, Wolfensberger and Glenn (1975) developed Program Analyses of Services Systems (PASS), an assessment device designed to determine the degree to which human services fit the normalization philosophy. Unfortunately, PASS is based on white, middle-class values, which tend to dominate the definition of what is "normal" (Landesman-Dwyer 1981). Pieper and Cappuccilli (1980, 52–54) suggest the following set of questions, based on PASS, to determine how normalized a community residence program is. The residence would be considered normalized if all or most of these questions could be answered "Yes."

- Did the residents choose to live in the home?
- Is this type of setting usually inhabited by people in the residents' age group?
- Do the residents live with others their own age?
- Is the home located within a residential neighborhood?
- Does the residence look like the other dwellings around it?
- Can the number of people living in the residence reasonably be expected to assimilate into the community?
- Are community resources and facilities readily accessible from the residence?
- Do the residents have a chance to buy the house?
- Do the managers of the place act in an appropriate manner toward the residents?
- Are the residents encouraged to do all they can for themselves?
- Are the residents encourged to have personal belongings that are appropriate to their age?
- Are residents encouraged to use community resources as much as possible?
- Are all the residents' rights acknowledged?
- Are the residents being given enough training and assistance to help them be growing, developing individuals?
- Would I want to live in the home? Here is the final test. If the residence appears good enough for you to want to live in it, it will probably be an appropriate living arrangement for persons with special needs. We should demand residential arrangements for persons with special needs that are comparable to those inhabited by most nondisabled citizens.

O'Connor (1976) notes that architectural features of the building, security, personal effects in the sleeping area, privacy in the bedrooms and bathrooms, institutional or homelike furniture, and the evaluator's judgment of the general management and atmosphere of the facility are also important criteria to consider when determining whether a community residence program is normalized. Using these criteria, O'Connor evaluated 611 community residence programs and found that 69 percent were normalized. Larger residences were generally less likely to be normalized, while those with a high staff-to-resident ratio were more likely to be normalized.

Community Residence Programs: Problems and Issues

The growth of community residence programs has fostered problems which threaten their continued existence. Opponents to deinstitutionalization range from neighbors of proposed community residences to professionals who are cautious about endorsing a concept that lacks an empirical data base (Zigler 1977). Several factors identified in the literature may affect the successful placement of individuals with mental retardation in community residence programs. Some of the more significant variables include the lack of community support, residents' behavior, size of the residence, and funding.

The first major obstacle to the development of community residence programs is the lack of community support. Residents believe that if mentally retarded persons are introduced into the community, crime rates will rise, property values will decrease, and the neighborhood will change for the worse (Sigelman, Spanhel, and Lorenzen 1979). Berdiansky and Parker (1977) found that residents in North Carolina opposed development of community residences because they feared physical danger to their families and the possibility of sexually deviant behavior among retarded persons. Various studies have shown that the inability of mentally retarded persons to adjust to community placement is related to maladaptive behavior (Close 1977). However, Crawford, Aiello, and Thompson (1979) indicate that research investigating resident characteristics is often contradictory and inconclusive. Windle, Stewart, and Brown (1961) report that the lack of support services is as much to blame as individuals' behavior.

In some localities, the introduction of community residences has led to legislated zoning obstacles (Howse and Albert 1982). Heal, Sigelman, and Switzky (1978) report that community oppposition may occur even after preliminary surveys indicate community acceptance. Even when efforts are made to prepare the community for a new residence, the likelihood of opposition is great (Baker, Seltzer, and Seltzer 1974; Seltzer 1984). As a result, some developers have opted for a Machiavellian approach in establishing community residences. The developer makes secret arrangements for the home to be built, then presents it to the community after the fact. The developers hope that the community will see that the residents are harmless, and will therefore feel less resistance (Berdiansky and Parker 1977).

Despite community concerns, Sigelman, Spanhel, and Lorenzen (1979) report there is little evidence to support the suggestion that crime rates will increase or property values decrease when residence programs are brought into a community. In fact, property values have been known to increase because of the care given to community residences (Landesman-Dwyer 1981; Ryan and Coyne 1985).

In relation to size of community residences, O'Connor (1976) found that homes with fewer than twenty residents were more normalized than facilities having more than twenty. However, opponents to community residence programs argue that smaller isn't necessarily better. Some small community residence programs have been found to be more restrictive than larger homes (Butler and Bjaanes 1978), while others approximate small institutions (Thorne 1979). Further, size of a community residence is not necessarily related to the quality of care (Bercovici 1981; Hull and Thompson 1980). Other factors such as staff-residence responsibilities and staff commitment need to be considered (Baroff 1980). Landesman-Dwyer (1981) suggests that the size of a community residence be evaluated in relation to the mentally retarded person's age, past experience, ability level and current life situation. She further states that there simply isn't enough data to support the concept that smaller is better.

In a national survey of over two thousand community residence administrators, Bruininks et al. (1980), found that funding was a major management problem. In a similar survey, O'Connor and Sitkei (1975) reported that inadequate funds were the highest ranked problem facing the establishment and operation of community residence programs. With the current federal administration's goal of containing the growth and current spending within human service fields, the future of community residence programs remains uncertain (Fiorelli 1982). Some studies have shown that the cost of care within community residence programs is far less than in institutions (Landesman-Dwyer 1981), while others have indicated that the cost is comparable (Bensberg and Smith 1984; Retish, Hoy, and Boaz 1978). Bruininks, Hauber, and Kudla (1980) note that community residences with fewer than twenty residents are more cost effective than those with more than twenty residents. Amid debates over which type of facility is more expensive to operate, what is often overlooked is the fact that little evidence suggests that program budgets are correlated to the amount of quality of services provided (Balla, Butterfield, and Zigler 1974; King, Raynes, and Tizard 1971).

Despite the representative problems and issues described in this section, the number of community residence programs is increasing and that increase is expected to continue (Putnam and Bruininks 1986). Blatt, Ozolins, and McNally (1979, 144) report that positive changes have been made in institutions, but conclude that dehumanizing conditions will remain as long as institutions exist, stating that

> . . . we demand that every institution for the mentally retarded in the United States be closed. We insist that a society which claims to be civilized can find the proper ways and means to include the people who have been institutional inmates in decent community environments. The inmates have suffered enough. Society has done enough damage.

In order to successfully accomplish the process of deinstitutionalization, a carefully prescribed transition program must be developed to adequately prepare the individual for community living and the community for the individual.

REFERENCES

Baker, B. L., Seltzer, G. B., & Seltzer, M. M. (1974). *As close as possible: Community residences for retarded adults*. Boston: Little, Brown & Co.

Balla, D. A., Butterfield, E. C., & Zigler, E. (1974). Effects of institutionalization on retarded children: A longitudinal cross-institutional investigation. *American Journal of Mental Deficiency, 78,* 530–549.

Bank-Mikkelson, N. E. (1968). Services for mentally retarded children in Denmark. *Children, 5,* 198–200.

Baroff, G. S. (1980). On size and the quality of residential care: A second look. *Mental Retardation, 18,* 113–117.

Bensberg, G., & Smith, J. (1984). Comparative costs of public residential and community residential facilities for the mentally retarded. *Education and Training of the Mentally Retarded, 19,* 45–48.

Becovici, S. M. (1981). Qualitative methods and cultural perspectives in the study of deinstitutionalization. In R. H. Bruininks, C. E. Meyers, B. B. Sigford, & R. C. Lakin (Eds.), *Deinstitutionalization and community adjustment of mentally retarded people.* (Monograph No. 4). Washington, D.C.: American Association on Mental Deficiency.

Berdiansky, H. A., & Parker, R. (1977). Establishing a group home for the mentally retarded in North Carolina. *Mental Retardation, 15,* 8–11.

Blatt, B. (1970). *Exodus from pandemonium.* Boston: Allyn & Bacon.

Blatt, B. (Ed.) (1973). *Souls in extremis.* Boston: Allyn & Bacon.

Blatt, B., & Kaplan, F. (1966). *Christmas in Purgatory.* Boston: Allyn & Bacon.

Blatt, B., Ozolins, A., & McNally, J. (1979). *The family papers: A return to purgatory.* New York: Longman, Inc.

Bruininks, R. H. (1981). *Alternatives for development or defeat: A symposium on research and residential environments.* Paper presented at the Annual Meeting of the American Association on Mental Deficiency, Detroit, MI.

Bruininks, R. H., Hauber, F. A., Kudla, M. J. (1980). National survey of community residential facilities: A profile of facilities and residents in 1977. *American Journal of Mental Deficiency, 84,* 470–478.

Bruininks, R. H., Kudla, N. J., Wieck, C. A., & Hauber, F. A. (1980). Management problems in community residential facilities. *Mental Retardation, 18,* 125–130.

Butler, E. W., & Bjaanes, A. T. (1978). Activities and the use of time by retarded persons in community care facilities. In G. P. Sackett (Ed.), *Observing behavior, Volume I: Theory and applications in mental retardation.* Baltimore: University Park Press.

Close, D. W. (1977). Community living for severely and profoundly retarded adults: A group home study. *Education and Training of the Mentally Retarded, 12,* 256–261.

Conroy, T. (1977). Trends in deinstitutionalization of the mentally retarded. *Mental Retardation, 15,* 44–46.

Crawford, J. L., Aiello, J. R., & Thompson, D. E. (1979). Deinstitutionalization and community placement: Clinical and environmental factors. *Mental Retardation, 7,* 59–63.

Drew, C. J., Logan, D. R., & Hardman, M. J. (1984). *Mental retardation: A life cycle approach.* St. Louis: Times Mirror/Mosby.

Dybwad, G. (1970). Architecture's role in revitalizing the field of mental retardation. *Journal of Mental Subnormality, 16,* 1.

Edgerton, R. B., Eyman, R. K., & Silverstein, A. B. (1975). Mental retardation system. In N. Hobbs (Ed.), *Issues in the classification of children.* (Vol. 2). San Francisco: Jossey-Bass.

Eyman, R. K., & Borthwick, S. A. (1980). Patterns of care for mentally retarded persons. *Mental Retardation, 18,* 63–66.

Fiorelli, J. S. (1982). Community residential services during the 1980s: Challenges and future trends. *The Journal of the Association for the Severely Handicapped, 7,* 14–18.

Heal, L. W., Sigelman, C. K., & Switzky, H. N. (1978). Research on community residential alternatives for the mentally retarded. In N. R. Ellis (Ed.), *International review of research in mental retardation.* (Vol. 9). New York: Academic Press.

Heward, W. L., & Orlansky, M. D. (1984). *Exceptional Children* (2nd ed.). Columbus, Ohio: Charles E. Merrill.

Howse, J. L., & Albert, C. L. (1982). Locating community residences: A matter of home and family. *Proceedings of the Conference on International Assessment of Attitudes and Services for the Developmentally Disabled.* New York: Young Adult Institute Workshop, Inc.

Hull, J. T., & Thompson, J. C. (1980). Predicting adaptive functioning of mentally retarded persons in community settings. *American Journal of Mental Deficiency, 85,* 253–261.

Janicki, M. P., Mayeda, T., & Epple, W. A. (1983). Availability of group homes for persons with mental retardation in the United States. *Mental Retardation, 21,* 45–51.

King, R. D., Raynes, N. V., & Tizard, T. (1971). *Patterns of residential care: Sociological studies in institutions for handicapped children.* London: Routledge & Kegan Paul.

Kugel, R., & Wolfensberger, W. (Eds.). (1969). *Changing patterns in residential services for the mentally retarded.* Washington, D.C.: President's Committee on Mental Retardation.

Landesman-Dwyer, S. (1981). Living in the community. *American Journal of Mental Deficiency, 86,* 223–234.

MacMillan, D. L. (1982). *Mental retardation in school and society* (2nd ed.). Boston: Little, Brown and Company.

New York State Association for Retarded Children v. Carey. 383 F. Suppl. 715 (E. D., N.Y.), 1975.

NYSOMRDD (1982). *A comparison of New York's deinstitutionalization program with nationwide trends.* (Planning Unit Report 82–05). Albany, NY: New York State Office of Mental Retardation and Developmental Disabilities.

Nirje, B. (1969). The normalization principle and its human management implications. In R. B. Kugel & W. Wolfensberger (Eds.). *Changing patterns in residential services for the mentally retarded.* Washington, D.C.: President's Committee on Mental Retardation.

O'Connor, G. (1976). Home is a good place: A national perspective of community residential facilities for developmentally disabled persons. (Monograph No. 4). Washington, D.C.: American Association of Mental Deficiency.

O'Connor, G., & Sitkei, G. (1975). Study of a new frontier in community services. Residential facilities for the developmentally disabled. *Mental Retardation, 13,* 35–39.

Pieper, B., & Cappuccilli, J. (1980). Beyond the family and the institution. The sanctity of liberty. In T. Apolloni, J. Cappuccilli, & T. P. Cooke (Eds.), *Achievements in residential services for persons with disabilities: Toward excellence.* Baltimore: University Park Press.

Putnam, J. W., & Bruininks, R. H. (1986). Future directions in deinstitutionalization and education: A delphi investigation. *Exceptional Children, 53,* 55–62.

Retish, P., Hoy, M., & Boaz, B. (1978). Systems unlimited—Normalization exemplified. *Mental Retardation, 15,* 313–316.

Roos, P. (1970). Normalization, dehumanization, and conditioning: Conflict or harmony? *Mental Retardation, 8,* 12–14.

Ryan, C. S., & Coyne, A. (1985). Effects of group homes on neighborhood property values. *Mental Retardation, 5,* 241–245.

Seltzer, M. (1984). Correlates of community opposition to community residences for mentally retarded persons. *American Journal of Mental Deficiency, 89,* 1–8.

Shapiro, H. (1973). Circle of homes for the retarded in Cuyahoga County. *Mental Retardation, 11,* 19–21.

Sigelman, C. K., Spanhel, C. L., & Lorenzen, C. D. (1979). Community reactions to deinstitutionalization: Crime, property values, and other bugbears. *Journal of Rehabilitation, 45,* 52–54.

Thorne, J. M. (1979). Deinstitutionalization: Too wide a swath. *Mental Retardation, 17,* 171–175.

Thorsheim, M. J., & Bruininks, R. H. (1978). *Admission and readmission of mentally retarded people to residential facilities.* Minneapolis: University of Minnesota, Department of Psychoeducational Studies.

Turnbull, H. R., & Turnbull, A. P. (1975). Deinstitutionalization and the law. *Mental Retardation, 13,* 14–20.

Windle, C. D., Stewart, E., & Brown, S. (1961). Reasons for community failure of released patients. *American Journal of Mental Deficiency, 66,* 213–217.

Wolfensberger, W. (1969). The origin and nature of our institutional models. In R. B. Kugel & W. Wolfensberger (Eds.), *Changing patterns in residential services for the mentally retarded.* Washington, D.C.: U.S. Government Printing Office.

Wolfensberger, W. (1972). *The principle of normalization in human services.* Toronto: National Institute on Mental Retardation.

Wolfensberger, W. (1974). *The origin and nature of our institutional modes.* Syracuse, New York: Human Policy Press.

Wolfensberger, W., & Glenn, L. (1975). *Program analysis of service systems.* Toronto, Canada: National Institute on Mental Retardation.

Wyatt v. Stickney. 325 F. Suppl. 781 (M.D., Ala.), 1971.

Zigler, E. (1977). Twenty years of mental retardation research. *Mental Retardation, 15,* 52.

DISCUSSION QUESTIONS

1. Do you feel that *all* mentally retarded persons should be integrated into the community? Why?
2. Are mentally retarded adults being adequately prepared for community living? Why? What could be done to improve their preparation?
3. Do you feel that communities are being adequately prepared for the integration of mentally retarded individuals? Why? What could be done to prepare communities better?
4. What current attitudes in society lead to the rejection of community-based programs? How might you change these attitudes?
5. The community in which you live is very hesitant to allow the establishment of a community residence program. You have been asked to attend an open hearing on the topic. What would you say to the individuals present at this meeting?
6. Should state institutions for the mentally retarded be completely abolished as suggested by some professionals? Why?

Public Reactions to Housing for the Mentally Retarded

Jerome Margolis
Thalia Charitonidis

MacMillan (1977) has indicated that mentally retarded individuals have suffered personal indignity and have been shunted aside and segregated by society. Within the last few years, this state of affairs has slowly improved, as evidenced both by legislative commitment and by judicial decisions which support the rights of the handicapped individual. Yet the existence of a legal and philosophical commitment does not necessarily guarantee a positive change in public attitudes.

Findings of Mamula and Newman (1973) and Trippi, Michael, Colao, and Alvarez (1978) have shown that at least with respect to housing the public's negative attitudes have interfered with the right of handicapped individuals to live on an independent basis. In contrast, studies by Gallup (1976) and Kastner, Repucci, and Pezzoli (1979) have obtained findings in direct opposition. In each of those studies, more than 75 percent of the individuals surveyed indicated that they would not object to an educable, mildly, or moderately retarded person residing in their neighborhood.

It has become evident that equivocal information exists with regard to public reactions toward housing for mentally retarded individuals. Consequently, the focus of this study is to assess the true state of affairs with respect to prevailing community attitudes toward individualized housing for mentally retarded persons.

PARTICIPANTS

Survey participants numbered eighty individuals identified as either landlords or agents responsible for the rental of rooms or apartments advertised in local newspapers. The geographic area under consideration included the greater part of the eastern coast of New Jersey extending from the Oranges in the north to Lakewood and Toms River in the south. Both low and middle income communities were included in this study.

PROCEDURE

This research was designed to encompass three variables which might influence the attitudes of the respondents questioned: caller status (social worker vs. sibling); sexual status of the retarded individual (male vs. female); and the socioeconomic status of the dwelling location (low vs. middle). Each participant was randomly assigned to a combination of the three conditions, creating a design which allowed for an equal number of individuals in each of the categorical variables cited.

Telephone contact was made with each respondent on two separate occasions. The first call, initiated by a female interviewer, verified the availability of the advertised apartment. If the response was positive, data were obtained concerning monthly rent, utilities, lease and security arrangements, and food store proximity (i.e., within walking distance). The second call, completed by a male assuming the role of either the retarded individual's sibling or social worker, was made approximately twenty to thirty minutes later. The following oral statement was used:

I am calling about your advertisement in the newspaper. I am calling for my brother/sister/client who is a young, mentally retarded adult who has just completed a rehabilitation program and has secured a job in the (specific geographical location) area. I was wondering if your apartment was still available.

Throughout the study, when required, the retarded individual was described as having the following characteristics: twenty-four years old, no physically disabling condition, no gross visual stigmata, and differing from the norm in his or her ability to learn or understand information (i.e., slow learner).

A response was considered positive when no discrepancies were found in the comparison of data recorded from the first and second calls. Any attempt to discourage the second caller from pursuing the rental of the apartment was scored as a negative attitudinal response.

RESULTS

Of the eighty individuals surveyed, 58, or 72.5 percent, indicated a willingness to accept a mentally retarded individual as a tenant. Employing a chi square analysis for discontinuous data, it was found that none of the categorical variables employed yielded significant differences (caller status: X^2 = 0.000, df = 1.p > .05; sexual status of the retarded individual: X^2 = 2.257, df = 1, p > .05; socioeconomic status; X^1 = 0.251, df = 1. p > .05).

DISCUSSION

It is encouraging to note that the current findings support those of Gallup (1976) and Kastner et al. (1979), and differ substantially from those of Trippi et al. (1978). Nevertheless, stereotypic attitudes toward the retarded were evidenced by those individuals who responded negatively to the housing inquiry. Specific concerns centered around the careless and destructive tendencies that are often attributed to mentally retarded persons. Other expressed attitudes included a perceived threat to personal safety, a projected decline in property value, and fear of a retarded person's "visibility," which might cause the neighborhood to be less attractive.

From a pragmatic point of view, family members and social workers associated with retarded individuals can look forward to a more favorable climate in terms of residential housing. It will therefore be necessary for them to direct their efforts toward fostering a greater degree of autonomous behavior in the handicapped person. In addition, professional educators will have the onus of developing programs (Crnic & Pym 1979) which will nurture necessary independent living skills required for successful normalization to occur (Wolfensberger 1972).

REFERENCES

Crnic, K. A., & Pym, H. A. Training mentally retarded adults in independent living skills. *Mental Retardation*, 1979, 17, 13–16.

Gallup, G. Organization report for the President's Committee on Mental Retardation. *Public attitudes regarding mental retardation*. In R. Nathon (Ed.), *Mental retardation: Century of decision*. Washington, DC: US Government Printing Office, 1976. (No. 040-000-00343-6.)

Kastner, L. S., Reppucci, N. D., & Pezzoli, J. J. Assessing community attitudes toward mentally retarded persons. *American Journal of Mental Deficiency*, 1979, 84, 137–144.

MacMillan, D. *Mental retardation in school and society*. Boston: Little, Brown & Co., 1977.

Mamula, R. A., & Newman, N. *Community placement of the mentally retarded*. Springfield IL: Charles C. Thomas, 1973.

Trippi, J., Michael, R., Colao, A., & Alvarez, A. Housing discrimination toward mentally retarded persons. *Exceptional Children*, 1978, 44, 430–433.

Wolfensberger, W. *The principle of normalization in human services*. Toronto: National Institute on Mental Retardation, 1972.

CHAPTER 6

Assessment Issues

INTRODUCTION

Special educators have long debated the efficacy of labels. Some professionals argue that labeling a child *mentally retarded, emotionally disturbed,* or *learning disabled* does not provide special educators with any information regarding the child's instructional needs. Other professionals argue that labeling is necessary for obtaining services for handicapped children and for acquiring funds to support these services.

The first section of this chapter, *Labeling and Classification of Handicapped Children,* begins with a discussion of the arguments for and against labeling and proceeds to a review of the research on the effects of labels on students and teachers. Alternatives to our present system of labeling and classification are also presented. Included is a reprint of the article *The Implications of the Language of Mental Retardation For LD* by the late Dr. Burton Blatt, a prolific writer, who addressed the use of labels in special education.

In addition, section two, *Nondiscriminatory Assessment: A Legal Perspective* covers nondiscriminatory assessment, an issue closely interrelated with the labeling process. This issue is approached from a legal perspective, beginning with an overview of landmark court cases and their implications for assessment. Guidelines and procedures for use when making assessment and placement decisions are also discussed. The chapter concludes with a reprint of an article entitled *Nondiscriminatory Assessment: A Formative Model* by James Ysseldyke and Richard Regan. The authors present their proposal for a model of nondiscriminatory assessment within the context of instructional intervention.

As with many of the issues and practices discussed in this text, there is no easy resolution to the problem of labeling. Labels have been in existence for decades and perhaps will remain for decades to come. We have come a long way from the use of such labels as *idiot, imbecile,* and *moron,* but more work must be done before we can either divest ourselves of labels altogether or at least develop labels capable of serving some without hurting others.

LABELING AND CLASSIFICATION OF HANDICAPPED CHILDREN

Labeling and classification are social acts that can serve to either place children in supportive interventions or identify them as abnormal individuals who need to be removed from community life (Reynolds 1984). These two diverse outcomes of labeling have resulted in much controversy about the effects of labeling. The importance of this issue was reflected by Hobbs (1975, 1) when he stated that "nothing less than the futures of children is at stake." However, while criticizing many elements of labeling, Hobbs also noted that without categories and labels all complex communicating and thinking stop.

Professionals, and a large segment of society in general, have rebelled against simplistic categorizations of people. In requesting a review of this practice, then U.S. Secretary of Health, Education, and Welfare Elliot Richardson called attention to the inappropriate labeling of children which had serious consequences for the child. This Project on Classification of Exceptional Children led to the publication of *The Futures of Children,* and a systematic review of the labeling of children (Hobbs 1975). The negatively loaded terminology used in the field of special education, i.e., mentally *retarded,* emotionally *disturbed,* socially *maladjusted,* learning *disabled,* hearing *impaired,* has resulted in widespread criticism of these labeling practices (Reynolds and Balow 1972).

While acknowledging that the complexities of this issue go beyond the scope of this section, the topics that will be discussed include arguments for and against labeling, an overview of the research on the effects of labeling on students and teachers, and alternatives to the current system of labeling and classification. Indepth coverage of many of these areas can be found in Hobbs (1975), MacMillan and Meyers (1979), Reynolds (1984), and Ysseldyke and Algozzine (1982).

Support for Labeling

Most authors agree that while the systems currently used to categorize and group children may be unsatisfactory, some forms of labels are essential, since they draw attention to the group they are designed to identify and permit an organized response to that group (Lucas 1974). Hobbs (1975, 13) states that "classification is essential to providing services for children, and a label may be a child's ticket to getting help."

Arguments supporting labeling strongly relate to the need to obtain services for students and to raise money for those services. As noted by Hallahan and Kauffman (1982), labeling tends to highlight problems for the public, resulting in more successful fundraising. While perhaps not the way it should be, the reality is that taxpayers may react more sympathetically and be more willing to support services for labeled groups. Also, local and federal support for special education services are both tied to categorical labels; in order to receive monies, children receiving special education services must be labeled. Historically, the aid to education formulas did not benefit handicapped children until they became identifiable through categorization (Lucas 1974).

Other often-voiced reasons for the use of labels with handicapped children have included facilitating communication among professionals, identifying common groups for research and advocacy activities, rallying volunteer organizations, encouraging the passage of legislation, and designing and evaluating programs (Hallahan and Kauffman 1982; Hobbs 1975; Reynolds 1984). In addition, labeling may help people tolerate differences; for example, Gottlieb and Leyser (1981) and Yeates and Weisz (1985) suggest that labels may help the general public justify and accept some inappropriate or helpless behaviors. It has also been hypothesized that belonging to an identified group may help labeled individuals to view themselves positively. For example, a physically handicapped person could compare his motor skills to those of other disabled people, rather than to those of able-bodied individuals. In general, those who support labeling state that labels do serve a descriptive purpose and will therefore continue to be applied in some form even if we change the present terminology.

Opposition to Labeling

Much of the controversy surrounding the use of labels focuses on the allegation that labels stigmatize, stereotype, and reflect a prejudicial attitude toward some individuals (Hallahan and Kauffman 1982; Lucas 1974; Reynolds and Balow 1972). Hobbs (1975, 3) cautions that "children who are categorized and labeled as different may be permanently stigmatized, rejected by adults and other children, and excluded from opportunities essential for their full and healthy development." Since many more ethnic minority children (than white children) are labeled, questions have been raised about this potentially discriminatory practice and about whether school officials use social class, race, and home environment in an arbitrary way when labeling children (Hallahan and Kauffman 1982; Smith et al. 1986).

Another concern is that labeling is a type of intellectual laziness that indicates a reluctance to make difficult educational decisions. Lucas (1974) emphasizes that labeling puts the burden of failure on the student, rather than on the school or society, and Reynolds and Balow (1972) state that labels can be used as an excuse for poor educational programs. Mercer (1970) notes that a label may be viewed as an inherent attribute of the person, rather than a means of categorizing that person within the larger social environment. Similar thoughts are expressed by Blatt (1985) who states that such labels as *learning disabilities, mental retardation,* and *mental illness* are only inventions, and that a person is only "learning disabled" or "mentally retarded" because some official has designated him as such.

The use of labels and categories may encourage the perception that all people within a category have the same personality and behavioral characteristics, when in reality, labeled individuals differ as much from one another as their nonlabeled peers (Hallahan and Kauffman 1982). Newcomer (1985) warns that the dichotomous labeling of children as either having or not having a handicapping condition encourages the assumption that all labeled children have the same negative qualities—for example, inattentiveness or task avoidance. Labeling tends to homogenize children (Lucas 1974) when there is little research to indicate that children within the same category share the same needs or that being given a different label indicates need for a different instructional program (Heller, Holtzman, and Messick 1982; Potter et al. 1983).

Problems also occur when people attach conflicting meanings to labels. At present, the system used for classification is based on either exclusionary or inclusionary principles, and students are placed in categories to the extent that they display or don't display certain characteristics (Ysseldyke, Algozzine, and Epps 1983). While classification systems "should have clear definitions" (Cromwell, Blashfield, and Strauss 1975, 14), this does not always happen. For example, Ysseldyke, Algozzine and Epps (1983) report that 85 percent of the normal students in their sample could have been classified as learning disabled using the definitions and criteria for this category, and 4 percent of their sample of learning disabled students did not meet any of the criteria for the learning disabled category. Many argue that if labels tend to be influenced by stereotypes, if they are of questionable reliability, and if they yield little useful information, then their use should be reevaluated (Hobbs 1975; Lucas 1974; Ysseldyke, Algozzine, and Richey 1982).

The final major concern about the use of labels has existed since Dunn (1968) asserted that labeling and placing mildly handicapped students in special classes could have possible negative effects on students' self-concepts. While most literature reviews on the effects of labeling have been inconclusive (Gottlieb and Leyser 1981; Hallahan and Kauffman 1982; MacMillan, Jones, and Aloia 1974), and have led to conflicting interpretations, the following sections will present an overview of some of the research studies on the effects of labeling on both students and teachers or other adults.

Effects of Labeling on Students

The classic article often cited when the effects of labeling are being discussed is the Rosenthal and Jacobsen (1968) study, from which emerged the term *Rosenthal effect* to designate a self-fulfilling prophecy. While often criticized for methodological flaws (Snow 1969; Thorndike 1968), this study reported that when teachers were told that certain students in their classes were potential bloomers, those students achieved higher scores on tests than the rest of the class. Rosenthal and Jacobsen believed these differences were a result of expectancy cues that the teachers conveyed to the children. Although attempts to replicate this study have not been successful (Fleming and Anttonen 1971; Hallahan and Kauffman 1982), it provided the basis for much research.

The results of subsequent studies have not been as dramatic as Rosenthal and Jacobsen's, nor have results always been consistent. While some researchers have found lower self-concepts in labeled students (Margalit and Zak 1984; Rogers and Saklofske 1985), others report no differences (Silverman and Zigmond 1983; Stone 1984). In most of these studies, methodological problems make the results difficult to interpret. These studies, while only representative of the available literature, indicate the inconclusiveness of results.

Rogers and Saklofske (1985) and Margalit and Zak (1984) compared the self-concepts of nondisabled and labeled learning disabled children and reported that the labeled students had lower self-concepts. In addition, the labeled students took less responsibility for their academic success or failure, and had lower expectations for their future performance (Rogers and Saklofske 1985). When examining both academic and general self-concepts of students labeled as *mentally retarded, learning disabled,* or *normal,* Carroll, Friedrich, and Hand (1984) concluded that the labeled children had lower self-concepts.

On the other hand, Silverman and Zigmond (1983) compared the self-concepts of labeled and nonlabeled adolescents and reported that the labeled students did not have a lower self-concept than the nonlabeled group. Similar effects were also demonstrated in a study by Stone (1984). Coleman (1983) found no differences on self-concept measures between handicapped and nonhandicapped children or between children placed in resource rooms and self-contained classes. However, it was noted that students who stayed in the regular class while experiencing academic problems had the lowest self-concepts. Using social comparison theory, Coleman hypothesized that it was not the label itself that caused poor self-concept, but rather, not having similar others to use as a comparison group.

While researchers have also examined the effects of labels on the attitudes of nonhandicapped children towards labeled children, MacMillan, Jones, and Aloia (1974, 247), in a literature review, note that the "evidence of the effect of labeling on peer acceptance is open to several conflicting interpretations." Research on the effects of labels as they are used in the schools is equivocal, and authors have discussed the difficulty in separating the effects of actual behavior that might influence attitudes of other children from the effects of the label itself (Reynolds 1984). All school programs are not the same, and while some programs may result in less stigmatizing of labeled children (Johnson and Johnson 1981), it is difficult to make any generalizations (Reynolds 1984).

Effects of Labeling on Teachers and Other Adults

Many studies have indicated that most of us tend to view labeled people differently from nonlabeled people (Foster and Keech 1977; Foster, Ysseldyke, and Reese 1975; Hallahan and Kauffman 1982) and that one's expectations can be biased by labels. Ysseldyke, Algozzine, and Richey (1982) reported that decisionmakers in schools had inordinately high estimates of the number of handicapped students and might be influenced by their expectations.

One approach that has been taken by many researchers in trying to ascertain the effects of labels is providing people with descriptions of hypothetical students, differing only on misinformation about the student's label or lack of label. While the research does indicate that this type of information can bias expectations, there is no conclusive evidence how this information influences the labeled person (Hallahan and Kauffman 1982).

This type of misinformation study has been conducted with teachers, employers, and other adults. Rolison and Medway (1986), for example, investigated the effects of varied information about a hypothetical male student on the expectations of 180 classroom teachers, and noted that the teachers had higher expectations when the student had no label, or was labeled *learning disabled,* than when the student was labeled *mentally retarded.* Schloss and Schloss (1984) used mock resumes to determine employers' expectations regarding individuals with varied handicapping labels. Employers were asked to predict the potential success on the job of a person enrolled in a regular high school program, an educational program for deaf students, or a program for mentally retarded individuals. Interpreting employers' responses as reflecting society's attitudes towards retarded people, Schloss and Schloss reported that the managers had higher expectations for the normal and deaf applicants than the mentally retarded job seekers. In another study using a mock report with the only difference being the labels *institutionalized* or *regular school student,* Schloss and Miller (1982) clearly demonstrated that public school teachers had different expectations based on only the changed label. The teachers recommended different curricula for the students when the label was changed and had lower expectations of long-term success for students labeled *institutionalized.*

While there is not necessarily any connection between a student's label and what he or she can actually do, people who work with exceptional children may derive negative expectations from labels which interfere with the student-teacher relationship (Reynolds and Balow 1972). Yeates and Weisz (1985) suggest that adults tend to expect helpless behavior from children labeled *mentally retarded.* They state that "generally, failures by retarded children are strongly ascribed to low ability, whereas those by nonretarded children were ascribed to low effort" (349). These studies suggest that new ways of classifying students may be necessary if they are to receive appropriate services. Several suggested ways to do this will be reviewed.

Alternatives to Present System of Labeling

In *The Futures of Children,* Hobbs (1975, 5) rejects the notion of abandoning all classification, and argues for "more precise categories and for more discriminating ways of describing children in order to plan appropriate programs for them" . . . and "safeguards to decrease the deleterious effects of classification procedures that can, in fact, have many beneficial outcomes." Lucas (1974) states that confusion occurs when psychometric performance, causative diagnosis, and etiology are all considered in labeling children, and stresses that the only relevant criteria for educators is what the student can and will do, and the implications this has for providing instruction. Related to this, Reynolds and Balow (1972) propose an alternative system that avoids placing stigmatizing labels on students and focuses on enhancing instruction. They suggest labeling the instructional systems or the teachers (i.e., the teaching laboratory or the resource teacher), rather than the children, to reflect the special programs and those who deliver them. This recommendation also emphasizes the need to base training on the competencies teachers need (skills in transcribing Braille, or mobility instruction) instead of on the characteristics of the students they teach (teacher of the blind).

Years ago, when it was decided that the best way to provide special education services was to sort students into groups on the basis of common characteristics (Ysseldyke, Algozzine, and Epps 1983), an elaborate classification system developed. However, since examination of this system failed to find links between problems and interventions, change is clearly called for (Hobbs 1975; Reynolds 1984). While some states have stopped using traditional categories and have shifted to describing students' special needs, Reynolds (1984) calls for classification in the schools to be based mainly on progress in the curriculum and to be oriented strictly to problems in instruction. The Project on the Classification of Exceptional Children (Hobbs 1975) recommends a comprehensive system for the classification of children with emphasis on the services needed to assist the child, his family, and school. Reynolds and Wang (1983) suggest a slightly different approach, advocating the distribution of waivers to allow school districts to try new classification and service delivery approaches without the loss of funding.

As this last suggestion indicates, many logistical difficulties linked to funding still interfere with alternatives to traditional labeling. The legislative structure that supports special education is written in language that stresses categories for funding. If a defensible system for making decisions about program eligibility is to be developed, special educators and other advocates will need to stretch the legislative guidelines and categories of the past in ways that encourage more flexibility (Hobbs 1975; Reynolds 1984; Reynolds and Balow 1972; Ysseldyke, Algozzine, and Epps 1983).

REFERENCES

Blatt, B. (1985). The implications of the language of mental retardation for LD. *Journal of Learning Disabilities, 18,* 625–626.

Carroll, J., Friedrich, R., & Hand, J. (1984). Academic self-concept and teachers' perceptions of normal, mentally retarded, and learning disabled elementary school students. *Psychology in the Schools, 21,* 343–348.

Coleman, J. (1983). Self-concept and the mildly handicapped: The role of social comparisons. *Journal of Special Education, 17,* 37–45.

Cromwell, R., Blashfield, R., & Strauss, J. (1975). Criteria for classification systems. In N. Hobbs (Ed.), *Issues in the classification of children (Vol. 1).* San Francisco: Jossey-Bass.

Dunn, L. (1968). Special education for the mildly retarded—Is much of it justifiable? *Exceptional Children, 35,* 5–24.

Fleming, E., & Anttonen, R. (1971). Teacher expectancy as related to the academic and personal growth of primary-age children. *Monograph of the Society for Research in Child Development, 36,* Ser. No. 145.

Foster, G., & Keech, V. (1977). Teacher reactions to the label of educable mentally retarded. *Education and Training of the Mentally Retarded, 12,* 307–311.

Foster, G., Ysseldyke, J., & Reese, S. (1975). I wouldn't have seen it if I hadn't believed it. *Exceptional Children, 41,* 469–473.

Gottlieb, J., & Leyser, Y. (1981). Facilitating the social mainstreaming of retarded children. *Exceptional Education Quarterly, 1,* 57–69.

Hallahan, D., & Kauffman, J. (1982). *Exceptional Children.* Englewood Cliffs, NJ: Prentice Hall.

Heller, K., Holtzman, W., & Messick, S. (1982). *Placing children in special education: A strategy for equity.* Washington, D.C.: National Academy Press.

Hobbs, N. (1975). *The futures of children.* San Francisco: Jossey-Bass Publishers.

Johnson, R., & Johnson, D. (1981). Building friendships between handicapped and nonhandicapped students: Effects of cooperative and individualistic instruction. *American Educational Research Journal, 18,* 415–423.

Lucas, C. (1974). The use and abuse of educational categories. In R. Jones & D. MacMillan (Eds.). *Special education in transition.* Boston: Allyn and Bacon.

MacMillan, D., Jones, R., & Aloia, G. (1974). The mentally retarded label: A theoretical analysis and review of research. *American Journal of Mental Deficiency, 79,* 241–261.

MacMillan, D., & Meyers, C. (1979). Educational labeling of handicapped learners. In D. Berliner (Ed.), *Review of research in education.* Washington, D.C.: American Educational Research Association.

Margalit, M., & Zak, I. (1984). Anxiety and self-concept of learning disabled children. *Journal of Learning Disabilities, 17,* 537–539.

Mercer, J. (1970). Sociological perspectives on mild mental retardation. In H. C. Haywood (Ed.), *Social-cultural aspects of mental retardation.* NY: Appleton-Century-Crofts (Prentice Hall).

Newcomer, P. (1985). LD or not LD. *Learning Disability Quarterly, 8,* 82–83.

Potter, M., Ysseldyke, J., Regan, R., and Algozzine, B. (1983). Eligibility and classification decisions in educational settings: Issuing "passports" in a state of confusion. *Contemporary Educational Psychology, 8,* 146–157.

Reynolds, M. (1984). Classification of students with handicaps. In E. Gordon (Ed.), *Review of research in education.* Washington, D.C.: American Educational Research Association.

Reynolds, M., & Balow, B. (1972). Categories and variables in special education. *Exceptional Children, 38,* 357–366.

Reynolds, M., & Wang, M. (1983). Restructuring "special" school programs: A position paper. *Policy Studies Review, 2* (Special No. 1), 189–212.

Rogers, H., & Saklofske, D. (1985). Self-concepts, locus of control and performance expectations of learning disabled children. *Journal of Learning Disabilities, 18,* 273–278.

Rolison, M., & Medway, F. (1986). Teachers' expectations and attributions for student achievement: Effects of label, performance pattern, and special education intervention. *American Educational Research Journal, 22,* 561–573.

Rosenthal, R., & Jacobsen, L. (1968). *Pygmalion in the classroom.* NY: Holt, Rinehart and Winston.

Schloss, P., & Miller, S. (1982). Effects of the label "institutionalized" vs. "regular school student" on teacher expectations. *Exceptional Children, 48,* 363–364.

Schloss, P., & Schloss, C. (1984). Job description and handicapping condition. *Journal for Vocational Special Needs Education, 6,* 9–11.

Silverman, R., & Zigmond, N. (1983). Self-concept in learning disabled adolescents. *Journal of Learning Disabilities, 16,* 478–481.

Smith, R., Osborne, L., Crim, D. & Rhu, A. (1986). Labeling theory as applied to learning disabilities: Survey findings and policy suggestions. *Journal of Learning Disabilities, 19,* 195–202.

Snow, R. (1969). Unfinished Pygmalion. *Contemporary Psychology, 14,* 197–198.

Stone, B. (1984). Ecological view of self-concept. *Remedial and Special Education, 5,* 43–44.

Thorndike, R. (1968). Review of Pygmalion in the classroom. *American Educational Research Journal, 5,* 708–711.

Yeates, K. & Weisz, J. (1985). On being called "mentally retarded": Do developmental and professional perspectives limit labeling effects? *American Journal of Mental Deficiency, 90,* 349–352.

Ysseldyke, J., & Algozzine, B. (1982). *Critical issues in special and remedial education.* Boston: Houghton Mifflin Co.

Ysseldyke, J., Algozzine, B., & Epps, S. (1983). A logical and empirical analysis of current practice in classifying students as handicapped. *Exceptional Children, 50,* 160–166.

Ysseldyke, J., Algozzine, B., & Richey, L. (1982). Judgment under uncertainty: How many children are handicapped? *Exceptional Children, 48,* 531–540.

DISCUSSION QUESTIONS

1. Some people state that a label may be a child's ticket to getting help. Do you think labels are necessary for getting services? Why? What other approaches could facilitate the provision of services?
2. Do you think labels stigmatize handicapped people in a negative way? Why? Suggest alternative labels that might be more positive.
3. Do you think people tend to believe that all people with the same label have the same abilities or characteristics? Explain. How might this be changed?
4. The research studies that provide misinformation about a person's label indicate that people make different judgments depending on the assigned label. Do you think you would do this? What would be the reasons you, or others, would probably give for doing this?
5. Think of the way we use labels around young children (e.g., "Didn't you hear me call you? What are you, deaf?") Can you think of some examples? What do you think children learn from this type of comment, and what can we do about it?

The Implications of the Language of Mental Retardation for LD

Burton Blatt

THE SITUATION

Don't make the mistake. Rick Heber didn't settle the matter. Herbert Grossman isn't settling the matter. In days long past, neither

Note. The Implications of the Language of Mental Retardation for LD by B. Blatt, 1985, *Journal of Learning Disabilities, 18,* pp. 625–626. Copyright 1985 by PRO-ED Inc. Reprinted by permission.

did Tredgold, Goddard, Wallin or Doll. And in the days to come, neither will you or I. *Mental retardation* is how we wish to define it. And it sounds exactly how we want to name it. We're allowed to redefine or rename it anytime we get an official quorum to agree, which we've been wont to do incessantly, and which we actually do periodically. Mental retardation is our invention—very real, of course, as are so many other human inventions. However, people not only reinvent very old wheels, but also such very new wheels that the fresh product is altogether different from the original in form, substance, and purpose. So, too, mental retardation—at least from time to time. So, too, learning disabilities—even more so; hence this attempt to foster analogies from my field to yours.

THE TERMS

Over the years, many terms have been used to label this thing, this state, we now call *mental retardation*. To look for the origins of those terms is like looking for the origins of language. That is, although there was a time when our ancestors did not have language, and today we have it, it would be fruitless to look for the point at which language arose. So the labels and metaphors we use to communicate concerning mental retardation developed naturally more than they were created intentionally. But while we don't know well enough how the field got started and grew, much less how the language was created to understand it, we do know that some terms are used interchangeably and others in specific context when speaking to this problem. As most readers know, the favorite generic label *today* is *mental retardation*. In the past, but here and there to this day, the following terms were/are used to identify the problem: *mental deficiency, mental subnormality, feeble–mindedness, mental handicap,* and *slow learner.* In the past, the term *moron* was used to identify those we now generally call the *retarded,* and whom the schools call the *educable mentally retarded* or *EMR.* In the past, the term *imbecile* was used to identify those the schools now label the *trainable* mentally retarded or *TMR.* Today the *severely mentally retarded* and/or *profoundly mentally retarded* have replaced the *idiot* as a designation for the most seriously retarded. Of course, as labels have been employed to identify various groups and subgroups on the intellectual hierarchy, there are numerous group-

ings to categorize by etiology (or causation) of disability. For example, some nomenclature schemes differentiate between people with demonstrable clinical syndromes and those who are aclinical (without obvious pathology). Still other schemes differentiate on the basis of level of independence, physiognomy, or where the person lives (e.g., in an institution or in the community). There were even terms used to separate those in the institution who work (worker boy or girl) from those who don't.

Certainly related to the Babel we have created as our language of mental retardation is the incomprehensibility of much of our history as a field. For example, Victor, *The Wild Boy of Aveyron,* was important not because one can learn from his life that wild boys are noble and educable, but that one can learn from this story that all people are noble and educable (Itard 1932). That distinction doesn't appear in the textbooks which recount the story of Victor and his teacher; and to miss that distinction is to miss the main point of Itard's work. After all, why should we be surprised if deliberate and systematic training succeeded in helping a child change, even a severely handicapped child, even a wild boy? A visit to any circus demonstrates to the most reluctant nativist that lions can be tamed, elephants can be trained to do things that elephants don't typically do, seals learn tricks, and dogs master the most intricate routines. There is even some evidence that dolphins communicate with each other and monkeys communicate with us. The most compelling lesson to be learned from the saga of *The Wild Boy of Aveyron* is *not* that capability is educable but, rather, that there are incapable people on earth who need and deserve our attention—and we have been ignoring them. The great surprise should not be that Victor learned, but in the very fact of our astonishment that he did learn. What might be also surprising to people today is that a medical doctor once would devote a significant period of his life to so mundane an activity as teaching one severely handicapped child. That's almost unbelieveable in our generation. Yet, despite the most illuminating and sensitive recent books about Victor on what Shattuck calls *The Forbidden Experiment* (1980), the field of mental retardation itself continues to perseverate on the "educability" issue. Was this a psychotic child, an idiot child or a hoax? We in the field ponder without resolution a question that Itard, himself, asked and answered *to his satisfaction:* "This must be a human creature." And so, the field of mental retardation is left with little more than being "stuck" on unraveling Itard's curriculum. Did Locke contribute more to Itard's thinking than Condillac? Or we speculate on what eventually happened to the child whom Itard's housekeeper, Madame Guerin, took care of—after Itard, in despair, fled the situation. Despite the illuminating histories from those outside of the field in recent years, we in mental retardation still worry about whether Itard's wild boy was or wasn't an incurable idiot. But the lesson we must eventually learn if we are to help such people is that every child, even a wild child, is "a human creature." And on that issue, we spend little or no time worrying about the meaning of such an assertion, much less the consequences if we were to deny it.

Confused language begets confused thinking. In our day, the bricks of Babel were used to build the mental retardation industry. For some people, the analogy of the Tower of Babel to the mental retardation monolith is not inconceivable.

THE UNDERSTANDINGS

Mental retardation, learning disabilities, mental illness, those and other disabilities are inventions—important, useful, effective, but inventions. A person is mentally retarded because an agency or some official body designated him or her as mentally retarded. One is labeled retarded, learning disabled, you name it, in the same way one is labeled a college student, or a Democrat, or a Republican, or a Rotarian—by being pulled or admitted to the group. What does mental retardation mean—actually? What we—professionals in consort with government and consumers—mean it to mean. Ditto learning disabilities. Once upon a time, mental retardation was incurable and irremediable and occurred at birth or early age. Today, it can happen almost anytime—at least through adolescence, and there are large government grants aimed at not only preventing but reversing the condition. Once upon a time, we said that mental retardation included 3 percent of the population. Later we revised that to permit as much as 16 percent of the population to be labeled "retarded." But on reconsideration, we changed the definition again, so today no more than 2 percent of the people are so labeled. And if you think mental retardation is mercurial insofar as the way we have changed our language, and thus modified our population, examine the history of the learning disabilities movement. After the shock, one will either laugh or cry or, most probably, say, "What the hell!"

REFERENCES

Itard, Jean Marc Gaspard. The Wild Boy of Aveyron, translated by George & Muriel Humphrey, with an introduction by George Humphrey, New York: The Century Company, 1932. (paperback edition, Appleton-Century-Crofts, 1962)

Shattuck, R. The Forbidden Experiment: The Story of the Wild Boy of Aveyron, New York: Giroux, 1980.

NONDISCRIMINATORY ASSESSMENT: A LEGAL PERSPECTIVE

While the debate over psychological and educational testing has been going on for many years (Block & Dworkin 1976; Cronbach 1975; Haney 1981; Jensen 1969;

Kamin 1974), the issues of test validity and how tests are used have received re-
newed attention recently. This expanded interest, particularly over the use of intelligence tests and assessment procedures in general, may be traced to litigation
which has prompted careful scrutiny of testing procedures, the purposes for which
tests have been developed and used, and the processes by which placement decisions have been made for special education students. Lawsuits have played a major
role in shaping the direction of psychological and educational testing and special
education procedures (Fafard, Hanlon, and Bryson 1986).

While the specific issues in each of the various lawsuits vary somewhat, there
are some central themes. For instance, many of the cases stem from allegations that
Constitutional rights have been violated, particularly those rights guaranteed by the
Equal Protection clause of the U.S. Constitution. Also, several court cases have
examined whether the procedures for identifying, classifying, and placing students
in special education classes are adequate and fair. Plaintiffs have argued that the
assessment instruments and procedures used to make placement decisions have
been discriminatory and have led to unfair representation of various minority
groups in special education classes. In supporting their contentions, plaintiffs have
questioned the appropriateness of administering tests in English to students who
are of limited proficiency in English, or whose primary language is other than
English. They have also cited the fact that various minority groups are unfairly
overrepresented in special education programs.

Needless to say, court cases have had a tremendous impact on how state education departments and school districts reach decisions regarding the identification
and placement of students who are deemed in need of special education. Of particular importance to this section are the issues raised by some of the court cases as
they relate to the assessment of children. Indeed, assessment procedures have been
at the center of arguments regarding whether the procedures used for identifying
and classifying students into special education programs are discriminatory and
biased—thereby leading to discrimination in placement, and ultimately to the denial of Constitutional rights. As a result of many court battles, it is now mandated
that educational and psychological assessments be conducted in a nonbiased and
nondiscriminatory manner. How nonbiased assessment has been defined, interpreted, and how it continues to evolve will be presented later in this section.

Clearly, not all the issues and arguments regarding litigation and the development of nondiscriminatory assessment can be presented in this brief section. However, in order to better understand how issues of nondiscriminatory assessment
have developed, an overview of landmark court cases will be presented. Following
this, issues on nondiscriminatory assessment as they relate to court decisions and
current practices in special education will be discussed. Finally, several guidelines
and practices will be suggested as a beginning framework for those who make
assessment and placement decisions regarding special education students.

Overview of Significant Court Cases

The relevant court cases on the topic of nondiscriminatory assessment have generally focused on placement decisions. In some cases, the question has been whether

certain minority groups were overrepresented in special education classes, and, if so, whether this phenomenon was justified. The role of testing—especially intelligence testing—in placement has been scrutinized to determine whether the tests and procedures used lead to a denial of Constitutional rights.

In *Hobson v. Hansen* (1967), the use of a tracking system and standardized tests to place students was questioned (Salvia and Ysseldyke 1985). In this case, it was alleged that use of standardized tests led to "disproportionate placement of poor and minority students in both lower educational tracks and in special education" (Salvia and Ysseldyke 1985, 42). As Reschly (1978, 5) notes, this case set the stage for later developments, since it was the first case in which the courts "considered technical issues related directly to psychological testing." In this decision, the judge acknowledged that while tests are only one factor in making placement decisions, testing was the most important consideration in making track assignments (*Hobson v. Hansen* 1967). This ruling was important since it found that a tracking system was, indeed, unconstitutional. However, the basis for this decision was not that tests themselves were biased, but rather, that since the tests used were "standardized primarily on and are relevant to a white middle-class group of students, they produce inaccurate and misleading test scores when given to lower class and Negro students" (*Hobson v. Hansen* 1967, 514).

Thus, the first case in which testing procedures came under attack found that tests played a prominent and possibly eminent role in the identification and placement of students. As a result, the subtle implication contained in this decision was that tests must be used for the purposes for which they were developed, and must have been standardized on the populations with whom they will be used in making decisions. Failure to follow these precepts invalidates results and muddies the placement process. However, at the time of *Hobson*, overrepresentation of minorities in special education classes was generally considered the result of "cultural" or "familial" influences, not of possible problems with assessment procedures. Indeed, the full impact of the *Hobson v. Hansen* decision, and its ramifications, seems to have been generally ignored at the time (Reschly 1978).

A second case that had implications for special education procedures as well as for assessment techniques was *Diana v. State Board of Education* (1970). Reschly (1978) identified this case as the initial litigation that specifically related to overrepresentation of minorities in special education programs. *Diana* was a class action suit filed on behalf of students with limited proficiency in English who were placed in classes for mildly retarded students. The plaintiffs alleged that inappropriate assessments were being conducted and that the assessment techniques which were being used for bilingual and minority students reflected the values of the majority. While this suit was settled out of court, the final agreement nevertheless had significant implications for assessment procedures. That agreement required that assessments be conducted in the primary language of the students being tested, and that those test items deemed unfair to that population were to be deleted. Students in special education classes in California at the time of *Diana* were reassessed in a timely manner, using these guidelines, to determine if their placement was indeed appropriate.

Several other lawsuits (*Dyrcia S. v. Board of Education* 1979; *Jose P. v. Ambach* 1979; *United Cerebral Palsy v. Board of Education* 1979) were also filed alleging that minority students were being denied their constitutional rights. *Dyrcia* was filed on behalf of limited English proficiency students, and the *United Cerebral Palsy* case was filed on behalf of physically handicapped students. Together with *Jose P.*, these suits charged violations of law on such procedural matters as lack of timeliness in evaluations, inadequacies of Individual Education Plans, infractions of the least restrictive environment mandates, and failure to provide appropriate bilingual and cultural programming for students. As a result of these decisions, it was ordered that evaluations be conducted in a timely manner and that assessments be conducted by examiners who were proficient in the language or mode of communication of the student being evaluated. School Based Support Teams (SBSTs) were instituted to ensure that decisions were made by multidisciplinary teams, and to develop procedures for the assessment of non-English speaking students (Fafard, Hanlon, and Bryson 1986).

Lora v. Board of Education (1977) was filed to correct abuses in the identification and placement of black and Hispanic students in segregated special day schools. This suit stemmed from the fact that, while 35 percent of the student population was black, the population of the special day schools in question was 68 percent black. The judge ruled that constitutional rights had indeed been violated, and that the system used to make special education placements was racially segregated and discriminatory. The court ordered that teachers be retrained, that new materials be introduced, and that experts from the field of communications be consulted so that due process rights and procedures could be effectively communicated to those speaking the major language of the city. In terms of conducting assessments in a nondiscriminatory fashion, examiners were instructed to use sensitivity in determining the proper language for conducting assessments, and in selecting materials for assessing personal and social adjustment. The schools also were ordered to pay closer attention to placing students in the least restrictive environment, and when making referrals, to describe a student's behavior in such a way that it could be directly observed and compared to that of other students. In addition, structured observations of the students in the setting in which the problem was reported to occur were mandated. Personnel administering tests were required to be fluent in the primary language of the student, and assessment techniques were to be used only for those purposes for which they were intended. Test norms were to be scrutinized on the basis of cultural, linguistic, ethnic, cognitive, emotional and sensory factors, and the team responsible for making placement decisions was to rule out ethnic and cultural factors in determining the need for special education placement (Wood, Johnson, and Jenkins 1986).

Thus, court cases were certainly moving special education professionals in the direction of nonbiased and nondiscriminatory assessments. The mandate was clear: No one test or testing procedure was sufficient to make a placement decision, and test purposes, development, and standardization procedures needed to be examined. Further, placement decisions were to be made by multidisciplinary teams who would consider more than just a student's IQ.

The court case which may eventually be shown to have had the most important implications for assessment procedures is *Larry P. v. Riles* (1979). This case has been ongoing, and decisions have been handed down as recently as September 1986 (*Larry P. v. Riles* 1986). According to Prasse and Reschly (1986), the plaintiffs

> were able to easily demonstrate that black children were being placed in programs for the mildly retarded at a rate which significantly exceeded a comparison to the percentage of black children in the school-based population, and that the rate was excessive when contrasted with the placement of white children in the same programs for the mildly retarded. (334)

Prasse and Reschly (1986, 336) underscored the importance of the *Riles* decision when they stated that it represented "the most serious challenge to professional educators' and psychologists' use of intelligence tests in the process of placing children in programs for the mildly retarded."

From the time of the original *Larry P.* suit, important legislation was passed regarding the legal rights of handicapped persons (Section 504 of the Rehabilitation Act of 1973 and The Education for All Handicapped Children Act of 1975, P.L. 94-142) that included provisions for nondiscriminatory assessment. These laws included guidelines for multifaceted and multidisciplinary approaches to information gathering, as well as the stipulation that tests were to be used only for the specific purposes for which they were developed and only with those students who were represented in the standardization procedures. The decision in *Larry P.* included sweeping mandates for the state of California, not the least of which was that because standardized IQ tests were racially and culturally biased, and therefore not valid for determining the placement of black children in classes for educable mentally retarded students (Prasse and Reschly 1986), students so placed must be reevaluated, without the use of standardized intelligence tests, to see whether their placement in these classes had been appropriate. Perhaps even more far reaching is the recent order modifying the original judgment and stating that

> school districts are not to use intelligence tests in the assessment of black pupils who have been referred for special education services. . . . In lieu of IQ tests, districts should use alternative means of assessment to determine identification and placement. Such techniques should include, and would not be limited to, assessment of the pupil's personal history and development, adaptive behavior, classroom performance, academic achievement, and evaluative instruments designed to point out specific information relative to a pupil's abilities and inabilities in specific skill areas. (*Larry P. v. Riles* 1986, 4)

While the *Larry P.* decision has clear implications in the state of California, Prasse (1986) points out that the law is dynamic rather than static, and that not all cases concur with the decision in the *Larry P.* case. This is evident in *Parents in Action on Special Education (PASE) v. Hannon* 1980. While the issue in question was similar to that in *Larry P.,* in *PASE,* the judge ruled in favor of the defendants and found little evidence that items on the WISC-R were biased. As noted by Berk, Bridges, and Shih (1981), the judge in *PASE* acknowledged that IQ tests dominated the identification and placement process, but did not find the tests discriminatory. As a result of these conflicting rulings and ongoing controversy about the role of IQ tests in American schools, it is obvious that far more litigation lies ahead. It will be a challenge to keep abreast of developments in the courts as they pertain to special education assessment practices.

Implications of Court Findings for Special Education and Nondiscriminatory Assessment

Clearly, the court cases have implications for anyone who will be conducting psychological and/or educational assessments, or who will be taking part in identification and placement decisions for students in special education programs. But many court decisions regarding standardized testing have been criticized by professionals in the field. For example, Lambert (1981), who was a witness in the case, took issue with the *Larry P.* decision, and argued that individual intelligence tests do not discriminate against minorities. Bersoff (1984) asserted that, given the parameters of the court, any intelligence test developed would fail the test itself, but Bersoff concluded that the courts were correct in their judgment that tests were used on populations other than those on which they were standardized. This is more a matter of a failure on the part of test users, however, than on the part of tests themselves. Reynolds (1982) argues that the apparent overrepresentation of minorities in special education classes may not be due to failure of IQ tests, and, in fact, there may not be discrimination since the numbers may reflect the higher percentage of minorities who are referred. He also notes, however, that problems in language bias have yet to be thoroughly researched. Problems in the present system of classification have also been noted, with the advantages and disadvantages of altering the category labels pointed out (Zigler, Bulla, and Hodapp 1984). In addition to discussing classification issues, these reseachers conclude that mentally retarded children are appropriately defined on the basis of measures of intellectual abilities. They do call for greater differentiation among students who require special education, especially those in the mentally retarded range, and caution that a single label does not effectively distinguish among the heterogeneous needs of these students. Duffey et al. (1981) point out that there is as yet little agreement as to what constitutes nonbiased assessment. While many attempts have been made to develop culture-free and culture-fair tests not influenced by the language, social status, and education of those persons to whom they are being administered (Cattell 1973; Freeman 1962), Duffey et al. (1981) highlight the difficulties in developing such tests. They also indicate that many problems noted by the courts relate more to test use rather than to the tests themselves.

Another outcome of the court cases contesting assessment and placement decisions has been the proliferation of research studies which examine the psychometric properties of various tests, with particular attention to whether these tests, given their psychometric properties, are suitable for use with minority groups (Arffa, Rider, and Cummings 1984; Greenberg, Stewart, and Hansche 1986). Various researchers have investigated assessment and intervention strategies for students with limited proficiency in English (Langdon 1983; Wilen and van Maanen Sweeting 1986), advancements in adaptive behavior measures (Gully and Hosch 1979; Heath and Obrzut 1986), and multifaceted, pluralistic (Mercer 1979), process (Meyers, Pfeffer, and Erlbaum 1985), and context (Messick 1984) assessment. Just as Prasse (1986) notes, these areas are rapidly changing. The litigation has provided an impetus for research into the improvement of assessment procedures and technology.

In addition to spurring research in related fields, court challenges have had far-reaching effects on the identification and placement of special education students in areas beyond the geographical confines of the legal jurisdictions. Position papers have flourished, attesting to the widespread influence of court challenges on professionals in the field (Finn and Resnick 1984; Reschly 1984; Snow 1984; Tonnesen 1979). Finally, while most of the issues surrounding labeling and overrepresentation of minorities in special education classes have dealt with mildly mentally retarded students, Tucker (1980) points out that problems of overrepresentation may be shifting from classes for mentally retarded students to programs for learning disabled students.

Guidelines for Conducting Nondiscriminatory Assessment

As has been pointed out by several researchers (Prasse 1986; Tonnesen 1979), it is important that those involved in special education remain involved in the evolution of special education law and practices, not only for their own interests but also to aid the development of practices and procedures that affect children in special education.

In recent years, the need for direction in educational and psychological assessment has increased. This need has been recognized, and guidelines for nondiscriminatory assessments have been developed and presented (Duffey et al. 1981; Helton 1984; National Association of School Psychologists 1984; Salvia and Ysseldyke 1985). While arriving at one specific definition of what constitutes nonbiased or nondiscriminatory assessment is difficult, certain components may be extrapolated from the different sets of guidelines reported, as well as from the various pieces of legislation and litigation themselves.

Certainly, decisions should not be made on the basis of a single test or test score, and decision-making must be considered an integral component of the assessment process. Salvia and Ysseldyke (1985, 5) define assessment as "the process of collecting data for the purpose of (1) specifying and verifying problems and (2) making decisions about students." Of particular note is the definition of assessment as a *process,* a point that has received considerable support in the literature (Reschly 1978; Reynolds 1982; Ysseldyke and Regan, 1980). Assessment tools must be standardized on the population with which they will be used. While this may seem quite obvious now, Salvia and Ysseldyke (1985) point out that until the 1972 revision of the Stanford-Binet Intelligence Scales, no black children had been included in the standardization sample.

The need for a dynamic, process-oriented, and multifaceted approach has also been widely noted (Feuerstein 1979; Meyers, Pfeffer, and Erlbaum 1985; Sewell 1986), with greater emphasis on what skills or knowledge students have and have not attained, and under what conditions. Care must be taken to ensure that students who have limited proficiency in the English language are not penalized. Finally, measures of adaptive behavior, which assess levels of personal independence and social responsibility (Reschly 1982, 1985) are vital, especially in assessments of mentally retarded children.

Exciting developments have taken place and, no doubt, will continue to occur in special education with respect to placement decisions and assessment techniques. This section has highlighted only a few of the very important issues, but it is clear that those entering the field of special education will need to carefully monitor future guidelines on nondiscriminatory assessment as they emerge.

REFERENCES

Arffa, S., Rider, L. H., & Cummings, J. A. (1984). A validity study of the Woodcock-Johnson Psycho-Educational Battery and the Stanford-Binet with black preschool children. *Journal of Psychoeducational Assessment, 2,* 73–77.

Berk, R. A., Bridges, W. P., & Shih, A. (1981). Does IQ really matter? A study of the use of IQ scores for the teaching of the mentally retarded. *American Sociological Review, 46,* 58–71.

Bersoff, D. N. (1984). Social and legal influences on test development and usage. In B. S. Plake (Ed.), *Social and technical issues in testing: Implications for test construction and usage.* Hillsdale, NJ: Lawrence Erlbaum Associates.

Block, N., & Dworkin, G. (1976). *The IQ controversy.* New York: Random House.

Cattell, R. (1973). *Technical supplement for the Culture Fair Intelligence Tests scales 2 and 3.* Champaign, IL: Institute for Personality and Ability Testing.

Cronbach, L. (1975). Five decades of public controversy over mental testing. *American Psychologist, 30,* 1–14.

Diana v. State Bd. of Ed., 70 C. 37v (N.D.C.A. 1970).

Duffey, J. B., Salvia, J., Tucker, J., & Ysseldyke, J. (1981). Nonbiased assessment: A need for operationalism. *Exceptional Children, 47,* 427–434.

Dyrcia, S. v. Bd. of Ed., 79 C. 2562 (E.D.N.Y. 1979).

Emihovich, C. A. (1983). The color of misbehaving: Two case studies of deviant boys. *Journal of Black Studies, 13,* 259–274.

Fafard, M. B., Hanlon, R. E., & Bryson, E. A. (1986). *Jose P. v. Ambach:* Progress toward compliance. *Exceptional Children, 52,* 313–322.

Feuerstein, R. (1979). *The dynamic assessment of retarded performance.* Baltimore: University Park Press.

Finn, J. D., & Resnick, L. B. (1984). Issues in the instruction of mildly mentally retarded children. *Educational Researcher, 13,* 9–11.

Freeman, F. S. (1962). *Theory and practice of psychological testing* (3rd Ed.). New York: Holt, Rinehart and Winston.

Greenberg, R. D., Stewart, K. J., & Hansche, W. J. (1986). Factor analysis of the WISC-R for white and black children evaluated for gifted placement. *Journal of Psychoeducational Assessment, 4,* 123–130.

Gully, K. J., & Hosch, H. M. (1979). Adaptive Behavior Scale: Development as a diagnostic tool via discriminant analysis. *American Journal of Mental Deficiency, 83,* 518–523.

Haney, W. (1981). Validity, vaudeville, and values: A short history of social concerns over standardized testing. *American Psychologist, 36,* 1021–1034.

Heath, C. P., & Obrzut, J. E. (1986). Adaptive behavior: Concurrent validity. *Journal of Psychoeducational Assessment, 4,* 53–59.

Helton, G. (1984). Guidelines for assessment in special education. *Focus on Exceptional Children, 16,* 1–16.

Hobson v. Hansen, 269 F. Suppl. 401 (D.D.C. 1967).

Jensen, A. (1969). How much can we boost IQ and scholastic achievement? *Harvard Educational Review, 39,* 1–123.

Jose P. v. Ambach, 3EHLR 551: 245, 27 (E.D.N.Y. 1979).

Kamin, L. (1974). *The science and politics of IQ.* Potomac, MD: Lawrence Erlbaum Associates.

Lambert, N. (1981). Psychological evidence in *Larry P. v. Wilson Riles. American Psychologist, 36,* 937–952.

Langdon, H. W. (1983). Assessment and intervention strategies for the bilingual language-disordered student. *Exceptional Children, 50,* 37–46.

Larry P. v. Riles, 495 F. Supp. 96 (N.D. Cal. 1979).

Larry P. v. Riles, No. C-71-2270 RFP (September 25, 1986).

Lora v. Bd. of Ed., 74 F.R.D. 565 (E.D.N.Y. 1977).

Mercer, J. (1979). *System of multicultural pluralistic assessment: Technical manual.* Cleveland: The Psychological Corporation.

Messick, S. (1984). Assessment in context: Appraising student performance in relation to instructional quality. *Educational Researcher, 13,* 3–8.

Meyers, J., Pfeffer, J., & Erlbaum, V. (1985). Process assessment: A model for broadening assessment. *Journal of Special Education, 19,* 73–89.

National Association of School Psychologists (1984). Standards for the provision of school psychological services—Appendix I. In A. Thomas and J. Games (Eds.). *Best practices in school psychology.* Kent, OH: National Association of School Psychologists.

PASE v. Hannon, 506 F. Supp. 831 (NLDL. Ill. 1980).

Prasse, D. P. (1986). Litigation and special education. An introduction. *Exceptional Children, 52,* 311–312.

Prasse, D. P., & Reschly, D. J. (1986). Larry P: A case of segregation, testing, or program efficacy? *Exceptional Children, 52,* 333–346.

Reschly, D. J. (1978). *Nonbiased assessment and school psychology* (Bulletin No. 8527). Bureau for Pupil Services, Division for Instructional Services. Madison, WI: Wisconsin Department of Public Instruction.

Reschly, D. J. (1982). Assessing mild mental retardation: The influence of adaptive behavior, sociocultural status, and prospects for nonbiased assessment. In C. R. Reynolds and T. B. Gutkin (Eds.), *The handbook of school psychology.* New York: John Wiley & Sons.

Reschly, D. J. (1984). Beyond IQ test bias: The national academy panel's analysis of minority overrepresentation. *Educational Researcher, 13,* 15–19.

Reschly, D. J. (1985). Best practices: Adaptive behavior. In A. Thomas and J. Grimes (Eds.), *Best practices in school psychology.* Kent, OH: National Association of School Psychologists.

Reynolds, C. R. (1982). The problem of bias in psychological assessment. In C. R. Reynolds & T. B. Gutkin (Eds.), *The handbook of school psychology.* New York: John Wiley & Sons.

Salvia, J., & Ysseldyke, J. E. (1985). *Assessment in special and remedial education* (3rd Ed.). Boston: Houghton Mifflin Co.

Sewell, T. E. (1986). *Testing for instructional outcome: How valid is the psychometric procedure?*

Paper presented at the Annual Conference of the American Psychological Association, Washington, D.C.

Snow, R. E. (1984). Placing children in special education: Some comments. *Educational Researcher, 13,* 12–14.

Tonnesen, N. F. (1979). Reform in special education: The problem of classification and placement. *Journal for Special Educators, 15,* 187–193.

Tucker, J. A. (1980). Ethnic proportions in classes for the learning disabled: Issues in nonbiased assessment. *Journal of Special Education, 14,* 93–105.

United Cerebral Palsy v. Bd. of Ed., 79 C. 560, (E.D.N.Y. 1979).

Wilen, D. K., & van Maanen Sweeting, C. (1986). Assessment of limited English proficiency Hispanic students. *School Psychology Review, 15,* 59–75.

Wood, F. H., Johnson, J. C., & Jenkins, J. R. (1986). The *Lora* Case: Nonbiased referral, assessment, and placement procedures. *Exceptional Children, 52,* 323–331.

Ysseldyke, J. E., & Regan, R. R. (1980). Nondiscriminatory assessment: A formative model. *Exceptional Children, 46,* 465–466.

Zigler, E., Bulla, D., & Hodapp, R. (1984). On the definition and classification of mental retardation. *American Journal of Mental Deficiency, 89,* 215–230.

DISCUSSION QUESTIONS

1. It is obvious that legal challenges have resulted in careful examination of assessment practices. Do you think this is the best way to influence change? Why? What might be more effective?

2. Assume you are in a state that bans the use of IQ tests. Develop and describe your plan for deciding whether a student is mentally retarded and in need of special education.

3. In American public schools, should minority children be required to learn the same things as all the other children? If so, is it discriminatory to test them with tests developed on non-minority children? Think about and discuss the relationship between these two questions.

4. Your school psychologist and administrator are concerned about this issue of nondiscriminatory assessment, and ask you to outline the major factors they need to consider. Do so.

5. While most of the issues of overrepresentation of minority students have focused on classes for the mildly retarded student, this problem with overrepresentation may be shifting now to classes for students with learning disabilities. Explain why this might be occurring.

Nondiscriminatory Assessment: A Formative Model

James E. Ysseldyke
Richard R. Regan

Recent and significant changes in public policy on the education of handicapped children are reflected in the provisions of Public Law 94-142, the Education for All Handicapped Children Act. This article focuses specifically on those provisions of the law typically referred to as the "Protection in Evaluation Procedures" provisions.

A review of Congressional testimony addressing the "Protection in Evaluation Procedures" indicates a much broader concern than simply the fairness of tests and test items as used with members of minority groups (Ysseldyke, 1978a). The broader issue is a concern with abuse in the entire process of using assessment data to make decisions about pupils.

Researchers and educators in the United States have exhibited considerable effort in attempts to identify fair tests for use with students from specific racial or cultural groups. In their attempts to cope with traditional assessment practices and to develop means of nondiscriminatory assessment, it seems that professionals and educational agencies have overlooked some very important facts. Efforts to develop nondiscriminatory assessment procedures have focused on tests and on attempts to eliminate biases from them. Yet, as has been noted elsewhere (Salvia and Ysseldyke 1978; Ysseldyke 1978a, b), nondiscriminatory assessment will not be achieved by developing "fair" tests.

Even if *the* fair test were available, there would still be considerable bias in the decision-making process. We believe that to meet both the letter and spirit of the law, psychologists and educators must begin to view assessment within the context of instructional intervention.

ASSESSMENT AND DECISION MAKING

Assessment is clearly and simply the process of collecting data for the purpose of making decisions about pupils (Salvia and Ysseldyke 1978). Vast amounts of data about children are collected within the educational setting and those data are used for the purpose of making decisions. Studied from a domain sampling model, the qualitative and/or quantitative nature of the data used in the decision-making process depends on the type of decision to be made (e.g., referral, screening). The whole process of assessment is a decision-making procedure—one in which assessment strategies and techniques should be dictated by the kinds of decisions to be made. Past and current practices in assessment-intervention with handicapped and nonhandicapped children clearly indicate that if educators are to serve all children within the confines of the educational environment effectively and efficiently, nondiscriminatory decision-making procedures must be initiated—procedures whose focus and emphasis are dictated by the decision(s) to be made and/or the function(s) to be served.

MEASURING INTERVENTION EFFECTIVENESS

Nondiscriminatory assessment can best be approximated by using data on intervention effectiveness, rather than data obtained from norm-referenced tests, to make most psychoeducational decisions. The conceptualization proposed here essentially restricts the use of norm-referenced tests to classification.

This conceptualization of nondiscriminatory assessment within the intervention process is made possible through the operationalization of the Deno cascade. It is based on the belief that requiring systematic planning, execution, and evaluation—within and across levels of service—of individual pupil programs is fundamental to the concept that the only meaningful class, for educational purposes, contains an N of one (Deno 1972). The data used to make decisions about an individual child should, for the most part, be data on instructional interventions that have and have not worked for the child.

The first step in this effort to establish nondiscriminatory assessment strategies and techniques is the suggestion that an enrollment policy be initiated mandating that all children, regardless of handicapping condition, have access to the continuum of educational services at the least restrictive point (i.e., the regular classroom). Since all children enter the school environment at the level of the regular classroom, a decision to move a child to the next level of service should be a data based decision. The classroom teacher should be required to document that the regular curriculum and at least three alternative instructional strategies have been tried and evaluated—demonstrating that academic and educational goals can or cannot be achieved at that level of service. Accountability can be incorporated within this conceptualization by asking teachers, prior to referring a child to a more intensive level of service, to sign a statement that they have attempted at least three instructional alternatives and that in their opinion the child will not make progress in the current placement.

This formulation expresses a firm commitment to the concept that no child, regardless of handicapping condition, should be relegated to a given level in the continuum based on his or her performance on norm-referenced tests. Rather, service should be provided on the basis of demonstrated and documented intervention effectiveness as the child moves through the continuum of services.

CONCLUSION

The essential advantage of the proposed approach lies in the kind of data used in decision making. A model for decision making has already been proposed by Cartwright, Cartwright, and Ysseldyke (1973). Within this approach, instructional intervention with individual children takes on the attributes of hypothesis testing. Systematic alteration of objectives, materials, methods, and techniques takes place until a set of procedures is identified that moves the child effectively toward accomplishment of the objectives. This process for the implementation of nondiscriminatory assessment within the intervention process should significantly reduce the number of children falsely identified and placed in alternative educational programs.

REFERENCES

Cartwright, G. P., Cartwright, C. A., & Ysseldyke, J. E. Two decision models: Identification and diagnostic teaching of handicapped children in the regular classroom. *Psychology in the Schools.* 1973. *10*, 4–11.

Deno, E. Strategies for improvement of educational opportunities for handicapped children: Suggestions for exploitation of EPDA potential. In M. C. Reynolds & M. D. Davis (Eds.), *Exceptional children in regular classrooms*. Minneapolis MN: University of Minnesota. 1972.

Salvia, J., & Ysseldyke, J. *Assessment in special and remedial education*. Boston: Houghton-Mifflin. 1978.

Ysseldyke, J. E. *Implementation of the nondiscriminatory assessment provisions of Public Law 94-142. A position monograph prepared for the Bureau of Education for the Handicapped. Washington DC: US Government Printing Office. 1978a.

Ysseldyke, J. Remediation of ability deficits in adolescents: Some major questions. In L. Mann, L. Goodman, & J. L. Wiederholt (Eds.). *The learning disabled adolescent*. Boston: Houghton-Mifflin. 1978b.

CHAPTER **7**

Behavior Management Issues

INTRODUCTION

One of the most difficult problems facing many teachers is the management of children's behavior in the classroom. Students may display a wide variety of inappropriate classroom behaviors, ranging from inattention to physical aggression, that interfere with learning. As a result, teachers, parents, physicians, and school administrators have turned to many different approaches to behavior management. This chapter presents an overview of several of the approaches used to manage students' behavior.

The first section, *Behavior Management: Use and Abuse,* presents an overview of behavior management techniques, with explanations of their purpose and intended results. Particular emphasis is given to the use and potential abuse of punishment and aversive techniques. The position statements on the use of aversives from four professional organizations—the Association for Retarded Citizens, the American Association on Mental Deficiency, the National Association of School Psychologists, and the Association for Persons With Severe Handicaps—are reprinted in this section.

The second section, *Nutritional and Diet Therapy for Individuals With Learning and Behavior Problems,* reviews the literature on the use of diet therapy to improve children's behavior. The use of diet therapies, in particular the Feingold diet, has been followed by many families with almost religious zeal, although its benefits remain highly controversial. The Feingold diet (with examples of its dietary restrictions) and other diet therapies are examined in this section, along with the possible benefits and drawbacks of the diet therapy approach to children and their families. The conflicting research results on the effectiveness of diet therapy are also discussed in this section and in the reprinted article by Divoky, *Can Diet Cure the L.D. Child?*

The third section in this chapter, *Drug Therapy For Exceptional Individuals,* examines ways that prescription drugs are being used to alter students' behavior. The use of stimulants in controlling hyperactivity is reviewed, along with the use of

185

psychotropic drugs, such as tranquilizers, to control aggression or other inappropriate behaviors. Use of these medications with children is still controversial, and is viewed by some authors as an inappropriate shortcut to behavior management. The reprinted article by Walker, *Drugging the American Child: We're Too Cavalier about Hyperactivity,* represents this perspective.

Behavior problems in the classroom often lead to frustration, anxiety, and burnout among teachers. To alleviate the problem, physicians and educators have developed a number of ways to cope with classroom management problems. While the effectiveness and controversial nature of these techniques has been challenged by many, others have adopted the procedures as standard practice.

BEHAVIOR MANAGEMENT: USE AND ABUSE

Behavior management has consistently ranked among the most important, difficult, and controversial issues that face those who are entrusted with the care of others. As pointed out by Schmid and Nagata (1983), the annual Gallup polls consistently rank classroom discipline at the top of the nation's school-related concerns. They stress that classroom discipline, or the lack of it, separates good teachers from bad, and that the stress of trying to maintain discipline contributes to such phenomena as teacher burnout (see *Chapter 2*). While few would argue that behavior management and discipline in the schools are important for carrying out the educational mission, the methods used to obtain and maintain discipline remain subjects for debate.

Closely related to the notion of discipline, and certainly one of the most emotionally laden topics in relation to managing behavior of students, is the use of corporal punishment. Court decisions such as *Ingraham v. Wright* (1977) brought the issues surrounding corporal punishment to public attention (Smith, Polloway, and West 1979). In *Ingraham,* the Court ruled that corporal punishment does not violate constitutional rights or protections against cruel and unusual punishment. This is consistent with the history of corporal punishment, which has traditionally been upheld in most cases, although it has been disapproved in cases which involved extenuating circumstances (Smith, Polloway, and West 1979). Questions may be raised, however, about the extent, frequency, severity, and the psychological advantages or disadvantages of corporal punishment as a means of behavior management. In fact, while conventional wisdom appears to support the use of corporal punishment, Smith, Polloway, and West (1979) note that corporal punishment has been attacked on grounds of moral, physical, and psychological harm.

The issue of corporal punishment becomes even more important when viewed in light of several other factors. First, since exceptional children, by definition, deviate from societal norms to a greater extent than do others, there may be a tendency for these individuals to be punished more extensively and more severely if corporal punishment becomes the method of choice in behavior management (Smith, Polloway, and West 1979). Second, Baroff (1986) states that there may be an ever-present danger of escalating the frequency and intensity of the punishment; if a given level of punishment does not alter a child's behavior, it might be logical to suggest that one reason the punishment did not work was because it was not severe enough. Clearly, such a question would seem to lend credence to Baroff's concerns.

While corporal punishment is but one technique under the rubric of behavior modification, it is appropriate for highlighting some of the arguments concerning behavior management. The many ethical, legal, and practical concerns about behavior management procedures become even more difficult to sort out when the behavior under question is potentially self-injurious or self-abusive, or manifested by individuals who are unable to speak for their own rights (Smith, Polloway, and West 1979).

The involvement of the courts lends further importance to issues surrounding behavior management. Martin (1975) notes that the courts have ended their long-standing tradition of noninterference in schools, and legal challenges based on constitutional rights of due process and equal protection under the law are occurring. Thus, court cases have had an impact on how and whether the behavior of individuals can be modified.

In discussing behavioral interventions and behavior modification, it is important to clarify what is meant by these terms. Indeed, any strategy or intervention that is intended to alter what a person does (i.e., how a person behaves) may be construed as behavior modification. However, different methods of altering behavior stem from different core assumptions, and the theoretical foundations, frameworks and underpinnings should not be confused. For example, psychoanalytic theory makes assumptions vastly different from those of behavioral theory. This section deals with behavior management techniques that evolved from the behaviorist tradition of psychology, and which have roots in classical and operant conditioning. As such, behavior management deals with observable behaviors and postulates no motives or unconscious processes. Historical reviews of behaviorist psychology and other schools of thought are readily available (Cullinan, Epstein, and Lloyd 1983), and the precursors of modern behavior theory can be traced to such classical writings as Watson (1913), Watson and Raynor (1920), and Skinner (1938, 1957, 1968). Applications of behavior theory to abnormal behavior can also readily be found (Ullmann and Krasner 1975).

In the following section, some unifying principles of behavior modification will be presented, followed by brief descriptions of the procedures and methods used to increase desirable behaviors or decrease unwanted behaviors. Finally, several ethical considerations regarding the use of behavior modification techniques will be outlined.

General Assumptions Underlying Behavior Modification

Considering the emphasis that those who employ behavior modification principles and techniques place on objective, observable, concrete behaviors, it is not surprising that one of the basic tenets of behavior modification is that "behavior is governed by its consequences" (Baroff 1986, 274). That is, a particular behavior may be viewed in terms of whether or not it is reinforced or encouraged. Whether dealing with behavior of young infants or the elderly, mildly or severely handicapped persons, learning disabled or mentally retarded persons, the basic principles of behavior modification do not change. Behavior is still postulated to be governed by its consequences. What will change is the nature and type of reinforcers that are viewed as effective in bringing about change (Baroff 1986).

Morris (1976) outlines a set of assumptions that generally appear to guide behavior modification techniques. First, it is assumed that behavior, and what may be termed behavior problems, are learned. This assumption contrasts with other models which may postulate biological predetermination or genetic predisposition of behavior. A person is assumed to be born *tabula rasa,* and behavior is a matter of conditioning. Morris (1976) argues that, although it is sometimes difficult to understand the nature of the reinforcement for a particular behavior, this does not justify the assumption that the behavior is biologically caused.

Second, behavior problems are assumed to be learned separately. Although there may be instances when it appears that more than one specific behavior is learned, or that behaviors are associated, behaviors are treated individually unless there is compelling evidence to do otherwise.

Third, it is assumed that behavior and behavior problems can be modified using behavior modification procedures. Morris states that "research does suggest that behavior modification procedures have wide application and merit consideration in the treatment of various behavior problems" (1976, 6). Baroff (1986) emphasizes that it is the very effectiveness of behavior modification procedures that often leads to controversy. The public has been exposed to the potential dangers of behavior modification procedures through their portrayals in novels such as Anthony Burgess' *A Clockwork Orange* (1963).

In addition, the behavior that people display in a particular situation is assumed to be typical behavior for that setting. That is, behavior is believed to be situation-specific and must therefore be generalized to other settings. Emphasis is also placed on behavior in the present, and the goals of behavior modification are concrete and very specific; these specific goals are referred to as target behaviors.

Finally, it is assumed that symptom substitution, the replacing of one (usually unwanted) behavior with another unwanted behavior, does not occur. Further discussions of the principles of behavior modification, with more exhaustive reviews and analyses, are available in Bandura (1969) and Walker and Shea (1984).

There are two broad categories of behavior modification procedures: reinforcers, which act to increase or maintain behaviors, and punishers, which decrease the frequency of or eliminate behaviors. The following sections discuss these in more detail.

Techniques Which Increase or Maintain Behaviors

Generally speaking, any procedure which increases the probability that a behavior will occur is considered a reinforcer. Thus, in behavioral terms, reinforcement is the process through which behaviors are maintained or increased. Reinforcers are determined by their effects on a given behavior, and there are two types of reinforcement: positive and negative.

Positive reinforcement of desired behaviors is perhaps the most basic behavior modification technique (Axelrod 1983; Ullmann and Krasner 1975). The concept is simple, and involves the introduction of a reward which is contingent on the display of the desired behavior. Slightly more confusing is the notion of negative reinforcement; perhaps because of the term *negative,* there is a tendency to associate negative reinforcement with punishment. However, they are not synonymous. It is important to remember that reinforcement, both positive and negative, is aimed at increasing or maintaining behavior. Thus, negative reinforcement increases or maintains a behavior, and is carried out by the removal or avoidance of a noxious, or aversive stimulus, not the application of it.

Other methods of increasing the frequency of desirable behaviors include shaping, or successive approximations, in which behaviors that resemble a target behavior are reinforced. Prompting is a technique whereby the person is assisted in performing the target behavior, and fading is the gradual removal of prompts (Axelrod 1983; Sulzer and Mayer 1972).

Using principles of positive reinforcement, a token economy, or a symbolic reward system, may be established (Morris 1976). Tokens are symbolic in that they may be associated with, and exchanged for, objects which are reinforcing. Token economy systems are preferable when one is working with groups of children and when there are many behaviors to be learned (Morris 1976).

Once the nature of the reinforcer is determined, a schedule of reinforcement must be developed. Elaborate systems involving ratio and interval schedules, which may be fixed or variable in nature, can be manipulated to achieve the fastest learning and the most enduring behavior. Schedules of reinforcement, with the characteristics described in more detail, are presented by Axelrod (1983), Sulzer and Mayer (1972), and Ullmann and Krasner (1975).

Bandura (1969, 1973) and Bandura and Walters (1963) did extensive work on the use of modeling and observational learning. These procedures involve exposing individuals to others engaging in prosocial or antisocial behaviors and then monitoring the children's behavior to determine if they exhibit those behaviors displayed by the models. These procedures have been used to both increase and decrease behaviors, and are discussed by Walker and Shea (1984).

Techniques Which Decrease the Frequency of Behaviors

When a displayed behavior is deliberately not followed by reinforcement, the process is known as extinction, or "the removal of those rewarding consequences which normally follow a particular behavior" (Morris 1976, 89). In discussing extinction, Axelrod (1983) notes that reduction in the frequency of the behavior is slow and gradual, and that spontaneous recovery occurs. Furthermore, extinction requires great consistency on the part of all who deal with an individual, and certain behaviors may be particularly resistant to extinction since they may be reinforcing in and of themselves. Ignoring unwanted behaviors, a frequently used method of extinction, may pose a problem for the behavior manager when the unwanted behavior is simply too dangerous to ignore.

Other methods used to decrease the frequency of unwanted behaviors include the rewarding of behaviors that are incompatible with them. For example, out-of-seat running may be decreased by rewarding in-seat, on-task behavior (Morris 1976).

At this point, some of the more problematic and controversial—although in some ways extremely effective—methods of behavior management must be discussed. Axelrod (1983, 28) notes the effectiveness of punishment procedures, and stated that "one might expect that the identification of procedures that can be used to diminish undesirable behaviors would be a cause for rejoicing. Such has not been the case." Solomon (1964) points out that punishment is a noxious stimulus that, by its inclusion, will diminish unwanted behavior and lead to new responses. Thus, the stimuli that are applied in punishment techniques are aversive (Solomon 1964; Sulzer and Mayer 1972). Primary aversive stimuli have included physical trauma, water sprays, electric shocks of high intensity, and bright lights, to name just a few examples.

The advantages of punishment include its effectiveness in immediately stopping unwanted behavior, and its use as an aid to assist the person in discriminating the desirable behavior from other behavior. Possible disadvantages to punishment include the child's modeling aggressive responses, developing unwanted emotional states such as fear, and acquiring a diminished self-concept (Bandura and Walters 1963). Morris (1976), like many others, suggests that physical punishment should be considered the least preferred behavior modification technique—with rare exceptions: "In some rare instances, however, physical punishment (e.g., a painful event like a slap or a loud noise) must be used" (104). In a similar vein, Walker and Shea (1984) point out that "punishment is perhaps the most misunderstood and emotionally explosive of the behavior modification techniques" (111), and state that they "are irrevocably opposed to the use of corporal punishment . . . and to psychological punishment, which at a minimum can erode the already fragile self-concept of the developing child" (113).

Time out from positive reinforcement and *response cost* techniques are yet other methods of reducing the frequency of certain behaviors. Time out involves removing the student from something reinforcing or the opportunity to receive reinforcement, and response cost results in the student's losing a specific amount of reinforcement when particular behaviors occur (Cullinan, Epstein, and Lloyd 1983). Lewellen (1980) describes three types of time out procedures: observational time out, where, for example, a child is seated at the perimeter of an activity; exclusion, in which the child leaves the reinforcement area and goes to an area of nonreinforcement, while still remaining within a class; and seclusion, which is segregation into a time out room for a brief period.

Overcorrection is a procedure developed by Foxx and Azrin (1973), and involves both a punishment and a corrective, or educational, component. In the restitution phase, the transgressor restores the environment to its previous state; in the positive practice phase, the desired behavior is practiced repeatedly. This procedure has been used effectively, for example, to reduce the incidence of talking out of turn or getting out of one's seat (Azrin and Powers 1975). While each of these behavior modification procedures may be effective in a variety of settings, there is not unanimous agreement on if, and when, several of them may ethically be used.

Ethical Considerations in Behavior Modification

As previously noted, the effectiveness of aversive techniques in behavior modification has led to widespread debate. Clearly, there is strong support for the use of positive techniques wherever possible, and for trying less restrictive treatments prior to aversive treatments—if those are to be used at all (Foxx 1982; Freschi and DiLeo 1982). Axelrod (1983), for example, suggests that response cost or time out procedures that can reduce unwanted behavior are preferable to aversives, but he also notes, "The conflict is that punishment procedures often work where reinforcement techniques do not. The failure to use punishment . . . can be contrary to a student's long-term best interests" (40). In discussing intervention strategies for mentally retarded infants and preschoolers, Baroff (1986) rules out corporal punishment and aversive stimulation, and states that "such procedures have absolutely no place in the management of children, and even with adults their use must be minimal and carefully monitored" (277). Baroff rejects any program of intervention which relies solely on aversive techniques.

However, others point out that at times, strong techniques are warranted and justified. In fact, it may be unethical, and a denial of treatment, *not* to use the techniques known to modify behavior. Sulzer and Mayer (1972) state that there are times when positive reinforcement techniques simply are not powerful enough to alter behavior. Walker and Shea (1984) caution, however, that it is unethical to use strategies that are stronger than needed, and Foxx (1982) classifies interventions along a continuum of least restrictive treatment.

Snell and Zirpoli (1987) justify the use of strong aversives with severely handicapped persons only in situations that are clearly life threatening, and where the use of other, less forceful, techniques are impossible. Along with others, they note the importance of adequate precautions and review processes (Harris 1985; Nolley et al. 1980).

The controversy on the use of aversives is certainly not surprising when one considers that techniques have included "hitting (head and hand slaps), cold showers, squirting lemon juice in the mouth, electric shock, and prolonged physical restraint" (Baroff 1986, 424). Baroff clarifies, however, that these techniques are generally reserved for use when other interventions have not been effective. An issue arises, however, when insufficient monitoring procedures exist, or when the success or failure of other techniques is open to interpretation. Compounding the controversy is the fact that many times, clients who are subjected to such treatments are institutionalized and unable to communicate to others.

Harris and Ersner-Hershfield (1978) describe one piece of equipment that is frequently used: a battery-operated prod that delivers an electric shock. The authors suggest that safety problems, often not cited in the literature, can occur if the current takes a dangerous path through the body or if persons accidentally touch part of the prod. Butterfield (1975) suggests that devices used for aversive conditioning are potentially lethal. Indeed, there have been reports of deaths of persons who have undergone various forms of aversive treatment (Autistic man dies 1985; Settlement reached 1986). Occurrences such as these have led professional organizations, including the Association for Persons with Severe Handicaps and the Association for Retarded Citizens, to call for the cessation of intrusive interventions and for a halt to the use of aversives (TASH: The Association for Persons with Severe Handicaps 1986, 1987).

Perhaps a greater appreciation for the position of those who argue for the continued use of aversives is attained when one understands that the behaviors being modified include many forms of self-injurious behavior such as head banging and self-mutilation, aggressiveness to others, severe and prolonged tantrums, vomiting and rumination, stripping, pica and coprophagy. Clearly, failure to alter these behaviors may well lead to self-harm. The question is, To what extent can the goal justify the intervention? Reviews of these and other arguments can be found in Morris and Kirby-Brown (1983); Schroeder, Mulick, and Schroeder (1979); and Whitman, Scibak, and Reid (1983). Unfortunately, studies using more positive interventions have produced somewhat mixed results (Measel and Alfieri 1976).

Perhaps more questions have been raised than answered. However, while the debates on behavior management will probably continue, it can only be hoped that those on both sides of the arguments are vehemently struggling for what they believe is correct, and are careful considering the dignity of the person involved in each behavioral intervention.

REFERENCES

Autistic man dies after punishment therapy (1985, July 26). *Marshfield News-Herald*, p. 5.

Axelrod, S. (1983). *Behavior modification for the classroom teacher* (2nd ed.). New York: McGraw-Hill.

Azrin, N. H., & Powers, M. A. (1975). Eliminating classroom disturbances of emotionally disturbed children by positive practice procedures. *Behavior Therapy, 6*, 525–534.

Bandura, A. (1969). *Principles of behavior modification*. New York: Holt, Rinehart, and Winston.

Bandura, A. (1973). *Aggression: A social learning analysis*. Englewood Cliffs: NY: Prentice-Hall.

Bandura, A., & Walters, R. H. (1963). *Social learning and personality development*. New York: Holt, Rinehart, and Winston.

Baroff, G. S. (1986). *Mental Retardation: Nature, cause, and management* (2nd ed.). Cambridge: Hemisphere Publishing Co.

Burgess, A. (1963). *A clockwork orange*. New York: Ballantine Books, Inc.

Butterfield, W. H. (1975). Electric shock-safety factors when used for the aversive conditioning of humans. *Human Therapy, 6*, 98–110.

Cullinan, D., Epstein, M. H., & Lloyd, J. W. (1983). *Behavior disorders of children and adolescents*. Englewood Cliffs, NY: Prentice-Hall, Inc.

Foxx, R. M. (1982). *Decreasing behaviors of severely retarded and autistic persons*. Champaign, IL: Research Press.

Foxx, R. M., & Azrin, N. H. (1973). The elimination of autistic, self-stimulatory behavior by overcorrection. *Journal of Applied Behavior Analysis, 6*, 1–14.

Freschi, D. F., & DiLeo, P. D. (1982). Treatment of self-abusive behaviors using positive intervention with an autistic boy. *Exceptional Children, 49*, 77–78.

Harris, K. R. (1985). Definitional, parametric, and procedural considerations in timeout interventions and research. *Exceptional Children, 51,* 279–288.

Harris, S. L., & Ersner-Hershfield, R. (1978). Behavioral suppression of seriously disruptive behavior in psychotic and retarded patients: A review of punishment and its alternatives. *Psychological Bulletin, 85,* 1352–1375.

Ingraham v. Wright, 430 U.S. 651 (1977).

Lewellen, A. (1980). *The use of quiet rooms and other timeout procedures in the public school.* Mattoon, IL: Eastern Illinois Area of Special Education.

Martin, R. (1975). *Legal challenges to behavior modification: Trends in schools, corrections, and mental health.* Champaign, IL: Research Press.

Measel, C. J., & Alfieri, P. A. (1976). Treatment of self-injurious behavior by a combination of reinforcement for incompatible behavior and overcorrection. *American Journal of Mental Deficiency, 81,* 147–153.

Morris, R. J. (1976). *Behavior modification with children: A systematic guide.* Cambridge, MA: Winthrop.

Morris, R. J., & Kirby-Brown, D. (1983). Legal and ethical issues in behavior modification with mentally retarded persons. In J. L. Matson & F. Andrasik (Eds.), *Treatment issues and innovations in mental retardation.* New York: Plenum.

Nolley, D., Boelkins, D., Kocur, L., Moore, M. K., Goncalves, S., & Lewis, M. (1980). Aversive conditioning within laws and guidelines in a state facility for mentally retarded individuals. *Mental Retardation, 18,* 295–298.

Schmid, R. E., & Nagata, L. M. (1983). *Contemporary issues in special education* (2nd ed.). New York: McGraw-Hill.

Schroeder, S. R., Mulick, J. A., & Schroeder, C. S. (1979). Management of severe behavior problems of the retarded. In N. R. Ellis (Ed.), *Handbook of mental deficiency: Psychological theory and research* (2nd ed.). Hillsdale, NJ: Laurence Erlbaum.

Settlement reached on care of autistic youths at school (1986, December). *New York Times,* p. 10.

Skinner, B. F. (1938). *The behavior of organisms.* New York: Appleton.

Skinner, B. F. (1957). *Verbal behavior.* New York: Appleton.

Skinner, B. F. (1968). *Technology of teaching.* New York: Appleton.

Smith, J. D., Polloway, E. A., & West, G. K. (1979). Corporal punishment and its implications for exceptional children. *Exceptional Children, 45,* 264–268.

Snell, M. E., & Zirpoli, T. J. (1987). Intervention strategies. In M. E. Snell (Ed.), *Systematic instruction of persons with severe handicaps,* (3rd ed.). Columbus: Charles E. Merrill.

Solomon, R. L. (1964). Punishment. *American Psychologist, 9,* 239–253.

Sulzer, B., & Mayer, G. R. (1972). *Behavior modification procedures for school personnel.* Hinsdale, IL: The Dryden Press, Inc.

TASH: The Association for Persons with Severe Handicaps (1986, February). ARC resolution on aversives. *Newsletter, 12,* p. 1.

TASH: The Association for Persons with Severe Handicaps (1987, February). Resolution on the cessation of intrusive interventions. *Newsletter, 13,* p. 3.

Ullmann, L. P., & Krasner, L. (1975). *A psychological approach to abnormal behavior* (2nd ed.). Englewood Cliffs, NJ: Prentice-Hall.

Walker, J., & Shea, T. (1984). *Behavior management.* St. Louis: Times Mirror/Mosby.

Watson, J. B. (1913). Psychology as a behaviorist views it. *Psychological Review, 20,* 158–177.

Watson, J. B., & Raynor, R. (1920). Conditioned emotional reactions. *Journal of Experimental Psychology, 3,* 1–4.

Whitman, T. L., Scibak, J. W., & Reid, D. (1983). *Behavior modification with the severely and profoundly retarded: Research and application.* New York: Academic.

DISCUSSION QUESTIONS

1. What safeguards would you suggest to prevent the abuse of behavior management technology? How would you implement these suggestions in schools and other facilities serving exceptional individuals?
2. Because of legal restrictions, some programs are not permitted to use aversives to stop inappropriate behaviors. As a result, some individuals have inflicted permanent damage on themselves (i.e., detached retinas) during periods of self-abuse. How do you react to this? In this case, are we really protecting the rights of the individual? What are the arguments for both sides of this issue?
3. Do you think teachers and administrators should be allowed to use corporal punishment (spanking, hitting, etc.) in schools? Why? What would be the benefits and the drawbacks of its use? Do you think parents have the right to use corporal punishment, or is it child abuse?
4. Some critics claim that students are too aware of being reinforced for their work and depend on this external reinforcement for motivation; as a result, students may only work when they know what reward they are working for. Do you think this is a problem? Why? Do you need a reward to work?
5. In many schools a student who behaves inappropriately in class is sent to the office for reprimanding. What are the problems with this approach? What might we be teaching the students? How can we change this situation?

Association for Retarded Citizens of the United States Position Statement on Behavior Management

During their national convention in October 1986 in Reno, Nevada the Association for Retarded Citizens of the United States (ARC), adopted a position statement on behavior management. This statement follows.

ISSUE

Behavior management programs include a variety of techniques to develop and main-

Note. From *ARC Position Statements on Programmatic Issues* (pp. 27–28) by the National Board of Directors, 1984. Copyright 1984 by the Association for Retarded Citizens of the United States. Reprinted by permission.

tain skills that will enhance an individual's opportunities for learning and self-fulfillment. Behavior management programs can also diminish behaviors that may impede individual learning and self-fulfillment. The ARC realizes the importance of positive behavior management programs in meeting individual needs, but recognizes that, regardless of the specific technique used, there is a potential for abuse and misuse of any behavior management procedures. Specifically the use of aversive and deprivation procedures is in direct conflict with the right of people with mental retardation to be free from harm. These procedures can cause a loss of dignity and prevent full participation in society. (ARC definition of aversive and deprivation appears below.)

POSITION

Prior to consideration of any behavior management program, the nature and extent of the perceived behavior problem must be determined. Potential causes such as physical or medical conditions, environmental factors, staffing problems, and inappropriate programming must be reviewed and addressed prior to development of a behavior management program.

For individuals with mental retardation, the ARC supports behavior management programs that are

- applied in a humane and caring manner with the ultimate goal of growth and habilitation;
- intended to enhance opportunities for self-determination and independence;
- based upon the thorough assessment of each individual's existing competencies and characteristics;
- effective in developing competence to cope with the environment and in fostering more complex adaptive behaviors;
- implemented by staff who have been trained and are qualified to effectively apply positive, nonaversive approaches;

- monitored continuously and systematically to ensure that the approach is consistent with individual needs and successful in achieving established goals;
- based on a positive approach to the development and maintenance of desired behavior.
- Further the ARC believes any aversive interventions that withhold essential nutrition and hydration, inflict pain, use chemical restraints in lieu of programming, or impose techniques which produce physical or psychological pain, humiliation, or discomfort must be eliminated. All means of review processes, including human rights committees independent of service providers, should be used during the transition from aversive and deprivation procedures to positive approaches.

In this resolution, ARC has noted that aversive refers to noxious, painful, unpleasant or intrusive stimuli or activities applied in response to maladaptive behavior. Deprivation refers to withholding, withdrawing, or delaying of any stimuli or activities which are pleasurable.

TASH Resolution on the Cessation of Intrusive Interventions

November, 1986

In order to realize the goals and objectives of the Association for Persons with Severe Handicaps including the right of each person with a severe

Note. TASH Resolution on the Cessation of Intrusive Interventions, 1987, *TASH Newsletter 13,* pp. 3, 9. Copyright 1987 by The Association for Persons With Severe Handicaps. Reprinted by permission.

handicap to grow, develop, and enjoy life in integrated and normalized community environments, the following resolution is adopted:

Educational and other habilitative services must employ instructional and management strategies which are consistent with the right of each individual with severe handicaps to an effective treatment which does not compromise the equally important right to freedom from harm. This requires educational and habilitative procedures free from chemical restraint, aversive stimuli, environmental deprivation or exclusion from services:

Therefore, TASH calls for the cessation of the use of any treatment option which exhibits some or all of the following characteristics: (1) obvious signs of physical pain experienced by the individual; (2) potential or actual side effects such as tissue damage, physical illness, severe physical or emotional stress and/or death that would properly require the involvement of medical personnel; (3) dehumanization of persons with severe handicaps because the procedures are normally unacceptable for persons without handicaps in community environment; (4) extreme ambivalence and discomfort by family, staff and/or caregivers regarding the necessity of such extreme strategies or their own involvement in such interventions; and (5) obvious repulsion and/or stress felt by peers who have no handicaps and community members who cannot reconcile extreme procedures with acceptable standard practice:

It is further resolved that The Association for Persons with Severe Handicaps' resources and expertise be dedicated to the development, implementation, evaluation, dissemination, and advocacy of educational and management practices which are appropriate for use in integrated environments and which are consistent with the commitment to a high quality of life for individuals with severe handicaps.

AAMD Adopts Position Statement on Aversive Therapy

The following American Association on Mental Deficiency (AAMD) statement on aversive therapy was unanimously passed by the Legal and Social Issues (LASI) Committee and adopted by the AAMD Board of Directors in December 1986.

Some persons who have mental retardation or developmental disabilities continue to be subjected to inhumane forms of aversive therapy techniques as a means of behavior modification. The American Association on Mental Deficiency (AAMD) condemns such practices and urges their immediate elimination. The aversive practices to be eliminated include some or all of the following characteristics:

1. Obvious signs of physical pain experienced by the individual;
2. Potential or actual physical side-effects, including tissue damage, physical illness, severe stress and/or death; and
3. Dehumanization of the individual, through means such as social degradation, social isolation, verbal abuse, techniques inappropriate for the individual's age and treatment out of proportion to the target behavior, because the procedures are normally unacceptable for nonhandicapped individuals.

The AAMD urges continuing research into humane methods of behavior management and support of existing programs and environments that successfully habilitate individuals with complex behaviors.

Note. The AAMD Position Statement on Aversive Therapy, 1987, *Mental Retardation, 25,* p. 118. Copyright 1987 by the American Association on Mental Deficiency. Reprinted by permission.

National Association of School Psychologists Resolution on Corporal Punishment

The following resolution was adopted on April 19, 1986, in Hollywood, Florida by The National Association of School Psychologists.

As the purpose of the National Association of School Psychologists is to serve the mental health and educational needs of all children and youth; and

The use of corporal punishment as a disciplinary procedure in the schools negatively affects the social, educational, and psychological development of students; and

The use of corporal punishment by educators reinforces the misconception that hitting is an appropriate and effective technique to discipline children; and

Corporal punishment as a disciplinary technique can be easily abused and thereby contribute to the cycle of child abuse; and

School psychologists are legally and ethically bound to protect the students they serve; and

Note. National Association of School Psychologists Resolution on Corporal Punishment. Copyright 1986. Reprinted by permission.

Research indicates that punishment is ineffective in teaching new behaviors, that a variety of positive and effective alternatives are available to maintain school discipline, and that children learn more appropriate problem solving behaviors when provided with the necessary models;

Therefore it is resolved that the National Association of School Psychologists joins other organizations in opposing the use of corporal punishment in the schools and in other institutions where children are cared for or educated;

And will work actively with other organizations to influence public opinion and legislative bodies in recognizing the consequences of corporal punishment, in understanding and researching alternatives to corporal punishment, and in prohibiting the continued use of corporal punishment;

And will encourage state affiliate organizations and individual members to adopt positions opposing corporal punishment, to promote understanding of and research on alternatives to corporal punishment including preventive initiatives, and to support abolition of corporal punishment at state and local levels.

NUTRITIONAL AND DIET THERAPY FOR INDIVIDUALS WITH LEARNING AND BEHAVIOR PROBLEMS

For many years, researchers have conducted studies examining the effects of nutrition on children's learning. As early as the 1950s, Keister (1950) and Tuttle, Daum, and Larsen (1954) reported that adequate nutrition improved children's attention, concentration, sociability, and scholastic achievement while lessening distractibility.

In a study of Eskimo children, Read (1973) noted that children who did not eat breakfast were more likely to be disruptive, inattentive, and lethargic in school. Malnourished children were found to acquire language later and score lower on IQ tests (Botha-Antoun, Babayan, and Harfouche 1968), as well as to show impaired perceptual and abstract abilities (Cravioto and DeLicardie 1970). However, while most professionals would agree that adequate nutrition is essential for normal child development, several controversial theories have recently been presented on the effects of diet on children's learning and behavior.

The Feingold Diet

Much of the controversy on diet therapies started after the publication of the book *Why Your Child Is Hyperactive* by Dr. Benjamin Feingold (1975). The diet proposed by Feingold, an allergy specialist at the Kaiser-Permanente (K-P) Health Care Program, was referred to as the K-P diet and involved eliminating foods and health products that contained natural salicylates, and over three thousand artificial colorings and flavors, and BHT preservatives. Feingold stated that some children's learning and behavior problems, particularly hyperactivity, were a result of an allergic or toxic response to these substances in the children's diet. In addition to many fruits, vegetables, and processed foods, the diet also eliminated mouthwashes, toothpastes, and flavored medications.

According to Feingold (1975), hyperactive children could be predisposed to this allergic or toxic reaction to chemicals in foods, and those children so predisposed could experience dramatic improvement in their behavior if their diets excluded the offending substances. The diet's instructions included initially eliminating all foods from Group I, which contain natural salicylates, and Group II, which contain artificial colors, flavors, and preservatives like BHT (Feingold, 1975). Examples of these foods are presented in the following list.

Foods Eliminated on the K-P Diet

- Group 1—Almonds, apples, apricots, tomatoes and all tomato products, cucumbers and pickles, blackberries, boysenberries, gooseberries, raspberries, strawberries, cherries, currants, grapes and raisins or anything made from them such as wine or jelly, nectarines, oranges, peaches, and plums.
- Group 2—All cereals with artificial colors and flavors, all instant breakfast foods, all manufactured bakery products, packaged baking mixes, bologna, salami, hot dogs, sausages, meat loaf, ham, bacon, pork, all barbecued poultry, frozen fish that is dyed or flavored, manufactured ice cream, puddings, dessert mixes, flavored yogurt, all manufactured candy, cider, wine, beer, soft drinks, diet drinks, tea, prepared chocolate milk, margarine, colored butter, mustard, anything mint flavored, soy sauce, chocolate syrup, catsup, chili sauce, all colored cheeses, most over-the-counter medications, all toothpastes and powders, all mouthwashes, cough drops, antacid tablets, and perfumes (Feingold 1975).

It is necessary to check all food labels carefully to assure that all food eaten is free of these substances. The diet must be adhered to totally and a diet diary must be kept noting everything the child eats. To make the diet easier for the child, Feingold recommends that the whole family go on it. If the diet is followed without infractions, Feingold states that positive responses should be noted within seven to twenty-one days. While the foods in Group II must be eliminated for life, the foods in Group I can be reintroduced one at a time after two to six weeks on the diet. If the child does not show a negative response to the food, it can remain in the child's diet. Feingold claims that from 30 to 50 percent of children respond dramatically to his diet with reduction of hyperactive symptoms and perceptual cognitive disturbances, and improved academic achievement and motor control (Ross and Ross 1982).

By 1983, more than 200,000 children were following this diet (Mattes 1983), and it was claimed that not only hyperactivity, but also other conditions such as retardation, autism, and even bed wetting would respond positively to this diet.

Questions about the Diet Effectiveness

As the use of this diet spread, so did the controversy on its effectiveness. The food industry and the Federal Drug Administration established committees to review the evidence on the effectiveness of the Feingold diet. Because of discrepancies in the research, the Consensus Development Conference at the National Institute of Health decided to study the issue of diet and hyperactivity. This conference concluded that while many studies linked adverse behaviors to the presence of certain food additives in the diet, the number of children potentially affected was small compared to Feingold's claims, the effects were seldom observed in controlled tests, and there was insufficient evidence to identify which groups of children might respond to the diet (Food additives 1982).

Many researchers have examined the effectiveness of the K-P diet with inconsistent results. In a carefully controlled study, Harley et al. (1978) reported that while the subjects' parents often rated their children as "improved," the objective measures in the study did not indicate any changes. However, Feingold disputed these results claiming that the hyperactivity patterns were not measured well and that there were actual improvements in more than 25 percent of the subjects (Gaylin 1977).

Conners (1980) stated that while Feingold's claims were impressive, they were based on many anecdotal reports and subjective measures. In 1975, the National Advisory Committee on Hyperkinesis and Food Additives recommended scientific challenge studies to evaluate the outcomes of diet therapies. Following these studies, Conners (1980) concluded that while some hyperactive children showed improvement on the K-P diet and seemed to have an adverse reaction to some food dyes, the dramatic results claimed by Feingold were not supported.

The results of the research may pose more questions than they answer. Stine (1976), Rose (1978), and Rapp (1978), for example, reported a relationship between artificial food colors and increases in both frequency and duration of hyperactive behaviors. These results were most prevalent in children under the age of six, and the methodology usually used rating scales completed by parents and teachers to measure changes in behavior.

Many critics of these pro-diet studies claim that the rating scales used are subjective and/or poorly researched. In addition, the research has been criticized for small sample sizes, poor experimental controls, and use of untrained observers. Levy and Hobbs (1978), Mattes and Gittleman (1981), and Harley et al. (1978) all conducted studies that found no consistent effect on behavior when the Feingold diet was subjected to strict challenges. Adams (1981) challenged both the efficacy of the K-P diet and the validity of relying on parents' reports in evaluating children's responsiveness to the diet. In a well-designed double-blind crossover study using fourteen objective measures, no significant differences were found between children who violated the diet and those who had no diet infractions. Another frequently voiced criticism of the diet focuses on the difficulty in controlling a young child's intake of prescribed foods. As Taylor (1979) comments, obtaining data that is truly free of dietary infractions is difficult.

In an attempt to examine and summarize the overall results indicated in the many studies on the efficacy of the Feingold diet, Kavale and Forness (1983) conducted a meta-analysis of twenty-three studies and concluded that diet modification was not an effective intervention for hyperactivity. Their findings suggested that the uncontrolled studies showed greater treatment effects than the controlled studies, and they cautioned that the findings from uncontrolled studies—though psychologically persuasive—should not be taken as evidence of the success of diet therapy.

In response to these charges of nonsubstantive proof of the diet's efficacy, Rimland (1983) wrote in defense of additive-free diets. He stated that reviews suggesting the K-P diet was of little value were unwarranted, damaging, and incorrect. He noted that while most of the experimenters eliminated about ten dyes during their study, Feingold recommended eliminating nearly three thousand additives. In addition, he stated that in many tests, the dosages of extracts were much lower than what an average individual would consume in one day, according to FDA norms. In Rimland's opinion, the researchers who found no beneficial effects from the diet did not recognize and control relevant variables.

Other Diet Interventions

Many other studies have examined the effects of dietary components on children's behavior. According to clinical ecologists, seven out of ten people with mental problems are allergic to foods, chemicals, or inhalents, and their hypersensitivities to these substances may intensify or directly cause brain dysfunction. Levin and Zellerbach (1985) are convinced that allergic reactions are one of the main causes of violence in America. Rapp (1978) also states that many foods, including gluten and artificial ingredients can affect children's behavior, and reports that more than 70 percent of the hyperactive children she has studied had evidence of allergy in their personal and family history, as well as positive allergy skin tests.

In a study of juvenile offenders, David (1983) demonstrated that dietary changes—including elimination of refined sugars and dairy products—reduced sinus stuffiness, improved skin conditions, increased energy levels, and reduced such behavior problems as hostility, aggressiveness, irritability, and depression. This study reported that as a result of the diet modification, there was an 80 percent decrease in the number of juvenile offenders constantly in serious trouble, and nearly twice as many subjects were rated as well-behaved while on the controlled diet. Of course, it was impossible to tell what other factors might have also affected their behavior.

Lester, Thatcher, and Monroe-Lord (1982) conducted a study suggesting that when children consumed refined carbohydrates, their intellectual functioning was negatively affected. This study reported a negative correlation between full-scale IQ scores and the proportion of refined carbohydrates in the total food calorie intake.

Studying a nine-year-old retarded child with autistic behaviors, Bird, Russo, and Cataldo (1977) employed a gluten-free diet because the child's parents reported that restricting wheat gluten improved their son's behavior. However, when this diet was implemented under controlled conditions, the results showed little relationship between the gluten-restricted diet and decreased frequency of the autistic behaviors.

In the Alabama Diet-Behavior Program, researchers evaluated the effects of reducing sugar in the diets of 488 incarcerated juveniles. Over a 22-month period, those on the reduced sugar diet demonstrated a 35 percent reduction in antisocial behavior. Those subjects identified as property offenders benefitted most from the diet, with a 53 percent decrease in their offending behaviors (Schoenthaler, 1983). Prinz, Roberts, and Hantman (1980) report that sugar ingestion is more consistently associated with aggressive, destructive, and restless behaviors than were diets with salicylates and additives. Crook (1984) further suggests that sugars may have the most diverse effects on behavior.

Another type of dietary therapy was proposed by Cott (1972) who used orthomolecular therapy—also known as megavitamin therapy—with autistic, schizophrenic, and learning disabled children. This treatment involved administering massive dosages of various vitamins such as niacin, ascorbic acid, pyridoxine, calcium pantothenate, B3, B6, C, and E to provide for the optimum molecular composition of the brain. Cott reported that this treatment often works when other forms of treatment have failed, and it can result in reduced hyperactivity, increased communication, cooperation, and desire to learn. While many researchers have questioned the use of megavitamins and have attributed the results of megavitamin therapy to a placebo effect (Rimland 1971), those involved with the treatment approach state that the effects can clearly be seen since disturbed behavior begins again when the children stop receiving the vitamins.

While it is clear that many people have reported observing the effects of diet and nutrition on children's behavior, it is still not clear what is causing the behavior changes. For example, Crook (1984) states that while he has repeatedly observed the effects of diet on hyperactivity, he cannot explain the cause of the phenomenon. Conners (1980) also states that while there may be some substance to the Feingold claims, the effects are inconsistent, although Conners concedes that in his own work, he did find a link between ingestion of artificial colors and learning performance.

The general trend in the research seems to indicate that the studies that rely on more subjective measures show more positive results, while those that use well-designed controls show less correlation between diet and behavior. However, the data do suggest that small numbers of children benefit from diet therapy—though not the large numbers of children reported by some researchers.

As a result of the conflicting findings, the Consensus Development Conference at the National Institute of Health cautions against routine application of modified diet as a preferred treatment approach (Thorley 1983). However, they also suggest that sufficient concerns have been raised about the effects of additives on behavior to recommend that standardized tests be devised and insisted upon before food additives are approved. Until such testing and approval occurs, the panel recommends that the public monitor the food additives that they consume.

While stating that the diet therapy presented by Feingold poses no known risks to children, The National Institute of Health panel adds that no diet is advisable until a thorough physical and psychosocial evaluation of the child and family has been done (Hyperactivity—diet link questioned 1982). Divoky (1978) expresses fears that people may tend to automatically blame children's problem behavior on food substances rather than questioning their own child rearing or teaching practices. Wender (1977) also expresses concern that parents' modification of a child's diet may postpone more appropriate medical, psychological, or educational interventions. Obviously, much more research needs to be done before diet therapy replaces the other forms of treatment such as behavior modification, psychotherapy, or even drug therapy.

In some cases, it may be that trying to follow the strict diets imposes order, purpose, and consistency on families' lives. This could provide hope to families whose frustration with their children's problems has led them to try the unproven diet therapy. This hope may be an important variable that the research hasn't measured. Whatever approach is followed though, it is crucial that traditional treatment approaches still be implemented for the child's benefit.

REFERENCES

Adams, W. (1981). Lack of behavioral effects from Feingold Diet violations. *Perceptual and Motor Skills, 52,* 307–313.

Bird, B., Russo, D., & Cataldo, M. (1977). Considerations in the analysis and treatment of dietary effects on behavior: A case study. *Journal of Autism and Childhood Schizophrenia, 7,* 373–382.

Botha-Antoun, E., Babayan, S., & Harfouche, J. (1968). Intellectual development related to nutritional status. *Journal of Topical Pediatrics, 14,* 112–115.

Conners, C. K. (1980). *Food additives and hyperactive children*. New York: Plenum Press.

Cott, A. (1972). Megavitamins: The orthomolecular approach to behavior disorders and learning disabilities. *Academic Therapy, 7*, 245–258.

Cravioto, J., & DeLicardie, E. (1970). Mental performance in school age children: Findings after recovery from severe malnutrition. *American Journal of Diseases of Children, 120*, 404–410.

Crook, W. (1984). Diet and hyperactivity. *Journal of Learning Disabilities, 17*, 66.

David, O. (1983). The relationship of hyperactivity to moderately elevated lead levels. *Archives of Environmental Health, 38*, 341–346.

Divoky, D. (1978). Behavior and food coloring: Lessons of a diet fad. *Psychology Today, 12*, 145–148.

Feingold, B. (1975). *Why your child is hyperactive*. New York: Random House.

Food additives and hyperactive kids. (1982, April). *FDA Consumer*, p. 13.

Gaylin, J. (1977, October). Research disputes link between hyperactivity and food additives. *Psychology Today*, pp. 46, 152.

Harley, J., Ray, R., Tomasi, L., Eichman, P., Matthews, C., Chun, R., Cleeland, C., & Traisman, E. (1978). Hyperkinesis and food additives: Testing the Feingold hypothesis. *Pediatrics, 61*, 818–828.

Hyperactivity–diet link questioned. (1982, January 23). *Science News*, p. 53.

Kavale, K., & Forness, S. (1983). Hyperactivity and diet treatment: A meta-analysis of the Feingold hypothesis. *Journal of Learning Disabilities, 16*, 324–330.

Keister, M. (1950). The relation of midmorning feeding to behavior of nursery school children. *Journal of the American Dietetic Association, 26*, 25–29.

Lester, M., Thatcher, R., & Monroe-Lord, L. (1982). Refined carbohydrated intake, hair cadmium levels, and cognitive functioning in children. *Nutrition and Behavior, 1*, 3–13.

Levin, A., & Zellerbach, M. (1985). *The type one type two allergy relief program*. New York: Berkley Publishers.

Levy, F., & Hobbs, G. (1978). Hyperkinesis and diet: A replication study. *American Journal of Psychology, 135*, 1559–1560.

Mattes, J. (1983). The Feingold Diet: A current reappraisal. *Journal of Learning Disabilities, 16*, 319–323.

Mattes, J., & Gittleman, R. (1981). Effects of artificial food colorings in children with hyperactive symptoms: A critical review and results of a controlled study. *Archives of General Psychiatry, 38*, 714–718.

Prinz, R., Roberts, W., & Hantman, E. (1980). Dietary correlates of hyperactive behavior in children. *Journal of Consulting and Clinical Psychology, 6*, 760–769.

Rapp, D. (1978). Does diet affect hyperactivity? *Journal of Learning Disabilities, 11*, 56–62.

Read, M. (1973). Hunger, school feeding programs, and behavior. *Journal of the American Dietetic Association, 63*, 386–391.

Rimland, B. (1971). High dosage levels of certain vitamins in the treatment of children with severe mental disorders. In D. Hawkins & L. Pauling (Eds.), *Orthomolecular Psychiatry*. San Francisco: W.H. Freeman.

Rimland, B. (1983). The Feingold Diet: An assessment of the reviews by Mattes, by Kavale and Forness, and others. *Journal of Learning Disabilities, 16*, 331–333.

Rose, T. (1978). Functional relationships between artificial food colors and hyperactivity. *Journal of Applied Behavioral Analysis, 11*, 439–446.

Ross, D., & Ross, S. (1982). *Hyperactivity: Current issues, research, and theory* (2nd ed.). New York: John Wiley & Sons.

Schoenthaler, S. (1983). Alabama Diet-Behavior Program: An empirical evaluation of Coosa Valley Regional Detention Center. *International Journal of Biosocial Research, 5,* 78–87.

Stine, J. (1976). Symptom alleviation in the hyperactive child by dietary modifications: A report of two cases. *American Journal of Orthopsychiatry, 46,* 637–645.

Taylor, E. (1979). Food additives, allergy, and hyperkinesis. *Journal of Child Psychology and Psychiatry, 20,* 357–363.

Thorley, G. (1983). Childhood hyperactivity and food additives. *Developmental Medicine and Child Neurology, 25,* 531–534.

Tuttle, W., Daum, K., & Larsen, R. (1954). The effects on school boys of omitting breakfast—physiological responses, attitudes, and scholastic attainment. *Journal of the American Dietetic Association, 30,* 674–677.

Wender, E. (1977). Food additives and hyperkinesis. *American Journal of Diseases of Children, 131,* 1204–1206.

DISCUSSION QUESTIONS

1. It would seem unlikely that a good diet could harm anyone. Why do you think the idea of diet modification has resulted in such controversy?
2. Many people describe the "Feingold Associations" as having followers with quasi-religious beliefs. How and why do you think these beliefs evolved, and why do they continue to exist while the research seems so questionable?
3. Have you ever noticed changes in your own behavior as a result of diet changes? Changes in others?
4. What do you think would be the most difficult part of this diet therapy? The easiest?
5. A parent is interested in trying diet therapy with her child. What advice would you give her?
6. Write down what you have eaten today (or yesterday). Compare your food with what is allowed on the K-P diet. Would you have to change your eating habits very much? What changes would be the most difficult for you?

Can Diet Cure the LD Child?

Diane Divoky

Dr. Ben F. Feingold believes that synthetic food additives cause hyperactivity and learning disabilities in children, and over the last five years the semiretired San Francisco pediatric allergist has made a lot of converts.

Note. Can Diet Cure the LD Child? by D. Divoky, 1978, *Learning, 6,* pp. 56–57. Copyright 1978 by Springhouse Corporation. Reprinted by permission.

Why Your Child Is Hyperactive, the book in which he argues his hypothesis, has sold 115,000 copies in hardback since Random House published it three years ago, and the popular media have spread his message far and wide.

The additive-free regimen he recommends for "hyperactive" children, known as the K-P diet (named for the Kaiser-Permanente Medical Care Program, for which he worked for the last twenty-five years) or the Feingold diet, is now famous enough to have a book of its own, *How To Feed Your Hyperactive Child* (Doubleday 1977), chock-full of menus, lists of safe brands of food, and recipes for everything from salted butter to lollipops. The national Feingold Association of the U.S. has a membership of 10,000 families and 120 local affiliates.

As long as one does not dwell too long on Feingold's evidence, it's easy to understand why his thesis has become so enormously popular. Over the last several years, doctors and educators have created an epidemic of hyperactivity and learning disabilities; almost every dilemma besetting the schools—from poor reading to poor discipline—has been turned on its head to be seen as a psychomedical problem caused by faulty central-nervous-system operations. Before 1965 there were virtually no children described as "learning disabled" or diagnosed as victims of "minimal brain dysfunction"; now, with the labels rife and special public funds available, as many as a quarter of the youngsters in a district may be described that way. Parents often are quick to see their difficult and impulsive children as victims of vague neurological handicaps.

Once the medical model takes over, the standard treatment for these youngsters can be a combination of stimulant drugs (Ritalin, Dexedrine) and counseling, plus some special accommodations in school. But the only element of this combination that seems to "work" (that is, make the child slow down and focus) are the drugs, and many parents have become justifiably anxious about potential side effects—insomnia, weight loss, crying jags, stomachaches, mood swings, and the zombielike quality that often masks a child's personality. Isn't there a better way to make a child manageable in school and at home?

At the same time parents are asking that question, increasing numbers of people have become concerned about the "unnaturalness" of their diets and about the possible harmful effects of highly processed and additive-loaded foods.

Along comes Feingold. Not only is he going to get hyperactive kids off drugs but he's going to do it with a wonderfully appealing treatment: additive-free, healthful food. Basically, the Feingold hypothesis goes this way: It is not just an accident that since World War II the rise in the use of synthetic colors and flavors in foods coincides with the incidence of learning disabilities and hyperactivity. By some unknown mechanism, food additives—in combination with natural salicylates found in many fruits and some vegetables—cause an adverse hyperactive reaction in certain sensitive children. By removing these substances through an elimination diet, the majority of hyperactive and learning disabled children—sometimes, Feingold says, as many as 80 percent—can be helped, many of them dramatically.

With such an attractive, wholesome treatment for what Feingold calls the H-LD child, it apparently doesn't matter that Feingold's theory is based not on a controlled study but simply on anecdotes of cases he's treated in his practice.

Is the Proof in the Pudding?

Researchers have had a difficult time testing the validity of the hypothesis. What, for example, is the significance of the cases that Feingold cites to argue his cure? The four "hyperactive" boys he focuses on as success stories in his book are a heterogeneous group of difficult kids, from six to seventeen years old, with no common symptoms. Feingold describes them in the most subjective ways: "a small, terrifying Mr. Hyde"; "wild beyond control" or "placid to the point of being dull"; a "repertoire of aggression and unhappiness including stomping, kicking walls while in temper tantrums, general surliness, telling big lies about small problems." Feingold makes no distinction between hyperkinesis and learning disabilities, or among the myriad behaviors that lead to one label or the other. He does not attempt to guess what part of his diet affects which aspect of the child's behavior or to distinguish between the children it helps and those it doesn't.

To guarantee the control of a child's diet as part of a rigorous study might require assigning a full-time monitor to stalk him around the clock; such a figure would, of course, produce enormous changes in behavior, even without diet modification. And to change a child's diet at home, one must change not only the eating and food-shopping habits of an entire family, but also the quality of interfamiliar relationships. As Dr. Sheldon Margen, professor of human nutrition at the University of California, Berkeley, notes in the *Journal of Nutrition Education* (April/June 1975): "Food is one of the most emotionally charged substances we deal with, and it is naive to believe that a change in diet brings about only physiological changes. Psychological factors are particularly potent when the change in diet affects the entire family." To determine the effect of the one variable—change in additive consumption—amidst all the changed variables is nearly impossible.

Bernard Weiss, a professor of radiation biology and biophysics at the University of Rochester, who with Margen is now conducting a study of the efficacy of the Feingold diet, admits that the results will reflect more than just dietary intake: "The fathers [in the study] have become more cooperative and participate more in child care and family life. The mothers are no longer just housewives; they've become behavioral observers. Our intervention has been massive."

In spite of these complications, the studies completed so far have shown little difference between the behavior of children on the K-P diet and those on other regimens. In June 1977 the National Advisory Committee on Hyperkinesis and Food Additives reported: "The evidence available so far generally refutes Dr. Feingold's claim that artificial food colorings in the diet substantially aggravate the behavior of children with learning disability and hyperkinesis."

Meanwhile, the believers are not to be swayed. The subject of a recent press release from the Feingold Association of the U.S. was a new and ambiguous study of the K-P diet out of the University of Pittsburgh School of Medicine. The study basically found no differences in the responses of the sixteen children in challenge experiments that had some kids receiving additive-free diets while others got placebo diets. The researchers did highlight one suggestive finding: To a limited degree, there was a difference in behavior for a brief period of time in a few of the younger children, when rated by parents. The psychologists called for more research to explore this new observation. The Feingold Association, however, leaped from this morsel of evidence to a sweeping conclusion: "What this means is that a simple, nutritious diet (high in protein, low in sweets and other carbohydrates, virtually devoid of 'junk' food) will turn a problem-plagued existence into a normal life for most hyperactive children."

Well, a simple nutritious diet is something all children deserve. And good food is certainly a more palatable cure for aggressively active kids than amphetamine-type drugs. But the Feingold partisans may have lost more than they've gained by buying into the entire medical model. Drs. Melvin D. Levine and Craig B. Liden of the Children's Hospital Medical Center in Boston warn in the August 1976 issue of *Pediatrics:* "Caution should be advised with regard to the Feingold diet. The widespread popularization of the hypothesis is regrettable . . . more data must be sought. At present, there is no substitute for describing a child well and avoiding labels. . . . The premature endorsement of 'food subtractives,' like the impulsive recommendation of drugs, may mask underlying cognitive deficiencies or emotional maladjustments while risking toxic effects and malnutrition. This is the danger we face in craving easy answers to a complex, fundamental, and widespread form of failure in childhood. . . . Simplistic cures are unlikely."

DRUG THERAPY FOR EXCEPTIONAL CHILDREN

Drugs have been used to treat exceptional children for many reasons. Anticonvulsants are administered to control seizures; tranquilizers and other psychotropic drugs are given to control mood, behavior, or thought processes; and stimulants are prescribed to control hyperactivity. While many of the treatments reflect tremendous progress in research in the treatment of exceptional children, some of these therapies remain controversial. In particular, the advantages and disadvantages of using stimulants to reduce hyperactivity in children or tranquilizers to manage the behavior of mentally retarded individuals are still being evaluated. It is these two types of drug therapy that will be focused on in this section.

Stimulant Therapy for Hyperactive Children

Hyperactivity is a problem observed in many school children today. Typically these children are labeled as having an "attention deficit disorder with hyperactivity" (American Psychiatric Association 1980) and exhibit excessive activity, inattention, and impulsivity which often results in social and academic achievement problems.

While many experts are frustrated trying to define hyperactivity and delineate it from other behavioral problems (Prinz, Connor, and Wilson 1981), it is clear that hyperactivity affects many children in the schools today. It is estimated that from 5 to 28 percent of school-age children (Murray 1976) and up to 40 percent of children referred to mental health clinics are being identified as "hyperactive" (Backman and Firestone 1979).

A large number of these children are taking prescribed drugs to help control their excessive or inappropriate behaviors. Barkley (1981) estimated that from one to two percent of children in schools, or six hundred thousand children were taking prescribed drugs; however, Walker (1975) estimated that 10 to 15 percent of students in school districts were taking prescribed medication to help manage their behaviors. The most popular type of pharmacological treatment is the use of stimulant medication such as methylphenidate (Ritalin), dextroamphetamine, or pemoline (McDonald 1978), although minimal effects have been attributed even to caffeine (Kavale 1982). These medications have a paradoxical effect, since, although stimulants, they tend to decrease excessive activity in a child.

While it was generally assumed that hyperactive and distractable behaviors were due to an excess of environmental stimulation that the hyperactive child was unable to filter, recent research has indicated that activity may function to increase sensory input missing from the environment (Zentall and Zentall 1976). It seems that the hyperactive child is not driven to activity in high stimulation environments, but rather, adequate stimulation may actually reduce certain hyperactive behaviors. Koester and Farley (1981) suggest that hyperactive children may have low arousal levels, and that they therefore continually seek a high degree of stimulation from the environment as a means of increasing their arousal levels. The results of these studies may explain why the stimulant medications have the paradoxical effect. Increasing a child's internal stimulation through drug therapy seems to *decrease* that child's need to seek external stimulation, thereby decreasing the child's excessive activity.

The use of stimulant therapy to treat hyperactivity remains controversial. The issue of stimulant drug therapy has polarized researchers since the 1960s (Kavale 1982). While medical personnel (American Academy of Pediatrics 1970, 1975) consider stimulant drugs to be an effective treatment for hyperactivity, Sroufe (1975) questions their interpretations because of methodological problems with the research. Others (Hentoff 1972; Schrag and Divoky 1975) criticize stimulant drug use from ideological and moral perspectives.

For many reasons, the use of stimulant medication has been growing rapidly. First, in many cases these drugs provide rapid symptom relief and have fewer and less harmful side effects than major tranquilizers. In addition, they are less expensive and less time consuming to administer than other nondrug therapies, and provide quick relief for the adults in the child's world (Hartlage and Telzrow 1982; McDonald 1978). All of these reasons are based on the assumption that the drug treatment is indeed effective. While there are many contradictory reports, some studies have demonstrated the generally positive effects of stimulant medication in decreasing hyperactive behaviors. Kavale (1982) studied the efficacy of stimulant drug treatment for hyperactivity by conducting a meta-analysis of 135 studies which used stimulant drug therapy.

Because of the difficulty interpreting the diverse outcome measures reported in the 135 studies, Kavale (1982) refined his results by reporting the effectiveness of stimulant therapy in three outcome categories: behavioral, cognitive, and physiological. The behavioral outcomes exhibited positive changes, indicating that the average subject receiving stimulant medication was better off than approximately 70 percent of control subjects. While the positive effects found in the cognitive outcomes were not as large as those found for the behavioral outcomes, they suggested that the average child treated with drugs was better off than 69 percent of the control subjects. This study also reported moderate increases in IQ scores and achievement measures for those subjects treated with drugs; however, these results had not been reported in previous reviews (Barkley 1977). The physiological measures indicated negative consequences for the drug treated subjects on their circulatory and respiratory systems, as shown by increases in pulse, respiration, and blood pressure, as well as suppression of height and weight. However, other physiological measures, such as galvanic skin response, averaged evoked potential, and electroencephalogram readings were consistently positive for the drug-treated subjects, supporting the suggestion that stimulant drug therapy has an energizing effect which might lower stimulation thresholds (Kavale 1982).

In spite of positive results reported in many studies examining the effectiveness of stimulant therapy for hyperactivity, there are still many emotionally charged issues. One dominant concern is the issue of symptom removal versus a cure for hyperactivity. Walker (1975) states that stimulants merely mask the symptoms of hyperactivity without curing the condition, and questions the scientific sense of supressing hyperactivity without diagnosing and correcting the underlying medical or psychological problem. Conners (1973) states that stimulant therapy does not allow the child to learn how to control his own behavior, and also decreases the motivation of parents and teachers to find other ways to treat the problem. Ross and Ross (1976) express concern that a child who learns that his or her problem can be solved by taking a pill will possibly resort to similar solutions later in life. However, Aman (1984) and Weiss (1981) state that this does not seem to be the case. While there seems to be no evidence that drug therapy produces a susceptibility to drug use in later life, this concern merits additional research.

Another concern about the use of stimulant drugs relates to the different dosages required by children for various tasks. Gadow (1983) reports that for some children, the optimal drug dose for cognitive performance is less than one-half the dose for suppression of conduct problems. Many of the studies that report improvement in behavior titrated the prescribed dosage according to conduct, not learning. In fact, the ideal dosage to regulate behavior problems may actually impair cognitive performance. In their study, Sprague and Sleator (1977) found a decrement in learning in those children given larger dosages of Ritalin. Pelham et al. (1980) also reported that children's reponses deteriorated at higher stimulant dosages.

O'Donnell (1982) identifies the rebound effect as another disadvantage of stimulant therapy. This refers to the child's irritable behavior during the afternoon hours when the medication wears off. Simms (1985) also discusses problems that occur when children forget to take their medication at lunch, or take more than prescribed in order to "become smarter."

While stimulant therapy has had considerable success in calming hyperactive children, there is concern about its effect on children's academic performance. Gadow (1983) reports that while stimulant therapy may increase academic productivity in some children, thereby leading to better grades, follow-up studies of drug-treated children have repeatedly failed to show an increase in academic achievement. Aman (1984) reviewed ten studies and found that the children showed improvement on only two out of twenty-six measures of reading as a result of medication. In an article analyzing the effects of stimulant therapy on mathematical achievement, Barkley and Cunningham (1978) reported that only two out of fourteen studies demonstrated improved mathematical performance as a result of the drug administration. Pelham (1977) examined spelling and reported that the number of correctly spelled words did not increase as a result of Ritalin therapy.

Many contradictory findings remain on the issue of stimulant therapy for hyperactive children. Some variations may be explained by differences in the identification techniques, methodologies, types of drugs and dosages, ages of the children, and types of outcome measures used. As a result of these equivocal findings, many people are recommending that nonmedical strategies be tried before drug therapies are implemented (Walden and Thomson 1981). Many alternative therapies have been found quite effective in reducing hyperactive behavior; in some cases, they have been shown to be as effective, or more effective than stimulant therapy, although the results regarding alternative therapies are not consistent either. A few of these therapies will be examined here.

Alternative Therapies to Reduce Hyperactivity

Many researchers have explored the use of behavioral approaches to behavior management. Rapport, Murphy, and Bailey (1982) found that a response cost behavioral program was more effective than Ritalin in reducing hyperactivity in the classroom and at home. Christensen (1975) demonstrated that behavior modification produced more work-oriented behavior and less disruptive behavior than drug therapy. Slightly different results were found by Backman and Firestone (1979), who noted that the most effective way of removing hyperactive behavior was through a combination of medication and behavior modification. They stated that the second most effective treatment was medication alone, and the least effective therapy was behavior therapy plus a placebo.

Other alternative treatment approaches have been used to reduce hyperactivity with varying success; these include play therapy, insight therapy, biofeedback, relaxation techniques, environmental restructuring, cognitive monitoring, and social reinforcement. Although approximately 60 to 70 percent of hyperactive children show improvement in behavior with drug therapy, there still seems to be no reliable way of predicting which children will respond favorably (Hartlage and Telzrow 1982).

No Simple Answers

In spite of the potential success of other therapies and the uncertainties connected with stimulant therapy, physicians, clinicians, and educators continue to request drug therapy for hyperactive children because of this approach's rapid response and high success rates in improving home and school behaviors (Connors and Taylor 1980). Although the literature presents complex and sometimes contradictory findings, the research has, in general, demonstrated beneficial effects for hyperactive children treated with stimulant drugs (Kavale 1982). Many ethical questions, however, still need to be carefully resolved by all concerned with hyperactive children.

Many researchers are concerned that drug therapy may be an easy escape for teachers and parents (Schrag and Divoky 1975). It is important that convenience not become a more critical issue than providing an appropriate learning environment—in either the school or the home. Walden and Thomson (1981) suggest that nonmedical approaches be tried before medication is used; this would avoid prescribing stimulants as a way of masking the child's problems. While drug therapy may improve the child's accessibility to education and counseling, it does not eliminate all the problems encountered by the hyperactive child.

One of the few things that is apparent in this controversy is that simple answers do not exist. Many factors need to be considered before making recommendations for medication. If drug therapy is a convenient, but imperfect approach to the treatment of hyperactivity (Wood and Frith 1984), it is the responsibility of all involved with exceptional children to strive for the best solutions available, even if those solutions are less convenient.

Pharmacological Treatment of Mentally Retarded Individuals

While the previous section on stimulant therapy reflects a large body of literature, only recently has critical attention been given to the study of the pharmacological treatment of mentally retarded people. Tu (1979) suggests that no other population in modern society has been exposed to such a large number and variety of drugs as have individuals with mental retardation. Of particular concern are the psychotropic drugs, which are prescription medications administered to produce changes in mood, behavior, or thought processes.

These drugs were originally intended for the treatment of severe mental illnesses, such as schizophrenia, depression, or mania, but, as a result of the success of medications with these populations, the use of psychotropic drugs has inappropriately generalized to mentally retarded people, since some of their inappropriate behaviors are similar to those exhibited by psychotic persons. Because of the success of these drugs in treating psychiatric disorders, their use with mentally retarded people proliferated during the 1960s and 1970s. Although this type of treatment may be viewed as a more humanistic alternative to some of the more restrictive restraints previously used, some people allege that this pharmacotherapy employs medication as a chemical straightjacket that has no therapeutic value (Breuning, Davis, and Poling 1982). Now, with the discovery of the possible long-term side effects resulting from these treatments, and the input of legal advocacy groups representing mentally retarded people, the issue has become even more complex.

Several classes of medications are typically used with the therapeutic intention of supressing undesired behaviors or facilitating the desired behaviors of mentally retarded persons: the anxiolytics or minor tranquilizers; antidepressants and antimanics; stimulants; antiepileptics; and the major tranquilizers or neuroleptics. All of these drugs, except the antiepileptics, are used for behavior management; the antiepileptics are designed to manage a variety of convulsive disorders. Since many people with mental retardation also have seizure disorders, the administration of the antiepileptics to those who do have seizures may be invaluable. However, the use of the antiepileptics to manage nonepileptic behavior, or to prevent seizures in a person who has never been observed to have seizures, is of no documented value (Breuning, Davis, and Poling 1982).

The anxiolytics, antidepressants/antimanics, and stimulants are infrequently used for behavior control with mentally retarded people. Although it is generally thought that anxiolytics are of little or no value in the treatment of hyperactivity, acting-out behavior, or self-destructiveness, they have the side effects of sedation and physical and psychological dependence (Breuning, Davis, and Poling 1982; Lipman 1982). Research on the use of antidepressant/antimanic drugs for behavior management has shown varied effects, with some improvement in hyperactive behavior reported with lithium. However, this type of drug has the side effects of interfering with the metabolic absorption of other drugs and possibly causing kidney toxicity. In some cases, stimulants are used to treat mentally retarded people who display behavior that is considered disruptive or hyperkinetic; however, this medication is known to inhibit the metabolism of anticoagulants, anticonvulsants, and some antidepressants (Lipman 1982).

The neuroleptics, or major tranquilizers, when effective, produce a specific improvement in mood and behavior without sedation or addiction. It appears that these drugs are used with mentally retarded people because of a superficial similarity between their behavior and that of people with mental illness; yet, there is no certainty that the treatment will be equally effective for both groups (Breuning, Davis, and Poling 1982). With mentally retarded people, the primary value of neuroleptics seems to be in their ability to produce a relatively nonselective sedation, since there are few specific behaviors that are selectively improved. However, they do have the major side effects of inducing tardive dyskinesia, an impairment in the ability to move, as well as interfering with learning.

Several surveys have been conducted to determine the amount of drug use with people with mental retardation, and, in general, they show that 40 to 50 percent of the institutionalized mentally retarded population are receiving neuroleptic drugs and 23 to 50 percent are taking antiepileptics (Breuning, Davis, and Poling 1982; Tu 1979). Tu (1979) also estimates that between one-half and two-thirds of those on psychotropic drugs have been prescribed the drugs too liberally. While it would seem logical that there would be a lower percentage of noninstitutionalized mentally retarded individuals taking medication, no data could be found on this, suggesting a need for further research.

In addition, Tu (1979) also found that 52 percent of the mentally retarded people included in the survey were being given more than one medication. This was being done in spite of the fact that objective evidence regarding the effects of using many of the drugs in combination is lacking, the therapeutic response to this multi-drug therapy is generally poor, and many adverse effects—including the aggravation of seizures—have been reported. In addition, 30 percent of Tu's sample of institutionalized mentally retarded persons had been on psychotropic medication for more than ten years without drug "holidays" to assess the effect of the medication.

A closely related problem is the possible long-term side effects resulting from the continual administration of neuroleptic drugs. Of particular concern are the dyskinesias, which although not life-threatening, do interfere with adaptive function. Aman and Singh (1985) and Bruening, Davis, and Poling (1982) estimate the prevalence of tardive dyskinesia among mentally retarded people to be between 17 and 30 percent. To add further confusion, the dyskinetic symptoms often closely resemble the stereotypic body movements that the drug is attempting to eliminate.

While lack of adequate staff or training, and exaggerated hopes for pharmacotherapy have all been cited as possible reasons for excessive drug administration, the causes are still uncertain (Tu and Smith 1979). While it might be tempting to take a strong antidrug stance on the use of medication to control the behavior of mentally retarded persons, there are many beneficial effects. For example, while major tranquilizers may actually interfere with behavior modification techniques (Lipman 1982), they are also capable of reducing stereotyped movements and suppressing aggressive and self-destructive behaviors (Aman, White, and Field

1984; Lipman 1982). In addition, the change in behavior, while perhaps not statistically significant from a research point of view, may be significant enough from the perspective of a parent or caretaker to warrant the risk of possible side effects (Anderson et al. 1985).

While drug therapy for mentally retarded people should not be viewed just as a chemical straightjacket, neither should its use be taken lightly. Since pharmacological interventions may be beneficial for some people with mental retardation, the optimal treatment may be one that balances the use of psychotropic drugs with ongoing behavioral interventions. Drug therapy could then be viewed as a supplemental therapy which helps to control excessive inappropriate behaviors until programming efforts can suceed, at which time medication could be gradually reduced or eliminated. If used with care, psychotropic drugs may achieve a more positive image and come to be viewed as therapeutic tools rather than devices of coercion and repression. It is the responsibility of all professionals working with mentally retarded people to monitor drug use and its effects.

REFERENCES

Aman, M. (1984). Hyperactivity: Nature of the syndrome and its natural history. *Journal of Autism and Developmental Disorders, 14,* 39–56.
Aman, M., & Singh, N. (1985). Dyskinetic symptoms in profoundly retarded residents following neuroleptic withdrawal and during methylphenidate treatment. *Journal of Mental Deficiency Research, 29,* 187–195.
Aman, M., White, A., & Field, C. (1984). Chlorpromazine effects on sterotypic and conditioned behavior of severely retarded patients—A pilot study. *Journal of Mental Deficiency Research, 28,* 253–260.
American Academy of Pediatrics Committee on Drugs. (1970). An evaluation of the pharmacologic approach to learning impediments. *Pediatrics, 46,* 142–144.
American Academy of Pediatrics Council on Child Health (1975). Medication for hyperkinetic children. *Pediatrics, 55,* 560–562.
American Psychiatric Association (1980). *Diagnostic and statistical manual of mental disorders* (3rd ed.). Washington, D.C.: American Psychiatric Association.
Anderson, L., Campbell, M., Grega, D., Perry, R., Small, A., & Green, W. (1985). Should autistic children be treated with haloperidol? Dr. Anderson and associates reply. *American Journal of Psychiatry, 142,* 883–884.
Backman, J., & Firestone, P. (1979). A review of psychopharmacological and behavioral approaches to the treatment of hyperactive children. *American Journal of Orthopsychiatry, 49,* 500–504.
Barkley, R. (1977). A review of stimulant drug research with hyperactive children. *Journal of Child Psychology and Psychiatry and Allied Disciplines, 18,* 137–165.
Barkley, R. (1981). *Hyperactive children: A handbook for diagnosis and treatment.* New York: Guilford Press.
Barkley, R., & Cunningham, C. (1978). Do stimulant drugs improve the academic performance of hyperkinetic children? *Clinical Pediatrics, 17,* 85–92.
Breuning, S., Davis, V., & Poling, A. (1982). Pharmacotherapy with the mentally retarded: Implications for clinical psychologists. *Clinical Psychology Review, 2,* 79–114.

Christensen, D. (1975). Effects of combining methylphenidate and a classroom token system in modifying hyperactive behavior. *American Journal of Mental Deficiency, 80,* 266–276.

Conners, C. K. (1973). What parents need to know about stimulant drugs and special education. *Journal of Learning Disabilities, 6,* 349–351.

Connors, C., & Taylor, E. (1980). Pemoline, methylphenidate, and placebo in children with minimal brain dysfunction. *Archives of General Psychiatry, 37,* 922–930.

Gadow, K. (1983). Effects of stimulant drugs on academic performance in hyperactive and learning disabled children. *Journal of Learning Disabilities, 16,* 290–299.

Hartlage, L., & Telzrow, C. (1982). Neuropsychological disorders in children: Effects of medication on learning and behavior in hyperactivity. *Journal of Research and Development in Education, 15,* 55–65.

Hentoff, N. (1972, May 25). Drug-pushing in the schools: The professionals. *The Village Voice,* pp. 20–22.

Kavale, K. (1982). The efficacy of stimulant drug treatment for hyperactivity: A meta-analysis. *Journal of Learning Disabilities, 15,* 280–289.

Koester, L., & Farley, F. (1981). Hyperkinesis: Are there classroom alternatives to drug treatments? *Elementary School Guidance and Counseling, 16,* 91–97.

Lipman, R. (1982). Psychotropic drugs in mental retardation: The known and the unknown. In K. Gadow and I. Bialer (Eds.), *Advances in learning and behavioral disabilities* (Vol. 1). New York: JAI Press, Inc.

McDonald, J. (1978). Pharmcologic treatment and behavior therapy: Allies in the management of hyperactive children. *Psychology in the Schools, 15,* 270–274.

Murray, J. (1976). Is there a role for the teacher in the use of medication for hyperkinetics? *Journal of Learning Disabilities, 9,* 30–35.

O'Donnell, H. (1982). The hyperactive child and drug treatment. *Reading Teacher, 36,* 106–110.

Pelham, W. (1977). Withdrawal of a stimulant drug and concurrent behavioral intervention in the treatment of a hyperactive child. *Behavior Therapy, 8,* 473–479.

Pelham, W., Schnedler, R., Bologna, N., & Contreras, A. (1980). Behavioral and stimulant treatment of hyperactive children: A therapy study with methylphenidate probes in a within-subject design. *Journal of Applied Behavior Analysis, 13,* 221–236.

Prinz, R., Connor, P., & Wilson, C. (1981). Hyperactive and aggressive behaviors in childhood: Intertwined dimensions. *Journal of Abnormal Child Psychology, 9,* 191–202.

Rapport, M., Murphy, A., & Bailey, J. (1982). Ritalin vs. response cost in the control of hyperactive children: A within-subject comparison. *Journal of Applied Behavior Analysis, 15,* 205–216.

Ross, D., & Ross, S. (1976). *Hyperactivity: Research, theory, and action.* New York: John Wiley & Sons.

Schrag, P., & Divoky, D. (1975). *The myth of the hyperactive child.* New York: Pantheon Books.

Simms, R. (1985). Hyperactivity and drug therapy: What the educator should know. *Journal of Research and Development in Education, 18,* 1–7.

Sprague, R., & Sleator, E. (1977). Methylpenidate in hyperkinetic children: Differences in dose effects on learning and social behavior. *Science, 198,* 1274–1276.

Sroufe, L. (1975). Drug treatment of children with behavior problems. In F. Horowitz (Ed.), *Review of Child Development Research* (Vol.4). Chicago: University of Chicago Press.

Tu, J. (1979). A survey of psychotropic medication in mental retardation facilities. *Journal of Clinical Psychiatry, 40,* 125–128.

Tu, J., & Smith, J. (1979). Factors associated with psychotropic medication in mental retardation facilities. *Comprehensive Psychiatry, 20,* 289–295.

Walden, E., & Thomson, S. (1981). A review of some alternative approaches to drug management of hyperactivity in children. *Journal of Learning Disabilities, 14*, 213–217.

Walker, S. (1975). Drugging the American child: We're too cavalier about hyperactivity. *Journal of Learning Disabilities, 8*, 354–358.

Weiss, G. (1981). Controversial issues of the pharmacotherapy of the hyperactive child. *Canadian Journal of Psychiatry, 26*, 385–392.

Wood, J., & Frith, G. (1984). Drug therapy? Let's take a closer look. *Academic Therapy, 20*, 149–157.

Zentall, S., & Zentall, T. (1976). Activity and task performance of hyperactive children as a function of environmental stimulation. *Journal of Consulting and Clinical Psychology, 44*, 693–697.

DISCUSSION QUESTIONS

1. What guidelines would you recommend be followed before using drug therapy with hyperactive children? Individuals with mental retardation?
2. Describe a child you think might merit further evaluation for possible drug therapy.
3. A parent says her son is "driving her crazy," and she heard from a neighbor that there are medications to help control his behavior and make him do better in school. What questions would you ask the parent and what advice would you give?
4. You had Billy in your class last year, and while he was an active child who needed much structure and reinforcement, he functioned fine as long as you were prepared for him. You just heard that this year's teacher is referring him for possible Ritalin therapy. Would you do anything? What?
5. The institution staff where you work is very hesitant to change the medications of any of the mentally retarded students with whom you work. However, three of your students are constantly falling asleep. The staff is concerned that lowering the dosage of medication will result in a return of inappropriate and agressive behaviors. What would you do?

Drugging the American Child: We're Too Cavalier about Hyperactivity

Sydney Walker, III, M.D.

Hyperactivity is a collection of symptoms, not a disease. It has a number of causes. Without exhaustive diagnostic tests, a physician may grab for the expedient pill, mask the real problem, and let the child down hard.

The history of medicine is full of treatment fads that we now recognize as ridiculous and unfortunate. For centuries physicians treated many diseases by bleeding their patients, many of whom responded by dying. Pernicious anemia, which is caused by a vita-

Note. Drugging the American Child: We're Too Cavalier About Hyperactivity by S. Walker, 1974, *Psychology Today*, pp. 43–48. Copyright 1974 by the American Psychological Association. Reprinted by permission.

min B-12 deficiency, used to be attributed to "oral sepsis"; the cure was to pull out all the patient's teeth. History will record another disastrous fad from our own times—the use of Ritalin and amphetamines to subdue children who are hyperactive.

Hyperactivity, also known as hyperkinesis and minimal brain dysfunction, is not a disease; it is merely a label for a constellation of signs and symptoms that can occur for various reasons. The hyperactive child's behavior is driven, uncontrolled. He may have a short attention span, throw temper tantrums, and have difficulty sleeping, learning, sitting still, and responding to discipline. These symptoms may be present in whole or in part, to greater or lesser degrees. They may be present throughout the day, in the morning or at nighttime only, or after meals. They can occur in children of both sexes, though they are observed more frequently in boys.

THE EXPEDIENT APPROACH

Hyperactivity has become an epidemic in this country. Conservative estimates put the number of afflicted at about 5% of all American school children, or almost a million and a half youngsters. Some estimates are much higher, and the number is increasing. Even more alarming, 10 to 15% of the students in some school districts are taking potentially dangerous drugs by prescription from a family doctor, frequently at the urging of school authorities.

The hyperactive child is often sent to a general practitioner or pediatrician who lacks the time, training, or inclination to get at the root of the child's problem. The expedient approach is to conduct a cursory examination, then write a prescription for Ritalin (methylphenidate) or an amphetamine. Paradoxically, these stimulants seem to suppress symptoms of hyperactivity in children. They sometimes lose their effectiveness with time, though. The physician typically reacts by increasing the dosage until the child's unruly behavior is once again under control.

The picture is much the same if the child goes to a neurologist or psychiatrist. Neurologists tend to look for specific, "hard" neurological signs of disease, without taking other factors into account. If they fail to find what they are looking for, they resort to one of the stimulant drugs. Psychiatrists, on the other hand, may look closely at the hyperactive child's personal and family life, but neglect to give him a complete physical or neurological exam. When psychotherapy doesn't work, the answer, once again, is stimulant medication.

In my medical practice I see many hyperactive children. I have never prescribed stimulants for these patients, and I never will.

TIME AND TROUBLE

Stimulants merely mask the symptoms without curing the disease. Some physicians believe that at the present stage of medical knowledge, this is all we can hope to do. That is not true. I have found that the hyperactive child's problem can almost always be identified and treated if the physician is willing to take the time and trouble to run through diagnostic tests and evaluate the resulting quantitative data. That means he must use all the sophisticated instrumentation now available to the medical profession, and he must listen carefully to what the patient and his parents have to say. It is best if he is trained in both neurology and psychiatry, since the underlying problem can turn out to be psychiatric, neurological, neurochemical, or neurophysiological. Arriving at the proper diagnosis is like solving a perplexing mystery; every clue must be considered.

Since hyperactivity usually indicates some sort of subtle brain dysfunction, it makes sense to look for malfunctioning in the neurophysiological processes related to the brain. For example, we know that oxygen is the most critical element in normal brain functioning, and that anemias, heart abnormalities, and other medical disorders can interfere with the passage of oxygen to the brain. Since improper oxygenation can cause changes in behavior, it is a logical suspect in hyperactivity.

VEIN ENGORGEMENT

Take the case of D., a five-year-old girl whose parents brought her to me because she had difficulties in school, threw tantrums, and was generally hyperactive. A neurologist had diagnosed this child as schizophrenic. He told her parents that he could find nothing physically wrong with her, so they should take her home, love her, and make the best of an unhappy situation. The neurologist did not do any neurological studies.

I questioned D.'s parents carefully. I discovered that as an infant, D. had tired while sucking at the bottle. She had a history of holding her breath, always tired easily, and had trouble keeping up with her playmates. Interestingly, her fatigue and disruptive behavior seemed to grow worse in the mountains where the air is thin, but improved at sea level.

The next step was a complete physical and neurological examination. Enlarged photographs of the back of the eye showed that certain veins in back of the retina were engorged. An ophthalmologist had mistakenly diagnosed this condition as excess pigment in the eye, without doing the requisite tests that would have told him the retinal veins were congested with blood.

Vein engorgement at the back of the eye sometimes signals a cardiac problem. I did find a moderate heart murmur, which a pediatrician had previously detected but considered benign. An electroencephalogram (EEG) showed the child's brainwave patterns to be slowed and dysrhythmic, though curiously improved during sleep. These findings were further indication of an oxygenation problem.

I do not want to imply that the diagnosis was easy and straightforward. Some signs, including an elevated level of calcium in the blood and a peculiar malformation of the forehead, turned out to be false leads. Also, no one sign pointed unambiguously to the correct diagnosis. It was necessary to take the entire pattern of clues into account.

D.'s story has a happy ending. Because I suspected poor oxygenation due to a heart problem, I sent her to a cardiologist. He determined that she had an extra vessel between the heart and the lung which was preventing a normal flow of oxygen to the brain. D. underwent surgery to correct this defect, and her hyperactivity, fatigue, rages, and tantrums disappeared. She began to participate in normal school activities, and is progressing well without medication. But without a multidimensional approach to diagnosis, this child would have gone on as a hyperactive, hopeless "schizophrenic," and in a few years would have died from her cardiac problem.

LOW LEVEL OF GLUCOSE

Another condition that can lead to hyperactivity is an inability to tolerate and assimilate glucose (sugar). The body gets this vital fuel from carbohydrates, which are present in many foods. Several organs in the body are involved in carbohydrate metabolism, and several types of disorders can interfere with it, ranging from diabetes to the extreme opposite, hypoglycemia, or low blood sugar.

The level of glucose in the blood stream directly influences the functioning of brain and other nerve cells in complicated ways. If the level is abnormal, there may be subtle symptoms of brain dysfunction, including hyperactivity.

That was the case with R., an eight-year-old boy whose parents brought him to me with complaints that the child threw tantrums and was aggressive both at home and at school. R. was also grouchy and difficult to reach, particularly in the morning and around meal times.

A local pediatrician had recommended that R. take stimulant drugs, but his parents wisely sought a second opinion before they began to administer medication. I took a complete family history, and discovered that an uncle and some cousins had diabetes. Then I ran a number of physical, neurological and biochemical tests. Again, there were some signs that proved misleading. The important finding, though, was that R. had an abnormally low level of glucose in his blood, while the level of insulin, a substance that regulates the metabolism of glucose, was too high. Ironically, this condition is often a precursor of diabetes, a disease characterized by the opposite condition—high glucose and low insulin levels.

Since other tests ruled out various other kinds of carbohydrate abnormalities, we concluded that the boy was prediabetic. I placed him on an appropriate high-protein, low-carbohydrate diet. His hyperactivity soon abated, his aggressive tantrums stopped, and he began to perform well in school. I am continuing to check him every six months for the possible development of juvenile diabetes, a particularly erratic, difficult-to-manage form of diabetes that often causes blindness. So far, he is doing well.

Without a multidimensional approach to diagnosis, this child would now be taking stimulant medication for "hyperactivity" and his carbohydrate problem would be undetected.

After oxygen and glucose, the most important requirement for the proper functioning of brain and nerve tissue is an adequate level of calcium in the body. Calcium is vital for the maintenance of proper cell-membrane polarity (positive or negative electrical charge) in the central nervous system. It is also involved in various metabolic processes, by which each cell biochemically breaks down food substances and converts them to usable energy. If the body does not get or use enough calcium, there can be behavioral symptoms, including hyperactivity.

INEDIBLE SUBSTANCES

S., a nine-year-old boy, had this problem. He had been labeled hyperactive at the age of four. When his parents brought him to me, S. had taken Ritalin for two and a half years. The dosage had gradually been increased to 15 mg three times a day, causing sleeplessness, agitation, and a decrease in appetite.

I learned that S.'s mother had *lost* eighteen pounds during her pregnancy. I also discovered that S. had a condition called pica, an appetite for inedible substances such as chalk or clay. Both these facts pointed to a possible dietary deficiency. Also, S.'s pica might have resulted in the ingestion of toxic materials, such as lead.

Once again, various clues proved to be irrelevant. For instance, three of S.'s relatives were diabetic, but in this case that fact was not significant for the eventual diagnosis. And some signs, such as the absence of certain reflexes, indicated an impairment of the central nervous system but did not pinpoint its exact nature.

An EEG revealed some unusual electrical discharges in the right temporal region of the brain. Such discharges are often taken to indicate a seizure disorder attributable to lesions in the brain. I did not jump to that conclusion, however, since seizure disorders can be due to other causes as well, including toxicity, infection, and metabolic disturbances. Biochemical studies showed that S. had an unusually low level of calcium in his blood, though urine calcium was normal.

Taken together, the various signs and symptoms in this case seemed to reflect a calcium problem. I increased the S.'s calcium intake by the simple expedient of having him drink more milk. Within two months, his behavior improved. He was able to stop taking Ritalin, his appetite returned, and his blood calcium level returned to normal. Had these changes not taken place, we would have gone on to search for more subtle calcium problems, of which there are many; fortunately he did improve.

Without a multidimensional approach to diagnosis, though, this child would still be taking Ritalin, and would still be suffering from a calcium deficiency.

CYANOTIC AT BIRTH

I have described some common origins of hyperactivity, but there are many others. Sometimes the patient has a glandular problem. Sometimes he is the victim of lead or carbon monoxide poisoning. Sometimes there are lesions in the brain.

If the physician listens closely to the patient, the patient may tell him what's wrong. I recall a ten-year-old boy who had to be placed in a special class at school because he suffered from hyperactivity and profound learning problems. Sometimes the teacher would put him in the corner until he calmed down. When this child talked about his difficulties, he spoke of having the "heebie-jeebies" periodically during the day. Apparently no one thought that was very important, but it turned out to be significant indeed.

By the time I saw him, the boy's mother had taken him to several doctors. They had prescribed Mellaril (a tranquilizer), amphetamines and Ritalin, all to no avail.

The child's history contained indications of possible brain damage. At birth he had been cyanotic, i.e., blue, because of imperfect oxygenation of the blood. Cyanosis can cause damage to brain tissue. Also, his development during childhood had been somewhat slow.

The physical, neurological and biochemical tests were all negative, except that an EEG revealed generalized, unstable output of high voltage electrical discharges from the brain whenever the boy was told to breathe deeply and whenever he was exposed to stimulation from light. These findings indicated that he had brain lesions which were causing subtle seizure activity. The seizures were not obvious to others since they did not cause flagrant motor activity, but the heebie-jeebies were the child's own subjective perception of what was going on in his brain.

Many seizure disorders can be treated without anticonvulsant drugs, but in this case an anticonvulsant was necessary. Once the boy was put on appropriate medication, his EEG improved and his school performance changed dramatically. He is now back in a regular class, and has no more school difficulties.

HAIR WHORL

Sometimes the causes of hyperactivity are not medical at all, but psychiatric or situational. Traumatic childhood experiences and unresolved conflicts can contribute. And it is not unusual for a child who is anxious, over/stimulated or frustrated in his studies to display uncontrolled behavior, fidgeting, a short attention span, or temper tantrums.

A case in point is that of G., a seven-year-old boy who was fidgety and disruptive. In addition to his behavioral problems, G. was having trouble with reading and spelling. He tended to reverse mirror image letters like *b* and *d,* or *d* and *g,* saying "god" when he should have said "dog," and he sometimes started to read and write from the wrong side of the page. Because of all his problems, G. found himself in a class for the neurologically handicapped. He was treated with Mellaril and Ritalin, without results.

A neurological examination revealed that although G. was left-eyed and left-footed, and used his left hand for eating, he favored his right hand for writing. The hair whorl, which is usually on the crown of the head on the side opposite from the dominant hand, was in the middle. And the boy showed confusion in right-left orientation. All these signs, and the fact that other tests were negative, suggested a condition known as mixed dominance, in which neither side of the brain is clearly dominant. Mixed dominance can cause dyslexia, or difficulty with reading. In G.'s case, the resulting frustration led to behavioral problems.

Fortunately, the reading problems caused by mixed dominance are often treatable if the diagnosis is made before the patient reaches adolescence, when the brain loses much of its adaptability. I referred G. to a reading clinic where he could get special reading therapy on a one-to-one basis. After eight weeks of therapy, his behavior improved; he stopped taking medication, and he returned to a normal classroom. He has since moved to the head of his class.

TIGHT UNDERWEAR

It should be clear by now that there is no simple list of causes for hyperactivity. As research into the disorder continues, we can expect to discover new etiologies. For example, Ben F. Feingold, chief emeritus of the Department of Allergy at Kaiser-Permanente Medical Center in San Francisco, recently reported that many hyperactive patients improve if they avoid foods that contain artificial colors and flavors.

We must also keep in mind that hyperactivity can be a convenient label for children who are hard to control for other reasons. Frequently a rigid school teacher sees a normal, active, curious child as overactive. Some children are unruly and inattentive in school not because they are hyperactive, but because they are hungry, or even because their underwear is too tight. One child I saw had behavior problems due to sleeplessness, which in turn was caused by pinworms.

All these examples demonstrate that it makes no scientific sense to suppress hyperactivity with drugs, without diagnosing and then correcting the underlying medical or psychological problem. That is putting the cart before the horse. But there is another reason to avoid the drugs: they can be dangerous.

Ritalin is the most commonly prescribed medication for hyperactivity. Its exact chemical properties are not clearly understood, but it does have an amphetaminelike effect on the nervous system. A recent study indicates that Ritalin is a more potent hallucinogen per unit of weight than LSD, and can cause withdrawal symptoms if taken in excess. The U.S. Department of Justice's Bureau of Narcotics and Dangerous Drugs put Ritalin and amphetamines under hard narcotics controls in 1971, because of their potential for abuse.

A recent advertisement in the *American Journal of Psychiatry* states that Ritalin should not be used to treat children under six for minimal brain dysfunction, since "safety and efficacy in this age group have not been established." The ad warns that "sufficient data on safety and efficacy of long-term use of Ritalin in children with minimal brain dysfunction are not yet available." It also states that "although a causal relationship has not been established, suppression of growth, i.e., weight gain and/or height, has been reported with long term use of stimulants in children. Therefore, children requiring long-term therapy should be carefully monitored." If the safety and efficacy of Ritalin have not been established, then what is the rationale for its use?

WHOLESALE DRUGGING

There are other dangers as well. Animal studies indicate that amphetamines can cause constriction of brain vessels, increase the likelihood of a convulsive seizure, and influence carbohydrate metabolism in an unknown way. They also alter the output of growth hormone, and affect the sensitive biochemical balance in the brain and central nervous system. It may well be that stimulant drugs produce greater harm in the long run than the hyperactive symptoms they are meant to control.

Many physicians now recognize the dangers in the longtime practice of prescribing amphetamines for overweight adults, yet most physicians continue to use them for hyperactive children. I believe, though, that if the logic of my argument is evaluated fairly, both professionals and lay people must come to share my worry and dismay about the wholesale drugging of children whom adults find difficult to manage.

CHAPTER 8

Ethical Issues

INTRODUCTION

The fields of special education and medicine are changing so rapidly that many of the advances are creating ethical dilemmas for those involved. Some of the ethical issues presented in this chapter may raise questions many readers would prefer not to think about. The issues presented in the following three sections require each reader to think about his or her own values and to reach personal conclusions. And some readers may feel they can't reach any conclusion without more time to discuss and think about these topics that are so important to handicapped children and adults.

The first section, *Withholding Medical Treatment from Severely Handicapped Individuals,* covers one of the most difficult issues facing us today. Medical technology has become so advanced that it is possible to treat, sometimes successfully and sometimes unsuccessfully, many children who would not have survived in the past. This raises many complex issues, such as quality-of-life concerns, attempts to define humanness, and many conflicting legal interpretations of the appropriateness of medical treatment for some people. There are many perspectives on this topic, and most of them are discussed, at least briefly, in this section. Wolfensberger's perspective is clearly articulated in the reprinted article, *A Call to Wake Up to the Beginning of a New Wave of Euthanasia of Severely Impaired People.*

The second section, *Moral and Ethical Implications of Human Sexuality for Handicapped Individuals,* addresses the problems with and the need for recognizing the sexual nature of handicapped individuals. This topic has often been avoided in the hope that if it is not mentioned, maybe it will go away. With more and more handicapped people integrated into community life, the need to discuss this issue is becoming crucial. Problems, solutions, and other concerns about the sexuality of handicapped persons are reviewed in this section.

The last section in this chapter, *Plastic Surgery for Children with Down's Syndrome,* reviews the relatively new but increasing use of cosmetic surgery with Down's Syndrome children. Proponents of cosmetic surgery for children with Down's Syndrome suggest that making these children look more like other children can assist their social acceptance. However, there are many critics of these procedures. This section describes what is involved in this surgery, as well as its potential benefits and drawbacks. Photographs reprinted from three medical journals are provided to assist the reader in drawing conclusions about this procedure.

With the rapid advancement of medical technology, greater acceptance of the principle of normalization, and litigation affirming the rights of handicapped citizens, professionals are beginning to examine the ethical issues facing special education. Once ignored, these human rights issues are beginning to surface and must now be addressed by persons in several professions.

WITHHOLDING MEDICAL TREATMENT FROM SEVERELY HANDICAPPED INDIVIDUALS

The right of handicapped persons to a public education has been affirmed by litigation (PARC v. Commonwealth of Pennsylvania 1971; Mills v. Board of Education 1972) and legislation (Public Law 94-142). However, according to Wolfensberger (1980), a more critical right, the right to life, is being threatened by the liberalization of abortion, the administration of psychoactive drugs, and the denial of medical treatment. One of these threats, the withholding of medical treatment from handicapped children—a procedure which often results in their deaths—will be examined in this section.

Historical Perspective

The contemporary practice of withholding medical treatment from handicapped infants is, in many ways, a continuation of the historical practice of infanticide, the killing of young children. In ancient times, the Greeks actively promoted the destruction of handicapped infants because of concerns that defective infants would pass on their defects to the next generation. Aristotle stated, "As to the exposure and rearing of children, let there be a law that no *deformed* child shall live . . ." (cited in McKeon 1941, 1302). In classical Rome, it was thought that it made no sense to preserve the life of weak, sick, or defective infants, but the Romans abandoned the infants in deserted places rather than actively killing them. In fact, Weir (1984), in his thorough review, points out that many societies have encouraged the selective killing of handicapped infants at birth. Perhaps one of the most unusual justifications of this practice was presented by the Nuer tribe in Africa, who considered handicapped infants nonhuman "hippopotamuses" who were born to human parents by mistake. Therefore, their practice of returning these "hippopotamuses" to their natural habitat by throwing them into a river was not questioned.

Weir (1984) also points out the distinctions societies have made in attempting to find socially acceptable ways to facilitate handicapped infants' deaths. Many societies have distinguished between acts of direct killing and more passive acts such as abandonment or exposure. Therefore, it has often been possible to bring about the death of an infant and avoid legal punishment. For example, in Renaissance

Italy, unwanted infants were often turned over to wet nurses; in eighteenth century France, unwanted infants were admitted to understaffed and overburdened found-ling hospitals, and in the twentieth century, nontreatment decisions were some-times made by parents or doctors in neonatal intensive care units.

Euthanasia

Euthanasia is defined as the "act or practice of killing individuals who are hopelessly sick or injured for reasons of mercy" (Hardman and Drew 1978, 393). Confusion arises between active and passive euthanasia (Downing 1969); active euthanasia is the application of a means, such as administering a lethal drug dose, to end a life, while passive euthanasia permits a person to die without extraordinary means of medical intervention (Beauchamp and Perlin 1978). From a medical point of view, Rachels (1975, 78) explains that "it is permissable, at least in some cases, to withhold treatment and allow a patient to die, but it is never permissable to take any direct action designed to kill the patient." Legally, the distinction is viewed as the differ-ence between acts and omissions (Hardman and Drew 1980).

In spite of the legal and medical viewpoints, one factor that must be considered is whether the treatment would be viewed as extraordinary in the case of a nonhan-dicapped individual (Diamond 1977; Rickham 1969). Rapid advances in neonatal surgery during the past several decades have enabled doctors to save an increasing number of newborn infants with severe congenital malformations through ordinary surgical techniques (Rickham 1969). However, in many cases, handicapped chil-dren with conditions that are surgically correctable are allowed to die. For example, in the "Johns Hopkins" case (Gustafson 1973) and the "Baby Doe" case (Weir 1984), Down's Syndrome infants with intestinal or esophageal blockages, which were correctable by surgery, starved to death when their parents refused permis-sion for surgery. A severely handicapped infant died while his case was being ar-gued in Maine Superior Court, although his tracheoesophageal fistula was repair-able by surgery (McCormick 1974). While these were highly publicized cases, reports can be found pertaining to other infants with Down's Syndrome (Shaw 1973), myelomenigocele (Hide, Williams, and Ellis 1972; Zachary 1968), prematur-ity (Duff and Campbell 1973), and other genetic and congenital defects (Robertson and Fost 1976).

Doctors have long withheld medical support from malformed infants, allowing them to die at birth and telling the parents that their babies were stillborn (*The hardest choice* 1974), but physicians are now admitting the practice of withholding treatment from handicapped infants. In one intensive care unit, neonatologists admitted that in one year they allowed one-third of twenty-four infants to die by withholding treatment (Colin 1974). Duff and Campbell (1973) state that forty-three deaths (14 percent) in the special care nursery of the Yale-New Haven Hospi-tal over a twenty-nine-month period were related to withholding treatment. Hodgman, a professor of pediatrics stated, "If we have a baby that I know is malformed beyond hope, I make no attempt to preserve life" (*The hardest choice* 1974, 84).

However, members of the Reagan administration's Department of Health and Human Services, responding to the "Baby Doe" case, where a Down's Syndrome infant was denied medical treatment, ordered doctors and hospitals to provide life prolonging medically necessary treatment for severely handicapped infants except in cases where death appears inevitable. In addition, this "Baby Doe" regulation gave federal investigators around-the-clock access to hospital records and facilities. According to this regulation, which received support from many advocacy groups and opposition from many hospital groups, withholding medical treatment was justified only if the infant was chronically and irreversibly comatose, if treatment would merely prolong an inevitable death, or if the treatment was so extreme and so likely to be futile that it would be inhumane to administer it (Weil 1984). However, on June 9, 1986, the United States Supreme Court struck down the Reagan administration's "Baby Doe" regulations. In its first ruling on this moral issue, the High Court followed a legalistic path. It stated that since there was no evidence that hospitals had discriminated against handicapped infants or had refused treatment sought by parents, there was no reason for federal intervention in a sensitive area usually left to state agencies. There are many implications to this decision and most individuals involved feel that many more such cases will come before the Supreme Court (Malcolm 1986).

Support for Withholding Medical Treatment

The proponents of withholding medical treatment from handicapped infants present five arguments for passive euthanasia. The first is that the defective infant does not fulfill the criteria for humanness (Duff and Campbell 1973; Englehardt 1973; Fletcher 1974; McCormick 1974; Stevens and Conn 1976; Tooley 1972; Walmsley 1978; Whytehead and Chidwick 1977). These criteria vary. Tooley (1972) presents these five properties as necessary for "personhood": a capacity for desires about one's future, a capacity to have a concept of self, the actuality of being a conscious subject of experiences, a capacity for self-consciousness, and the actuality of being a continuing subject of experiences and other mental states. Fletcher (1974) offers these four personhood criteria: neocortical function, self-consciousness, relational ability, and happiness. Fletcher states, "Any individual of the species *homo sapiens* who falls below the IQ 40 mark in a standard Stanford-Binet test, amplified if you like by other tests, is questionably a person; below the 20 mark, not a person" (1974, 52).

The second argument offered in support of passive euthanasia is that the quality of life of the handicapped individual may be so diminished that no one would choose to live under such circumstances (Hardman and Drew 1978; Rickham 1969; Robertson 1975); related to this, Duff and Campbell (1973) propose death as a more humane alternative to the quality of institutional life that might be faced by many severely handicapped individuals.

Third, passive euthanasia proponents point to the legal concept of wrongful life, arguing that nonexistence would be preferable to the compromised life of many handicapped children (Englehardt 1973). In wrongful life court cases, severely handicapped children, with the aid of legal guardians, sue for damages for their very existence calculated on the basis of their expected life spans. Capron (1980) characterizes the children's position in these cases as follows: "I'd rather not be here suffering as I am, but since your wrongful conduct preserved my life, I am going to take advantage of my regrettable existence to sue you" (89).

The fourth and fifth arguments are that euthanasia would relieve families of the social, psychological, and economic burdens of raising a handicapped child (Robertson 1975), and finally, would resolve the competing equities issue (Boggs 1977) of allocating human and financial resources to those with the greatest probability of contributing to society (Rickham 1969).

Opposition to Passive Euthanasia

Arguments are also presented by the opponents of passive euthanasia for handicapped infants. The strongest and most basic argument is that based on the sanctity of human life. Jakobovits (1980, 24–25) states that the sanctity of life principle allows for no exceptions since, "the title to life is absolute from the moment of birth." Ramsey (1978) presents a similar concept, the equality of life principle, under which individuals may not be compared or evaluated as inferior merely because of their defects.

Others cite the violations of human rights that may occur when nontreatment decisions are made (Affleck 1977; Dybwad 1972), particularly when the infants have no say in the decision (Hardman and Drew 1980; Shaw 1973). When decisions are made by parents, physicians, other parties, or society, the selected treatment may be that which serves best the interests of those parties; the interests of the primary party, the handicapped infant, may be secondary to the wishes of individuals whose lives are not at stake in the decision (Weir 1984).

Concerns have also been voiced regarding the irreversability of decisions based on potentially inaccurate predictions of future functioning (McCormick 1974). Because assessment devices are not very accurate during the early childhood years, attempts to determine the potential mental and physical functioning levels of handicapped infants based on clinical judgments are questionable. Although Lorber (1971) proposes a regression formula for deciding who should receive medical treatment, the error margin is great (Affleck 1977). Because of the high stakes and the uncertainty about prognosis, many people involved with this issue feel that it is better to err on the side of caution.

Diamond (1977, 133) counters the wrongful existence theory stating that "there is no evidence that the handicapped child would not rather go on living." While the court cases involved with the wrongful life arguments have had mixed decisions, many of the justices have maintained it is wrong to assume that nonexistence would ever be preferred to continued existence, even with severe handicaps (Weir 1984).

Others fear that passive euthanasia will lead to selective extermination as preached in Nazi Germany (*Deciding when* 1973), or even to the destruction of female infants as practiced in many countries (Weir 1984). From the families' perspective, raising a handicapped child may be stressful, but parents and siblings also report that their lives are enriched by sharing the experience (Lebacqz 1972). Other families stress that most parents are too upset at the time to understand the problem and their full range of options (Hardman and Drew 1980).

The final and perhaps most straightforward argument is a legal one, since parents or physicians who opt for euthanasia could be charged with murder or manslaughter, neglect, or child abuse (Robertson 1975; Robertson and Fost 1976). Although as of 1984, no parent or physician in the United States had been prosecuted for neonatal euthanasia, there have been cases where parents were prosecuted for directly killing an abnormal child who survived the neonatal period (Weir 1984).

Legal Factors

Although not many judicial decisions focus specifically on euthanasia of children with severe handicaps, many points of criminal and civil law apply (Guess et al. 1984). First, the constitution states that all people have a right to the equal protection of the law; therefore handicapped newborns have at least the same rights to treatment as nonhandicapped newborns. While there may be many debates over intentions, the result of withholding treatment to a handicapped child is to cause the child to die. The criminal codes throughout the United States generally define the intentional taking of a human life as homicide. If the death is caused by intentional means, charges of murder can be brought; if the death results from disregarding the consequences of failing to act, charges of involuntary manslaughter can be brought. Criminal charges may apply to either action or inaction. Other charges can be brought under the child abuse laws in each state. In these cases, the parents, physicians, or other health care practictioners can also be charged with manslaughter if treatment or failure to treat results in the death of a child. In addition to the criminal charges of first- and second-degree murder and manslaughter, the charges of conspiracy and accessory before the fact can also be brought.

The final legal point to be examined is the enforcement of federal laws prohibiting discrimination towards handicapped persons. President Reagan stated that Section 504 of the Rehabilitation Act of 1973 forbade recipients of federal funds from withholding from handicapped citizens, simply because they were handicapped, any benefit or service that would ordinarily be provided to nonhandicapped citizens. While there are more technical points to these legal issues than can be discussed in this section, a more complete review can be found in Guess et al. 1984.

Economic and Social Factors

One perspective on the treatment of handicapped children considers a cost analysis comparing the assets an individual contributes to society to the community resources that individual uses. Some consider a person with severe handicaps a drain on society's scarce resources. If the costs outweigh the benefits, the value of supporting a severely handicapped individual's life may be questioned (Powell, Aiken, and Smylie 1982). Regardless of who is responsible for caring for a severely handicapped child, the already staggering cost of this commitment is increasing (Guess et al. 1984). For example, Budetti et al. (1981) in studying the technology of neonatal intensive care units, found that the procedures were not cost effective because the consumption of 133 severely handicapped survivors outweighted the productive potential of 835 nonhandicapped survivors.

While the cost of providing services varies greatly, it is clear that both the community and family pay large amounts to maintain the lives of severely handicapped persons. However, this cost analysis approach ignores other perspectives that view the individual's rights and needs as coming before those of society (Guess et al. 1984). Powell, Powell, and Aiken (1982) state that from the individual perspective, severely handicapped infants would have rights to existence independent of the effect their life would have on society.

Another consideration of social consequence is the impact the birth and presence of a child with a severe handicap has on the family. While there are many relevant studies, the findings are inconsistent (Blackard and Barsch 1982; Guess et al. 1984). Regardless of the specifics, the family of a handicapped child may face extra stresses that can complicate the traditional problems that families encounter; however, this potential stress does not necessarily affect the family negatively. All that can be said for certain is that a handicapped child will influence the family. Whether this impact is positive or negative or may be influenced by many other factors (Guess et al. 1984).

Who Should Make the Decision

Decision making is difficult with so many complex factors to be considered. Further, the question of who should make the decision to treat or not to treat a handicapped infant is still unanswered.

Many physicians and ethicists involved with this issue think that the parents of the child are the appropriate decision makers, and they usually choose not to override the parental decision (Weir 1984). Others, however, feel that the parents are the least qualified decision makers, and argue that while they may be familiar with the family dynamics, they may be emotionally distressed at the time, lack knowledge about the medical facts and potential abilities of the child, and have a conflict of interest between their own interests and those of the handicapped child.

Because of their specialized knowledge and experience in treating handicapped children, many people involved with this controversy think that the physician is best prepared to make treatment or nontreatment recommendations (Weir 1984). In addition to being more knowledgeable, physicians may be able to be more objective since they are not as emotionally involved as the parents would be. However, physicians may not always make accurate diagnoses, and they may not fully understand the future capabilities of the child. Some physicians who have observed the treatment of many handicapped children may try to protect the infant and family from the potential suffering and problems that may face them by recommending nontreatment, while others may be more willing to try experimental treatments to further the research base of medicine. Physicians may also differ in their readiness to examine the legal requirements of treatment and parents' wishes. Thus, while physicians may have more experience than parents in these cases, it is clear that they may also have difficulties with making treatment or nontreatment decisions.

Several cases of nontreatment have been decided by the courts. While this may allow for the two opposing viewpoints presented to be presented by objective, knowledgeable witnesses, many parents and physicians object to this approach since it reduces parental autonomy and the use of medical discretion in making decisions (Weir 1984). While many attorneys accept the use of the courts to protect handicapped infants' rights, others feel that the outcomes of the cases are often influenced by the personal views of the judges.

It is clear that no one person is always able and qualified to make a nontreatment decision. That is one reason many hospitals have formed committees to be responsible for making treatment decisions. These committees generally consist of physicians, nurses, social service personnel, hospital administrators, clergy, and sometimes, special educators. A committee is more likely than a single person to have access to all the relevant information: the medical facts, information about the family, and data on school and placement alternatives (Weir 1984). The greatest problem with committees has to do with the need for rapid decisions, since even short delays may result in death or further deterioration of an infant's condition. If a hospital has an existing committee that can meet on short notice, the process can work; if committee members cannot be available for rapid decisions, then the committee approach loses many of its advantages.

Support for Active Euthanasia

An additional issue to examine is that of support for active euthanasia in some nontreatment cases. Once a nontreatment decision has been made, the infant's death usually follows. However, nontreatment does not always result in the death of the child, at least not immediately. In those cases, what should be done for infants who are dying slowly and suffering?

While there are often distinctions between "killing" and "letting die" from both moral and legal perspectives, the outcome of either decision may eventually be the same. While the intentional killing of handicapped infants is distasteful to many people, those who are killed quickly do not suffer a slow death, such as that experienced by the Down's Syndrome infants who starved to death when surgery to correct their incomplete esophaguses was denied (O'Neil 1978). While it is not possible to address all the possible scenarios, it is important to consider what circumstances, if any, would justify action that brings about a rapid and painless death for a nontreated handicapped infant.

Related Issues

As medical technology progresses, so do the legal, moral, and ethical issues. The preceding discussions have barely touched on some of the controversies surrounding medical treatment of handicapped children. There are many. Among the most pressing questions are these: Who has the authority to determine whether treatment is withheld from handicapped individuals? And what are the legal ramifications of such actions? (Hardman and Drew 1980)

While this section has focused primarily on infants, and has not yet touched on the nontreatment of older handicapped individuals, there are several such cases that merit mentioning. For example, Walter Sackett (1971), a Florida legislator, suggested that five billion dollars could be saved over the next fifty years if up to 90% of the residents in Florida's state institutions were allowed to die as a result of nonagressive treatment of medical problems such as pneumonia. In a recent court battle that extended over a three-year period, a twenty-eight-year-old woman with cerebral palsy finally won the right to refuse to be force fed to keep her alive. The court ruled that

> Elizabeth Bouvia's decision to forgo medical treatment or life support through mechanical means belongs to her. . . . We do not believe it is the policy of this state [California] that all and every life must be preserved against the will of the sufferer (Chambers 1986, A28).

While these cases are different from those that deal with the treatment of infants, since the involved persons have lived on their own without extraordinary medical treatment or have given their own consent for the nontreatment, the issues are closely related.

And while answers are hard to come by, the questions raised are important to anyone who has contact with handicapped individuals. How society, in general, responds to these questions will be determined in part by how the professionals involved with these individuals respond. While it is easier to wait until faced by the situation, it is important for us to think about the questions and our own answers now.

REFERENCES

Affleck, G. (1977). The right to survive. *Mental Retardation, 15,* 52.

Beauchamp, T., & Childress, J. (1979). *Principles of biomedical ethics.* New York: Oxford University Press.

Beauchamp, T. L., & Perlin, S. (1978). *Ethical issues in death and dying.* Englewood Cliffs, NJ: Prentice-Hall, Inc.

Blackard, M., & Barsch, E. (1982). Parents' and professionals' perceptions of the handicapped child's impact on the family. *The Journal of the Association for the Severely Handicapped, 7,* 62–70.

Boggs, E. M. (1977, January). *Competing equities: An issue raised by, but not going beyond, Section 504.* Memorandum to the Legislative and Social Issues Committee of the American Association on Mental Deficiency.

Budetti, P., McManus, P., Barrand, N., & Heinen, L. (1981). Background Paper #2: Case studies of medical technologies; Case study #10: The cost and effectiveness of neonatal intensive care. From *The Implications of Cost-Effectiveness Analysis of Medical Technology.* Washington, D.C.: Office of Technology Assessment, Congress of the United States.

Capron, A. (1980). The continuing wrong of "wrongful life." In A. Milunsky and G. Annas (Eds.), *Genetics and the Law II.* New York: Plenum Press.

Chambers, M. (1986, April 17). Appeals panel says quadriplegic has right to end force feeding. *The New York Times,* p. A28.

Colin, B. D. (1974, May). Life sustaining care withheld from infants. *Pediatric News,* pp. 1, 42–43.

Deciding when death is better than life. (1973, July 16). *Time,* pp. 36–37.

Diamond, E. F. (1977). The deformed child's right to life. In D. J. Horan and D. Mall (Eds.), *Death, dying, and euthanasia.* Washington, D.C.: University Publications of America, Inc.

Downing, A. B. (1969). *Euthanasia and the right to death: The case for voluntary euthanasia.* London: Peter Owen Limited.

Duff, R. S., & Campbell, A. G. (1973). Moral and ethical dilemmas in the special care nursery. *The New England Journal of Medicine, 289,* 890–894.

Dybwad, G. (1972). Basic legal aspects and provision for medical, educational, social, and vocational help to the mentally retarded. *Australian Journal of Mental Retardation, 2,* 97–105.

Engelhardt, H. T. (1973). Euthanasia and children: The injury of continued existence. *The Journal of Pediatrics, 83,* 170–171.

Fletcher, J. F. (1974). *Four indicators of humanhood—The inquiry matures.* The Hastings Center Report, Institute of Society, Ethics, and the Life Sciences, *4,* 4–7.

Guess, D., Dussault, B., Brown, F., Mulligan, M., Orelove, F., Comegys, A., & Rues, J. (1984). *Legal, economic, psychological, and moral considerations on the practice of withholding medical treatment from infants with congenital defects.* Seattle, Wa.: The Association for Persons with Severe Handicaps.

Gustafson, J. M. (1973). Mongolism, parental desires, and the right to life. *Perspectives in Biology and Medicine, 16,* 529–557.

Hardman, M. L., & Drew, C. J. (1978). Life management practices with the profoundly retarded: Issues of euthanasia and withholding medical treatment. *Mental Retardation, 16,* 390–396.

Hardman, M. L., & Drew, C. J. (1980). Parent consent and the practice of withholding treatment from the severely defective newborn. *Mental Retardation, 18,* 165–169.

Hide, D. W., Williams, H. P., & Ellis, H. L. (1972). The outlook for the child with myelomeningocele for whom early surgery was considered inadvisable. *Developmental Medicine and Child Neurology, 14,* 304–307.

Jakobovitz, I. (1980). Jewish views on infanticide. In M. Kohl (Ed.), *Infanticide and the value of life.* Buffalo, N.Y.: Prometheus Books.

Lebacqz, K. (1972). *Editorial correspondence: Mongoloid children and the burden of the family.* The Hastings Center Report, Institute of Society, Ethics, and the Life Sciences, *2,* 12–13.

Lorber, J. (1971). Results of treatment of myelomeningocele. *Developmental Medicine and Child Neurology, 13,* 279–303.

Malcolm, A. (1986, June 11). Ruling on Baby Doe: Impact limited. *The New York Times,* p. A16.

McCormick, R. A. (1974). To save or let die: The dilemma of modern medicine. *Journal of the American Medical Association, 229,* 172–176.

McKeon, R. (Ed.). (1941). *The basic works of Aristotle.* New York: Random House.

O'Neil, R. (1978). The moral relevance of the active/passive euthanasia distinction. In D. Smith and L. Bernstein (Eds.), *No rush to judgement: Essays on medical ethics.* Bloomington, Ind.: The Poynter Center.

Powell, T., Aiken, J., & Smylie, M. (1982). Treatment of involuntary euthanasia for severely handicapped newborns: Issues of philosophy and public policy. *The Journal of the Association for the Severely Handicapped, 6,* 3–10.

Rachels, J. (1975). Active and passive euthanasia. *The New England Journal of Medicine, 292,* 78–80.

Ramsey, P. (1978). *Ethics at the edge of life.* New Haven: Yale University Press.

Rickham, P. (1969). The ethics of surgery in newborn infants. *Clinical Pediatrics, 8,* 251–254.

Robertson, J. A. (1975). Involuntary euthanasia of defective newborns: A legal analysis. *Stanford Law Review, 27,* 213–269.

Robertson, J. A., & Fost, N. (1976). Passive euthanasia of defective newborn infants: Legal considerations. *The Journal of Pediatrics, 88,* 883–889.

Shaw, A. (1973). Dilemmas of "informed consent in children." *New England Journal of Medicine, 289,* 885–890.

Stevens, H. A., & Conn, R. A. (1976). Right to life/ Involuntary pediatric euthanasia. *Mental Retardation, 14,* 3–6.

The hardest choice. (1974, March 25). *Time,* p.84.

Tooley, M. (1972). Abortion and infanticide. *Philosophy and Public Affairs, 37,* 51.

Walmsley, S. A. (1978). A life and death issue. *Mental Retardation, 16,* 387–389.

Weil, W. (1984, July). The Baby Doe decisions. *Health,* 58.

Weir, R. F. (1984). *Selective nontreatment of handicapped newborns: Moral dilemmas in neonatal medicine.* New York: Oxford University Press.

Whytehead, L., & Chidwick, P. F. (Eds.) (1977). *Considerations concerning the passage from life to death.* An Interim Report by The Task Force on Human Life, Winnipeg.

Wolfensberger, W. (1980). A call to wake up to the beginning of a new wave of "euthanasia" of severely impaired people. *Education and Training of the Mentally Retarded, 15,* 171–173.

Zachary, R. B. (1968, August 3). Ethical and social aspects of treatment of spina bifida. *The Lancet,* pp. 274–276.

DISCUSSION QUESTIONS

1. Many lawyers feel that those responsible should be legally prosecuted when a severely handicapped child dies because medical treatment was withheld or not aggressively followed.
   a. Do you agree with this?
   b. What exceptions would you make to your answer?
   c. What circumstances would you have to consider in making your decision?
2. Many people have suggested that a committee should be established to decide which children should be treated or not treated—in other words, who should live and who should die.
   a. Who do you think should be on the committee and why?
   b. What criteria should they consider in making the decisions?
3. As mentioned in the section, the courts have recently ruled that an adult women, with normal intelligence and severe cerebral palsy, be allowed to make her own decision about force feeding to keep her alive.
   a. Do you agree with this decision and why?
   b. What if she were suffering from a severe emotional problem?
   c. What if she were also mentally retarded?
4. *Case History.* H.R. was a two-day-old infant who was vomiting his feedings and green fluid. He was born to a forty-five-year-old mother who had thought she was through meno-

pause and safely out of the range of pregnancy. The family had two normal teenagers, the parents were in good health, and the pregnancy was uneventful. The baby had the unmistakable stigmata of Down's syndrome, a diagnosis confirmed by chromosome examination. In addition, he had a slight heart murmur.

Radiologic examination confirmed the baby had an intestinal obstruction that could only be corrected by surgery. The well-educated parents had expressed their intentions of institutionalizing the baby prior to the discovery of the intestinal problem. When asked to sign the consent form for the surgery, the father signed saying, "I have no alternative, do I?" The surgery was successful and ten days later the infant was on his way to the state institution (Beauchamp and Childress 1979).

a. Knowing that the parents intended to institutionalize the child, do you think the physicians should have encouraged the surgery? Why?

b. Were there any other factors that should have been considered in this case?

5. *Case History.* A baby was born with congenital heart disease, asphyxia at birth, diagnosed brain damage, and numerous other problems. The parents requested that life-prolonging measures be discontinued. However, the physicians said that nothing they were doing was extraordinary and continued ventilatory assistance, antibiotic medication, surgical procedures, and blood transfusions long after the parents considered the situation to be hopeless. After the child was removed from the respirator, the parents were given the child to take home. For weeks they listened to a high-pitched wailing from the child, administered anticonvulsive medicine daily, hoped in vain for some signs of improvement, and fed the child through a stomach tube.

The parents debated their alternatives and rejected the idea of continuing medical care at home since there were no signs of improvement. They rejected the idea of institutionalizing the child since they did not want to visit "a twenty-year-old vegetable lying on a mat in a rehab center somewhere." They also rejected the idea of allowing the child to die from an untreated infection because of the prolonged suffering it would cause. They finally decided to kill their child by increasing the dosage of anticonvulsant medicine and stopping feeding. The child died in six days. When later asked about killing their child, they said "We never doubted that our decision was for the child's best interests. We did it out of love." (Weir 1984, 249.)

a. Do you think the hospital was right to ignore the parents request to discontinue treatment? Why?

b. Do you think any of the treatments were extraordinary in this case?

c. Do you think these parents should be prosecuted for killing their child? Why?

d. What support might have changed the outcome of this case and why?

A Call to Wake Up to the Beginning of A New Wave of "Euthanasia" of Severely Impaired People

Wolf Wolfensberger

Those who ally themselves with severely handicapped or otherwise deeply rejected people can take satisfaction in the fact that major breakthroughs have been experienced in the extension of public funding to the education of severely handicapped children, and even in their inclusion in the public education system. However, a major new calamity now looms over the current scene which renders such advances less significant: the powerful gathering of forces that would assault the very lives of people who are profoundly, severely, and even moderately afflicted; and the beginnings of systematic and large-scale "death-making" of afflicted people.

In the context of a brief editorial, I can only sketch a few aspects of these developments. These include the following:

1. The liberalization of abortion in general has resulted in explicit sanction (often outright encouragement) of the abortion of (potentially) handicapped infants; in turn this has led to the now widespread practice of some forms and stages of infanticide which include (a) the abortion of viable fetuses, and of fetuses in the last weeks of pregnancy; (b) efforts to kill living and viable aborted infants; and (c) any number of measures applied after birth to maximize the likelihood that a handicapped newborn will not survive.

2. In hospitals (even those run by religious bodies), mentally retarded people, people with other handicaps, and elderly people are commonly denied relatively elementary life supports such as antibiotics, basic resuscitation, or even the simplest medical procedures. In fact, the likelihood is relatively high that persons afflicted with multiple devalued conditions will not leave a hospital alive—even if their affliction and/or illness is relatively moderate. In many locales in North America, it is dangerous to admit to a typical general hospital a moderately retarded person who is above the age of sixty. Secretly and without involving relevant relatives, advocates, or the other human service providers responsible for the handicapped individuals, death-dealing decisions about such individuals are commonly made by medical personnel. Often, the only way to assure the safety of such afflicted persons in hospitals is to place at their bed a twenty-four hour "guard," e.g., family, advocates, friends, private duty nurses, or members of that person's supportive human service circle such as group home staff.

3. Handicapped people are given massive doses of psychoactive drugs, so that they die from drug effects—even though the death certificate will list only the complications, such as cardiac arrest, pneumonia (caused by paralysis of the throat which lets food into the windpipe), etc.

4. Elderly people are subjected to conditions and abuses which make healthy

Note. A Call to Wake Up to the Beginning of a New Wave of "Euthanasia" of Severely Impaired People by W. Wolfensberger, 1980, *Education and Training of the Mentally Retarded, 15,* pp. 171–173. Copyright 1980 by the Division on Mental Retardation, The Council for Exceptional Children. Reprinted by permission.

elderly people sick and feeble, and sick and feeble elderly people dead. Innumerable human service, nursing home, and institutional practices contribute to this. Many elderly people in the community are too poor to eat appropriately, which once more contributes to all sorts of secondary causes of death; violence against elderly people is rampant; in the nursing homes, not enough eating time may be allowed for feeble residents; etc.

5. Infirm people are precipitously moved around from one place to another, which is known to drastically increase the death rate. The list could go on.

The erosion of the sense of sanctity of the lives of afflicted people is proceeding at great pace. People should deeply contemplate the calamitous meaning of the 1980 Supreme Court decision regarding Philip Becker: rejecting and absentee parents may legally refuse life-sustaining medical procedures to be performed on their handicapped offspring, condemning a child to (a most likely slow and gruesome) death. We thus return to the concept of child-as-chattel who can be killed at the whim of the parent, as was the case in pagan Greece and Rome.

We should also be aware that for the first time in about 2500 years, the medical profession is abandoning its radical commitment to life, and is massively participating in death-making, even to the point where in state after state, new capital punishment laws are being enacted under which medical personnel would actively participate in the execution of prisoners by means of poisonous injections. Ominously, more and more transport systems for invalid people are adopting police terminology, uniforms, etc.

Three dynamics appear to prevent many people from recognizing the new wave of death-making: they have been insulated from the evidence; they have seen the evidence, but it has been so disguised that they could not perceive the truth; even if they saw the evidence, and even if it were not dis-

guised, they simply cannot believe that large-scale "euthanasia" could become a reality in our society.

Disguises of the new "euthanasia" movement have included measures (to mention only some samples) such as the following: (a) the use of all sorts of babble that detoxifies the many forms of homicide. Killing may be interpreted as good science, good medicine ("healing intervention," "therapeutic"), compassion ("helping to die"), good law, and even solid theology, religion, and Christianity (e.g., Whytehead 1979; Whytehead and Chidwick 1977). (b) The disfigurement (e.g., injection of dyes) of infants prior to abortion, so that attending personnel will not view the aborted infant as human. (c) A major disguised form of death-making is for handicapped people to be dumped into the community without support systems. There, many are severely victimized in any number of ways (having their income and property taken away, being sexually abused and physically assaulted, etc.); many enter into a violent street culture in which they are weak members; many end up in penury, hunger, and poor health. (d) Few people are able to see the connections between legitimized and medicalized mass psychoactive drugging of people, and their resulting secondary incapacitation and death.

Legislative protection of the lives of the handicapped has eroded gradually, but two major breakthroughs so far have been the liberalization of abortion, and the passage of "death and dignity" type legislation. One such act that has probably gone further than any other is the 1978 Death with Dignity Act of Arkansas. I believe that this act now makes relatively active euthanasia a matter that can be legitimized by judicial decision. In other words, I believe we are now beyond the realm of legislation and into the realm of court interpretation—where judicial rulings have also gradually moved more and more toward a pro-death position, as the Becker case clearly indicates.

What is to be done? The necessary action falls on many levels, depending upon a person's state of awareness, station in life, and calling. Some obvious measures include the following: (a) increasing one's awareness of the relevant dynamics, facts and realities; (b) personal radicalization on the issue; (c) educating the unaware segments of the public to the prevailing realities and dangers; (d) boldly, overtly and explicitly confronting death-making everywhere and on all levels; (e) channeling the emphasis upon legal action in areas of educational inclusion, institutional quality, and community integration to issues pertaining more directly to questions of life and death; (f) engaging in symbolic—even dramatic—life affirming actions, if need be even civil disobedience vis-a-vis laws and authorities allied to death.

REFERENCES

Whytehead, L. *Report of the task force on human life.* Winnipeg, Manitoba (Canada): General Synod of the Anglican Church of Canada, 1979.

Whytehead, L., & Chidwick, P. F. *Considerations concerning the transit from life to death.* Winnipeg, Manitoba (Canada): Task Force on Human Life, General Synod of the Anglican Church of Canada, 1977.

MORAL AND ETHICAL IMPLICATIONS OF HUMAN SEXUALITY FOR HANDICAPPED INDIVIDUALS

The education of handicapped individuals is laden with many controversial issues, but none has traditionally been more controversial than that of sex education for the handicapped. With the passage and implementation of Public Law 94-142, special educators are focusing their attention on the normalization and deinstitutionalization of handicapped persons. As this trend toward placement within the least restrictive environment continues, handicapped individuals will encounter more opportunities for sexual contacts and loving relationships (Bass 1974).

In the past, handicapped individuals, particularly people with mental retardation, have often not been allowed to assume responsibility for their own sexual growth (Perske 1974); their sexuality has been ignored, denied, or subverted (Schmid, Moneypenny, and Johnston 1977). Opponents of the normalization principle suggest that mentally retarded persons would commit sexual offenses if they were returned to a community setting; however, there is little evidence that this would occur. If the principle of normalization is to be achieved, persons with handicapping conditions will need practical knowledge of their own sexuality and the responsibilities that go with it (Alcorn 1974).

Historical Perspectives and Attitudes

Historically, handicapped individuals have not been permitted to assume responsibility for their own sexual growth (Perske 1974). Attitudes toward the handicapped person's sexual development have emphasized physical, emotional, and intellectual desexualization (Russell and Hardin 1980). Maddock (1974) attributes such negative attitudes toward the sexual expression of handicapped persons to three things: uncontrolled reproduction, undisciplined sex drive and custodial mentality.

The first concern, uncontrolled reproduction, has led to the eugenics movement with the goal of sterilization. Goddard (1912) proposes that mentally retarded males be castrated and mentally retarded females receive ovariectomies. Perske (1973) reports that one midwestern institution officially recorded 656 castrations between 1894 and 1944, many of which were performed to prevent masturbation. Cooke (1973) reports that surgical sterilization of mentally retarded people was permitted by statute in twenty-eight states, twenty-three of which allowed sterilization without consent. Mentally retarded persons residing in state institutions were often given the option of release in exchange for the agreement to be sterilized. Virginia legislators recently discovered that more than seven thousand people were involuntarily sterilized between 1924 and 1972 under a state program to eliminate "social misfits" (*New York Times* 1981).

Advocates of sterilization argue that we need to protect mentally retarded people from unwanted parenthood and its responsibilities, to protect the rights of the unborn child by assuring that the child will not be raised by a mentally defective person, and to protect society from economic burdens, overpopulation, and generations of mental defectives. These pervasive attitudes can best be summarized by Chief Justice Oliver Wendell Holmes (1927) who states:

> It is better for all the world, if, instead of waiting to execute degenerate offspring for crimes, or to let them starve for their imbecility, society can prevent those who are manifestly unfit from continuing their kind. The principle that sustains compulsory vaccination is broad enough to cover cutting the fallopian tubes . . . three generations of imbeciles are enough (*Buck v. Bell,* 274 U.S. 200)

The second concern, undisciplined sex drive, relates to society's view that mentally retarded individuals have greater sex drives than nonhandicapped people. As a result, society has treated mentally retarded individuals as "sexual monsters" who need to be repressed. There is no empirical proof that this concern is warranted.

The third concern, custodial mentality, views the mentally retarded individual as incapable of learning and developing. Rather than teaching the mentally retarded person about sex and sexuality, persons who abide by this belief maintain that "the handicapped need to be shielded from situations which might awaken their dormant sexual desires and lead them into a life of frustration" (Maddock 1974, 275). Advocates of this philosophy believe that ignoring the sexuality of the mentally retarded will make it disappear; in other words, the less a handicapped person knows about sex, the less opportunity he will have to be sexually irresponsible (Gordon 1974).

Much recent attention has been given to sex education for the handicapped preschool child (Ware, Woods, and Gamsu 1977), school age child and adolescent (Rothenberg, Franzblau, and Geer 1979), and adult (Tegtmeier 1977). The concern for sex education is crossing all categorical boundaries; articles have been written about the need for sex education for the learning disabled (Rothenberg, Franzblau, and Geer 1979), multiply handicapped (Fischer 1975), mentally retarded (Kempton 1977), physically handicapped (Thornton 1979), hearing impaired (Pearson 1979), visually impaired (Knappett and Wagner 1976), and emotionally disturbed individuals (Kalma 1976).

Arguments for Sex Education

Proponents of sex education stress that ignorance—not knowledge—stimulates inappropriate behavior (Gordon 1975). Research has shown that many handicapped individuals lack fundamental knowledge of human body functions and the concepts of intercourse, pregnancy, and childbirth that normal children learn incidentally (Brantlinger 1985; Edmonson and Wish 1975; Fischer and Krajicek 1974; Sengstock and Vergason 1970). Sex education programs have been said to enhance self-esteem and socialization, improve personality development, reduce anxiety and the probability of sexual exploitation, and encourage responsibility, maturity, and a respect for sex (McNab 1978). Haavik and Menninger (1981) have found that sex education programs can improve the learning of trainable mentally retarded students over a two- to three-year period in the areas of body identification, social skills, self-care, manners, and knowledge of growth and reproduction.

In addition to the interpersonal advantages of a sex education program, some professionals feel that parents want help with their child's sexual development. The four common concerns most often cited by parents regarding their child's sexuality include: their own inability to answer questions raised by their child; masturbation; fear that their child will be a threat to the community; and fear that their child will be sexually exploited (Sengstock 1967). Vockell and Mattick (1972) report that

> Sex education happens automatically: the only questions are whether it will happen haphazardly or designedly, whether it will come from persons who care for the child or from persons with less worthy motives, whether the child will understand or be confused and frightened by what he learns (130).

Arguments Against Sex Education

Although there is generally less opposition to sex education for handicapped persons than for nonhandicapped persons (Bass 1977), the sexual needs of handicapped individuals are generally not understood by the general population (Brekke 1979; Heshusius 1982). This lack of understanding is best exemplified in the way the handicapped person has been treated historically.

Opponents of sex education have expressed fears that sex education will awaken dormant and unfulfillable sexual desires, put ideas into children's heads, and lead to uncontrolled reproduction and undisciplined sex drives in handicapped individuals (Kirkendall 1970). Van Pelt (1977) states that many sex education programs confuse love with sex, and Phillips (1976) reports concerns over sex education's encouraging premarital sophistication and promiscuity.

Wolfensberger (1972) identifies the following five reasons why people might feel uncomfortable with the sexuality of the mentally retarded: having sex might result in handicapped offspring; mentally retarded parents would be inadequate parents; mentally retarded individuals are intellectually subnormal and cannot marry in the "human sense"; relationships between mentally retarded persons might not be "normal"; and such relationships might violate religious and theological mores. Such beliefs result from our society's cultural rejection of sex in general, and from the tendency to equate sex with deviancy. Extremist groups, such as the John Birch Society, have adopted the aforementioned views in their opposition to sex education. Their arguments against sex education include fear of increased venereal disease in society, increased illegitimacy, and an increasing number of children born handicapped (Gordon 1971).

Who Should Provide Sex Education

The question of who should provide sex education to handicapped individuals is also controversial. Sengstock and Vergason (1970) state that there are advantages to teaching sex education in the schools; teachers know how children learn and are able to select appropriate materials. Studies report that many parents want the schools to teach sex education to their handicapped children (Goodman, Budner, and Lesh 1971; Hall, Morris, and Barker 1973). Because of prejudice, confusion, ignorance and fear, many parents are not comfortable with teaching sex education themselves (Dupras and Tremblay 1976). Some parents have asked the schools for help in forming parent groups that could assist them in understanding the sexuality of their children (Turchin 1974). Fischer and Krajicek (1974) have found that parents tend to underestimate their handicapped children's knowledge about sex.

Sellin (1979) states that parents should be responsible for teaching sexual content to their children, whether they are comfortable with it or not. Those who are against including sex education in the school curriculum add that it invades the privacy of the family, teaches attitudes and values that may conflict with those of the home, and is usually too crisis-oriented (Phillips 1976). Further, Knappett and Wagner (1976) criticize sex education in the schools as being inadequate.

While many teachers have favorable attitudes toward sex education for handicapped individuals (Meyen and Retish 1971), a number have not received any comprehensive preparation in teaching sex education (May 1980). Professionals (Johnson 1973; Meyen 1970) have suggested some traits and roles that should be considered in preparing professionals to be effective teachers of sex education with exceptional individuals; however, their attention has focused primarily on inservice training for teachers, not on preservice preparation.

Johnson (1973) states that hardly any teacher preparation institutions have been systematically training teachers to instruct in the area of sex education. Meyen (1970, 5) reports that "very few teachers had received any training at all in sex education in their undergraduate preparation. In fact, most indicated that they had given little thought to this responsibility until they encountered the problems posed by their pupils in the classroom." If the needs of handicapped people are to be met, coursework on human sexuality should be required as part of teacher preparation programs (Blom 1971). Without training, many teachers might give little thought to the handicapped person's sexuality until they encountered problems (Meyen 1970).

As the literature indicates, handicapped people have the same sexual needs and desires as nonhandicapped people, and they are capable of "normal" sexual behaviors (Bass 1974). Unfortunately, handicapped individuals are receiving little or no training in handling sex responsibly (Bass 1974). As a result, negative attitudes toward their sexuality continue.

If the needs of exceptional individuals are to be met, professionals must be trained in the area of sex education, and societal attitudes must change. Public Law 94-142 has paved the way for handicapped people to receive a free and appropriate public education in the least restrictive environment; part of that education must be a sound program of sex education. "We cannot afford to be naive about sex and the handicapped if we hope they will eventually become independent, functional members of the community" (McNab 1978, 305).

REFERENCES

Alcorn, D. (1974). Parental views on sexual development and education of the trainable mentally retarded. *Journal of Special Education, 8,* 119–130.

Bass, M. (1974). Sex education for the handicapped. *Family Coordinator, 23,* 27–33.

Bass, M. (1977). *Developing community acceptance of sex education.* San Diego, California. (ERIC Document Reproduction Service No. ED 153 089).

Blom, G. (1971). Some considerations about the neglect of sex education in special education. *The Journal of Special Education, 5,* 363–364.

Brantlinger, E. (1985). Mildly mentally retarded secondary students' information about and attitudes toward sexuality and sexuality education. *Education and Training of the Mentally Retarded, 20,* 99–108.

Brekke, B. (1979). *An assessment of the need for sex education for the mentally retarded in North Dakota.* Grand Forks, North Dakota University. (ERIC Document Reproduction Service No. ED 176 521).

Buck v. *Bell* (1927). Supreme Court Reports, No. 584, 274, U.S. 200.

Cooke, R. E. (1973). Ethics and laws on behalf of the mentally retarded. In Haslam, R. H. A. (Ed.). *The Pediatric Clinics of North America, 20,* 259–268.

Dupras, A., & Tremblay, R. (1976). Path analysis of parents' conservatism toward sex education of their mentally retarded children. *American Journal of Mental Deficiency, 81,* 162–166.

Edmonson, B., & Wish, J. (1975). Sex, knowledge and attitudes of moderately retarded males. *American Journal of Mental Deficiency, 80,* 172–179.

Fischer, H. (1975). Sex education and the multiply handicapped child. In J. Teske, *Presentations for parents, 1974–1975.* Denver, Colorado. (ERIC Document Reproduction Service No. ED 163 676).

Fischer, H., & Krajicek, M. (1974). Sexual development in the moderately retarded child: Level of information and parental attitudes. *Mental Retardation, 12,* 28–30.

For the retarded, a case for the courts. *New York Times,* February 22, 1981. p. E7.

Goddard, H. (1912). *The Kallikak family.* New York: MacMillan.

Goodman, L., Budner, S., & Lesh, B. (1971). The parents' role in sex education for the retarded. *Mental Retardation, 9,* 43–46.

Gordon, S. (1971). Missing in special education: Sex. *Journal of Special Education, 5,* 351–354.

Gordon, S. (1974). *Sexual rights for the people . . . who happen to be handicapped.* New York: Center on Human Policy.

Gordon, S. (1975). Sex education. *Exceptional Parent, 5,* 16–17.

Haavik, S., & Menninger, K. (1981). *Sexuality, law, and the developmentally disabled person.* Maryland: Paul H. Brookes Publishing Co.

Hall, J., Morris, H., & Barker, H. (1973). Sexual knowledge and attitudes of mentally re-tarded adolescents. *American Journal of Mental Deficiency, 77,* 706–709.

Heshusius, L. (1982). Sexuality, intimacy, and persons we label mentally retarded: What they think—what we think. *Mental Retardation, 20,* 164–168.

Johnson, W. (1973). Sex education of the mentally retarded. In F. de la Cruz & G. LaVeck (Eds.), *Human sexuality and the mentally retarded.* New York: Brunner/Mazel.

Kalma, L. (1976). Sex education within biology classes for hospitalized disturbed adolescents. *Exceptional Children, 42,* 451–455.

Kempton, W. (1977). The sexual adolescent who is mentally retarded. *Journal of Pediatric Psychology, 2,* 104–107.

Kirkendall, L. (1970). Does sex education arouse unwholesome curiosity? In I. Rubin and L. Kirkendall (Eds.), *Sex in the childhood years.* New York: Association Press.

Knappett, K., & Wagner, N. (1976). Sex education and the blind. *Education of the Visually Handicapped, 8,* 1–5.

Maddock, J. (1974). Sex education for the exceptional person: A rationale. *Exceptional Children, 40,* 273–278.

May, D. (1980). Survey of sex education coursework in special education programs. *Journal of Special Education, 14,* 107–112.

McNab, W. (1978). The sexual needs of the handicapped. *The Journal of School Health, 48,* 301–306.

Meyen, E. (1970). Sex education for the mentally retarded: Implications for programming teacher training. *Focus on Exceptional Children, 1,* 1–5.

Meyen, E., & Retish, P. (1971). Sex education for the mentally retarded: Influencing teach-ers' attitudes. *Mental Retardation, 9,* 46–49.

Pearson, C. (1979). Sex education: A survey of parents with deaf adolescents. *American Annals of the Deaf, 124,* 760–764.

Perske, R. (1973). *New directions for parents of persons who are retarded.* London: Abingdon Press.

Perske, R. (1974). Sexual development. *Exceptional Parent, 4,* 36–39.

Phillips, P. (1976). *The aspirations and dilemmas involving sex education for the mentally retarded.* (ERIC Document Reproduction Service No. ED 172 506).

Rothenberg, G., Franzblau, S., & Geer, J. (1979). Educating the learning disabled adolescent about sexuality. *Journal of Learning Disabilities, 12,* 10–14.

Russell, T., & Hardin, T. (1980). Sex education for the mentally retarded. *Education and Training of the Mentally Retarded, 15,* 312–314.

Schmid, R., Moneypenny, J., & Johnston, R. (1977). *Contemporary issues in special education.* New York: McGraw-Hill.

Sellin, D. (1979). *Mental retardation: Nature, needs, and advocacy.* Boston: Allyn and Bacon, Inc.

Sengstock, W. (1967, May). *Sex education for the mentally retarded.* Paper presented at the Institute on Sex and the Mentally Retarded. Cleveland, Ohio.

Sengstock, W., & Vergason, G. (1970). Issues in sex education for the retarded. *Education and Training of the Mentally Retarded, 5,* 99–103.

Tegtmeier, W. (1977). Sex education with retarded adults. *Special Children, 3,* 19, 21–36.

Thornton, C. (1979). A nurse-educator in sex and disability. *Sexuality and Disability, 2,* 28–32.

Turchin, G. (1974). Sex attitudes of mothers of retarded children. *Journal of School Health, 44,* 490–492.

Van Pelt, J. (1977). A parents' look at independent living. *Australian Journal of Mental Retar-dation, 4,* 1–3.

Vockell, E., & Mattick, P. (1972). Sex education for the mentally retarded: An analysis of problems, programs, and research. *Education and Training of the Mentally Retarded, 7,* 129–134.

Ware, L., Woods, R., & Gamsu, E. (1977). *A sex education program in a therapeutic preschool.* (ERIC Document Reproduction Service No. ED 161 199).

Wolfensberger, W. (1972). *The principle of normalization in human services.* Toronto: National Institute on Mental Retardation.

DISCUSSION QUESTIONS

1. A proposal to introduce sex education into the special education curriculum is being discussed at the next school board meeting. Each of the following people has the opportunity to express his or her point of view. What would each say?
   a. A teacher who feels that sex education for individuals who are handicapped is important.
   b. A teacher who feels uncomfortable teaching sex education.
   c. A parent who believes a coordinated sex education program would enhance his/her child's education.
   d. A parent who is opposed to having a sex education curriculum in the school.
   e. A member of the community who is opposed to having a sex education curriculum in the school.
2. What content should be included in a sex education program for persons who are handicapped? Why?
3. Who should teach sex education? Why?
4. Should individuals who are handicapped marry and have families? What variables would you consider?

PLASTIC SURGERY FOR CHILDREN WITH DOWN'S SYNDROME

Down's Syndrome is the most common of the chromosomal causes of mental retardation, with as many as fifty physical signs characterizing the condition (Cleland 1978). While the number of signs differs from one case to another, the overall physical appearance of individuals with Down's Syndrome is strikingly similar (Robinson and Robinson 1976). However, in spite of these similarities, individuals with Down's Syndrome show a wide variation in abilities; their IQs range from the mild to profound levels of retardation, and there is also variation in the ages at which they reach developmental milestones (Smith and Wilson 1973).

As a result of recent educational and medical efforts, many children with Down's Syndrome are able to function at much higher levels than in the past, with increasing numbers of them being taught to read, write, and function at near normal levels (Pines 1982). However, one obstacle to their full acceptance in both school and society may be their characteristic appearance. In an attempt to reduce this social stigma, and the expectations associated with certain physical characteristics, surgeons have been performing corrective facial plastic surgery on children with Down's Syndrome since the 1970s (Lemperle and Radu 1980). Since the first description of this facial plastic surgery was presented by Hohler (1977), hundreds of children have had this surgery in Germany, Israel, Australia, Canada, and most recently, in the United States (Lemperle and Radu 1980; Olbrisch 1982; Rozner 1983; Shapiro 1982). Descriptions of these operations have not been restricted to the medical literature, but have extended to popular magazines (Pines 1983; Shapiro 1982), newspapers (Pines 1982), and parents' magazines (*Exceptional Parent* 1983). However there has been little discussion of this surgery in the special education literature, even though many professionals may be called upon for advice from parents and may be working with the children. These plastic surgery procedures, their effectiveness, and the ethical issues involved in this normalization attempt are outlined in this chapter. Photographs of Down's Syndrome children before and after the surgery can be found at the end of this section.

The Plastic Surgery Procedures

All of the procedures that will be described are standard plastic surgery procedures. The only novelty is that they are being used to modify some of the facial characteristics of children with Down's Syndrome (Rozner 1983).

One of the most important procedures for improving appearance, speech, and breathing is reduction of the size of the tongue. By cutting out a large rhomboid at the tip of the tongue, the tongue volume is reduced by at least 50 percent. While the wound closes in about a week, the tongue remains swollen for four to six weeks before assuming its smaller size (Ross 1983).

The characteristic epicanthic fold (of the upper eyelid) may be eliminated in two ways. In some cases, inserting a silicone or rib cartilage implant to raise the bridge of the nose is sufficient to obliterate the folds. In other cases, children require an additional surgical procedure, a Z-plasty, directly on the eyelids. Implants are also used in many cases to correct receding chins, enhance flat jawbones, and raise cheekbones (Lemperle and Radu 1980; Olbrisch 1982; Ross 1983; Shapiro 1982). Some of these implants may need to be replaced as the children grow and reach puberty.

Other surgical procedures are done on various soft tissue areas of the face. For example, drooping lower lips can be corrected by cutting out part of the lip; the fatty tissue under the chin can be removed by curettage which sculpts the fat of the full neck; and dysplasia of the ears in both position and size is corrected by otoplasties (Lemperle and Radu 1980; Olbrisch 1982; Ross 1983).

Effectiveness of the Surgery

While Lemperle and Radu (1980) report that the surgery is so simple and risk-free that no child with Down's Syndrome should be deprived of it, there are some possible complications. For example, some children have severed their tongue sutures by chewing, some implants have become infected or dislocated, some children have experienced pain and difficulty in swallowing for a few days after the surgery, and at least one child suffered from aspiration pneumonia following surgery—although preventative antibiotics are now administered to avoid this problem (Olbrisch 1982; Ross 1983).

Most of the follow-up reports have been based on subjective data. On a questionnaire sent to families of 102 children followed by Lemperle and Radu, over 75 percent of the respondents report that the children are better able to keep their mouths closed, have better speech and eating habits, have less inflamed lips, fewer respiratory infections, and improved moods (Olbrisch 1982). Other anecdotal reports have said that, after surgery, the children are no longer teased by other children and that parents therefore allow the children to socialize more (Hohler 1977). Pines (1982) reported improved behavior in one boy after he saw his appearance, and enormous strides in social development in a girl after the surgery. Lemperle and Radu (1980) state that both parents and children tend to be satisfied by the results; the children often spend much time looking in mirrors, and telling people about the surgery. In addition, they describe one child as saying, "Now I am perfectly normal."

One plastic surgeon reviewing these results, questions claims of functional gains, since raising the bridge of the nose with an implant does not improve the air flow, nor does tongue reduction necessarily improve speech (*Exceptional Parent* 1983). More than tongue size is involved in speech; speech also requires muscle coordination and thinking, neither of which is affected by the surgery (Shapiro 1982). The Down's Syndrome Congress has called for carefully controlled studies on the effectiveness, medical risks, and emotional effects of the surgery before it is accepted (*Exceptional Parent* 1983).

Implications

While it has been stated that the purpose of the plastic surgery is to normalize the child's face, not beautify it (*Exceptional Parent* 1983), there are many implications in this type of normalization. First, from a practical point of view, is it ethical to subject children, who cannot consent, to a potential physically and emotionally painful operation that is not medically necessary? While it may not be possible to know whether a child would wish to have the surgery since it is usually done at a young age, it has been reported that the operation is done, as are many other operations, because the doctors believe it is for the long-term benefit of the patient (Editorial 1983). However, surgeons and parents are cautioned not to overestimate the benefits of the surgery, since it will not improve the child's learning skills. Functional and aesthetic benefits are best weighed separately in considering the operations.

Second, what are the parents' and children's expectations following surgery? Belfer (1980) expresses concern that the surgery might interfere with parents' acceptance of their child's limitations, and that it could lead to denying the child's problems—either consciously or unconsciously. This denial in turn might inhibit the development of parent-child relationships, keep the child out of remedial programs that address his/her educational and social needs, and lead to parental disappointment and dissatisfaction. And what of the expectations of the children themselves? For example, the child who stated, "Now I am perfectly normal" may be vulnerable to disappointment later if he/she is not able to respond normally in some situations (Belfer 1980; *Exceptional Parent* 1983). Since the reason for social difficulties is not limited to appearance, but also involves a person's lower IQ and associated behaviors, surgery alone will not eliminate all the problems. On the other hand, if the child's physical appearance is changed so that people don't immediately recognize and stigmatize the child, too much may be expected of him or her, leading to frustration (Ross 1983).

Finally, from an ethical and philosophical perspective, while plastic surgery can alter children's appearances, thereby diminishing the automatic expectations associated with their physical attributes (Ross 1983), the problem is really that society, not the child, needs to change. But it is easier to make the minority adapt to the majority; hence, this surgical intervention. If, as Feuerstein states (Pines 1982), this surgery provides children with the opportunity to be seen as individuals, rather than just members of an inferior group, then we must study the effects of this on the children, and if those effects are beneficial, offer surgery as an option when desired. However, neither enthusiasm nor skepticism regarding these facial plastic surgery procedures should interfere with controlled research and objective follow-up studies.

It is still necessary for us to improve the negative attitudes demonstrated by society towards retarded and other handicapped people. Most handicapping conditions cannot be eliminated or made less visible by surgery; educating children and adults about the abilities and needs of exceptional individuals will have more widespread, lasting impact on society than surgery on a relatively few individuals. Further, educating ourselves seems a less extreme approach to the normalization of individuals with Down's Syndrome and other handicapping conditions.

REFERENCES

Belfer, M. (1980). Discussion: Facial plastic surgery in children with Down's Syndrome. *Plastic Reconstructive Surgery, 66,* 343–345.

Cleland, C. (1978). *Mental retardation: A developmental approach.* Englewood Cliffs, N.J.: Prentice Hall.

Editorial. (1983, June 11). Plastic surgery in Down's Syndrome. *Lancet,* p. 1314.

Exceptional Parent. (1983). Plastic surgery intervention with Down's Syndrome persons: Summary of a conference, *13,* 9–14.

Hohler, H. (1977). Changes in facial expression as a result of plastic surgery in mongoloid children. *Aesthetic Plastic Surgery, 1,* 245–250.

Lemperle, G., & Radu, D. (1980). Facial plastic surgery in children with Down's Syndrome *Plastic Reconstructive Surgery, 66,* 337–342.

Olbrisch, R. (1982). Plastic surgical management of children with Down's Syndrome: Indications and results. *British Journal of Plastic Surgery, 35,* 195–200.

Pines, M. (1982, August 31). Down's Syndrome masked by surgery. *The New York Times,* p. C-3.

Pines, M. (1983). Plastic surgery for Down's children. *Psychology Today, 17,* 85.

Robinson, N., & Robinson, H. (1976). *The mentally retarded child* (2nd ed). N.Y.: McGraw Hill.

Ross, T. (1983). Down's Syndrome—disguising the facts. *Nursing Mirror, 157,* 46–49.

Rozner, L. (1983, June 11). Facial plastic surgery for Down's Syndrome. *Lancet,* p. 1320–1323.

Shapiro, J. (1982, December 27). New faces for Down's kids. *Macleans,* p. 38.

Smith, D. & Wilson, A. (1973). *The child with Down's Syndrome.* Philadelphia: Saunders.

DISCUSSION QUESTIONS

1. The three children with Down's Syndrome in the following pictures have had facial plastic surgery. The pictures that are reprinted here were originally published in plastic surgery journals as examples of the benefits of the procedures. The pictures on the left were taken before the surgery, and those on the right were taken after the surgery had been completed and healed. Describe the differences you see in the children before and after surgery.

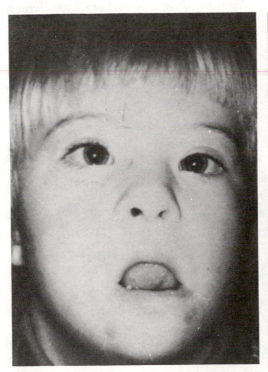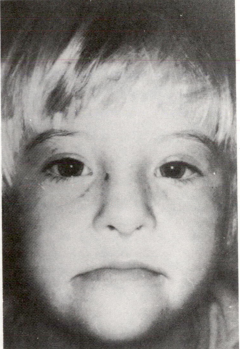

Figures 8.1a and b A six-year-old girl before and after surgery. *(From Facial Plastic Surgery in Children With Down's Syndrome by G. Lemperle and D. Radu, 1980, Plastic and Reconstructive Surgery, 66, pp. 337–342. Photos reprinted by permission.)*

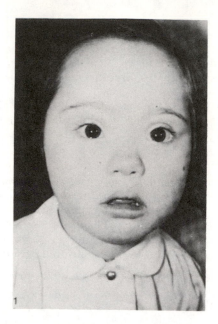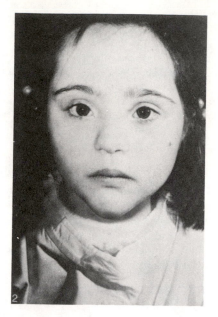

Figures 8.2a and b A five-year-old child before surgery; the same child at age nine after the surgery. *(From Changes in Facial Expression as a Result of Plastic Surgery in Mongoloid Children by H. Hohler, 1977, Aesthetic Plastic Surgery, 1, pp. 245–250. Photos reprinted by permission.)*

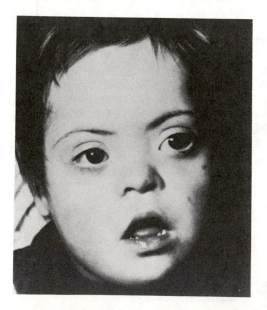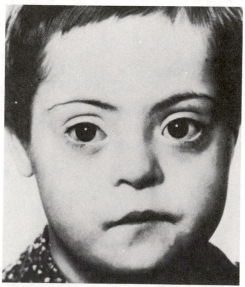

Figures 8.3a and b A four-year-old girl before surgery; a post-operative picture of the same child. *(From Plastic Surgical Management of Children With Down's Syndrome: Indications and Results by R. R. Olbrisch, 1982, British Journal of Plastic Surgery, 35, pp. 95–200. Photos reprinted by permission.*

2. Do you think that the surgery as illustrated by these three cases will be beneficial to the children? Do you think it is worth the discomfort that the children had?

3. A parent of a child with Down's Syndrome has just returned from a parent group meeting where there was a speaker discussing the benefits of plastic surgery for children with Down's Syndrome. The idea sounded interesting, but the parent wonders if it would be useful for his/her child. As a result, he/she goes to talk with the child's teacher.

   a. What questions would you expect the parent to ask?

   b. How would the teacher answer each of the questions?

4. How would you respond to a Down's Syndrome child, who, after having plastic surgery, said, "Now I am perfectly normal"? How do you think a parent should respond? The child's teacher? A physician?

5. A newspaper article stated, "When you see a 'retarded' person, you know it. The 'look' is there . . . but for some, the 'look' has disappeared, thanks to modern plastic surgery to sculpt a more 'normal' face." How do you react to a statement like this? How do you think the "typical" newspaper reader reacted?

6. What attitudes in society lead to recommending plastic surgery to change the appearance of a child with Down's Syndrome?

7. Do you think cosmetic surgery is appropriate for other groups of exceptional individuals? Who and why?

CHAPTER 9

Computer Technology and Special Education

INTRODUCTION

Microcomputer technology has experienced tremendous growth during the last few years—perhaps more than most people could have anticipated. Computers are being used for administrative functions, instruction, and with technical aids and devices to compensate for sensory loss. The wide application of computer technology in special education is improving our service delivery system while at the same time preparing handicapped individuals to better deal with an increasingly technologically oriented society. Proliferation of computer technology in the schools has also had an impact on teachers, who must now become computer literate to better meet the needs of the children they are serving.

Chapter nine focuses on the growth of microcomputer technology in the schools with particular emphasis on computer-assisted management, computer-managed instruction, and computer-assisted instruction. In addition, the use of microcomputers with aids and technical devices for the sensory impaired is discussed. The chapter concludes with a discussion of the benefits and potential limitations of computer technology.

Microcomputer technology has the potential to significantly improve the lives of teachers, parents, administrators, and handicapped children. With technological advancements being made on a daily basis, the possibilities and implications of the technology for education are endless; however, we must also recognize that there are limitations to that technology. How we decide to use the technology afforded us will eventually determine the degree to which the field of education will benefit.

COMPUTER TECHNOLOGY

Microcomputers are rapidly becoming commonplace in educational environments. As of December 1982, Blaschke (1982) reported that 150,000 microcomputers were available in the public schools; approximately 25,000 of them were used in special education. By the 1985–86 school year, it was estimated that approximately 500,000 microcomputers would be in the schools. Maddux (1984) indicated that at that time 160,000 microcomputers were used in special education. Mokros and Russell (1986) state that 88 percent of the schools in their survey used microcomputers with learning disabled or emotionally disturbed students. This influx of computer technology can be attributed, in part, to the reduced cost of owning and operating a computer (Joiner et al. 1980) and to the demonstrated success of computers with exceptional children (Hannaford 1987).

As a result of technological advances in computer applications with exceptional children, special educators have been faced with the challenge of becoming computer-literate, knowledgeable in instructional classroom management systems, and most of all, comfortable with the technology (Budoff and Hutten 1982). The purpose of this section is to examine the uses, advantages, and limitations of microcomputer systems. Additional information on this topic appears in Chapter 10.

Microcomputer Applications

Microcomputer applications in special education can be grouped into three broad categories: computer-assisted management or CAM, computer-managed instruction or CMI, and computer-assisted instruction or CAI (Behrmann 1984; Hofmeister and Thorkildsen 1986). CAM is used by administrative personnel to manage day-to-day program operations, including data collection, organization, storage and retrieval of student records, inventory and resource allocation, scheduling and report writing (Taber 1983). CMI is used by teachers in writing individualized educational programs (IEPs) and related reports, as well as in data collection and analysis (Behrmann 1984). CAI is used for direct, interactive instruction with students (Burke 1982).

Computer-Assisted Management

Evidence indicates that increasing numbers of special education administrators are becoming familiar with and adopting computer management systems to ease the demands of day-to-day accountability to local, state, and federal agencies (*Hot Topics* 1981). Computer-assisted management programs provide administrative personnel with an effective and cost efficient means of storing, organizing, and retrieving large amounts of data for decision-making purposes. For example, administrators can analyze specific services or educational objectives by a child's age, handicapping condition or any number of other variables (Ragghianti and Miller 1982). To assist the special education administrator with this process, a number of software packages have been developed, including the Monitor System (Whitney and Hofmeister 1981), Student Scheduling and Tracking System (Bolton 1982), and Turnkey's Modularized Student Management System (Morin 1984). A management program should be designed to incorporate several planning or reporting functions. Ragghianti and Miller (1982) recommend that the system be output- and evaluation-oriented, that its data collection procedures relate directly to the identification and placement process, and that the system meet the record- and data-keeping needs of the school or agency.

Other uses of CAM systems include student tracking, budget and financial report writing, cataloging of materials, and word processing (Behrmann 1984; Bennett 1982; Ragghianti and Miller 1982; Taber 1983). Behrmann (1984) notes that one of the greatest benefits of computer technology for administrators is the access it provides to more and better information. Access to bibliographic data bases such as ERIC, Bibliographic Retrieval Services (BRS), Handicapped Exchange (HEX) and Vital Information (VI) can offer the administrator timely information on the handicapped population. Another source of information is Special NET. Established in 1982, Special NET is a telecommunications network that can be accessed by microcomputer on a subscription basis. It offers administrators a Comprehensive System of Personnel Development Bulletin Board, which includes information on congressional activities, instructional practices, availability of resources, job openings, or upcoming conferences. To use Special NET, individuals must subscribe to the service and have access to a microcomputer with a modem for telephone capability.

Computer Managed Instruction

Burke (1982, 188) defines computer managed instruction (CMI) as ". . . the systematic control of instruction by the computer. It is characterized by testing, diagnosis, learning prescriptions and thorough record keeping." Behrmann (1984) identifies computerization of individualized educational programs (IEPs) and analysis of student performance data as two major uses of CMI for special education.

When using CMI for IEP development, teachers can select objectives from a data bank or write their own. Some programs even have the capability to monitor progress toward selected goals (Behrmann 1984). One must be careful however, not to lose sight of the child for the sake of convenience and efficiency.

Analysis of student data is particularly useful for the classroom teacher. As mandated by Public Law 94-142, teachers must have a method for evaluating a child's progress toward his or her designated IEP goals. Software programs such as Aimstar provide teachers with systematic recordkeeping procedures. Teachers select the data to be recorded and determine the objectives and the rate at which they are to be accomplished. A program printout provides the teacher with information on whether each child is meeting goals at the prescribed rate (Behrmann 1984). Bennett (1982) identifies the Goal-Based Management System as one of the best CMI software programs.

Computer-Assisted Instruction

Computer-assisted instruction (CAI) came into existence during the early 1960s when access to mainframe computers was increasing. Before long, CAI was identified as one of the most common instructional applications in special education (Hanley 1983). Burke (1982) defines CAI as

. . . any method of learning in which a computer is the primary delivery system. The definition has been narrowed somewhat by tradition, so that for most people it probably means direct instruction in which the student is on-line to a computer (197).

Anastasio and Morgan (1972) indicate that high cost, learning failure, and inadequate software have limited use of CAI in the past. The resurgence of CAI can be attributed, in part, to reduced cost, higher reliability (Budoff and Hutten 1982), its documented effectiveness with a wide variety of exceptional children (Carmen and Kosberg 1982; Steele, Battista, and Krockover 1982; Torgesen and Young 1982) and such beneficial instructional features as being self-paced, adaptive, highly interactive, and providing immediate feedback (Burns 1984).

Burns (1984) reports that the effectiveness of CAI has been examined in the literature from five perspectives: effects on achievement; attitudes toward CAI and its subject matter; content retention; cost; and learning time. Unfortunately, studies of these variables have led to confusing, often contradictory findings.

In a review of research on CAI, Edwards et al. (1975) reported that when CAI replaced all or part of traditional instruction, 45 percent of the studies reported achievement goals in favor of CAI. Culclasure (1982) investigated the effects of CAI on the reading ability of thirty-six mentally retarded adults; results indicated that the group which received CAI performed better in reading comprehension than the group which had received traditional instruction. Haus (1983) examined the effectiveness of CAI on math instruction with mildly retarded junior high school students who were performing three to five years below grade level and reported that students made gains in mathematics computation where CAI was used. Other researchers, however (Dence 1980; Herbert 1982; Vinsonhaler and Bass 1972), found no significant improvement in achievement levels of students using CAI.

In relation to student attitudes, a number of studies (Dence 1980; Herbert 1982; Holmes 1982; Magidson 1977) reported positive attitudes toward CAI. Clement (1981) attributes these positive attitudes to the fact that CAI is self-paced, that it does not "embarrass" students when mistakes are made, that it provides immediate feedback and that it is free from subjective evaluation. However, Kulik, Kulik, and Cohen (1980) in a meta-analysis of fifty-nine studies (seven studies examined student attitudes) found a negligible difference in attitudes toward CAI.

In a review of existing literature, Edwards et al. (1975) found that students had higher retention rates with traditional instruction than with CAI. However, contradictory findings were reported by Gleason (1981) and Dence (1980). They found that students taught with CAI had content retention rates at least equivalent to if not higher than those taught with traditional instruction.

The variables of cost and reduction of learning time reflect less contradictory evidence in support of CAI. Caldwell (1980) and McIsaac and Baker (1981) both conclude that microcomputers are most cost effective for CAI than mainframe computers. Others report that the use of computers in instruction have the added benefit of reducing students' learning time by 30 to 50 percent over traditional instruction (Burns and Bozeman 1981; Chambers and Sprecher 1980; Gleason 1981).

Given the prior disappointments with CAI, caution is urged (Budoff and Hutten 1982; Hofmeister 1982). Much of the research conducted on CAI has been limited by lack of validated software, modest sample sizes, and lack of detailed accounting of CAI program costs (Hofmeister 1982). Research on CAI may also be clouded by differential effects among variables such as sex, achievement levels, and curricular content (Burns and Bozeman 1981; Malone 1980).

Technical Aids and Devices

With the passage and implementation of Public Law 94-142, more children are receiving a free and appropriate public education in the least restrictive environment commensurate with their needs. This environment, to the greatest extent possible, should allow students with handicapping conditions to interact with their nonhandicapped peers. In order to facilitate this interaction, Section 604 of Public Law 94-142 provides for the use of technical aids and devices.

Rapid advances in technology have made it possible to use microcomputers along with electronic switches, communication devices and mobility aids. Because of the expansion of the electronics industry, new electronic communicators are continually being designed that can be activated in many ways, depending on the needs of the user (May and Marozas, in submission). For example, Fons and Gargagliano (1981) report that speech synthesizers such as the Phonic Mirror HandiVoice, the Talking Typewriter and the Type 'n Talk can improve the communication skills of persons with handicapping conditions. These devices may range from basic tape recording systems to complex matrix scanners which can be operated by a child's elbow, jaw, tongue, hands, feet, breath or even by electrical changes in the surface of the skin (Bigge 1982).

For children with visual impairments, the Kurzweil Reading Machine (KRM) has proved promising. Introduced in 1976, the KRM "uses an electronic scanner with speech synthesizer to read printed material aloud. It is programmed for one thousand exceptions and can read 200 different type faces at up to 250 words per minute" (Cushman 1981, 42). The KRM can read books, magazines, letters, and most printed documents. Unfortunately, the cost of the KRM makes it prohibitive for individual ownership (Behrmann 1984). Computer-printed enlarged print, Braille translators, talking calculators, and mobility devices such as the laser cane have also proved invaluable to persons with visual impairments.

To assist hearing-impaired individuals, Weitbrecht developed a modem which converts key strokes to Baudot codes for transmission over communication lines (Hagen 1984). Behrmann (1984) reports that this device is limited in usefulness because few people use the code and the expense is too great. A similar system, using a code established by the American Standard for Communication Information Exchange (ASCIE), can be used by a greater number of people because it has the advantage of being a "mainstream" system. Despite this advantage, it is not compatible with the Baudot system (Behrmann 1984). To alleviate this problem, several companies and research centers have begun experimenting with devices that have the capability to decipher both codes. One such device is a modem developed by the Amateur Radio Research and Development Corporation (AmRAD) for use with an Apple computer (Apple Computer Inc., no date).

Snell (1983) reports that many electronic devices provide students with immediate visual, auditory, and tactile feedback following a response. In addition to providing immediate reinforcement, these devices give physically handicapped children a sense of control through the use of switches. Switches allow the child who is physically handicapped to control electronically operated toys, tape recorders, games, or electrical appliances. Behrmann and Lahm (1983) indicate this technology teaches children that they can control their environment by making things happen.

Hannaford (1987) reports that wheelchairs with computer systems are now being developed. These wheelchairs will be capable of automatically monitoring speed and avoiding obstacles. Other computer systems can monitor the posture of a physically handicapped individual and automatically adjust the person's posture to accommodate his or her specific needs (Hannaford 1987).

The microcomputer can also be very beneficial to more mildly handicapped students with handwriting and spelling problems. Children with handwriting problems can use the computer as a word processor. A number of grammar and spelling programs—such as Sensible Grammar or MegaWorks the Spelling Checker—can assist the child who has difficulty with grammar or spelling (Hannaford 1987).

Limitations of Computer Technology

Microcomputer technology has played and will continue to play a significant role in the education of exceptional children. The realizable benefits of this technology, however, are contingent upon the identification, selection and use of appropriate software (Hannaford and Taber 1982). Unfortunately, microcomputer hardware development has far outstripped software development (Sturdivant 1980). "The development of educational software is so disappointing that one wonders whether the concept of teaching with micros is as widespread as the supporters claim" (Frenzel 1981, 26).

Bagley (1981) notes that far more emphasis is placed on the technical features than on the educational features of instructional software. For example, "It is not uncommon to find educational software that responds to students' mistakes with such remarks as 'wrong answer, dummy' " (Hannaford and Taber 1982, 138). Considering the amount of failure experienced by many exceptional children, such remarks can only be detrimental to their self-concept. Compounding the problem is the fact that most computer-assisted instruction is presented visually. Children with reading disabilities experience difficulty because of the necessity to rely on written text (Hofmeister 1982).

Another problem with educational software is the fact that much of it is designed for use with a particular brand of computer (Hannaford and Taber 1982). Therefore, one cannot assume that a software program designed for an Apple computer can be used on an IBM computer or vice versa. Hannaford and Taber (1982) report that if software programs are to be effective, both developers and consumers must be informed about such programs' educational compatability, design, and technical adequacy.

In addition to problems with educational software, the Minnesota Educational Computer Consortium (1979) points out that many microcomputers lack the capability to store and retrieve large quantities of data and to perform repetitive calculations. Others (Joiner et al. 1980; Nisen 1979), have expressed concern over X-ray emission and cathode ray tube flicker.

Benefits of Computer Technology

Microcomputers have their limitations, particularly when educators use them for instructional purposes. Despite these concerns, microcomputers offer many potential benefits to the teacher, child, and administrator.

One of the greatest potential benefits of the microcomputer is its individualized nature of instruction (Loewen 1981). Because of day-to-day demands, many teachers have difficulty finding time to provide individualized instruction. Microcomputers allow for this needed individualization, while at the same time providing children with instruction that is nonthreatening (Budoff and Hutten 1982) and nonembarrassing.

Microcomputers have a built-in motivational quality (Reith 1986). Program features such as color, motion, and sound gain and hold a child's attention (Hannaford and Taber 1982), a factor which has been identified as an essential element of learning (Gagne, Wagner, and Rojas 1981). In addition, the microcomputer provides the teacher with a reward system when a child has completed more traditional work (Budoff and Hutten 1982).

Particularly beneficial to special needs children is the fact that microcomputers have the capacity to operate a wide variety of special devices. Microcomputers can be connected to and control film projectors, tape recorders, amplifiers, voice synthesizers, and speech input units (Budoff and Hutten 1982). These options allow children who are physically or sensorially impaired to better interact with their nonhandicapped peers.

Administrators appreciate that microcomputers assist in decision-making and that they are cost effective. Microcomputers allow administrators to track students, develop budgets and financial reports, catalogue materials, and store and retrieve large amounts of data more effectively and efficiently.

The 1980s have been witness to incredible growth in microcomputer technology. Microcomputers offer great potential for improving our special education service delivery system (Bennett 1982); however, their limitations must be recognized. Special educators must face the challenge given to them by an ever-increasing technological world (Cobb and Horn 1986). They can best meet this challenge by becoming computer-literate and applying their knowledge to better meeting the needs of exceptional children. "Technology has the potential for improving the quality of life for exceptional persons but there is nothing inherent in technology to make this happen—the benefit is dependent on how technology is used" (Hannaford 1987, 17).

REFERENCES

Anastasio, J., & Morgan, J. S. (1972). *Factors inhibiting the use of computers in instruction.* Princeton, NJ: Educom.

Apple Computer, Inc. (no date). *Personal computers for the physically handicapped: A resource guide.* Author, 10260 Brandley Dr., Cupertino, CA 95014.

Bagley, C. (1981). The expert's view of computer-based instruction. *NSPI Journal, 20,* 38–39.

Behrmann, M. M. (Ed.). (1984). *Handbook of microcomputers in special education.* San Diego, CA: College-Hill Press.

Behrmann, M. M., & Lahm, E. A. (1983). *Babies and robots: Teaching young multiply handicapped children to manipulate their environment.* Paper presented at the National Conference of the Association for the Severely Handicapped, San Francisco, California.

Bennett, R. E. (1982). Applications of microcomputer technology to special education. *Exceptional Children, 49,* 106–113.

Bigge, J. (1982). *Teaching individuals with physical and multiple disabilities* (2nd ed.). Columbus, Ohio: Charles E. Merrill.

Blaschke, C. L. (1982). Microcomputers in special education: Trends and projections. *Journal of Special Education Technology, 5,* 25–27.

Bolton, B. (1982). Solving administrative problems: Student scheduling and tracking system for the microcomputer. *Educational Computer Magazine, 2,* 24–26.

Budoff, M., & Hutten, L. R. (1982). Microcomputers in special education: Promises and pitfalls. *Exceptional Children, 49,* 123–128.

Burke, R. L. (1982). *CAI sourcebook.* Englewood Cliffs, NJ: Prentice-Hall.

Burns, M. B. (1984). A justification for the use of computer-assisted instruction with the physically handicapped. In M. M. Behrmann and L. Lahm (Eds.), *Proceedings of the national conference on the use of microcomputers in special education.* Reston, VA: The Council for Exceptional Children.

Burns, P. K., & Bozeman, W. C. (1981). Computer assisted instruction and mathematics achievement: Is there a relationship? *Educational Technology, 21,* 32–39.

Caldwell, R. M. (1980). Guidelines for developing basic skills instructional materials for use with microcomputer technology. *Educational Technology, 20,* 7–12.

Carmen, G. O., & Kosberg, B. (1982). Educational technology research: Computer technology and the education of emotionally handicapped children. *Educational Technology, 22,* 26–30.

Chambers, J. A., & Sprecher, J. W. (1980). Computer-assisted instruction: Current trends and critical issues. *Communications of the ACM, 23,* 332–342.

Clement, F. J. (1981). Affective considerations in computer-based instruction. *Educational Technology, 21,* 28–32.

Cobb, H. B., & Horn, C. J. (1986). Planned change in special education technology. *Journal of Special Education Technology, 8,* 18–27.

Culclasure, D. F. (1982). A pilot project to evaluate the use of low-cost microcomputers to improve the effectiveness of ABE services provided mentally handicapped adults (Final Report). San Antonio, TX, San Antonio State Hospital. (ERIC Document Reproduction Service No. ED 228542).

Cushman, R. (1981). Seeing eye. *Creative Computing, 7,* 142–145.

Dence, M. (1980). Toward defining the role of CAI: A review. *Educational Technology, 20,* 50–54.

Edwards, J., Norton, S., Taylor, S., Weiss, M. & Van Dusseldorp, R. (1975). How effective is CAI? A review of the research. *Educational Leadership, 33,* 147–153.

Fons, K., & Gargagliano, T. (1981). *Articulate automata: An overview of voice synthesis.* Troy, MI: Votrax.

Frenzel, L. E. (1981). Learning with micros. *Interface Age, 26.*

Gagne, R. M., Wagner, W., & Rojas, A. (1981). Planning and authoring computer assisted instruction lessons. *Educational Technology, 21,* 17–26.

Gleason, G. T. (1981). Microcomputers in education: The state of the art. *Educational Technology, 21,* 7–17.

Hagen, D. (1984). Microcomputer resource book for special education. Reston, VA: Reston Publishing.

Hanley, T.V. (1983). *Microcomputers in the schools: Implementation in special education.* Arlington, VA: SRA Technologies.

Hannaford, A. E. (1987). Computers and exceptional individuals. In J. Lindsey, *Computers and exceptional individuals.* Columbus, Ohio: Merrill Publishing.

Hannaford, A. E., & Taber, F. M. (1982). Microcomputer software for the handicapped: Development and evaluation. *Exceptional Children, 49,* 137–142.

Haus, G. J. (1983). The development and evaluation of a microcomputer-based math assessment and remediation program for mildly mentally handicapped junior high school students. *Dissertation Abstracts International, 44,* 728-A.

Herbert, M. (1982). Microcomputer-assisted instruction: Equal may be better. *Business Education Forum,* 31–33.

Hofmeister, A. M. (1982). Microcomputers in perspective. *Exceptional Children, 49,* 115–121.

Hofmeister, A. M., & Thorkildson, R. (1986). Microcomputers in special education: Implications for instructional design. *Journal of Special Education Technology, 7,* 32–36.

Holmes, G. (1982). Computer-assisted instruction: A discussion of some of the issues for would-be implementors. *Educational Technology, 22,* 7–13.

Hot Topics (1981). Reston, VA: The ERIC Clearinghouse on Handicapped and Gifted Children, The Council for Exceptional Children.

Joiner, L. M., Sedlack, R. A., Silverstein, B. J., & Vensel, G. (1980). Microcomputers: An available technology for special education. *Journal of Special Education Technology, 3,* 37–42.

Kulik, J. A., Kulik, C. C., & Cohen, P. A. (1980). Effectiveness of computer-based college teaching: A meta-analysis of findings. *Review of Educational Research,* 525–544.

Loewen, D. (1981). *Microcomputers in teaching handicapped students.* Paper presented at the annual convention of the Association for Educational Data Systems, Minneapolis, May 5–8. (ERIC Document Reproduction Service No. ED 201410).

Maddux, C. (1984). Using microcomputers with the learning disabled: Will the potential be realized? *Educational Computer,* pp. 31–32.

Magidson, E. M. (1977). One more time. CAI is not dehumanizing. *Audiovisual Instruction,* 20–21.

Malone, J. W. (1980). What makes things fun to learn: A study of intrinsically motivating computer games. Palo Alto, CA: Xerox Palo Alto Research.

May, D. C. & Marozas, D. S. (in submission). Electronic devices in the classroom: Are they effective? *Journal of the Division of the Physically Handicapped.*

McIssac, D. N., & Baker, F. B. (1981). Computer-managed instruction system: Implementation on a microcomputer. *Educational Technology, 21,* 40–46.

Minnesota Educational Computing Consortium (1978). *Report of the MECC microcomputer task force.* Lauderdale, Minn: Author.

Mokros, J., & Russell, S. (1986). Learner-centered software: A survey of microcomputer use with special needs students. *Journal of Learning Disabilities, 19,* 185–190.

Morin, A. (1984). Education turnkey systems/mean: Involvement in special education technology use broadens. In M. Behrmann and L. Lahm (Eds.), *Proceedings of the National Conference on the use of microcomputers in special education.* Reston, VA: The Council for Exceptional Children.

Nisen, W. G. (Ed.). (July 1979). *The Harvard Newsletter on Computer Graphics,* p. 8.

Ragghianti, S., & Miller, R. (1982). The microcomputer and special education management. *Exceptional Children, 49,* 131–135.

Reith, H. (1986). *An analysis of the instructional and contextual variables that influence the efficacy of computer-based instruction for mildly handicapped secondary school students.* Paper presented at the Special Education Technology Conference, Washington, D.C.

Snell, M. (1983). *Systematic instruction of the moderately and severely handicapped.* Columbus, Ohio: Charles E. Merrill.

Steele, K. J., Battista, T., & Krockover, G. H. (1982). The effect of microcomputer-assisted instruction upon the computer literacy of high ability students. In A. Lane, *Readings in microcomputers and special education.* Guilford, CT: Special Learning Corporation.

Sturdivant, P. (1980). *Microcomputers: Promoting their use in elementary and secondary schools.* Paper presented at the annual convention of the Association for Educational Data Systems, St. Louis, April 13–16. (ERIC Document Reproduction Service No. ED 192718).

Taber, F. M. (1983). *Microcomputers in special education: Selection and decision-making process.* Reston, VA: The Council for Exceptional Children.

Torgeson, J. K., & Young, K. A. (1982). Priorities for the use of microcomputers with learning disabled children. In A. Lane, *Readings in microcomputers and special education.* Guilford, CT: Special Learning Corporation.

Vinsonhaler, J., & Bass, R. (1972). A summary of ten major studies of CAI drill and practice. *Educational Technology, 12,* 29–32.

Whitney, R., & Hofmeister, A. M. (1981). *MONITOR: A computer-based management system for special education.* Association for Educational Data Systems--1981 Convention Proceedings, Minneapolis, MN, 279–286.

DISCUSSION QUESTIONS

1. What do you feel has been the single greatest achievement of microcomputer technology in use with/for exceptional children? Why?

2. What are some of the major limitations of microcomputer technology? How might we overcome these obstacles?

3. Do you feel comfortable with computer technology? Why?

4. You are an administrator of a special education program that is examining the possibility of purchasing a computer-assisted management software program. What considerations would you take into account before buying a program?

5. You have been selected by your principal to give an inservice program entitled "Microcomputer Applications With Special Education Students." Develop an outline of the key concepts you would present.

CHAPTER 10

Emerging Issues and Trends in Special Education

INTRODUCTION

We have all heard the saying "The more things change, the more they remain the same." Because of their controversial nature, and because of continual changes within the field of special education, many of the issues discussed in the previous nine chapters will inevitably remain with us for years to come. While some of these topics could be labeled "emerging issues" and discussed within the framework of this chapter, we have chosen to focus here on issues not fully addressed in the preceding chapters. Some of the issues discussed in Chapter ten are changing rapidly or are new or neglected areas of special education. Our intent is to present issues which cover the life span of special education. To this end, the topics addressed include the issues of early childhood special education, transition from school to adult life, handicapped offenders, the elderly mentally retarded, technology, and Acquired Immune Deficiency Syndrome (AIDS) children as a possible special education population.

Chapter 10 concludes with a reprint of the article *Future Directions in Deinstitutionalization and Education: A Delphi Investigation.* The authors discuss the results of their Delphi study that attempted to predict which future events would affect educational services for exceptional individuals. Results of the study indicate that deinstitutionalization will continue, community-based programs will increase in number, technological advances will have profound effects on reducing the physical limitations of the sensorially impaired, and more students with handicapping conditions will spend time in the regular education classroom.

The field of special education is experiencing rapid growth and expansion. With this growth, the field will continue to be faced with problems and issues in the years to come. These issues provide special educators with goals for the future—goals which must be met to ensure the best possible education for all individuals with handicapping conditions.

EMERGING ISSUES AND TRENDS

Speculation about the future is always difficult, and some would argue, risky as well. It is much easier to deal with the issues at hand. However, anticipating the emerging issues facing special educators can be healthy since knowing what lies ahead can help us to deal with the inevitable. This chapter is difficult to write since there are so many emerging trends in the field of special education. For example, many of the topics addressed in the previous nine chapters of this text are also "emerging" issues (e.g., plastic surgery, merging regular and special education). Changes are occurring rapidly in our profession—perhaps, in some cases, too fast. These changes are affected by political, social, economic and philosophical trends in the United States. As with any field, growth and expansion will continue to yield new problems and issues in the years to come. Six areas of rapid change are discussed in this chapter.

Changes in Early Childhood Special Education

On October 8, 1986, President Reagan signed into law P.L. 99-457, the Education of the Handicapped Amendments. This legislation extended educational services to handicapped children under the age of five and authorized the expenditure of $50 million on services to this population in fiscal year 1987. In addition, the legislation called for the development of a state interagency coordinating council and development of an individualized family services plan in states that accepted the federal funds. Although most special educators would agree that the legislation is admirable, others have expressed concern. For example, in New York State, private agencies have for several years provided an extensive network of educational services for children under the age of five. These agencies are now concerned that their programs will be regulated out and that parents will no longer be allowed to choose which program their child will attend. Until the regulations are handed down from the federal to state governments, the impact of the legislation is uncertain.

With the passage and eventual implementation of P.L. 99-457, and the overall rapid growth of early childhood special education, comes the need for adequately trained personnel. In 1976, Ackerman and Moore stated that overall, 90,000 teachers were needed to serve preschool handicapped children. With the passage of P.L. 99-457 and the general shortage of teachers, one can only anticipate a much greater demand for preschool special education teachers in the years to come. Many states do not offer certification in early childhood special education (Bricker 1986), yet public schools and private agencies are providing services to young handicapped children. Those teachers prepared to work with normal infants or young children or with older handicapped children may not be adequately prepared to meet the special needs of preschool handicapped infants and young children (Karnes 1975). If quality services are to be provided to young handicapped children, personnel training programs will need to keep pace with national trends, and state education departments will need to establish certification requirements.

Emphasis on Transition from School to Adult Life

The availability of transitional services for handicapped youth has become a major concern for parents, professionals, and policy makers (Johnson, Bruininks, and Thurlow 1987). Rusch and Phelps (1987) report that of the approximately 300,000 handicapped youth who leave high school each year, the majority will experience unemployment or severe underemployment. Citing a report to the Senate Subcommittee on the Handicapped, Rusch and Phelps (1987) indicate that 67 percent of the persons with handicapping conditions between the age of sixteen and sixty-four are not working, and if they are, 75 percent are likely to be employed on a part-time basis. This situation is further complicated by the fact that only 50 percent of handicapped youth will obtain a postsecondary education, in contrast to 80 percent of their nonhandicapped peers (Hodell 1984; White et al. 1982). Because of underemployment, unemployment, and lack of postsecondary training, many handicapped youths are being placed in sheltered workshops and adult day care programs. The annual cost of such services can run as high as $12,000 per person (Phelps et al. 1982).

Efforts to minimize the problems faced by handicapped youth have been made through federal initiatives. The Vocational Education Act and its Amendments of 1968 and 1976 encourage the participation of handicapped youth and adults in vocational programs. The Rehabilitation Act of 1973 mandates that vocational rehabilitation agencies improve programs by involving clients in the design and delivery of services. More recently, Section 626 of P.L. 98-199 (Amendments to the Education of the Handicapped Act Amendments of 1973) appropriated $6.6 million to the Office of Special Education and Rehabilitation Services (OSERS) to spend in the form of grants and contracts to assist in the development of quality transitional services. As part of this initiative, OSERS has established model demonstration programs throughout the country. In addition, OSERS identifies critical components of quality transitional programming, including collaborative efforts between educational and community service agencies, effective high school programs which emphasize independent living skills, and a wide range of adult service programs (Will 1984).

Despite these federal initiatives, handicapped youth are not making a successful transition to adult life. This problem can be attributed, in part, to the lack of vocational assessment during the school years, the lack of career-oriented IEP goals, the lack of cooperative programming to assure a comprehensive service delivery structure, and the lack of counseling and career planning services (Cobb and Phelps 1983; Rusch, Mithaug, and Flexer 1986; Rusch and Phelps 1987).

Attempts at removing the barriers to optimal transitional services for handicapped youth are beginning to take place. The University of Illinois at Urbana-Champaign recently formed the Secondary Transition Intervention Effectiveness Institute. The purpose of this institute is to study the problems and issues relative to transitional services through the year 1990 (Rusch and Phelps 1987). Although the institute is in its infancy, it is one of the first systematic attempts at addressing the concerns of handicapped youth. Johnson, Bruininks, and Thurlow (1987) report that effective transition will occur only if consistent policy goals are developed at all levels; valid and reliable information is used to guide decision-making; evaluations are conducted of participant outcomes, cost effectiveness, and program benefits; and more management strategies are developed. Change must occur systemwide and must be based on what we have learned from our history of service delivery (Knowlton and Clark 1987).

Awareness of Handicapped Offenders' Needs

It is estimated that between 28 percent (Rutherford, Nelson, and Wolford 1985) and 42 percent (Morgan 1979) of persons incarcerated in state juvenile correctional programs are handicapped. Most of these persons would be categorized as learning disabled, mentally retarded, or behaviorially disordered (Nelson 1987). Despite the high prevalence of handicapped offenders in the criminal justice system, personnel who work with these people often do not understand them (Keilitz and Miller 1980). In fact, the handicapped offender tends to be more prone to physical, sexual, and economic abuse from other inmates (Santamour and West 1979; Snarr and Wolford 1985), and to be neglected educationally (Nelson 1987).

Historically, correctional facilities have ignored special education needs; placed the handicapped offender with those labeled as psychopaths, sociopaths or socially deviant; or changed the educational process to better meet the correctional system's needs (Wolford 1987). The special education needs of inmates have been ignored for three reasons. First, there is great difficulty in implementing the major provision of P.L. 94-142 (i.e., What is the "least restrictive environment" for an incarcerated individual?). Second, many people believe that inmates do not deserve the same educational benefits afforded their noncriminal peers. And third, even if they deserve educational programs, there is a shortage of qualified personnel to work with incarcerated persons (Nelson 1987). Rutherford, Nelson, and Wolford (1985) note that only 28 percent of the teachers in correctional facilities are certified in special education. Sutherland (1985) and Leone (1986) indicate that programs to train correctional special education teachers have only recently been developed. Other factors known to inhibit the development and implementation of special education programs in correctional facilities include the lack of interagency cooperation; inadequate screening procedures, lack of funds, and a high population turnover rate (Kerr, Nelson, and Lambert 1987; Leone 1986; Rutherford, Nelson, and Wolford 1985; Warboys and Shauffer 1986).

Under the parameters set forth by P.L. 94-142, all handicapped offenders have the opportunity to continue their education (Edgar, Webb, and Maddox 1987). However, fewer than 10 percent of correctional programs are in compliance with the law (Rutherford, Nelson, and Wolford 1985). Wolford (1987) suggests that in order to achieve quality special education programming in correctional facilities, careful monitoring of services and public advocacy will need to take place. Effective correctional special education programs will not be maintained in the years to come without public and professional assistance and attention (Wolford 1987).

The Growing Needs of the Elderly
Mentally Retarded Population

Historically, services for mentally retarded individuals have focused primarily on the needs of the young (Segal 1977). In the past, if mentally retarded people lived to be elderly, they often ended up in an institution because there were no nursing homes available or because existing nursing homes refused to accept retarded clients (Wolfensberger 1985).

Professionals today are becoming more concerned with the quality of life experienced by adult mentally retarded individuals. This is due, in part, to recent medical advances and the movements of normalization and deinstitutionalization discussed in Chapter 5. Today many people with mental retardation are living to be senior citizens and are residing in the community.

Considerable disagreement exists as to the probable size of the elderly mentally retarded population. In 1978, DiGiovanni, using a one-percent general population prevalence rate for mental retardation, estimated that there were between 50,000 and 382,000 elderly mentally retarded people in the United States. In 1984, using a three-percent prevalance rate for mental retardation, Seltzer and Seltzer estimated that there were between 1,100,000 and 1,380,000 elderly mentally retarded people.

The elderly mentally retarded population does not represent a homogeneous group, and as a result, their needs must be determined and met on an individual basis. Following a conference on the gerontological aspects of mental retardation, Hamilton and Segal (1975) reported that the five following service needs were the most important for the elderly mentally retarded population: health related needs, social-emotional needs, housing needs, vocational needs, and recreation and leisure needs.

Like the rest of the population, mentally retarded people are living longer, but not necessarily better. In fact, many elderly mentally retarded people are not receiving the care they need (Stone and Newcomer 1985). Segal (1977) attributes these problems to a lack of professionals trained to work with elderly mentally retarded people, negative community attitudes, lack of community awareness of the problems confronting this population, and the fact that many service programs do not recognize elderly mentally retarded people as clients.

While the need for services for elderly mentally retarded people is becoming more widely recognized, many obstacles still exist. In particular, there is limited research on the specific service needs of this population, as well as the type of programs being provided to them. Some programs and services for older persons are available from the local community's agency for the aging; however, persons who are developmentally disabled experience problems when they try to gain access to these programs (Segal 1977). The needs of this rapidly growing population must be faced as we move into the next era of special education.

Technology

Future advances in special education technology can be discussed in terms of six subtopics: integrated software, interactive videodiscs, networking, artificial intelligence, prosthetics, and teacher preparation. To date, the development of microcomputer hardware has far exceeded that of software (Hannaford and Taber 1982). As truly integrated educational software becomes more readily available, it will allow independent programs to coexist and interact with each other; allow educators to combine programs (e.g., word processing and spelling correction programs); and allow users to combine information management with control of other devices such as lights and appliances (Behrmann 1984).

Interactive videodiscs are rapidly becoming one of the most important new technological advances. With the capability of storing up to 54,000 high quality frames per side, the applications of this technology are multifaceted. Hofmeister and Thorkildsen (1987) indicate that videodisc technology can be used for assessment, instruction, and teacher preparation. In relation to assessment, standardized tests could be developed using a videodisc to assure more standardized administration procedures (Behrmann 1984). In the area of instruction, a number of curricular packages using videodiscs have been developed in such areas as telling time (Hofmeister, Atkinson, and Hofmeister 1975), problem solving (Nugent and Stone 1981) and reading (Prinz and Nelson 1984). In personnel preparation, videodisc-based teacher training programs are now being developed and field tested at Utah State University (Hofmeister and Thorkildsen 1987).

Networking is becoming increasingly popular. It is expanding beyond information sharing to the incorporation of video and voice capabilities. In special education, networking will expand to include electronic publications, teleconferencing, and the use of interactive cable television (Behrmann 1984).

Significant advancements are also being made in artificial intelligence. Systems already exist that have the capability of storing and retrieving large amounts of "human knowledge" for decision-making purposes. Hannaford (1987, 18) reports that "this new technology may develop small computers to serve as 'cognitive prostheses' to handicapped persons whose memory, conceptual abilities, or problem-solving capabilities are limited or lost."

Perhaps one of the greatest advances in technology is in the area of prosthetics. This technology allows persons with sensorial and physical impairments to function more independently and effectively in their environments. Microprocessors are being combined with artificial organs (e.g., the bioear) to provide for sensory compensation (Behrmann 1984). Speech synthesizers are continually being refined for those with communication problems, and Hannaford (1987) reports that wheelchairs with computer systems are being developed. Robots such as Heathkits' HERO I, increasingly being used in education, allow the user to manipulate his or her environment. Microprocessor implants in the human body are being explored to allow body parts to function where no human function remains (Behrmann 1984).

Technology will continue to play a significant role in the education of exceptional children. As a result, special educators face the challenge of becoming computer literate (Budoff and Hutten 1982) in order to deal with an ever-more technologically oriented society. Although there is a general consensus that teachers must be knowledgeable about computers (Molnar 1978), there is little agreement regarding what constitutes "computer literacy" (McCann and Kelemen 1984). Heward,

Test and Cooke (1981) report that teachers need to be knowledgeable in the operation of hardware, instructional techniques/applications, and production of software. Others (Hofmeister and Thorkildsen 1981) argue that teachers need only to know how to apply the technology.

These conflicting viewpoints aside, computer technology is here to stay. Therefore, efforts at promoting computer literacy need to be examined more closely. The development and implementation of preservice and inservice training programs on computer technology has been identified as a high priority for teacher preparation programs and school administrators (McCann and Keleman 1984). However, to date, there is a dearth of valid teacher preparation programs which provide training in the use of microcomputer technology (Uhlig 1982). Behrmann (1984) identifies lack of funding, resistance to change, and the resistance to learning about technological advances as three factors which limit the application of technology in education.

An Emerging Population—Students with Acquired Immune Deficiency Syndrome

Acquired Immune Deficiency Syndrome (AIDS) was first reported in the United States in 1981. Since that time, the United States Department of Health and Human Services (1986a) has received reports of 28,098 cases of AIDS: 27,704 adults and 394 children. It has been estimated that another 500,000 to one million people have been infected with AIDS but have not yet manifested symptoms of the disease (U.S. Department of Health and Human Services, 1986b).

A number of controversial issues have arisen since the identification of AIDS. Among these are the issues of compulsory blood testing, quarantine, identification of AIDS carriers by some visible sign, and most recently, the question of whether or not schools should admit students with AIDS. In 1987, the New Jersey Supreme Court ruled that schools must admit students with AIDS unless they were incontinent, unable to control drooling, had a history of biting or hurting others, or were "unusually physically aggressive" (*Education of the Handicapped* 1987). To date, of those children identified as having the AIDS virus, none are known or suspected to have been infected in schools, day-care programs, or foster care settings (Koop 1986). C. Everett Koop, the Surgeon General of the United States, states that "no blanket rules can be made for all school boards to cover all possible cases of children with AIDS and each case should be considered separately . . ." (24). In addition, the U.S. Supreme Court, in *School Board of Nassau County v. Arline*, a ruling applicable to those infected with AIDS, stated that a person with a contagious disease could be considered handicapped under Section 504 of the 1973 Rehabilitation Act (*Education of the Handicapped* 1987). The implications of this ruling for special educators is yet unknown, but it may introduce another growing group of students to special education.

With the implementation of the normalization and least restrictive environment concepts, many handicapped individuals have begun living independently within the community. As a result, these persons now face the same decisions regarding their sexuality and the consequence of their actions as their nonhandi-capped peers. Schools therefore need to develop and implement comprehensive sex education programs (including instruction on AIDS) for both handicapped and nonhandicapped students. AIDS has become a nationwide concern and only the future will determine the full impact of the disease.

REFERENCES

Ackerman, P., & Moore, M. (1976). Delivery of education services to preschool handicapped children. In T. Tjossem (Ed.), *Intervention strategies for high risk infants and young children.* Baltimore: University Park Press, 1976.

Behrmann, M. (1984). *Handbook of microcomputers in special education.* California: College-Hill Press.

Bricker, D. D. (1986). *Early education of at-risk and handicapped infants, toddlers, and preschool children.* Illinois: Scott, Foresman and Company.

Budoff, M., & Hutten, L. R. (1982). Microcomputers in special education: Promises and pitfalls. *Exceptional Children, 49,* 123–128.

Cobb, R. B., & Phelps, L. A. (1983). Analyzing individualized education programs for voca-tional components: An exploratory study. *Exceptional Children, 50,* 62–63.

DiGiovanni, L. (1978). The elderly retarded: A little-known group. *The Gerontologist, 18,* 262–266.

Edgar, E. B., Webb, S. L., & Maddox, M. (1987). Issues in transition: Transfer of youth from correctional facilities to public schools. In C. M. Nelson, R. B. Rutherford & B. I. Wolford (Eds.), *Special education in the criminal justice system.* Columbus: Merrill Publish-ing Company.

Education of the Handicapped. (1987, April 1). *Court Document.* Alexandria, VA: Capitol Publications, Inc.

Education of the Handicapped. (1987, April 29). *New Jersey high court upholds regulations on students with AIDS.* Alexandria, VA: Capitol Publications, Inc.

Hamilton, J., & Segal, R. (Eds.). (1975). Proceedings of a consultation. *Conference on the gerontological aspects of mental retardation.* University of Michigan.

Hannaford, A. E. (1987). Computers and exceptional individuals. In J. D. Lindsey (Ed.), *Computers and exceptional individuals.* Columbus: Merrill Publishing Company.

Heward, W. L., Test, D. W., & Cooke, N. L. (1981). Training inservice teachers to use technology. *Teacher Education and Special Education, 4,* 15–26.

Hodell, S. (1984). Adult adjustment of the learning disabled versus the nonhandicapped five years after high school. Unpublished doctoral dissertation, Northern Arizona Univer-sity.

Hofmeister, A. M., Atkinson, C., & Hofmeister, J. (1975). *Programmed time telling.* Eugene, OR: E-B Press.

Hofmeister, A. M., & Thorkildsen, R. J. (1981). Videodisc technology and the preparation of special education teachers. *Teacher Education and Special Education, 4,* 34–39.

Hofmeister, A., & Thorkildsen, R. (1987). Interactive videodiscs and exceptional individuals. In J. D. Lindsey (Ed.), *Computers and exceptional individuals* Columbus: Merrill Publishing Company.

Johnson, D. R., Bruininks, R. H., & Thurlow, M. L. (1987). Meeting the challenge of transition service planning through improved interagency cooperation. *Exceptional Chil-dren, 53,* 522–530.

Karnes, M. (1975). Education of preschool age handicapped children. In W. McCare, R. Burnham, & R. Henderson (Eds.), *Special education: Needs, costs, methods of financing. Report of a study*. Urbana: Bureau of Educational Research, College of Education, University of Illinois.

Keilitz, I., & Miller, S. L. (1980). Handicapped adolescents and young adults in the criminal justice system. *Exceptional Education Quarterly, 2,* 117–126.

Kerr, M. M., Nelson, C. M., & Lambert, D. (1987). *Helping adolescents with learning and behavior problems*. Columbus: Merrill Publishing.

Koop, C. E. (1986). *Surgeon general's report on Acquired Immune Deficiency Syndrome*. U.S. Department of Health and Human Services.

Knowlton, H. E., & Clark, G. M. (1987). Transition issues for the 1990s. *Exceptional Children, 53,* 562–563.

Leone, P. E. (1986). Teacher training in corrections and special education. *Remedial and Special Education, 7,* 41–47.

McCann, S. K., & Kelemen, E. J. (1984). Microcomputers: New directions and methods for the preparation of special education personnel. *Teacher Education and Special Education, 7,* 178–184.

Molnar, A. R. (1978). The next great crisis in American education: Computer literacy. *The Journal.*

U.S. Department of Health and Human Services (1986a). Update: Acquired Immune-deficiency Syndrome—United States. *Morbidity and Mortality Weekly Report, 35,* 757–766.

U.S. Department of Health and Human Services (1986b). *Facts about AIDS*. Pamphlet.

Morgan, D. J. (1979). Prevalence and types of handicapping conditions found in juvenile correctional institutions: A national survey. *Journal of Special Education, 13,* 293–295.

Nelson, C. M. (1987). Handicapped offenders in the criminal justice system. In C. M. Nelson, R. B. Rutherford & B. I. Wolford (Eds.), *Special education in the criminal justice system.* Columbus: Merrill Publishing Company.

Nugent, G., & Stone, C. (1981). Think it through: An interactive videodisc for the hearing impaired. *Proceedings of the Johns Hopkins First National Search for Applications of Personal Computing to Aid the Handicapped.* Los Angeles, CA: IIEE Computer Society Press.

Phelps, L. A., Blanchard, L. C., Larking, D., & Cobb, R. B. (1982). *Vocational programming and services for handicapped individuals in Illinois: Program costs and benefits*. Springfield: Illinois State Board of Education.

Prinz, P. M., & Nelson, K. E. (1984). *A child-computer teacher interactive method for teaching reading to young deaf children*. (Working papers, Vols. I & II). Washington, DC: International Symposium on Cognition, Education and Deafness. (ERIC Document Reproduction Service No. ED 247-720).

Rusch, F. R., Mithaug, D. E., & Flexer, R. W. (1986). Obstacles to competitive employment and traditional program options for overcoming these obstacles. In F. Rusch (Ed.), *Competitive employment: Issues and strategies.* Baltimore: Paul H. Brookes.

Rusch, F. R., & Phelps, L. A. (1987). Secondary special education and transition from school to work: A national priority. *Exceptional Children, 53,* 487–492.

Rutherford, R. B., Nelson, C. M., & Wolford, B. I. (1985). Special education in the most restrictive environment: Correctional/special education. *Journal of Special Education, 9,* 51–71.

Santamour, M. B., & West, B. (1979). *Retardation and criminal justice: A training manual for criminal justice personnel*. Washington, DC: President's Committee on Mental Retardation.

Segal, R. (1977). Trends in services for the aged mentally retarded. *Mental Retardation, 5,* 25–27.

Seltzer, M., & Seltzer, G. (1984). The elderly mentally retarded: A group in need of service. In G. Getzel & J. Mellor (Eds.), *Gerontological social work practice in the community*. New York: Haworth Press.

Snarr, R. W., & Wolford, B. I. (1985). *Introduction to corrections*. Dubuque, IA: William C. Brown.

Stone, R., & Newcomer, R. (1985). Health and social services policy and the disabled who have become old. In M. Janicki & H. Wisniewski (Eds.), *Aging and developmental disabilities: Issues and approaches*. Baltimore: Paul H. Brookes.

Sutherland, D. (1985). Training programs for correctional/special educators. *Journal of Correctional Education, 36,* 64.

Uhlig, G. (1982). Microcomputer literacy and teacher education in the southeastern United States. (ERIC Document Reproduction Service No. ED 226-721).

Warboys, L. M., & Shauffer, C. B. (1986). Legal issues in providing special educational services to handicapped inmates. *Remedial and Special Education, 1,* 34–40.

White, W. J., Alley, G. R., Deshler, D. D., Schumaker, J. B., Warner, M. M., & Clark, F. L. (1982). Are there learning disabilities after high school? *Exceptional Children, 11,* 273–274.

Wiebe, J. H. (1987). The software domain. In J. D. Lindsey (Ed.), *Computers and exceptional individuals*. Columbus: Merrill Publishing Company.

Will, M. (1984). *OSERS program for the transition of youth with disabilities: Bridges from school to working life*. Washington, DC: Office of Special Education and Rehabilitative Services (OSERS), U.S. Department of Education.

Wolfensberger, W. (1985). An overview of social role valorization and some reflections on elderly mentally retarded persons. In M. Janicki & H. Wisniewski (Eds.), *Aging and developmental disabilities: Issues and approaches*. Baltimore: Paul H. Brookes.

Wolford, B. I. (1987). Correctional education: Training and education opportunities for delinquent and criminal offenders. In C. M. Nelson, R. B. Rutherford & B. I. Wolford (Eds.), *Special education in the criminal justice system*. Columbus: Merrill Publishing Company.

DISCUSSION QUESTIONS

1. What three issues relating to special education do you feel are most important to address in the late 1980s and early 1990s? Why?
2. What impact do you feel P.L. 99-457 will have on the future of early childhood special education?
3. In what ways can parents, professionals, and policy makers best facilitate the transition of handicapped youth into adult life?
4. Do you feel that handicapped offenders should be afforded the same educational provisions as their nonincarcerated peers? Why?
5. Should we invest a great deal of time and energy in providing services to elderly mentally retarded individuals when our efforts might be better felt in the areas of early childhood education, transitional service delivery, or technology? Why?
6. Do you feel that technology is advancing too rapidly for man's own good? Why?
7. A child with AIDS has been placed in your classroom. What is your reaction? Do you feel that this child should be educated with children who have not been exposed to the AIDS virus? Why? Will you attempt to have the child removed from your classroom?

Future Directions in Deinstitutionalization and Education: A Delphi Investigation

Joanne W. Putnam
Robert H. Bruininks

Deinstitutionalization and the provision of appropriate educational services in the least restrictive environment are two aspects of a single movement to grant persons with handicaps increased participation and integration in society. The process of deinstitutionalization, supported as a federal and state policy since the administration of President John F. Kennedy, involves practices that reduce and prevent the need for residential living in large institutional environments and strategies that promote more normal living environments in smaller settings less isolated from community life (Lakin & Bruininks 1985). The process of deinstitutionalization has had a major impact upon public schools, especially because it increased substantially the numbers of severely handicapped students in special education service programs (Hill and Bruininks 1984). Schools must now collaborate with other service delivery systems to identify and provide comprehensive and effective services for this new school population. Also, techniques are needed to facilitate the learning, social integration, and overall adjustment of persons with handicaps in school and other community settings.

Unfortunately, efforts toward deinstitutionalization and implementation of P.L. 94-142 have remained relatively independent in terms of research work, interest group activity, and government agency responsibility. With little cooperation existing among edu-

cational and social service systems, problems have arisen, such as duplication of services, unrelated or conflicting agency goals, or failure to jointly maximize financial and programmatic resources. Although there is a generally recognized need to place handicapped persons into least restrictive settings and provide a free and appropriate education, opinions vary widely regarding how these policies can best be achieved. For example, disagreement exists over the role that public institutions will play in the future and the degree of social or academic integration that should take place in public schools.

One way to remove some of the communication barriers associated with bureaucratic structures or technical language is to involve professionals from different disciplines in joint problem-solving and decision-making activities. The Delphi technique was devised to aid planners and researchers in such endeavors (Dalkey and Helmer 1963; Delbecq, Van de Ven, and Gustafson 1975). A Delphi study involves soliciting opinions from well-informed individuals through several rounds of structured mail surveys and has been used for the purpose of solving problems, clarifying major issues, setting goals, and forecasting future events. This method has been particularly successful in pooling diverse opinions because it is accomplished through planned absence among participants. Problematic aspects of face-to-face decision making are avoided, such as the strong biasing influences of individual personalities on the judgments of others. Other strengths of the Delphi technique are that (a) participants need not be in the same geographic location to participate in the process, (b) feedback to participants can be con-

Note. Future Directions in Deinstitutionalization and Education: A Delphi Investigation by J. W. Putnam and R. H. Bruininks, *Exceptional Children, 53*, pp. 55–62. Copyright 1986 by the Council for Exceptional Children. Reprinted by permission.

trolled, and (c) statistical manipulation of responses is possible.

The Delphi technique was employed in several investigations relating to deinstitutionalization (Girardeau et al. 1978; Roos 1978). The study by Roos (1978) involved thirteen panelists and focused on the future of deinstitutionalization. Predictions made in this investigation supported the implementation of the developmental model and normalization, and a trend toward using smaller residential facilities. Girardeau et al. (1978) reached conclusions similar to those of Roos (1978), suggesting that deinstitutionalization would continue to take place. They noted that panelists believed the single issue which would have the most profound impact on deinstitutionalization was the implementation of Public Law 94-142.

Previous Delphi studies of policy trends were conducted in earlier years when expenditures and programs grew rapidly for handicapped children and youth. While these studies documented important trends and dimensions of public policy, little attention was given to assessing jointly the trends in deinstitutionalization and changes in special education services. Moreover, studies occurred prior to the recent major retrenchments in educational and human services at federal, state, and local levels. The recent emphasis on the difficulties for handicapped youth in transition between schooling and adult life and commonly documented deficiencies in adult service programs demonstrate the need for additional policy studies that address both the entire life cycle of disabled individuals and the services provided by different agencies.

The study presented in this article was designed to assess many of the complex trends and issues involving integration of handicapped people in educational and residential living programs. The Delphi technique was used for the purpose of systematically assessing the opinions of consumers and professionals in diverse fields regarding such future trends, policy issues, and problems in implementing deinstitutionalization and education of handicapped children and youth.

METHOD

Subjects

Initial selection of participants was made on the basis of their national reputations and responsibilities, extensive writing on deinstitutionalization and special education services, or nominations through phone contacts with leaders of national organizations concerned with handicapped people. This initial listing was compiled to ensure broad representation of perspectives and geographic location of respondents. Of the fifty persons initially invited to participate, forty-one returned the first questionnaire and thirty-three returned both questionnaires. Eight participants involved in the first round of the survey were unable to complete and return the second questionnaire within the given schedule. Categories and numbers among respondents in each category were state mental retardation program directors (4); advocate organizations (3, e.g., Association for Retarded Citizens); state special education directors (3); local special education directors (2); parents (4); federal government managers (3); university professors (9), in the fields of educational psychology, special education, psychology, and social work; researchers (3); and university graduate students (2).

An effort was made to obtain broad geographic representation of panel members (e.g., residing in Illinois, Kansas, Minnesota, Vermont, New York, Nebraska, Texas, California). Also, persons were included who were known to differ in opinions and philosophical persuasions regarding the process of deinstitutionalization and community integration of handicapped people.

Procedures

The Delphi technique involves a number of stages, including questionnaire development, repeated mail surveys, data collation, and analysis. A design team consisting of ten researchers, professors, and doctoral students from the University of Minnesota formulated a preliminary set of predictive statements for the first round of the Delphi exercise. The resulting questionnaire presented (a) forecasts for deinstitutionalization and residential services spanning the entire life cycle and (b) statements regarding trends in education directed more at children and youth below 25 years. A pilot survey of about twenty-five experts from throughout the United States was conducted at a Working Conference on Deinstitutionalization and Education of Handicapped Children and Youth, held in Minneapolis, and resulted in editing and refinement of the questionnaire. Nine of the experts participating in the pilot survey also served as members of the final Delphi panel. The following is a list of categories included in the questionnaire:

1. Philosophical, Conceptual, and Legal Trends
2. Residential, Educational, and Community Services
3. Service System Perspectives (Case Management, Interagency Coordination, Monitoring, Regulatory Issues, and Financial Considerations)
4. Intervention Strategies
5. Personnel Preparation and Program Staffing
6. Attitudes

The first questionnaire, containing seventy-two statements, was mailed in January 1983 to the selected panel of participants, who were asked to review the list of statements and rank them in terms of their *likelihood of occurrence and desirability*. Survey instructions provided an illustration of how to properly rate the statements. Respondents were first asked to indicate the probability of occurrence for the predictive statement during a specific time interval. Time intervals were (a) 1983–1985, (b) 1986–1990, (c) 1991–1995, (d) 1996–2000, and (e) later than 2000.

Panelists were then asked to indicate the desirability of that particular trend, as it was written, on a five-point scale:

1. Extremely undesirable
2. Undesirable
3. Neutral
4. Desirable
5. Extremely desirable

Spaces were provided for additional respondent comments and new items, along with ratings for any additional statements.

An abbreviated, second-round version of the first survey was mailed out in April 1983. It consisted of statements for which consensus on the desirability dimension was not reached (less than 80 percent agreement). Also incorporated into the second questionnaire were predictive statements participants had added to the first questionnaire.

For both surveys, statements were considered desirable if agreement was reached by 80 percent of the experts and likely to occur if predicted by 70 percent of those responding to the questionnaires. Categories one and two, and four and five were combined for the desirability scale, resulting in a three-point scale from "extremely undesirable" (1), to "neutral" (2), to "extremely desirable" (3), with median scores used for statistical analyses.

RESULTS

Thirty-three persons participated in both rounds of the Delphi survey. In the process of coding the data, some responses were found to be uninterpretable, completed incorrectly, or omitted, and, therefore were not incorporated into the final analysis. One survey was completed incorrectly and became a missing case; thus the data analysis included thirty-two surveys. The number of valid entries for the statements on each questionnaire ranged from 29 to 32.

Consensus on Probability of Occurrence and Desirability

Overall, there was considerably less consensus among panel members regarding the probability of a trend's occurrence during specified time intervals than for the degree of its desirability or undesirability. Standard deviations of assigned probabilities for given time intervals (e.g., 1983–1985, later than 2000) ranged from 20.3 percent to 59.4 percent on the first survey. As was expected, there was less variability on the second survey, with standard deviations ranging from 14.3 percent to 28.6 percent, most likely due to sharing the written comments contributed by panelists on the first survey.

Twenty-five statements (34.7 percent) from the first questionnaire appeared on the second, along with five new statements contributed by panelists. Over 80 percent agreement was achieved for eleven (33 percent) of the items on the second round. Over 65 percent agreement was obtained on six additional items. Especially controversial sections on this survey, in terms of desirability ratings on items, were the sections on financial considerations and attitudes.

Overall, panelists predicted that trends perceived to be undesirable would not take place. The one prediction receiving an undesirable rating and expected to occur only during the 1983–1985 time interval stated that the U.S. Justice Department would continue to decrease assistance to plaintiffs for litigation to accelerate and support deinstitutionalization.

Philosophical, Conceptual, and Legal Trends

The following trends were perceived as desirable or extremely desirable and predicted to occur during the time intervals given in parentheses.

1. Our terminology (professional and layman), as it relates to different types of handicaps, will become functional (e.g., moderately handicapped) rather than specific to particular handicaps (e.g., autistic, educable mentally retarded). (By 2000)
2. Institutional settings for persons who

represent no physical threat to others will be viewed as a totally unacceptable strategy to provide for persons who are not fully independent. (By 1991)
3. Acknowledgement of basic human rights and basic human services will be a major focus of legal advocacy efforts. (By 1983)
4. Regulation of services will shift from monitoring processes to monitoring outcomes, giving programs greater flexibility and greater responsibility in meeting targets. (By 1996)
5. Special educators and human service professionals will take the position that programming in the least restrictive environment is ultimately a fundamental civil right. (By 1996)

Panelists did not expect the deinstitutionalization movement to lose momentum due to (a) the difficulty of providing effective services in the community for children with severe medical and behavioral problems (1.5, undesirable) or (b) a curtailment in specialized services due to intermittent periods of low economic growth (1.4, extremely undesirable). Panelists did not anticipate general public support for the use of euthanasia with severely medically involved infants, a trend which received the lowest rating on desirability (1.2, extremely undesirable) of all the survey items. The federal role in policy making was not predicted to diminish, yet panelists disagreed somewhat on the desirability of such involvement, which was rated as 2.2 (undesirable) on both surveys. Service programs for persons with handicaps were not expected to be substantially deregulated, and several panelists expressed a strong need for continued federal protections.

Residential, Educational, and Community Service

Overall, panel members held the opinion that community-based educational and residential services would be made more available to persons with handicaps. The following predictions were rated as desirable or extremely desirable.

1. As children remain with their families and attend neighborhood public schools, other community-based services (e.g., respite, therapeutic recreation) will become available to them in natural settings and not simply in conjunction with residential placements. (By 1991)
2. Most handicapped children and youth will reside in family or foster family care situations until they are adults. (By 1986)
3. The average age of first admission to the residential service system will increase to about 23 years (currently about 18 years). (By 1996)
4. Responsibility for preschool programs for handicapped children will be placed with state departments of education in about 75 percent of the states. (By 1996)
5. Educational services for mildly handicapped learners will be moved from special education into regular education along with other remedial programs like Title I. (By 2000)
6. Assuming that IEPs will still be required, about 85 percent of all students for whom IEPs are written will spend some of their school day in regular education programs (compared with about 70 percent in 1980). (By 1991)
7. Employment options for handicapped persons will increase by at least one-third as a result of advances in micro-technology (By 2000)

A most controversial item, which speculated that schools would become community service centers for life-long learning and integration of educational and human services, was rated as desirable (3.9) by panel members yet not expected to occur. Another item rated as extremely desirable (4.8), but not predicted to occur, stated that severe developmental delay would no longer be prevalent in handicapped persons because of quality services throughout the life span.

Service System Perspectives

The following service system trends were predicted to occur:

1. Service delivery patterns will be oriented to child-needs and not disciplinary interests and traditions. (By 2000)
2. Careful study will be given to the effects of programs across service systems (e.g., the effects of education and support programs on the retention of children in their natural families, or the effects of the availability of habilitative day programs and the availability of community-based placements). (By 1996)
3. Specific services will be contracted to the agency (public or private) that has demonstrated the ability to deliver them most cost-effectively. (By 2000)
4. There will be increased requirements for performance standards as a condition of public support for training (not custody), including benefit-cost studies and client-growth measures as a condition for reimbursement. (By 2000)
5. Increased stress on life-long learning and employment will force greater integration of services between schools and human service agencies, especially for people between 18 and 25 years. (By 1996)
6. When multiple agencies/programs are involved with a single client, a single habilitation plan will be developed with input from each of the major agencies/programs providing service to the client. (By 1996)

The idea that a single monitoring system would be developed for evaluating each child's progress across different service delivery systems drew numerous comments and criticisms from panel members and was not expected to occur. The use of student outcome measures as a method for evaluating teachers also was not predicted to occur. Several participants suggested that a variety of outcome measures for services should be used, such as family outcomes, cost effectiveness, and other measures in monitoring programs.

With respect to financial considerations, the panel did not foresee a decrease in per student real dollar expenditures for educating school-age children and youth (extremely undesirable, 1.3) or an elimination of categorized funding for handicapped students (undesirable, 2.3). The use of voucher and tax reduction strategies was not an anticipated trend and received a neutral desirability rating (3.1). Panelists also did not expect to see a consolidation of management and funding for services delivered to persons with handicaps, a prediction which received a neutral desirability rating (2.8). In general, comments stressed that broader societal economic trends would determine future expenditures in services for handicapped persons.

Intervention Strategies

A relatively strong consensus developed among panel members regarding the desirability of most trends related to intervention strategies. The following trends were expected to take place.

1. Instruction of handicapped persons will increasingly occur in natural environments and situations, using natural cues and correction procedures. (By 1996)
2. Identification of instructional priorities-critical skills or "key stone" behaviors, related to multiple improvements/goals will be a research priority. (By 1991)
3. Technological advances will enable the design of learning and living environments that substantially eliminate functional limitations resulting from sensory and physical disabilities. (By 1996)
4. Certificates of completion, such as attendance certificates, will be used for handicapped youth failing to meet criteria for high school diplomas. (By 2000)

5. There will be a significant growth in research that focuses on the cost effectiveness and efficiency of various instructional strategies (e.g., one-to-one instruction versus group instruction) in educating handicapped persons. (By 1996)
6. There will be greater emphasis on training that enhances functioning in extra-school settings rather than sequential developmental learning sequences. (By 1996)
7. Regular education will initiate "cooperative" curriculums between persons with handicaps and nonhandicapped people. (By 2000)

Panel members disagreed on the desirability of certificates of completion for handicapped children failing to meet criteria for high school diplomas. One panelist suggested that vocational training and competitive placement will be more important in future work experience than having a certificate, while another wrote that it is important to issue certificates, provided they also reflect acquired skills. Interestingly, panelists did not predict that the percentage of special education teachers doing direct instruction in regular classrooms would double (desirable, 3.9).

Personnel Preparation and Program Staffing

The data indicate that panelists are generally pessimistic regarding future events related to personnel preparation and program staffing. The only trend expected with a probability of at least 68 percent during the 1983–1985 time period was judged to be undesirable. This item stated that education and human services would continue to attract less able college entrants because working conditions, salaries, and benefits are less desirable than those in private sector professions. Using paraprofessionals to deliver services in programs for persons with handicaps was a particularly controversial issue. The median desirability rating was in the undesirable

(2.4) range on the first questionnaire and in the neutral (2.7) range on the second questionnaire. A decline in the influence of employee bargaining units in education and human services also was not an expected trend (neutral desirability, 3.3). The general opinion was that (a) handicapped persons themselves should be given more responsibility for program planning and administration, (b) an increase in career ladder options would be desirable for direct service personnel in human services, and (c) greater attention in management and research efforts should be directed to developing strategies for increasing the productivity of human service and educational personnel.

Attitudes

All of the statements in this section were judged to be desirable or highly desirable.

1. Direct intervention into the attitudes of a community—whether through information or experience—will be a major component of programs serving groups of handicapped persons. (By 2000)
2. Shaping the attitudes of the next generation (today's school children) will be a major focus of those who advocate the integration and acceptance of handicapped people into society. (By 1991)
3. Nonhandicapped children who attend school and socially associate with severely handicapped peers will become an adult generation better capable of facilitating the social integration of handicapped persons into all community environments. (By 1991)
4. The cultural revolution that has increased the "valuing" of persons with handicaps will continue. (By 1996)
5. There will be increased understanding and acceptance of differences by nonhandicapped persons who grow up alongside handicapped persons in regular school classes. (By 1991)

6. Great societal willingness to support habilitative programs for handicapped people will come with increased face-to-face interactions between persons with handicaps and nonhandicapped people. (By 2000)

Direct intervention strategies to improve community attitudes was not expected to be a major component of programs serving persons with handicaps. Panelists were not hopeful that greater value would be placed on more heterogeneous friendships (e.g., between handicapped and nonhandicapped persons) than more traditional homogeneous intimate relationships. Another item, predicting a common attitude that families should assume primary financial responsibility, if at all possible, for their handicapped children, was most controversial. One parent of a handicapped child rejected the idea that families should bear no financial responsibility for their handicapped children, while others felt that society should assume a greater financial responsibility for the development and care of all children.

SUMMARY AND CONCLUSION

Major trends predicted in this Delphi forecasting survey were that the deinstitutionalization movement would not lose momentum and that institutionalization would be used only for individuals representing a serious physical threat to others. It was expected that community-based residential services would be made available to all persons with handicaps and that handicapped children and youth would increasingly remain in family or foster family situations until they were adults. Panelists predicted a continued federal government role in regulation and policy making, with a shift from monitoring processes toward monitoring outcomes in human and educational services. Panelists felt that programming in the least restrictive environment would be considered a fundamental civil right and it was even suggested that this concept would spread to regular education, freeing students and teachers from more confining structures.

There was some dissension over the use of functional versus specific language in referring to different levels and types of handicaps. With respect to social issues and problems associated with labeling and stigma, functional terminology was considered more appropriate than current practices (e.g., mildly handicapped, children with special needs). Many panelists indicated a belief that functional terminology is too vague to convey meaningful information for managing services, while others felt more general language should be adopted (e.g., children with special needs).

Given the present state of the economy and federal budget, it is perhaps significant that panelists did not anticipate decreases in expenditures for educating handicapped children and youth. Nonetheless, even stabilization of funding can be problematic if current funding levels are inadequate or if it prevents development of new programs. As might be expected, advances in technology were predicted to increase employment options for handicapped persons, as well as ameliorate substantially the effects of functional limitations resulting from sensory and physical disabilities.

It is noteworthy that panelists did not envision significant increases in the number of special education teachers involved in direct instruction within regular classrooms. However, they did foresee increases in the number of handicapped students spending time in regular classes and greater use of cooperative rather than competitive learning approaches with handicapped and nonhandicapped students. Successfully implementing cooperative learning interventions, however, will depend upon improved training of regular education teachers. Unfortunately, it is doubtful that many universities currently offer well-developed and validated training in areas pertinent to educating handicapped students in regular education environments. A substantial increase in the

movement of mildly handicapped students into regular education classes is not a predicted trend for the next fifteen-year time span. Some slowing in this trend is likely to occur with increasing emphasis on "back-to-the-basics" in school academic programs.

Panelists forecasted greater coordination among those serving persons with handicaps and the development of a single habilitation plan for clients. However, the idea that a single monitoring system would evaluate each child's progress across service systems resulted in numerous comments. Although panelists perceived this as a desirable trend, it was felt by many that monitoring was too complex to reduce to a single system, due, in part, to the many aspects of each unique person that could be monitored.

Although already considered an educational "best practice," instruction of handicapped children in natural environments and situations using natural cues and correction procedures was predicted to take place in the near future. Similarly, panelists indicated that researchers would likely examine the effectiveness of standard instructional strategies; for example, the one-to-one direct instruction format might be compared to small-group instructional approaches (such as cooperative group learning). Also, greater training in functional skills for handicapped youth was indicated as necessary to improve their performance in nonschool settings.

Panelists expected that improvements in attitudes would occur more through educating handicapped and nonhandicapped children together than through direct intervention aimed at changing community attitudes. Panelists also believed that by attending school with handicapped peers, nonhandicapped children would naturally become a more accepting generation of adults. However, they were not willing to state that greater value would be placed on more heterogeneous friendships (handicapped and nonhandicapped persons) as a supplement to homogeneous friendships.

The wide variability of responses on

some predictions indicates the difficulty panelists had in agreeing upon precise time intervals for a trend's occurrence. Such predictions, of course, have to be made somewhat
arbitrarily, and perhaps the criterion of a
median probability of occurrence rating of
70 percent for a time interval was overly
stringent. Whatever the reason, the end
result was that many trends were anticipated
to occur further in the future than may actually be the case.

A number of topics elicited strong and
often negative responses from panelists, as
indicated by their written remarks. Examples include (a) the use of functional versus
specific terminology as it relates to different
types of handicaps, (b) the use of paraprofessionals in the classroom, (c) employing student outcomes for evaluating teachers, (d)
the future of systems that require eligibility
determinations (diagnoses), (e) using a single
monitoring system for clients with handicaps, (f) the degree of financial responsibility
parents should have for their children with
handicaps, and (g) the use of euthanasia with
severely medically involved infants.

This survey identified a number of
trends and controversies related to achieving
fuller integration of handicapped children
and youth in schools and communities.
These issues provide a rich agenda for improving future services through policy development, research, and changes in practice.

REFERENCES

Dalkey, N., & Helmet, O. (1963). An experimental application of the Delphi method to
the use of experts. *Management Science, 9,*
458–467.

Delbecq, A. L., Van de Ven, A. H., & Gustafson, D. H. (1975). *Group techniques for program
planning.* Glenview, IL: Scott, Foresman and
Company.

Girardeau, F. L., Cairns, G. F., Rogers, B. &
Wiedenhofer, L. (1978). *Deinstitutionalization
in HEW region VII: The past and the future.*
Kansas City, Kansas: Department of Community Health and Kansas Center for Mental Retardation and Human Development.

Hill, B., & Bruininks, R. (1984). Maladaptive
behavior of mentally retarded individuals in
residental facilities. *American Journal of Mental Deficiency, 88*(4), 380–387.

Lakin, K. C., & Bruininks, R. (1985). Contemporary services for handicapped children
and youth. In R. H. Bruininks & K. C. Lakin
(Eds.), *Living and learning in the least restrictive
environment.* Baltimore: Paul H. Brookes.

Roos, S. (1978). The future of residential services for the mentally retarded in the United
States: A Delphi study. *Mental Retardation,
16,* 355–356.

Index